MEMOIRS

OF THE

LIFE AND WRITINGS

OF THE

REV. CLAUDIUS BUCHANAN, D. D.

MEMOIRS

OF THE

LIFE AND WRITINGS

OF THE

REV. CLAUDIUS BUCHANAN, D. D.

LATE

VICE-PROVOST OF THE COLLEGE OF FORT WILLIAM
IN BENGAL.

BY

THE REV. HUGH PEARSON. M. A.

GYAN

Published by

GYAN

Gyan Publishing House
5, Ansari Road
Daryaganj, New Delhi-110002
Phone: 011-47034999, 9811692060
E-mail: books@gyanbooks.com

Distribution Network
gyanbooks.com
India, USA, Canada, UK, Australia

ISBN: 978-93-6208-685-3 (PB)
First Published, 1817

2nd Impression 2024

Printed at: Gyan Press, Delhi.

MEMOIRS OF THE LIFE AND WRITINGS OF THE REV. CLAUDIUS BUCHANAN, D. D.
Author: REV. HUGH PEARSON

The Old Church of Parcor on the Coast of Malabar.

From an Original Drawing by Dr. Buchanan.

MEMOIRS

OF THE

LIFE AND WRITINGS

OF THE

REV. CLAUDIUS BUCHANAN, D. D.

LATE VICE-PROVOST OF THE COLLEGE OF FORT WILLIAM
IN BENGAL.

BY THE REV. HUGH PEARSON, D. D.

DEAN OF SALISBURY.

WITH NOTES RELATIVE TO THE

PRESENT STATE OF RELIGION IN INDIA;

AND

AN INTRODUCTION,

BY

CASPAR MORRIS, M. D.

"Οστις δ' ἐπὶ μεγίστοις τὸ ἐπίφθονον λαμβάνει ὀρθῶς βουλεύεται· μῖσος μὲν γὰρ οὐκ ἐπιπολὺ ἀντέχει· ἡ δὲ παραυτίκα τε λαμπρότης, καὶ ἐς τὸ ἔπειτα δόξα ἀείμνηστος καταλείπεται.

THUCYD.

Philadelphia:
GEORGE & BYINGTON, AND WM. STAVELY.
NEW-YORK: SWORDS, STANFORD AND CO.
. . . .
1837.

TO

WILLIAM WILBERFORCE, ESQ. M. P.

TO WHOSE EFFORTS IN PARLIAMENT

THE TRIUMPH OF THE CAUSE

TO WHICH THE LIFE OF DR. BUCHANAN WAS DEVOTED,

IS EMINENTLY TO BE ATTRIBUTED;

AND BY WHOSE PRIVATE FRIENDSHIP, AND PUBLIC SUPPORT,

HE WAS HONOURED;

THE FOLLOWING MEMOIRS

ARE, WITH SENTIMENTS OF THE HIGHEST RESPECT AND ESTEEM,

INSCRIBED BY

THE AUTHOR.

PREFACE

TO THE

ENGLISH EDITION.

The observation of Lord Bacon, as to the deficiency in the biographical department of literature in his day, is certainly not applicable to the present times. We have rather to complain of excess than of defect. While ample justice has been done to the lives of eminent persons, it must be confessed that accounts of obscure individuals have been unnecessarily multiplied.

The author of the following memoirs trusts that he will not be deemed liable to this charge. The person to whose life and writings they relate is already well known to the world, and has established an undoubted claim to posthumous regard. The prominent station which Dr. Buchanan occupied in India, and the zeal and ability with which he laboured to promote the interests of christianity in that country and throughout the eastern world, seem to demand some commemoration of his character and exertions; and, unless the writer of these pages is much mistaken in his judgment, they describe "a person in whom," to use the language of the celebrated author just alluded to, "actions, both great and small, public and private, are so blended together," as to secure that "genuine, native, and lively representation," which forms the peculiar excellence and use of biography.

There is this additional reason for giving to the public some account of Dr. Buchanan, that, from the nature of the subjects to which his attention was directed, he unavoidably incurred a considerable degree of displeasure on the part of those whose opinions or prejudices he felt it to be his duty to oppose. It is but reasonable, therefore, that his views and motives should be fully and fairly developed, that the world may have an opportunity of forming a just estimate of his character and labours.

How far the author of the following memoirs may have succeeded in this object, must be left to the public to determine. He is fully aware of the difficulty pointed out by a consummate judge of human nature,* of representing impartially sentiments or actions, respecting which much difference of opinion and feeling will necessarily exist, according to the knowledge and the dispositions of the reader upon the subject in question. It has undoubtedly been his aim to exhibit the character and conduct of Dr. Buchanan in their true light, and to enable the world to determine the degree of merit to which he may be justly entitled.

For this purpose he has endeavoured to render him, as much as possible, his own biographer, and has accordingly interwoven with the narrative of his life a series of extracts from letters to many of his friends and correspondents. Independently of the authentic and interesting nature of the information thus conveyed, where, as was eminently the case with Dr. Buchanan, the writer is upright in his general views, and simple in the expression of them, his correspondence formed one of the principal sources of the memoirs here presented to the public; some valuable private documents having been unfortunately lost. Other materials were derived from certain papers and memoranda referred to in the memoirs, from the more public events of Dr. Buchanan's life, and from his printed works. In the use of these various materials, relating to many different persons, events, and circumstances, the author cannot flatter himself that he has been invariably accurate. He can only say that upon every occasion this has been his intention and aim.

One part of the following memoirs will, it is presumed, be read with considerable interest, that which relates to the institution, progress, and effects of the College of Fort William, in Bengal; in the establishment, conduct, and superintendence of which Dr. Buchanan was intimately concerned during the period of its most extensive and effective operation. The proceedings of this institution are, it is believed, but little known in England, and deserve particular attention at the present moment.†

The account also of the journey of Dr. Buchanan to the

---

* Thucyd. Hist. ii. 35.

† It is remarkable that Professor Malthus, in stating as one of the principal reasons for the preference due to the East India Company's College in England, its superior adaptation to preserve regularity in the conduct, and economy in the personal expenses of the students, seems not to have been aware, that these were the very points in which the College of Fort William, during its first four years, peculiarly excelled. It is but just to the latter institution, that its original merits in both these important respects should be generally known.

coast of Malabar, and of his visit to the Syrian churches in the interior of Travancore, notwithstanding his own introduction of it to the public, will probably prove acceptable to the reader. More might easily have been added to this, and, indeed, to every part of the memoirs; but it may, perhaps, be thought by some that they have already exceeded their just limits.

It may not be unnecessary to observe, that these volumes contain the history of a man, whose leading characteristic was a sincere and devoted attachment to the gospel of Christ, as a living principle of faith and practice. While, therefore, it is hoped that those whose sentiments are substantially similar, will derive peculiar gratification from the perusal of the following memoirs, they may tend, as far as others are concerned, both to explain the nature of those paineiples, and to illustrate and recommend their excellence and value. Whatever is worthy, either of being admired or imitated, and there is much which is deserving of both in the character of Dr. Buchanan, is chiefly to be ascribed to his views and feelings as a christian; and though, as the author himself would avow, it is by no means necessary to coincide in every opinion expressed by Dr. Buchanan in these volumes, he is deeply persuaded, that the leading principles of his life and conduct are alone capable of producing genuine and exalted virtue, peace of conscience, and a well-grounded hope of eternal happiness.

With respect to his own undertaking, the author has only to state that he engaged in it at the request of the family and friends of Dr. Buchanan. They were, doubtless, induced to place this task in his hands from the circumstance of his having some years since had occasion to consider the great subject to which the life of that excellent man was devoted, which led to a subsequent acquaintance with him. And though he has to regret that his intercourse with Dr. Buchanan was less frequent and intimate than he wished, it tended greatly to increase that lively interest in his character, which the previous knowledge of his history had excited. He felt also that he owed a debt of gratitude and service to his memory, which he was anxious to have an opportunity of discharging; and however inadequately he may have acquitted himself of this obligation, he trusts that his intention will be approved; and that the following work, thus designed to record the excellencies of a benefactor and a friend, to adopt the affectionate apology of a Roman biographer, "Professione pietatis aut laudatus erit, aut excusatus."*

* Tac. in vit. Agric.

The author cannot close this preface, without shortly adverting to the subject which is so frequently brought under review in the following memoirs, the promotion of christianity in the East. Much as Dr. Buchanan was permitted to effect towards that great and important work, much yet remains to be accomplished. The foundation of our Episcopal establishment has indeed been laid in India; but it requires to be strengthened and enlarged, and a more goodly and majestic superstructure to be erected upon it. Churches are still wanting at the different European stations, and a considerable increase in the number of chaplains. The translation of the Scriptures and of useful tracts into the orential languages, should be encouraged and pursued. Schools should be instituted for the instruction of the young, more particularly in the knowledge of the English language; and the native christians, instead of being, as hitherto, neglected, and even repressed, should be accredited and supported.

These are but brief and imperfect suggestions, which it must be left to others, better qualified for the task, to expand and realize. The author would only, therefore, add, that it is for those who survive the lamented subject of this volume, and who deeply feel the value of his various labours, to study to repair his loss, to rescue from neglect or failure the plans which he conceived, and to continue that which he so successfully began.

In the meantime, may the following record of his pious and disinterested exertions, excite the zeal and strengthen the resolution of others to follow him in his benevolent career; and prove, under that divine blessing which its author fervently implores, in some degree the means of confirming and extending the kingdom of Christ, not only in India, but throughout the world at large.

St. Giles's, Oxford,
March 8, 1817.

CONTENTS.

PART I.

PART II.

PART III.

INTRODUCTION.

It is not the design of christian biography to exalt the individual whose character it portrays, but rather to magnify the results of the operations of the Holy Ghost, and to exhibit the fruits of his renewing and sanctifying influences on the hearts of those who are partakers of the like frailties and passions with ourselves, and thus to illustrate principles by individual instances, and offer encouragement to others to adopt the same motives of action, and aim at the same or higher attainments in christian character. The reader who can rise from the perusal of such a work, without having his own heart warmed with a higher sense of the love of Christ in rescuing one so far gone from the paths of holiness, and making him a vessel of honour, fit for the service of the sanctuary, and his own zeal for the extension of the kingdom of the Lord quickened by the example of what others have done in the cause, has failed to derive that benefit which it was intended to communicate; however much his fancy may have been amused, or his judgment convinced of the truth it contains.

To no work can such remarks be more properly applied than to the life of the Rev. Claudius Buchanan. Of commanding talents, ardent enthusiasm, and highly cultivated intellect, yet sunk by his own choice of evil into great depths of misery and degradation, both temporal and spiritual, the wonderful grace of God is astonishingly evidenced in "leading him by paths which he knew not" to the knowledge of the gospel, and then placing him in a prominent station in civil society; fulfilling almost literally the description of the Psalmist, "He raiseth up the poor out of the dust, and lifteth up the needy out of the dunghill that he may set him with princes, even with the princes of the people." Who that saw the deceitful youth leaving his home and friends with a wild scheme of arduous adventure and witnessed his arrival, friendless and almost penniless, in the great centre of corruption, where, to the eye of the superficial observer, scarce anything presents itself among the masses which congregate in it from every quarter of the earth, to relieve the moral darkness which appears to cover it as with a pall, could anticipate for him such a career as the providence of God was even then preparing for him? He will ever stand forth like Saul of Tarsus, a monument of the free and sovereign grace of God, who selects the instruments he will use in carrying on his work on earth according to his own pleasure, and often calls those, who, like the subject of this memoir, are able to adopt with sincerity the declaration of the same apostle, "unto me, who am less than the least of all saints, is this grace given," to occupy prominent stations in His church, that pride may be humbled, and self-righteousness abased for ever before Him; and it is of vital importance to the cause of the gospel, that while we survey with delight the noble army of those that have brought honour to the church by their lives, and hold up to public view the results of their labours as evidences that "God is with us of a surety," we should with equal diligence draw attention to the principles by which they were actuated, and exhibit them as "renouncing all works as a claim to merit," confessing them "all to have been mixed and sullied with sin and imperfection," and acknowledging that "whatever has been acceptable to God is His own, even the work of his Holy Spirit," and thus ascribing "all the glory to Father, Son, and Holy Ghost, for ever and ever."* But it is not only as a monument of grace in his individual character that we are to contemplate the subject of this memoir. Intimately connected with the commencement of those missionary efforts of the Church of England in the East, which have done such honour to her apostolic character, and which owe no small proportion of the power with which they have been urged onwards to his influence, the republication of the memoir of his life, after the lapse of nearly a quarter of a century, offers a suitable opportunity for reviewing the results of those operations, to the commencing and prosecuting of which he contributed so largely by his influence and personal exertion.

Instituted for purposes of commercial gain, it was too long the disgrace of the English East India Company that neither in its corporate capacity, nor in the individual cases of its servants, did

---

* See Dr. Buchanan's Will.

it realize the responsibility which necessarily attached to the influence it had acquired in the East; and acted as though the sole design of an overruling Providence in giving to Great Britain the empire of the East, was to fill the coffers of the people with the perishing riches of the world and to give to the nation a preponderance in the scale of earthly glory. Led on by that narrow, jealous spirit of selfishness, which is so diametrically opposed to the gospel of Jesus Christ, the Company not only made no efforts to extend the blessings of christianity to its heathen subjects, but interposed every possible obstacle to its introduction by others. When we see it, with bitter hatred of the truth, *prohibiting* its own regularly authorized chaplains from preaching to the natives, we are not surprised to find it refusing to allow passage in its vessels to the missionaries of other denominations who sought to supply the deficiency, nor to learn, that taking still another step it should have sought, when these devoted men had, by a circuitous route, established themselves in an adjacent but independent territory, under cloak of zeal for sound order and hatred to the principles of French philosophy, to prevent even the casual influence they might exercise in its territories; nor are we surprised to learn, that, under such a system, so overwhelming was the tide of worldliness and sensuality, that even the heathen were left behind in the gratification of every sinful lust, and that the greatest obstacle to the promulgation of the gospel was that which was occasioned by the unholiness of those who, calling themselves christians, "caused the name of the Lord to be blasphemed among the heathen" by their excess of riot and debauchery. But though to the eye of sense all was thus dark and dreary, that God, who "ruleth in the earth," and is ever working to educe good even from that which appears most evil in itself, had decreed that even here He would be praised. Light had begun to dawn on the moral darkness. A Grant among the civil servants of the Company, and a Brown among the clergy, had been raised up as the faint harbingers of that day which has since gone on to increase in light, though still far from having attained the lustre of the noon-day. During many years the opposing clouds rolled heavily around, and to those whose hopes were built on any foundation less firm than the unchangeable covenant of a God of truth, there appeared little reason to anticipate a triumph of the light. But Brown and Buchanan gave place to Martyn, and Thomason, and Corrie, and Crawford, and Goode, who, with ardent zeal and holy hands fanned, and fed, and trimmed the lamp until the same pure flame which once burned, a solitary taper, at the Mission Church, now rises with bright, steady, and increasing light from all the churches of the metropolis of the East. While from many an "up country" station, which once poured nothing but tenfold darkness upon the night of heathenism, the radiance is now beaming in faint but pure corruscations. The chaplains of the Company are no longer as once men more familiar with the gun, the bottle, and the card-pack than with the word of God; and some of the most elevated of the civil and military servants of the Company are "not ashamed of the gospel of Christ." Indeed it may be a question whether in any part of the christian church there can be found greater purity of life or soundness of doctrine than is here displayed. When we see the wealthy, the great, and the influential doing the work of evangelists, not only contributing freely of their money, but employing their own time in dispensing food to the hungry, and knowledge to the ignorant, that they may win souls to Christ, and lead them to seek for that "bread which cometh down from heaven," and those "wells of water which spring up to everlasting life;" and then behold the same individuals converting the rites of hospitality into occasions for conveying wisdom from on high, to scoffing, infidel guests, we cannot but say, this is the Lord's doing, and it is marvellous in our eyes. Time has been, and that within the memory of those now living, when it was not so, and when one christian man, having his lot cast in this modern Sodom, advertised in vain for a companion of like principles, in order that they might unite, together, as is there customary, in one domestic establishment. But behold the contrast. It is related of Joseph Dacre, Esq., a civil servant of the Company, that at the time of his death he left a congregation of four hundred professing native christians, converted by his instrumentality, besides many Europeans whom he had brought to the knowledge of the truth. His dying testimony was, "I have preached Christ with all my soul and now he alone is my confidence." "Jesus, I have sinned against thee. I have dishonoured thee, but thou still art my hope. And wilt thou let me go? Canst thou let me go? No! Thy mercy is a sea of boundless love." And a short before his death, with the prospect of soon standing before the judgment seat of Christ, he could say, "Had any one asked me within the last seventeen years, I think I may say twenty, what had been the object I had chiefly in view, I could have answered by divine grace, *the glory of God.*"

I have myself enjoyed the privilege of the acquaintance of one whose modesty would shrink from any degree of notoriety, highly connected and of great influence in society, a judge over an important district, who has been known to seek out a sick traveller, take him to his own tent, nurse and comfort his body, and then, when returning health gave opportunity, sit for hours by his bedside, reasoning with him "of temperance, righteousness, and a judgment to come," not permitting him to depart until he had brought him, (under the blessing of God) from the mazes of infidelity into the marvellous liberty of a son of God. And I have seen him, with the same noble spirit, spend day after day, among the orphan children of the common soldiers, with the same holy purpose of winning them to Christ. Indeed, so entirely has the tide of influence turned in favour of christianity that few are now to be found so hardy as to oppose its progress, or withhold their aid from the efforts which are making for its extension.

The opposition of the government, so rancorous as to lead to the prohibiting of its own chaplains from preaching the gospel to the heathen, has yielded, and though it is still stained with the guilt of a partial sanction of idolatry, yet there is now unlimited toleration of missionaries of every denomination; and in a farewell address of the late Governor, Lord William Bentinck, he makes *honourable* mention of the mission of the General Assembly of the Scotch Church. And though others doubtless must share with Dr. Buchanan in the glory of the change, it is generally conceded that it is chiefly attributable to the noble, self-denying, and unwearied assiduity with which, braving obloquy and reproach, he laboured to enlighten the mind of the British public on the real condition of the Indian provinces, and pointed out the means which his enlarged intellect and extensive observation rendered him so competent to suggest for its improvement.

But it is time we should turn our attention to that great change which has followed most directly the efforts of Buchanan himself, a change which he deemed of the utmost importance and which experience has shown he did not estimate too highly. When we recur to the decided hostility with which his proposal of an ecclesiastical Establishment for India was first met, and remember the continued opposition it encountered during so many years, and the bitter personalities with which the character of its proposer was assailed, not only through the medium of the press, but even on the floor of the House of Commons, and that too by persons of no little influence, we could not have anticipated that she should be already blessed with two bishops, in active discharge of their duties, and with the prospect of another to be soon added to the number, nor can we fail to admire the foresight displayed when in answer, doubtless to a suggestion of the possibility that an unsuitable person might be chosen to fill the highest office of the church, he could reply, "Place the mitre on any head, it will do good in India, and a spiritual bishop will in time arise." How delightful it is to trace the fulfilment of these sanguine hopes; to see a Middleton falling a victim to his self-sacrificing efforts to secure a college for the training up of an indigenous clergy; a Heber, whose refined and chastened taste (brought more and more under the influence of the gospel during his residence in India,) was so adapted to win the good will of all to the holy cause, in support of which he too fell, a martyr to his zeal; and passing over the short career of a Turner, and a James, to come down to the present time, when a Wilson in Calcutta, and a Corrie in Madras, stand forth as examples to the flock "over which the Holy Ghost has made them overseers" in purity of doctrine, holiness of life, and fervency of zeal, men of whom it may emphatically be said, they count not their lives dear unto themselves, but follow, undaunted, in the path on which they have seen no less than four of their predecessors fall martyrs to labours and cares which they themselves must encounter. Entering upon it too, the one, after years of faithful labour amid evil report and good report in the metropolis of the world had afforded reasonable grounds for a claim to retirement, and the other, after a life of still more arduous and self-denying exertion as the fellow-labourer of Martyn, Brown, Thomason, and Heber, whose toils and anxieties he shared with unflinching devotion to their common Lord. "Named with commendation in the primary charge of Bishop Middleton, twenty year since, the companion and friend of each succeeding prelate, and thrice supplying, so far as an archdeacon could, the vacant see," the patron of the Rev. Abdool Messee, and the Rev. Wm. Bowley, two of the most successful missionaries of modern times (whom he received to his house and his table, notwithstanding the sneers of pride pointed to their native origin as disqualifying them for such association,)—the hospitable friend of all those of every denomination, who passed through Calcutta on their way to labour among the more distant heathen, many missionaries of the American Board, being able to testify of his open-hearted simple kindness—the unwearied and liberal promoter of every public institution for the relief, "as well of the bodies as the souls" of his fellow beings—the affectionate counsellor of the young, to whom his house and his heart are always open, he stands forth, in the estimation of all who have been privileged to know him, as one who may adopt the language of the apostle, "Be followers together of me, and mark them which walk so as ye have us for an example." And yet so deep is his humility that in a recent private communication to the author of this feeble tribute to his worth, he can, in the spirit of the same apostle, count himself "less than the least of all saints;" and instead of being elated by his elevation to the Episcopal chair, speak of it as cause for still greater humiliation before God, in a deep sense of his unworthiness. Long may the Indian Church be blessed with such bishops; and when they have finished their course, and are called to the possession of the crown of righteousness laid up for them in heaven, may their mantles fall on those of like character, and with double portions of the same spirit.

But we cannot better display the result of this measure than in the words of the present Bishop of Calcutta, who in a late charge says:

"At the primary visitation of Bishop Middleton the chaplaincies in Bengal were fifteen, the clergy at work but ten or twelve. At the time of Bishop Heber, the chaplains allotted were twenty-six; but little more than half were actually in the field, with a few missionaries. Our chaplaincies are now thirty-seven, and those filled up thirty-two. The considerable places now regularly served are thirty-four; and including the Eastern settlements and Bishops College Chapel, and a few others, forty. To which number, if we add the smaller christian stations which are visited once, twice, or oftener in the year, the aggregate will be over ninety; while the whole amount of licensed clergy in the archdeaconry (of Calcutta) at present will be fifty-eight, and, with those absent on sick leave, sixty-five.

"In the presidency of Madras the augmentation has been equally gratifying. Out of eighteen stations only one of a very important character, Bellary, is without a chaplain, while above forty smaller spots are occasionally visited. If the Rev. missionaries are added, the number of clergy in residence would be thirty-five or forty." "My last accounts from Bombay left five absent or vacant of its fifteen chaplaincies. I hope, in a few months, to find the whole number of seventy-five are appointed, of whom, if about sixty are actually in India, I should trust the number of the clergy, with the Rev. missionaries, would be nearly one hundred and twenty."

Now, what could the most sanguine have anticipated more than we see here fulfilled? Twenty-five years since not a missionary of the Church of England on the ground and the chaplains prohibited from the promulgation of the gospel to the natives. Now no less than sixty ordained clergymen of the church engaged, directly and exclusively in missionary labour, not to mention the chaplains, many of whom are faithful and diligent missionaries to the heathen, in addition to the duties of their chaplaincies.

Nor must we omit, in this cursory survey of the results of the labours of Buchanan, to pause a moment in contemplation of an object which, though it did not present itself to his mind, yet sprang so immediately and exclusively from the efforts of the first bishop, that it may legitimately be considered the offspring of his labours. I allude to Bishops College, which, in the language of Bishop Wilson, "erected with a foresight and piety which will for ever illustrate the name of the first Bishop of Calcutta, stands on the margin of the river which washes our eastern metropolis, the noblest monument of British benevolence, waiting only to receive its flocking students and train them for missionary labor." Nor are its benefits only in anticipation, already have the first fruits been gathered. One missionary, who received his education entirely within its walls, having already gone forth as a labourer in the vineyard and offering at a late account as the result of his ministry no less than one hundred native converts waiting for baptism. Subsidiary to this, a High School in Calcutta, founded by Bishop Turner, is in successful operation, ready to pour forth youth, prepared on the spot, and habituated to the climate, who shall enter the college there to receive that complete education which it offers. Having thus traced down to the present time the good results of his unwearied efforts for the establishment of the Episcopate, we may next turn our attention to another, and even more important subject, the translation of the Word of God. What principle less persevering than Christian zeal but would have sunk under the various difficulties he was obliged to encounter in the commencement of his undertaking; and what but the most expansive and sanctified liberality would have been so profuse in its expenditure as he was in this most holy cause? And it must be remembered also, that this unwearied exertion was made in a climate proverbial for its enervating influence, and this expenditure encountered in direct opposition to those principles of worldly prudence which would have called for the accumulation of an independence while the opportunity was afforded, and in the midst too of a society in which a much smaller degree of christian zeal would have received a greater share of praise. Separated by half the globe from those who might be disposed to exact more from him, and to watch over him with an anxious solicitude, he stands forth as a monument of the preserving power of divine grace. And that same Spirit by which he was actuated and sustained, has carried on to completion, the work at which he thus assiduously laboured; and it is believed there is not now within the jurisdiction of the British government, a nation which may not hear, in its own language, the "wonderful works of God." Nor should we in this connexion, overlook the fact that it was the same ardent and persevering advocate of Episcopacy, and an Establishment as the best means of promoting the extension of christianity among both the native and European population of India, that stood forth as the champion of the Serampore missionaries, and was willing to entrust to their hands the important work of translation, when the reduction of the College of Fort William compelled those who were interested in this most important work to seek for other hands, to which it might be entrusted; thus affording undeniable evidence that a warm and decided attachment to what we ourselves believe, the only divinely-authorized form of church government, is perfectly compatible with the most enlarged liberality to those who conscientiously differ from us, and whom we cannot but believe to be thus far in error.

But we must now turn our attention to that which Dr. Buchanan himself esteemed an important result of his Indian residence, and which has afforded his adversaries more opportunity for attacking his character than any part of his labours, the account which he published of his visit, to the decayed christian churches on the coast of Malabar. What christian heart did not beat with joy and sympathy, when it was told of a body of christians in the mountain fastnesses of India, who had there maintained, in comparative purity, the faith and practice of primitive christianity in defiance not only of the idolatry by which it was surrounded, but even resisting to blood, the horrors of the Inquisition, rather than submit to the false doctrine of Rome? Who was not disposed to lift up his voice in thanksgiving to that God, by whom they had thus been kept? Who that heard of their humble acknowledgments, of their present fallen condition, and their willingness to be helped through the instrumentality of the Church of England, but indulged in ardent anticipations of the result? And who was not proportionably cast down when told that in all these points Dr. Buchanan had either suffered himself to be deceived by his own enthusiasm or had voluntarily deceived others. We find the very outset of his career marked by ardent enthusiastic feeling, and every subsequent step of his course shows the same character to have continued in a more chastened form throughout his life. It is not, therefore, at all surprising that we should find traces of it in those portions of his writings which are most calculated to call forth such feelings. But while we make these concessions, we must not be understood to admit, by any means, the truth of the allegations of the enemies of Dr. Buchanan, who are well designated—by one well competent to judge—as enemies of the cause in which he was engaged, and therefore bound to make the most of any imperfection they might find in its advocates. Cold, indeed, must have been the heart of him, who, as the first Western Christian put his foot within the sacred precincts of this Eastern Church, and remembered how many fights of affliction it had endured for the sake of the truth—who could witness the jealous care with which the word of God was kept and the anxiety manifested to possess it more abundantly—who conld listen to Abraham's remark upon the difference between the "religion of the heart and the doctrines of the head," and hear him say for "three hundred years we have been quarrelling with the Romish Church about supremacy, rites, and ceremonies, but the Bible has been out of the question. The Bible, sir, is what we want, in the language of our own mountains; with the Bible in his hand, every man may become the priest of his own family"—who could climb the hill of Ranniel, and, thence surveying the districts around, see humble yet neat christian churches almost hidden among the trees, and there partake of the simple hospitality of a christian man who had never been beyond "those mountains," and scarce could believe there were any christians in the world beside those with whom he was wont to associate—he who could witness these scenes and associate with such persons without enthusiasm must have been destitute of all susceptibility. It was natural that we should anticipate much good as the result of the more general diffusion of the word of God, and more general instruction of the priests. In these anticipations the whole christian church participated with Dr. Buchanan; but as yet they have not been realized. Through the exertions of Col. Monro, the Company's resident at Travancore, a college has been established for the instruction of the Catanars, and placed under the superintendence of the missionaries of the Church Missionary Society; these clergymen are also permitted to preach in the churches. The results of both these operations must necessarily be slow, but we cannot but be allowed still to hope that the blessing of the Holy Spirit may be shed out abundantly on these labors, and then shall they "not be in vain in the Lord:" and while it is evident, from later observations and more familiar intercourse, that they have lapsed further into error than Dr. Buchanan had supposed, this should, instead of cooling the zeal of Christians for their restoration, stimulate it to greater warmth and energy of action. Dr. Buchanan may be said to have died in their service—the last act in which he was engaged being the supervision of the printing of the New Testament in Syriac, in order to redeem the pledge which he made to them, when they so unwillingly entrusted to his care the manuscripts they had so long treasured, and which they had received from Antioch about the seventh century. Though pictures of the Virgin in their churches, and the acknowledgment of the value of the intercession of saints, prove them to have departed from the faith once delivered to their fathers, we cannot but still indulge the hope that this branch of the church may yet be restored to its pristine vigour and bring forth fruit to the praise and glory of God. And while we survey their fallen condition, and that of the sister churches of Armenia, Abyssinia, Greece, and Rome, and pray earnestly for their restoration, let us not forget to derive from it that practical lesson it is so well calculated to convey, and learn to be "watchful and strengthen those things that remain" in our own possession, lest a like condemnation come upon ourselves, and, while we justly look upon our privileges in the maintenance among us of so large a portion of primitive order, we lapse, like these our predecessors, into the form of godliness without the power. None but he who has stood amid the fumes of incense surrounded by a gaping, thoughtless crowd, and listened to the unintelligible jargon of the priest, bowing before a picture of the Virgin, instead of humbling himself in the presence of the only true God, can realize the humiliating feeling which is produced by the reflection that these are the descendants of the churches of Corinth and Philippi. And still more humbling is the feeling which is produced by the grosser levity of both priest and people in the Armenian Church, remembering their descent from those to whom Paul preached in Asia the "gospel of the grace of God." My heart has often sunk within me in witnessing these things, from the reflection that the glory of the Lord once shone on these churches still possessed of all the ordinances and rites of christianity, but totally destitute of that which alone gives them life and power. The Lord grant that our candlestick may never in like manner be put out of its place, and we left to cry, the temple of the Lord are we, while the glory has departed, and the light has been replaced by a darkness the more afflicting from the contrast. In the case of the Syrians, Dr. Buchanan well remarks that he was more pleased to trace the existence of that which still remained among them, as the little spark of good which might be kindled again into a flame by the kindly nursing of the English Church, than to seek how far they had fallen into error and darkness. He certainly overlooked the invocation of the Virgin, and the acknowledgment of the merits of the saints, or he could not have said—"The doctrines of the Syrian Church are few in number, but pure, and agree in essential points with the Church of England;" even with the qualification which immediately follows, "Though the body of the church appears to be ignorant and formal and dead, there are individuals who are alive to righteousness, who are distinguished from the rest by their purity of life, and are sometimes considered too rigid." It must be borne in mind, too, by those who are disposed to judge Dr. Buchanan hardly, that Col. Macaulay, and others whose opportunities for information were greater than his, were long under the same impression with himself, derived, doubtless, like his own, from the remarks of those who were "more alive to righteousness," or perhaps from the interested misstatements of those who were anxious to receive some temporal advantage which they hoped might result from such deception.*

---

* The London Missionary Register for December, 1836, received after the preparation of these sheets for the press, contains some recent accounts from the missionaries among the Syrian christians. The following extracts from their communications will exhibit clearly the present condition of these people, and the kind of instruction which is conveyed to the young Catanars in the seminary at Cotym:

"*Oct.* 7, 1834.—I received a visit to-day from Philippos, Catanar, of one of the Cottayam churches. We conversed on the errors of the Syrian Church. He seems to be fully sensible of them, although he unhappily appears to be but little troubled about their existence. On my mentioning the desirableness of a reformation, and the duty of the priests to promote it by all legal means, he coolly observed that that was the Metran's business—that any reformation must originate with him.

"*Oct.* 12—I preached to a very crowded congregation, in the Syrian church. There is evidently an increased attention to the word of God. The people begin to inquire of their priests, whether what Sahib says is true. "If it is not," they say, "why is he allowed thus to preach in our church? But if what Sahib says be true, why do not our priests tell us the same things?" I am inclined to believe that if ever there is a reformation here, it will begin among the laity, and not among the priests. By the priests, I have little doubt, there will be offered very strong opposition, and their influence among the people is very considerable. Still, let but the gospel be preached, simply and in love, and I cannot but believe that the Lord will appear for his own glory, to the joy of his people, and to the confusion of those who oppose themselves.

"*Oct.* 13—This day one of my servants came to me, to speak about christianity. He stated that he had long been convinced of its truth, and was now desirous of being baptized. I questioned him very closely, and was, upon the whole, much pleased with his answers: his knowledge of the doctrine of christianity is tolerably accurate. I know not what sinister motive he can have in thus coming forward. I told him that I could not recommend him to the Syrian Church; but that I should be happy to afford him further instruction in the truths of our holy religion; and that if he were found to be sincere, I should procure him baptism in our own church. For this encouragement he expressed himself thankful. He is married, and has two children; but his wife is opposed to christianity. He thinks, however, that she will not object to one of his children being baptized with him. May the Lord carry on, in this poor man's heart, the work which he seems to have begun!

Oct. 19: *Lord's Day*—I preached, as usual, in the Syrian church; but in much pain and weakness. There was a large number of men, women, and children present. Many of these are very regular in their attendance; and appear, at least, to receive the word gladly. If at one time more than another I feel tender commiseration for these poor Syrians, it is when I am addressing them in their own church. Here every thing around is calculated to remind you of their deeply-fallen condition. To-day I felt peculiarly earnest, while endeavouring to exhibit the ability and willingness of Christ *to save to the very uttermost all that come unto God by him.* I am very anxious not heedlessly to offend their prejudices: but still, if we preach at all, we must preach the whole truth: and, in order to make the truth evident, we must clear away their known errors: their refuges of lies must be exposed. Christ—not the Virgin, not merits of saints, not vows and fasts, not a wafer-god—Christ alone can help and save. Oh that we all, like St. Paul, may determine to *know nothing among* them *but Jesus Christ and him crucified!*

"At this period Mr. Woodcock was under the necessity of proceeding to the Nilgherries for the benefit of his health.

So many years have now elapsed since the grounds upon which the claims of missions to the heathen are founded have

---

"*Themes by youths in the Syrian College.*—The following themes by college boys were transmitted by the Rev. J. Peet, to illustrate their progress, and their views of divine truth.

"*On Justification by Faith.*—Justification by faith is the grace of God freely bestowed, and whereby He pardons all sins of men, and receives them holy in his sight without accounting sins; but it is not by the works and worthiness of men;—and we must consider with what. It is only by the free grace with which God hath offered the sacrifice of his own Son for the remission of our sins: for instance, Rom. iii. 24: 'Being justified by his grace through the redemption which is in Jesus Christ.' If we gain righteousness by works, it is not the free grace of God, for it is the payment of works: for instance, Rom. iv. 4: 'To him that worketh, is not reckoned the reward of grace, but of debt:' therefore by our works the grace is not gained. Of this, Rom. iv. 2: 'If Abraham was justified by his works, he has wherewith to glory; but not before God.' God commanded to Abraham, according to his commandment, 'that thou shalt get out of thine own country, and come into the land which I tell thee.' He believed God, and got out without doubting: this was reckoned to him for righteousness: of which Rom. iv. 3: 'For what the Scripture says: Abraham believed God, which was reckoned to him for righteousness.' Therefore we must pray to God to grant his Holy Spirit, that we also may walk in the footsteps of Abraham.

"*On the same subject.*—We must think what is said of justification by faith: it is the work of God's free grace. It is evident that we cannot be justified by any good works that we do. Eph. ii. 8, 9, mentions about this: 'You are saved by faith, by his grace; and that not of yourselves, but it is the free grace of God: it is not of works, lest any man should boast.' We must think what faith is, and how we can receive it: we must believe in Christ, with our perfect heart: many witnesses prove that we have remission of sin through his blood. If we examine how Job was saved from the deceit and temptation of Satan, he was only saved by faith; and not only he, but also Abraham, who is called the father of believers and the friend of God, 'believed in God, and it was reckoned to him for righteousness;' as it is said in Gal. iii. 6. Not only this, but faith is that by which we are confirmed in our mind concerning unknown things as things that are known. Even so we must certainly believe that there is no other Mediator between God and men, except Christ. When we believe so, we, who are sinners and offenders, will be received into the presence of Jehovah, armed with righteousness, as those that have no defect: the whole Scriptures record to this: about this it is spoken in the Epistle of John i. 12.

"In reference to this Theme, Mr. Peet remarks—

"A literal translation from a deacon's original Malayalim theme; and precisely as it was translated by an English scholar; first on a slate, and afterward written on this paper by him. My object in sending this is to show the state of learning at present.

"*On Praying to the Virgin Mary.*—It is not lawful to pray to the Virgin Mary, as we do to our God, who preserves us from harm by day and night: because she, being one of his creatures, could not save any man, or do any thing good, as the Almighty could. We, who are Christians, should not despise her, but honour her more than all other women; because she was the mother of our Saviour, and the blessed woman among all other women who were born in this world: and if we give those privileges and glory, which are due to God only, to any other creature, whether Virgin Mary or any saint, it is not only an horrible crime, but we despise and frustrate the merits of Christ which he hath shed for our salvation; and the scripture doth not teach us to trust in any other, but in Christ Jesus, for our salvation: and we are the transgressors of the scripture, if we do what it doth not teach us; for it teacheth us, in the first commandment which God gave to Moses, *Thou shalt have no other God before me*: from this we may learn that we must put our trust in no one, except the living God.

"Mr. Peet states that this theme was written without the slightest dictation of any kind."

been presented to the public, and so treacherous are our hearts in allowing such things to slip from the memory, that it may not be useless once more, on this occasion, to ask the attention of the readers of this volume to a cursory survey of them. In this, as in all other cases, the maxim of the Roman poet is true—

> "Segnius irritant animos demissa per aurem,
> Quam quæ sunt oculis subjecta fidelibus—"

and I feel assured that no heart, which has felt the power of sin, and known the saving efficacy of the blood of Christ applied to its own healing, can for one moment survey the actual condition of the heathen world, and hesitate as to the imperative nature of the obligation to extend to its polluted inhabitants the knowledge of the gospel. Having myself seen the abomination of idolatry, entering upon its consideration too with a heart steeled by long rooted prejudice in opposition to missionary effort, I have long-entertained the deliberate conviction that there is no sin of the christian church more universal—none which will draw upon it greater condemnation, than the cold indifference with which this great work, which has been solemnly committed to it by the Great Head of the Church, has been regarded: so long as it continues to be a principle of the Lord of truth and righteousness that "without holiness no man shall see the Lord"—that nothing which is impure or defileth shall enter within the walls of the New Jerusalem, so long must those, who know the pollution of the heathen world, mourn over the certainty of their exclusion from that happiness which the Lord hath purchased for those that love him. I pretend not to pass judgment upon every individual heathen: the Lord knoweth them that are his. But when we speak of masses we must speak in general terms. When the prophet in his despondence looked over Israel and thought, "I, even I alone, am left to call upon thy name," he was rebuked for his selfish, short-sighted want of faith, and told of seven thousand men who had not bowed the knee to Baal. Yet even the anxious glance of the prophet could not discern these members of an election by grace among the multitude—so now there may be and doubtless are, among the many hundreds of millions of the heathen world, some who, in anxious seeking after God, and doing by nature the things of the law, shall be accepted, and, coming from the east and the west, the north and the south, condemn those who with greater privileges abused or despised, shall see these enter into the kingdom of heaven, while they are themselves thrust out. But, when this is granted, have we granted any thing which shall in the slightest degree abate from the necessity of missionary effort? The testimony not of missionaries but of infidels, and even of the people themselves, is, that the mass of them are sunk into the lowest degree of wickedness and degradation—and this be it remembered not in ignorance and mental hebetude, but with minds intelligent and quick, and consciences far from seared. And what cry, other than that of those who are perishing, could come with a stronger appeal to the heart of the christian, than that of those who in anxious desire for salvation are seeking some way of acceptance, torturing their bodies for the good of their souls—groping in the dark in search of some light upon the way they are seeking which shall lead them to everlasting life and peace? To such a soul, wandering "now this way and now that," seeking the pearl of price, and willing to part with all to obtain it, "how beautiful upon the mountains would be the feet of him that brought glad tidings." Who does not long to tell to such an one the glorious news of the "blood of Christ cleansing from all sin"—to carry to such an one the invitation, "Come unto me, all ye that labour and are heavy laden, and I will give you rest?" So that the necessity to preach the unsearchable riches of Christ to the heathen may be founded on two perfectly distinct points of obligation: to those who are resisting that amount of light which still remains among them, and are not willing to retain God in their knowledge, it is necessary to exhibit his purity and holiness, and his hatred of sin, shown in the provision it was needful to make for the pardon of man's transgressions: and to those who are mourning under the conviction of unholiness and longing for deliverance from the power and guilt of sin, in order that they may be brought acquainted with the means of grace, and become possessors of the comfort and joy of a hope of glory. These arguments especially apply to those nations who, like the Hindoos and Chinese, are partially enlightened, possessed of acute and inquiring minds, and susceptible already of impressions which may be made upon their understandings, and addressed to their hearts—who, like the ancient Romans and Greeks, "by *wisdom* know not God." Equally cogent are the arguments which appeal to us in behalf of those nations who in the degradation of barbarism show but little to distinguish them from the brutes, living only for the gratification of animal appetites and passions, and exhibiting just enough of the characteristics of man to justify us in the belief that they are members of the human family, and as such possessed of souls destined to immortal existence, and susceptible of immortal joy and glory. To such the knowledge of the gospel, accompanied as it always is by the enlightening and sanctifying operations of the Holy Ghost, brings not only the assurance of future bliss but meliorating influences on their present condition. Let us but look back a few centuries to our own British, Saxon, and Celtic ancestry, and see them plunged in ignorance and idolatry as gross and degrading as that which now holds any portion of our fellow-men in its thraldom, and then contrast it with the light and knowledge which now afford us joy, and examine to what it is we owe the change, and we shall find the benign influences of the gospel at the foundation of it all; and, while we thus enhance our estimation of present blessings by the comparison, let us examine our own hearts and see whether we so value them as to be willing to make some sacrifice for the extension of the same to others. The natural philanthropy of the human heart should be sufficient to move us to some exertion at least to bestow upon others the blessings we so richly partake of ourselves. The conviction that

> "The quality of mercy is not strained,
> It droppeth like the gentle rain from heaven
> Upon the place beneath. It is twice blessed—
> It blesseth him that gives and him that takes,"

Should stir us up to some effort—or we should cease to pride ourselves on its possession. But if such motives should have weight on every feeling heart, what should be the amount of feeling in the christian's breast? Himself a monument of grace and mercy on the part of God, professedly partaker of the blessings purchased for all mankind by the blood of Jesus—how can he shut up his bowels of compassion from those who are allied to him by the ties of common humanity—profess to pity their degradation, and yet stretch forth no hand to help? Surely such want of consistency must draw down heavier condemnation than that which an apostle threatens to those who feel not for the bodily wants of their fellows.

And now, what remains for us but to examine, each one for himself, how far we are engaged in working together with God, for the promotion of the great object which He is labouring to effect, the restoration of his sovereignty in the world, and the bringing back of man from the degradation into which sin has plunged him, to the glory and honour which belonged to his original condition, and of which he is still susceptible? The cry of so many millions of fellow-creatures, destitute of all that constitutes our comfort in life, and hope in death, should alone be sufficient to arouse us from the lethargy in which we have so long been slumbering. Those generous, noble, expanded feelings, on which we are wont to pride ourselves as the tokens of our greatness, and which stand amid the desolation wrought by sin as the monuments of what man was when he came from the hand of his Creator in all the nobility and grandeur of the image of God; these, alone, should be sufficient to impel us to greater diligence in extending the blessings of the gospel. What, though the feeble cry of the new-born infant no longer pierce our ear, as it sinks in the polluted stream, or falls a prey to the devouring monster.—What, though the noise of the drum, and the shouts of a multitude of Priests of Baal, no longer drown the voices of infatuated females perishing in the flames.—What, though the headless trunks of human victims no longer lie before the hideous image of the "Black Mother," thirsting for blood—and the car of Juggernaut no longer rolls its cumbrous load, stained with the gore of self-devoted sacrifices. What are all these changes but triumphs of the cross? And shall we stop here, just as these signs of trembling give promise of victory? These are but the outposts of the enemy, and while the victory over them should cheer us to further conquest, far be it from us to rest here as though all had been achieved. Neither let us be disheartened because so little has yet been done—far from little is it when it is compared with the efforts which have been put forth to accomplish it. It is my firm conviction that so little has been effected only because so little effort has been made, and that, had not God been working with the little band of preachers, less still would have resulted. Who can say he has done what he could except perhaps here and there a widow who has cast in her mite? Let the thousands spent by professed christians, not for personal comfort, but for display and to maintain their station in the ranks of the world, compared with the insignificant sums expended for the extension of the gospel, be the answer. Where is the spirit of liberality which an apostle praised, leading, to the giving even "beyond that they were able?" and, above all, where are the self devoted men and women to go forth as heralds of the cross, bearing its glad tidings to those who, as yet, are "in darkness and the shadow of death," "feeling after God, if haply they may find him?" Let no one who professes to have been redeemed from the just penalty of his transgressions by the precious blood of Jesus, say all has been done till he has well examined whether he be not called of the Lord to join the army of the cross; and when he has decided that duty does not call him into the field, let him see well to it that he supports those who are there. Our own mission to the Chinese, how long are we to be content with *two* preachers of the gospel to so many *millions* of people? Where is the spirit which appeared just glowing with promise, when these two came forward to the work? May it not cease to burn brighter and brighter until its radiance has dissipated the gloom which has so long enshrouded the nation!* Then when the church of the Lord enters into the work with a spirit of holy emulation in stirring up her members to strive each one to be found faithful, whether in little or much, we shall see results follow which shall cause what has been effected to be forgotten in the comparison. The earnest appeal of the present Bishop of Calcutta in behalf of British India, may be applied with equal force to ourselves in behalf of the whole heathen world. Would to God it might stir up many of the *pious students of our colleges*, that "great might be the

*Since this was written the Foreign Committee has announced a third as ready to go forth. But "what are they among so many?" At the same time too it announces its fear of a deficiency of funds for the support of our present feeble foreign operations.

army of the preachers." "Oh that our cry could reach the land of our fathers! Oh that visions not of a single man of Macedonia, but of the hundred and thirty-four millions of Hindoos and Mohammedans who are under British sway or British influence, might present itself to the pious students at our universities, crying, 'Come over to India and help us!'

"Shall men call themselves christians and see the scholar, the philosopher, the mere traveller, spring forth on the distant expedition and not imitate their example for a much higher object? Shall commerce be never weary, never disconcerted in her enterprises, and shall christianity go to sleep? Shall the civil and military services of India be sought for with avidity by the first families in the kingdom, and shall the service of Christ be declined? Shall the privations of a voyage, the languor of an enervating climate, or the increased hazard of disease, never deter men for a moment in every other profession, and shall they deter them in this?"

Having enjoyed the unusual privilege of a domestication for several months in the families of the missionaries of the Church Missionary Society at Madras and Calcutta, I am able to bear testimony to that which has passed under my own personal observation, entering upon that observation too with a mind obscured by long indulged prejudice against all missionary efforts, and these in particular; the subjoined extracts, from letters written at the time, may illustrate the habits and manners of these devoted servants of the Lord Jesus, and justify the change which witnessing the scenes described produced on my own opinions.

"It was a lovely moonlight evening, about a week after our arrival in Madras, when, fatigued with the noisy, yet cheerless, merriment of the dinner table, I turned out for a solitary walk. Having exhausted the novelties of the place, and without any acquaintance with whom to pass an occasional hour, I began to feel that most dreary of all sensations, described by being 'a stranger in a strange land,' and having nothing to attach me to it I longed to be again at sea. As I wandered slowly and listlessly through the streets thronging with natives, my attention was aroused by the sound of the bell of a small chapel, which I knew to be attached to the mission stationed in this neighbourhood by the Church Missionary Society; I entered, and found, seated on mats placed on the floor, about fifty natives, of all ages and both sexes, neatly and cleanly clothed, and with every appearance of humble devotion, waiting the hour of social worship. Pausing in the vestibule, I stood, contemplating with rapturous feeling, a sight so pleasing. I saw the western world rolling back upon the East a portion of that knowledge which maketh wise unto salvation, which had originally emanated from it. I saw, from the land of darkness and the shadow of death, the first faint glimmerings of that light which shall one day cover the earth, dispelling from the minds of its benighted inhabitants the gloomy mists of superstition and idolatry in which for centuries they have been enveloped. Indulging glowing anticipations, I saw among the interesting youth who sat before me the future messengers of the glad tidings of peace, and, contemplating them with 'their feet shod with the preparation of the gospel,' saw them exposing their lives, willingly, to danger—and their persons to insult, in the glorious endeavour to bring others to that fountain of living waters opened in the house of David, for sin and for uncleanness, in which they themselves had been washed and purified. Such was the train of my reflections, when I was interrupted by a cordial and brotherly salutation from a gentleman ascending the steps from the little court-yard with which the chapel was surrounded, into the anti-room in which I stood. Finding he was the pastor of the little congregation now assembled, I requested his permission to stay during the service, which, though in an unknown tongue, was possessed of a deep interest. The attention manifested by the poor creatures, who were thus enjoying one of the greatest privileges afforded to the believer, was exceedingly pleasing. At the close of worship, as I was about leaving the church, the missionary sent to request I would favour him with my address, and on exchanging cards very kindly invited me to visit him at his station, which is about three miles from Madras, surrounded by a native population. I found he was the Rev. William Sawyer, a gentleman of good connexions, and handsome estate, the first of which he willingly sacrificed, and the last employed in the service of his Redeemer—

leaving friends and the comforts of civilized life to settle himself here among the poor benighted heathen—willing to spend and be spent in the endeavour to spread the knowledge of the blessed gospel of reconciliation among the votaries of a dark and horrid superstition. Having learned these circumstances, I did not hesitate to visit him early the following morning.

After riding a considerable distance through miserable villages of mud huts, and swampy paddy fields, on a quick turn of the road I saw at my side a beautiful Gothic chapel* of white stucco, and just behind it a lovely retired little spot, reminding me more of home and peace than any thing I had yet seen, a small one storied house, completely embosomed in trees, and surrounded by a neat shrubbery. A narrow lane, passing by the chapel and between two rows of cottages, inhabited by native christians, led to the house; at which I was received with that true welcome which a christian, and he only, knows how to give. But it was not in the exterior of this mansion of love, nor in the pleasing reception I met from its master, that the charm of the morning consisted. After passing an hour or two in delightful conversation—the more so when the circumstances in which I was placed were taken into consideration,—he invited me to accompany him in the performance of his morning duty, in visiting a school he has on the premises; and which is certainly one of the most interesting objects in India. Under an open shed, each busily employed in his proper task, we found about 25 boys, most of them natives, between the ages of 10 and 16. A few are the children of christian parents; others of idolaters, selected from a large body of children whom he has under the instruction of native teachers, in day schools, in the several villages by which he is surrounded, and which he daily visits. The principal part of his care, however, is bestowed on this central school. All who are admitted into it must renounce caste, and consent to remain entirely with him; adopting all the habits of christians, (excepting as they would interfere with harmless local customs,) but especially be regular in their attendance on family worship, which for their accommodation is in the Tamul

* Built at the private cost of Mr. S.

language, morning and evening, and at church on the Sabbath. They are first instructed in the principles of their native tongue, then in the various branches of a common English education, and some in Latin and Greek. I witnessed their examination in geography, grammar, reading, &c. and was astonished at their progress. The grand object, however, is to bring every thing to bear on the one point—the growth in that knowledge which maketh wise to salvation. The scriptures, of course, are much studied.

"Having spent the morning, I returned to our lodgings, and early the next day we sailed for Calcutta. On my return, I hastened to renew an intercourse which, though short, had been so full of interest, and did not hesitate to accept an invitation to remain, during our stay, with one whose character I so much esteemed. An opportunity was thus afforded me of inspecting more closely the establishment. Here all that passés around the children, day and night, is calculated to show them the superiority of that blessed religion, to instruct them in the tenets of which so much labour is bestowed. Secluded alike from the evil instructions of their connexions, and what is more, the pernicious example of those professed christians who, holding the truth in unrighteousness, cause the name of the Lord to be blasphemed among the heathen,—they see before them a brilliant evidence of the effects of the gospel of Jesus, where it is received in humility, in their teacher; who, 'constrained by the love of Christ,' is thus labouring to bring others to an acquaintance with the same blessed hope which supports himself under all his trials. The usual avocations of my friend were not interrupted by my residence with him, and I thus had an opportunity of witnessing his system in its application as well as its effects. Rising at half after four, every morning, he receives, in his chamber, the visits of such of the boys as may have been led, by the grace of God, to hunger and thirst after righteousness. An hour and a half is spent, with these, in conversation and private prayer. There is no compulsion in this; all are invited and received who love the Lord; and the nature of the interview is such, that none others wish to be present. About eight of the boys avail themselves of this privilege. At six the whole family is collected for worship, which is in the Tamul language; after which they breakfast, and the children go to their studies, under the immediate superintendence of a young man who has been educated by Mr. Sawyer, and is every way fitted for so important a duty. The greater part of the morning is spent by my friend in visiting his out-schools, which are under the care of the native christian men, so far as he can find them competent to the office; but he is still obliged to employ two or three heathen teachers. By daily visiting and catechising them, he labours to acquaint them with the principles of christianity, while they are acquiring such knowledge as fits them for respectable employments; and as any of them manifest a disposition to attend to better things, they are removed to his house, if the consent of their parents can be gained, and once in the week the teachers are required to bring all their scholars to the house that they may be examined and instructed by himself. In such employment the morning passes. After dinner a class of the boys is instructed in Latin and Greek* till four, when the little chapel at the road side is opened for the purpose of declaring the glad tiding of 'salvation by the remission of sins.' The native christians all collect, and generally a greater or less number of those who yet 'sit in darkness and the shadow of death' are attracted as they pass along; and, either entering or standing in crowds around the door, receive a portion of that seed, which, blessed by the fostering influence of the Sun of righteousness, shall spring up and bring forth much fruit. The time which elapses between the conclusion of this duty and nine o'clock, is spent either in study, conversation with any of the native christians who may want advice, or recreation. At nine the family is again collected, and, after expounding a portion of the Holy Scriptures, the duties of the day are ended, as they began, with prayer and thanksgiving."

"One of the most interesting of the native schools is that attached to the Baptist mission, under the care of Rev. George Pearce, near Cossipore, about three miles from Calcutta. In consequence of his determination to have it understood that his only object in coming among them was their conversion to christiani-

* With the view of qualifying them to act as catechists or missionaries.

ty, he announced to his boys that he should expect all who remained in his school to sign an agreement, to be ratified by their parents under a heavy penalty, that they would continue with him three years at least, and use christian books in learning. The consequence was that the whole school of more than fifty boys left him; for a few days he laboured under great discouragement; before long, however, he had the pleasure of finding them all return, and before I left India it was one of the largest and best conducted schools I had seen.

" But, one of the greatest changes that has been effected among the Bengalese, is in the education of their females. Till within a few years they had nothing, except the faculty of speech, to distinguish them as rational beings—their knowledge extended no further than the facts occurring under their daily observation. A large body of them are now in the mission schools, from among the lower castes, and the higher caste people are forced from shame to have their daughters educated at home. With them, however, there is one cause of difficulty not existing in connexion with the boys. The latter are stimulated to the necessary exertions by the hopes of being able to obtain situations as sircars. There is no stimulus of this kind to induce the girls to come forward; and as, from their present degraded condition, they cannot appreciate the advantages of education, it is found necessary to encourage them by rewards of clothes or rice, or small pieces of money. The most flourishing of these schools are those of the Ladies' Society of Calcutta, under the superintendence of Mrs. Wilson. This lady held the respectable situation of governess, in one of the most noble families of England, till, being moved with compassion for the Hindoo females, by the accounts which were forwarded of their degraded situation, she left her home and all its comforts to engage in the tuition of a people little advanced beyond savage life. A large building has lately been erected for a central school, in which she is to reside, and gather under her immediate care the more advanced girls from the different schools scattered over the town, and qualify them for teachers. This will be gaining a most important point, as they are now obliged to employ sircars, which is manifestly improper. From the daily routine of this lady you may judge of the labours of the faithful missionaries of both sexes. At 7 o'clock every morning her little carriage may be seen leaving home, and from that time until eleven, when it becomes so warm as to render it impossible longer to keep the children together, she is constantly engaged in instructing in one or other of her schools, 40 or 50 dirty, filthy dirty, little girls. At 4 o'clock in the afternoon the same routine commences, and the intermediate time is occupied in the instruction of a few little orphan girls whom she has adopted, and the necessary cares of a family.

"When she first arrived, she met with nothing but discouragement, even from the missionaries themselves, so hopeless did they deem the attempt to improve the condition of the females of India. She, however, persevered; and often relates, with great feeling, the incident which encouraged her amid all the opposition her plans encountered. Visiting one of the boys' schools in order to improve herself in the language, and become acquainted with the habits of the children, she observed the teacher (a native man) to speak harshly to a child at the door, ordering it away. On inquiring the cause, she was told it was a little girl who had been long troublesome from her desire to be taught as the boys were.

"By the liberality of the christian population of Calcutta a noble building has been erected for the accommodation of a central school in the midst of the native quarter of the town, and here, without any male protector, and separated by a long distance from any christian habitation, she resides with a family of heathen girls, whom she is training up in christian principles and habits under her own continued supervision. Many of them are orphans, who, having no earthly friend but herself, are thus left wholly under her influence. She has already seen enough of good resulting from her labours to render her thankful that she was called to endure the privations and labour she has cheerfully borne. And the conviction that, as yet, it is but the first swelling up of the fountain head which shall soon be enlarged by kindred springs into a noble stream, must give her inexpressible delight in the anticipation of the full result of her self-devotion, which will only be developed in the great day when secret things shall be revealed. Who that saw a single unprotected female leaving the comforts of civilized life and christian society, to venture forth alone, unsupported, nay, even frowned upon by many who were the most anxious for the promotion of the cause of missions—who that followed her to her port of destination, and saw her there received, it is true, with cordiality, but disheartened by the opinion of those who had been the longest engaged in the work, who considered her plan as impossible of execution—who that sat down with her in her first effort to instruct the one little girl so often repulsed from the boys' school, and still returning to solicit instruction, until the Providence of God brought her an instructor—who that accompanied her in her fatiguing and fruitless efforts to gain others in the filthy lanes and squalid huts of the lowest of the native inhabitants, but must admire the strength of that faith which could thus endure as seeing things which are invisible—and who that has travelled with her in her depression, and witnessed her labour, but must rejoice with her in the great work which has been accomplished by her instrumentality, when informed that the education of the females in the East is the work not only of the wives of all the missionaries now in India, and its dependencies, but of many ladies sent out by a society expressly constituted for the object? Such results have flowed from the persevering efforts of one faithful female."

The Church of Scotland occupies at present a most important position in the missionary field in India. The East India Company had established two colleges at Calcutta, the one for the instruction of Hindoos, and the other for Mohammedans, in the principles of science, from which they carefully excluded all christian instruction. Not satisfied with passive opposition, they had positively prohibited its introduction among the students! The result of this was just that which might have been foreseen. The absurdities of the heathen Mythology were too glaring to stand before the light of western science. But while the minds of the pupils were thus disenthralled from its bondage, they could not rest satisfied with the negative position in which they were placed, and soon formed a body of acute and intelligent infidels, anxious to disseminate their views in opposition to every system of religion among their countrymen. A coalition was formed between the then Archdeacon of Calcutta and some of the principal missionaries of other denominations resident in Calcutta, for the purpose of counteracting this evil influence, which resulted, by the blessing of the Lord, in bringing several of these young men into the ranks of christian truth. In view of these circumstances the Rev. Mr. Duff, the first missionary of the Church of Scotland to India, laboured sedulously among them. He says in his report to the assembly of the Church of Scotland,—

"The evidences in favour of christianity as a revelation from God having been admitted by several as irresistible, and by others no longer opposed, we last of all came to the grand terminating object of all our labours, viz. the announcement of the message itself, the full and free declaration of the essential doctrines of the gospel. It was then, and then only, as might have been expected, that vital impressions began to be made. Hitherto, we were engaged in the removal of obstacles that opposed our entrance into the temple of truth. Having now reached the threshold, we crossed it in order to discover and admire the beauties of the inner workmanship. Hitherto the intellect chiefly was called into exercise. We had now something suited to the feelings and the conscience. The word of God is the alone direct and efficacious instrument in awakening and regenerating a guilty and polluted world; and the Holy Spirit of God, the alone Almighty Agent in crowning this instrumentality with triumphs that shall issue in the glories of eternity. Accordingly, it was when unfolding, in simple and absolute dependence on divine grace, the scripture doctrine of the sinfulness, depravity, and helplessness of human nature, that the heart of the first convert became seriously affected under a sense of the guilt and vileness of sin; and, when unfolding the inexpressible love of the divine Redeemer to our apostate world, that another heart was touched, yea, melted under the display of such infinite tenderness. Thus it was that the gospel triumphed, and the doctrine of the cross, brought home to the heart and conscience, and sealed by the divine Spirit, maintained its high pre-eminence, as the only antecedent to the conversion of a soul towards God.

"And I must here add that, in the case of some of the individuals thus brought to a knowledge of the truth, there was exhibited a demonstration of the power of christianity, such as I have seldom, if ever, witnessed at home. The case of the third one that was baptized, and who now conducts an institution in one of the upper provinces, was somewhat peculiar, from the trying circumstances attending his separation from his friends. Ah! could any member of this assembly have been present on that memorable night, he would have seen what christianity could do, even for a poor brutish idolater. It was about nine in the evening; and if any one here has been in that far-distant land, he will know what the external scene was when I say, it was on the banks of the Ganges, and under the full effulgence of an Indian moon, whose brightness almost rivals the noon-day glory of the sun in these northern climes. Two or three had resolved, as friends, to go along with this individual, and witness a spectacle never before seen by us, and perhaps not soon again to be seen by Europeans. It was heart-rending throughout. Having reached the outer door of the house, the elder brother of this young man advanced towards him, and, looking at him wistfully in the face, began first to implore him by the most endearing terms as a brother, that he would not bring this shame and disgrace upon himself and his family, (which was a most respectable one.) Again and again did he earnestly appeal to him by the sympathies, and the tenderness, and the affection of a brother. The young man listened, and with intense emotion simply in substance replied, 'that he had now found out what error was, that he had now found out what truth was, and that he was resolved to cling unto the truth.' Finding that this argument had failed, he began to assert the authority of the elder brother, an authority sanctioned by the usages of the people. He endeavoured to show what power he had over him, if he cruelly brought this disgrace upon his family. The young man still firmly replied, '*I have found out what error is, I have found out what truth is, and I have resolved to cling unto the truth.*' The brother next held out bribes and allurements. There was nothing which he was not prepared to grant. There was no indulgence whatever which he would not allow him in the very bosom of the family—indulgences absolutely prohibited and regarded as abhorrent in the Hindoo system—if he would only stop short of the last and awful step of baptism, the public sealing of his foul and fatal apostacy. The young man still resolutely adhered to his simple but emphatic declaration!

"It was now, when every argument had finally failed, that his aged mother, who had all the while been present within reach of hearing, though we knew it not, raised *a howl of agony, a yell of horror,* which it is impossible for imagination to conceive. It pierced into the heart, and made the very flesh creep and shiver. The young man could hold out no longer. He was powerfully affected, and shed tears. With uplifted arms, and eyes raised to heaven, he forcibly exclaimed, '*No: I cannot stay!*' And this was the last time he ever had converse with his brethern or his mother!

"I could not help feeling then, and have often thought since, how wonderful is the power of truth—how sovereign the grace of God! If it be said that the Hindoo character is griping and avaricious, divine grace is stronger still, and is able to conquer it. If it is the yielding and fickle, ay, fickle as the shifting quicksands, divine grace can give it consistency and strength. If it is feeble and cowardly, divine grace can make the feeble powerful, and convert the coward into a moral hero. What signal testimony do such triumphs bear to the power of tne everlasting gospel!"

With this experience of the advantages to be derived from the introduction of science in her proper sphere, as the handmaid of christianity, he resolved to establish an institution in which she should hold this relation, in which the truths of christianity shall be taught simultaneously with that scientific truth which dissipates the clouds of error and superstition.

The American Board of Commissioners for Foreign Missions has in India twenty-one missionary stations, twenty-two missionaries, five teachers and printers, twenty-eight female assistants, fifty-seven native assistants, and two ordained native missionaries. They have under instruction in their schools nearly 8000 children, and the native members of their churches, at the various stations, amount to 280. The Wesleyan Methodists, the Independents of Great Britain, the Baptists, have all of them active and useful missions stationed in various parts of Hindostan. But by far the greatest amount of success has attended the labours of the Church Missionary Society, an institution of which Dr. Buchanan was a consistent and firm supporter. The Christian Knowledge Society, and the Society for the Propagation of the Gospel in Foreign Parts, both, also, institutions of the established Church of England, have many missionaries in the field. Connected with the missions of the former society in South India and Ceylon, there are, it is supposed, not less than 20,000 professed native christians. In the commencement of their operations, being unable to procure missionaries regularly ordained in the Church of England, they resorted to the employment of Lutheran clergymen, chiefly obtained from Halle, in Germany. The Church Missionary Society, from the same cause, resorted to the same source for its missionaries, who have proved eminently useful. Whole villages have been brought through their instrumentality to the renunciation of idolatry, and the adoption of christianity, which they have adorned by a holiness of life which has made them truly lights amid the darkness by which they are surrounded. For many years past the converts have maintained a society for the purpose of disseminating still further the gospel which they have proved precious to themselves, though even to the present time they are burdened with the imposition of heavier taxes than their heathen neighbours, owing to their strict adherence to the truth in reporting to the collectors their taxable property, instead of resorting to the expedients commonly employed to deceive them. In many instances too these officers, being heathens and accustomed to receive bribes that they may undervalue property, revenge themselves on the christian natives, who will not be partakers with them in this fraud upon the government, by overrating their property, and thus subjecting them to increased exaction. Yet, notwithstanding all these difficulties, the work progresses steadily, and by a late account no less than two hundred and fifty-six *families* had been added to the church in the short space of two months, and this, too, in the Tinnevilley district, where, most unhappily, some difference had occurred between the Lutheran missionaries, and the Episcopal authority, in consequence of the opinion of the bishop that unjustifiable concessions had been made to the native prejudices on the subject of caste. This large addition was made subsequently to the adoption of the more rigid system; surely nothing could more clearly demonstrate the solid foundation on which the work of the missionaries has been constructed, than the fact that, notwithstanding these difficulties, their converts continue steadfast in the faith. One most interesting circumstance is related in the last annual report of the American Board of Missions. A missionary, journeying to a distant station, found at Jalna a native christian congregation of forty or fifty members without any pastor. There had never been a missionary stationed at this point. Most of the members of this little church had come from Madras, and, by associating together, had not only maintained their ground, but increased. What more could be said of any congregation in our own favoured country, under similar circumstances?

In concluding this Introduction to the Memoir of Dr. Buchanan, it will not be inappropriate or uninteresting to notice a subject suggested by intelligence recently received. We have more than once had occasion to advert to the countenance afforded by the government to the idolatry of the Hindoos. Time after time appeals have been forwarded to the Court of Directors in England, on this subject, and it formed a prominent subject of discussion in the British Parliament at the time of the renewal of the charter.

The persevering industry of the friends of christianity appears likely at length to be crowned with success. Long every appeal even to humanity was resisted; the infant was left to perish, a "sacrifice to devils," 1 Cor. x. 20. Widows, victims to the cruelty of priests of "devils," were burned by *hundreds* annually with the sanction of professed christian judges; parents were destroyed by avaricious children, anxious to possess their substance, in the light of day, and beside the great thoroughfare of the capital of a christian government. These abominations have fallen before the progress of the gospel. Still christian men are content to receive large sums annually as taxes on idolatrous rites, thus giving their sanction to the same—and, as though it were not enough thus far to be partakers in the sin, a government, professedly christian, forces its servants, christians also, to be present at the celebration of idol worship, even, though by so doing, the Lord's day itself is desecrated; and in some instances, not content with the passive sanction of their presence, they are compelled to make an offering to the idol. It is calculated, by one well informed on the subject, that the annual revenue received from idol temples in the presidency of Madras alone does not fall short of $200,000. So lately as the middle of the last year, it appears, by a memorial presented by the christian inhabitants of Madras to Sir F. Adam, that the onerous task of drawing the idol car on days of festival, was only effected by the agency of the *police*, thousands of the poorer classes being *forced*, under the orders of the collectors and magistrates, from their homes for the performance of this special duty; and this interference is viewed by the great body of the people as a vexatious and oppressive act of power, to which they submit *only on compulsion*. The memorial, praying for the abolition of this and other equally objectionable customs, was signed by 11 chaplains, 39 missionaries, 30 civil servants of the company, 111 military officers, and 11 medical officers, and was presented by the bishop of Madras, with the expression of his entire approbation of its petitions and statements. One part of the petition had been anticipated by the Governor in consequence of the death of fifteen individuals over whom one of the cars was drawn in the month of March. Thanks to the indefatigable exertions of Mr. Poynder, the attention of the Court of East India Proprietors has again been drawn to these subjects, and the result has been such as to afford a cheering prospect that ere long this stain on the character of Great Britain will be obliterated. Standing forth as she does with a national church the bulwark of christianity, and a people foremost in every work which has for its object the temporal happiness and spiritual good of man, may she soon be purified from all blemish, and continue to be the rallying point for the friends of RATIONAL FREEDOM and SCRIPTURAL TRUTH.

Memoirs of the Rev. Dr. Buchanan.

PART I.

CHAPTER I.

IT is by no means uncommon in the history of those who have in any manner distinguished themselves among their contemporaries, to find them deriving no peculiar honour from their ancestors, but rather reflecting it upon them; and becoming themselves, if not the founders of a family, yet the sole authors of their fame. Of the truth of this observation, an instance is afforded by the subject of the following memoirs. His remote origin might perhaps be traced to some of those who have in different ages illustrated the name of Buchanan; but it is not known that he ever claimed any such distinction, nor is it a point which it is at all necessary to ascertain. If, however, the biographer of this excellent man is unable to deduce his descent from the possessors of worldly rank or talent, an honour which may be unjustly depreciated as it is sometimes unduly prized, he may at least assert, that his immediate progenitors were endowed with more than an ordinary share of christian piety; an honour, in his estimation, of a higher nature; and a blessing, which, as he peculiarly valued it, was not only a source of pleasing and grateful recollection, but might not improbably form one link in the chain of causes which led to his own distinguished worth and usefulness.

CLAUDIUS BUCHANAN was born at Cambuslang, near Glasgow, on the 12th of March, 1766. He was the son of Mr. Alexander Buchanan, a man of respectable learning, and of excellent character, who was highly esteemed in various parts of Scotland, as a laborious and faithful teacher, and who a few months previous to his death was appointed rector of the grammar school of Falkirk.

His mother was the daughter of Mr. Claudius Somers, one of the elders of the Church at Cambuslang about the period of the extraordinary occurrences which took place in that valley, in consequence of the preaching of the celebrated Mr. Whitfield, in the year 1742.* Notwithstanding the enthusiasm and extravagance which probably attended those remarkable scenes, it is unquestionable, that many were excited to a deep and lasting sense of real religion. Amongst this number was the grandfather of the subject of this Memoir; whose piety was imbibed by his daughter, the mother of Buchanan. By both these excellent persons he appears to have been carefully trained, from his earliest years, in religious principles and habits. He is described, by one of his surviving relatives, as having been distinguished from his youth by a lively and engaging disposition. He is said also to have recollected the serious impressions which were sometimes made upon his mind by the devotions of the paternal roof, and by the admonitions which his grandfather, from whom he derived his baptismal name, and who seems to have regarded him with peculiar affection, was accustomed to address to him occasionally in his study. And though, as it will afterwards appear, the instructions and example of these pious relatives were not immediately productive of any decided and permanent effect, he must be added to the number of those who ultimately derived essential benefit from having been brought up "in the nurture and admonition of the Lord;" and consequently as affording fresh encouragement to religious parents to pursue a course which has been so frequently crowned with success, and which is seldom, it may be hoped, altogether in vain.

In the year 1773, at the age of seven years, young Buchanan was sent to a grammar school at Inverary in Argyleshire, where he received the rudiments of his education, and is said to have made considerable proficiency in the Latin and Greek languages. He continued at Inverary till some time in the year 1779, when he was invited to spend the vacation with his school-fellow, John Campbell, of Airds, near the island of Mull; and in the following year he received an appointment, which would be deemed extraordinary in this part of the kingdom, but is by no means uncommon in Scotland. This was, to be tutor to the two sons of Mr. Campbell of Dunstafnage, one of whom was, in the year 1803, Captain of the East India Company's ship.

* See Gillies's Historical Coll. vol. ii. p. 339.

United Kingdom. As he had then only just completed his 14th year, his literary acquirements can scarcely be expected to have been extensive. Yet the very appointment to such an office, at so early an age, is in itself honourable to his character, and his continuance in it during nearly two years may suffice to show, that his conduct proved satisfactory to his employer. About this time he was again under considerable impressions of a religious nature, which he communicated to his excellent grandfather, who carefully cherished them, and assured him of his prayers. For a few months he continued in this promising course, spending much time in devotion amidst the rocks on the sea-shore near which he was then residing: but at length his serious thoughts were dissipated by the society of an irreligious companion, and his goodness, like that of many a hopeful youth, vanished "as a morning cloud, and as the early dew;" nor was it till many years afterwards, that painful and salutary convictions led him to seek that God whose early invitations he had ungratefully refused.

The residence of Buchanan at Dunstafnage might probably have been longer, had it not interfered with a necessary attention to the progress of his own education. In the year 1782 he therefore left the family of Mr. Campbell, and proceeded to the University of Glasgow; where he remained during that and the following year, diligently pursuing the various studies of the place. Whether his academical course was interrupted by the failure of his pecuniary resources, or was the result of deliberation and choice, is uncertain. It appears only that he left Glasgow in the year 1784, and went to the Island of Islay, for the purpose of becoming tutor to the sons of Mr. Campbell of Knockmelly. In the following year, from some cause, obviously not unfavourable to his character, we find him removed to Carradell in Kintyre, and performing the same office to the sons of Mr. Campbell of that place. In the year 1786, however, Buchanan returned to the college at Glasgow; and a certificate in that year, from the Professor of Logic, testifies not only that he had regularly attended upon the public lectures of that class, but that, in the usual examination and exercises, he had given commendable proofs of attention, diligence, and success in the prosecution of his studies; and that he had behaved with all suitable propriety of conduct and manners. At the conclusion of the academical session he returned to Carradell, and resumed his employment as a tutor; in which capacity it is presumed that he continued until the commencement of the autumn in the following year; when he quitted his native country, under very singular circumstances, and entered upon a project, on which, as it afterwards appeared, depended the future tenor of his life.

Mr. Buchanan had, from his earliest years, been intended by his parents for the ministry in the Church of Scotland: but being naturally of an ardent and excursive turn of mind, he, at the age of seventeen, during his first residence in the University of Glasgow, conceived the design of making the tour of Europe on foot; that being the only method of travelling, upon which his slender finances would allow him to calculate. His chief view in this romantic project was, doubtless, to see the world; yet not, as he afterwards declared, without some vague and undefined intention of applying the information which he might collect during his tour to some useful purpose. It was not, however, till nearly four years afterwards, during which, as we have seen, he was diligently employed in acquiring and imparting knowledge, that a circumstance occurred, which, though it did not originally suggest this design, certainly tended to hasten his departure from Scotland.* This was an imprudent attachment to a young lady, who happened to be on a visit to the family in which he was then residing, and who was superior to himself in birth and fortune. The affection was mutual, but the disparity of their rank and station seemed to form an insuperable barrier to their union. Mr. Buchanan became in consequence very unhappy, and in the height of his passion recurred to his favourite and long-cherished plan of a foreign tour; in the course of which, with all the sanguine expectation and the inexperience incident to his feelings and his age, he hoped to advance his fortune, and returning to his native country, to obtain the object of his wishes. Strange and unpromising as this project undoubtedly was, he was eager to accomplish it. But though his thoughtless ardour reconciled him to the culpable expedient of deceiving his parents, he was unwilling to leave them clandestinely. For the purpose, therefore, both of avoiding any opposition to his scheme, and of relieving them from uneasiness, he invented a story, which, engaged as he had long been in tuition, seemed by no means improbable. He pretended that he had been invited by an English gentleman

---

* A very different account of the circumstances, which led to Mr. Buchanan's emigration from his native country, has been given to the world: but the public may be assured, that it is entirely devoid of foundation in fact.

to accompany his son upon a tour to the continent; and as this engagement not only offered some present advantages, but held out flattering hopes of his future advancement in life, not inconsistent with their original intentions, his friends consented to the proposal, and permitted him to leave Scotland. Of this singular expedition, and of his subsequent history during several years, Mr. Buchanan long afterwards gave several distinct but consistent narratives, from which the following account is extracted. After briefly mentioning the circumstances which have been previously stated respecting his education and studies, and the scheme which he had devised for effecting his departure from his native country and friends, and his intended travels upon the continent, Mr. Buchanan suggests the obvious question, how he was to accomplish such a plan, destitute as he was of pecuniary resources. To this he replies, that the greater his difficulties were, the more romantic would his tour appear; and then proceeds as follows.

"I had the example of the celebrated Dr. Goldsmith before me, who travelled through Europe on foot, and supported himself by playing on his flute. I could play a little on the violin, and on this I relied for occasional support during my long and various travels.

"In August 1787, having put on plain clothes, becoming my apparent situation, I left Edinburgh on foot with the intention of travelling to London, and thence to the continent: that very violin which I now have, and the case which contains it, I had under my arm, and thus I travelled onward. After I had proceeded some days on my journey, and had arrived at a part of the country where I thought I could not be known, I called at gentlemen's houses, and farm-houses, where I was in general kindly lodged. They were very well pleased with my playing reels to them, (for I played them better than I can now,) and I sometimes received five shillings, sometimes half a crown, and sometimes nothing but my dinner. Wherever I went, people seemed to be struck a little by my appearance, particularly if they entered into conversation with me. They were often very inquisitive, and I was sometimes at a loss what to say. I professed to be a musician travelling through the country for his subsistence: but this appeared very strange to some, and they wished to know where I obtained my learning; for sometimes pride, and sometimes accident would call forth expressions, in the course of conversation, which excited their surprise. I was often invited to stay for some time at a particular place; but this I was afraid of, lest I might be discovered. It was near a month, I believe, before I arrived on the borders of England, and in that time many singular occurrences befel me. I once or twice met persons whom I had known, and narrowly escaped discovery. Sometimes I had nothing to eat, and had no where to rest at night; but, notwithstanding, I kept steady to my purpose, and pursued my journey.

Before, however, I reached the borders of England, I would gladly have returned; but I could not: the die was cast; my pride would have impelled me to suffer death, I think, rather than to have exposed my folly; and I pressed forward.

"When I arrived at Newcastle, I felt tired of my long journey, and found that it was indeed hard to live on the benevolence of others: I therefore resolved to proceed to London by water; for I did not want to travel in my own country, but on the continent.

"I accordingly embarked in a collier at North Shields, and sailed for London. On the third night of the voyage we were in danger of being cast away during a gale of wind; and then, for the first time, I began to reflect seriously on my situation."

During the violence of the storm, as he afterwards acknowledged to a friend, Mr. Buchanan felt as if the judgment of God, as in the case of Jonah, was overtaking him; but, unlike the repenting prophet, no sooner had the tempest of the elements subsided, than the agitation of his mind also passed away. He arrived safely in London on the second of September: "but by this time," he continues, in one of his letters referred to, "my spirits were nearly exhausted by distress and poverty. I now relinquished every idea of going abroad. I saw such a visionary scheme in its true light, and resolved, if possible, to procure some situation, as an usher or clerk, or any employment, whereby I might derive a subsistence: but I was unsuccessful. I lived sometime, in obscure lodgings, by selling my clothes and books; for I did not attempt to obtain any assistance by my skill in music, lest I should be discovered by some persons who might know me or my family. I was in a short time reduced to the lowest extreme of wretchedness and want. Alas! I had not sometimes bread to eat. Little did my mother think, when she dreamt that she saw her son fatigued with his wanderings, and oppressed with a load of wo, glad to lie down and sleep away his cares on a little straw, that her dream was so near the truth! What a reverse of fortune was this! A few months before, I had lived in splendour and happiness! But even in this extremity of misery my eyes were not opened. I saw indeed my folly, but I saw not my sin: my pride even then was unsubdued, and I was constantly anticipating scenes of future grandeur, and indulging myself in the pleasures of the imagination.

"After I had worn out many months in this misery, observing one day an advertisement in a newspaper, for a 'clerk to an attorney,' I offered myself and was accepted. I was much liked, and soon made friends. I then obtained a better situation with another gentleman in the law, and, lastly, engaged with a solicitor of respectable character and connexions in the city, with whom I remained nearly three years. During all this time I had sufficient allowance to appear as a gentleman; my desire for going abroad gradually abated, and I began to think that I should make the law my profession for life. But during a great part of this time I corresponded with my friends in Scotland, as from abroad, writing very rarely, but always giving my mother pleasing accounts of my health and situation."

Notwithstanding the preceding brief observation, that his allowance from his employers enabled him to make a genteel appearance, there are various intimations, in a memorandum book kept by Mr. Buchanan during a part of this period, that he was frequently a sufferer from the pressure of poverty: nor is this to be wondered at, when it is known, that the utmost salary which he received amounted only to forty pounds per annum. Accordingly, it appears, from several notes in the account book which has been referred to, that he was sometimes under the necessity of pledging articles of clothing, and in one instance his watch, for the purpose of procuring a little ready money; and even this painful expedient did not always afford him such a supply as to prevent him from occasionally recording, that he had been obliged to go without a breakfast or a supper; and once that he had neither breakfasted nor dined. It must, however, be acknowledged, that while this humble cash account is chiefly made up of his expenditure upon the necessaries of life, Mr. Buchanan seems to have wasted not a little of his scanty allowance on public amusements; amongst which the theatre frequently occurs, and sometimes debating societies.

From one of the brief memoranda contained in a pocket-book, from which the preceding circumstances are derived, and which are chiefly written in Latin, it appears that Mr.

Buchanan's father died on the 24th of August, 1788, precisely a twelvemonth after his own departure from Scotland. This event was probably communicated to him by his excellent mother, and must, it may be reasonably supposed, have awakened some peculiarly distressing feelings in the mind of her absent son; conscious as he must have been of the deception which he was practising upon their unsuspecting confidence. No symptom, however, of the ingenuous shame, which, it may be hoped, he could not but occasionally feel for such misconduct, is apparent in his diary. He merely mentions, that his widowed parent had written to him in the spring of 1789, upon the mournful subject of a monument to his late father: to which he replied by a letter, dated the 12th of May, *from Florence*, which he despatched on the 25th following. A subsequent entry notices his disappointment in not again hearing from his mother, whom, amidst all his wanderings from the path of integrity and virtue, he evidently regarded with unfeigned reverence and affection; while another states the arrival of an answer from her to a recent letter of inquiry from himself, which, either from the favourable account of his parent's welfare, or its salutary influence upon his own mind, appears to have afforded him much pleasure.

It cannot, however, be a matter of surprise to any one, who considers the imprudent manner in which Mr. Buchanan had left his native country, the deceit which he was practising upon his friends, the faint prospect which he could reasonably entertain of any considerable success in the world, and, above all, the pious education which he had received, to find, that the memoranda in question exhibit frequent marks of his inward perplexity and unhappiness. Thus, on the 10th of May, 1789, he records, in Latin, with an emphasis of expression which evidently proves the depth and sincerity of the feelings with which he wrote: "I have lived, I know not how, in a state of forgetfulness, or intoxication, to this day!" And on the 15th of July following, he briefly extends the same painful confession to that time. Within three days after the first of these dates, Mr. Buchanan was seized with a severe attack of fever, during which, he observes, that he had experienced, as might very naturally be expected, most uncomfortable reflections on his present situation. These, however, appear to have made no deep or lasting impression upon him, but, as in too many similar instances, to have vanished with the temporary alarm which occasioned them. Accordingly he soon afterwards states, that he had on that morning written part of a letter to his mother, and with the careless levity which in irreligious and impenitent minds returns, when they are relieved from the immediate fear of punishment, had altered his "plan of death and misfortune. to that of fortune and festivity."

He laments also, that on his recovery he had broken some salutary resolutions which he had made during his illness, and adds, with that fretful and impotent violence which characterizes those who are irritated rather than humbled by the consciousness of their weakness, and are ignorant of its only effectual remedy, "I *swear* I'll do so no more. O! that I knew how to persevere in good resolutions, as well as to make them! This has been my failing from my infancy." Who has not been compelled to make the same humiliating reflection, until acquainted with Him of whom the subject of these memoirs was as yet practically ignorant! without whom we can do nothing, but by whose gracious assistance the christian can do all things!

Amongst the various notices of his feelings and engagements, which occur in these memoranda, there are several, which prove that, amidst the incessant labour of an employment, which occupied nearly twelve hours of each day, Mr. Buchanan occasionally contrived to devote a part of his scanty leisure to literary pursuits. Unhappily, indeed, he was at this period so little under the influence of religion, that the Sabbath was too often spent in the study of Virgil and Horace; though at other times his reading on that sacred day appears to have been of a graver nature. But the latter hours of his evenings, which were not dedicated to amusement, seem to have been laudably employed in storing his mind with classical and general knowledge, and occasionally in improving his memory by artificial rules and practice.

Though the irreligious state, in which Mr. Buchanan was at this time living, led him too generally to neglect public worship, his early habits still induced him sometimes to enter the house of God. Upon one of these occasions he appears to have been much struck with the conduct of a young friend, who was so deeply alarmed while the preacher was displaying the terrors of the Lord in the future punishment of the wicked, that he rose up, leaving his hat behind him, and walked out of the church. It is understood that Mr. Buchanan considered this person as having been afterwards made spiritually useful to him.

Two short notes in the summer of the year 1789 indicate, that there were, even at that period, seasons in which he thought much and seriously upon his own state, and upon religious subjects; during which his reflections were sometimes gloomy and desponding, and resembling "the sighing of the prisoner" for deliverance; and at others cheered by a faint and distant hope of one day enjoying, through the infinite grace of God, the comforts of religion.

In the following year some traces occur, in the brief journal from which the preceding circumstances are extracted, of pious feeling in his mind. He notices a religious conversation with a friend, and adds, that he had in consequence thought seriously of a reformation. He mentions emphatically a season of private prayer, and his intention of purchasing a new Bible, when he could afford it; and while he confesses, on one occasion, with evident regret, his disinclination to religion, and alleges as one of the immediate causes, or symptoms, of this evil, the indulgence of morning slumbers, he observes, on another, that he had declined the invitation of a friend to a visit in the country on the following Sunday, upon religious principle, though he did not at the moment distinctly avow it. All these are circumstances indicative of a mind awaking from the deadly sleep of sin to the life of righteousness, and introductory to that important change of sentiment and conduct which was now approaching.

It is possible, indeed, that some may be at a loss to understand the meaning of this language, or to conceive the necessity of any other alteration in the religious character of Mr. Buchanan, than the correction of a few venial errors and trifling irregularities, or the supply of certain obvious omissions in his conduct. The determination of this question must undoubtedly depend upon the general views of those who consider it. In proportion as the standard of practical religion is either elevated or depressed, will be the judgment of every one as to the actual state, at this period of his life, of the subject of these memoirs. If slight views are entertained of the evil of sin, of the guilt, misery, and danger of a sensual and worldly life, and of the nature and extent of christian faith and holiness, the moral and religious deficiencies of Mr. Buchanan will certainly appear trivial and unimportant. But if, as the scriptures unequivocally assert, to live in the habitual neglect of Almighty God, though a formal acknowledgment of his being and attributes may be professed, is virtual impiety; to avow the name of christian, but to refuse the homage of the heart to Jesus Christ as a Saviour, is real unbelief; and occasionally to indulge in wilful sin, though the external manners may be decent and correct, is practical ungodliness; then was it evidently necessary, that a great and radical change should be effected in Mr. Buchanan's dispositions and conduct; then was it essential to his present and future happiness, that he should "repent and believe the gospel."

That this was the conviction of Mr. Buchanan himself, unquestionably the most competent judge of this interesting subject, plainly appears from his own declarations in the letters from which some preceding extracts have been made. "Since my coming to London," he observes, "until June last, I led a very dissipated, irreligious life. Some gross sins I avoided; but pride was in my heart; I profaned the Lord's-day without restraint, and never thought of any religious duty. Thus I lived till within these few months; exactly three years since my voluntary banishment from my native country; three tedious years; and for any thing I could have done myself, I might have remained in the same state for thirty years longer. But the period was now arrived, when the mercy of God, which had always accompanied me, was to be manifested in a singular manner. I had a very strong sense of religion when I was about the age of fourteen; and I used often to reflect on that period; but I had not, I believe, the least idea of the nature of the gospel. It was in the year 1790 that my heart was first effectually impressed, in consequence of an acquaintance with a religious young man."

Of the person thus briefly mentioned, and of the important effects which resulted from one remarkable meeting with him, the following is a more distinct and detailed account.

"In the month of June last," observes Mr. Buchanan, writing in February 1791, "on a Sunday evening, a gentleman of my acquaintance called upon me. I knew him to be a serious young man, and out of complaisance to him I gave the conversation a religious turn. Among other things, I asked him, whether he believed that there was such a thing as divine grace; whether or not it was a fiction imposed by grave and austere persons from their own fancies. He took occasion from this inquiry to enlarge much upon the subject; he spoke with zeal and earnestness, and chiefly in scripture language, and concluded with a very affecting address to the conscience and the heart. I had not the least desire, that I recollect, of being benefitted by this conversation; but while he spoke, I listened to him with earnestness; and before I was aware, a most powerful impression was made upon my mind, and I conceived the instant resolution of reforming my life. On that evening I had an engagement which I could not now approve: notwithstanding what had passed, however, I resolved to go; but as I went along, and had time to reflect on what I had heard, I half wished that it might not be kept. It turned out as I desired: I hurried home, and locked myself up in my chamber; I fell on my knees, and endeavoured to pray; but I could not. I tried again, but I was not able; I thought it was an insult to God for *me* to pray; I reflected on my past sins with horror, and spent the night I know not how. The next day my fears wore off a little, but they soon returned. I anxiously awaited the arrival of Sunday; but when it came, I found no relief. After some time, I communicated my situation to my religious friend: he prayed with me, and next Sunday I went with him to hear an eminent minister. This was a great relief to me; I thought I had found a physician: but, alas! though I prayed often every day, and often at night, listlessness and languor seized me. Sometimes hope, sometimes fear presented itself, and I became very uncomfortable. Going one morning to a bath, I found on a shelf Doddridge's Rise and Progress of Religion in the Soul. This book I thought just suited me. I accordingly read it with deep attention, and prayed over it. I next procured Alleine's Alarm to the Unconverted, and dwelt on it for some time. My religious friend then gave me Boston's Fourfold State. This I read carefully, and I hope it did me some good. I now secluded myself entirely from my companions on Sunday; and during the week, the moment business was done, I went home to my studies; and have since wholly withdrawn myself from pleasure and amusement. In this manner have I passed the seven last months, continually praying for a new heart, and a more perfect discovery of my sins. Sometimes I think I am advancing a little, at others I fear I am farther from heaven than ever. O the prevalence of habit! It is not without reason that it has been sometimes called a second nature. Nothing but the hand of the Almighty who created me can change my heart."

"About two months ago I wrote my mother some particulars of my state, and requested her prayers, for she is a pious woman. In her answer, written by my sister, is the following passage, 'My mother has heard much of Mr. Newton, Rector of St. Mary Woolnoth, London, and wishes that you would cultivate an acquaintance with him, if it is in your power.'"

It was, in fact, to this venerable man, that the letter, from which these as well as some preceding extracts have been made, was addressed. Nor must the occasion be omitted of paying a passing tribute of respect to the memory of that eminently pious and useful minister of Jesus Christ. The chosen and highly valued friend of Cowper could not indeed have been a common or uninteresting character. He was, in truth, far otherwise. However a world, incapable of appreciating spiritual excellence, may be disposed to treat his faith as a delusion, and his character as enthusiastic, the history of Mr. Newton will convince the candid inquirer, that the gospel is still "the power of God" to the conversion and salvation even of the chief of sinners; while the unblemished purity, the active benevolence, the exemplary fidelity, and the undeviating consistency of a course of more than forty years, sufficiently illustrate the holy and practical tendency of the doctrines which he had embraced; and prove that the grace which had brought peace to his conscience, and hope to his soul, had at the same time effectually taught him "to live soberly, righteously, and godly in the world."

The lively and substantial interest which Mr. Newton took in the situation and welfare of Mr. Buchanan, is one amongst many other instances of the christian kindness which habitually warmed his heart. The person who was thus addressing him was at that time an utter stranger. After mentioning, therefore, some of the particulars respecting his family, and his early history, which have been already stated, Mr. Buchanan thus proceeds.

"On the receipt of my mother's letter, I immediately reflected that I had heard there was a crowded audience at a church in Lombard street. Thither I accordingly went the next Sunday evening; and when you spoke, I thought I heard the words of eternal life: I listened with avidity, and wished that you had preached till midnight." Mr. Buchanan laments, however, that this pleasing impression was too soon effaced; and that, although he constantly attended Mr. Newton's sermons with raised expectations and sanguine hopes that he should one day be relieved from the burthen which then oppressed his mind, he had hitherto been disappointed. "But," he adds, with genuine humility, "I have now learned how unreasonable was such an early expectation: I have been taught to *wait patiently* upon God, who waited so long for *me*."

"You say," he continues, "many things that touch my heart deeply, and I trust your ministry has been in some degree blessed to me: but your subjects are generally addressed to those who are already established in the faith, or to those who have not sought God at all. Will you then drop one word to me? If there is any comfort in the word of life for such as I am, O shed a little of it on my heart. And yet I am sensible that I am not prepared to receive that comfort. My sins do not affect me as I wish. All that I can speak of is a strong desire to be converted to my God. O sir, what shall I do to inherit eternal life? I see clearly that I cannot be happy in any degree, even in this life, until I make my peace with God: but how shall I make that peace? If the world were my inheritance, I would sell it, to purchase that pearl of great price.

How I weep when I read of the prodigal son as described by our Lord! I would walk many miles to hear a sermon from the 12th and 13th verses of the thirty-third chapter of the second book of Chronicles."*

After apologizing for thus intruding upon one to whose attention he had no personal claim, Mr. Buchanan concludes as follows:

"My heart is overburthened with grief, and greatly does it distress me, that I must impart my sorrows to him who has so much himself to bear.† My frequent prayer to God is, that he would grant you strong consolation. To-morrow is the day you have appointed for a sermon to young people. Will you remember *me*, and speak some suitable word, that, by the aid of the blessed Spirit, may reach my heart? Whatever becomes of me, or of my labours, I pray God that *you* may prove successful in your ministry, and that *your* labours may be abundantly blessed."

The preceding letter was addressed to Mr. Newton anonymously; but so simply, yet so forcibly does it describe the state of a penitent, awakened to a just apprehension of his sin and folly, and earnestly desiring relief, that it could not fail to excite in the mind of a man of so much christian benevolence, a degree of lively sympathy with the feelings, and of interest in the welfare, of the writer. His letter, however, being not only without any signature, but without any reference to the place of his residence, the only method which occurred to Mr. Newton of conveying any reply to him was, by giving notice

---

* The following are the affecting verses alluded to by Mr. Buchanan: "And when he was in affliction, he besought the Lord his God, and humbled himself greatly before the God of his fathers, and prayed unto him: and he was entreated of him, and heard his supplication."

† Mr. Newton was at this time suffering under one of the severest domestic calamities.

in his church, that if the person who had written to him anonymously on such a day were present, and would call upon him, he should be happy to converse with him on the subject of his communication. This intimation Mr. Newton accordingly gave, and an early interview in consequence took place between them.

"I called on him," says Mr. Buchanan, in a letter to his mother, "on the Tuesday following, and experienced such a happy hour as I ought not to forget. If he had been my father, he could not have expressed more solicitude for my welfare.

Mr. Newton encouraged me much. He put into my hands the narrative of his life, and some of his letters; begged my careful perusal of them before I saw him again, and gave me a general invitation to breakfast with him when and as often as I could."

Of the meeting immediately subsequent to this first interview no account has been preserved. That it was mutually pleasing and satisfactory, is evident from the intercourse which afterwards took place between them, and which was ultimately productive of such important consequences.

"I cultivated," says Mr. Buchanan, "a close acquaintance with Mr. Newton, and he soon professed a great regard for me."

The grand subject, which would of course immediately occupy the attention of both, was the reality and the completion of the recent change in the moral and religious character of Mr. Buchanan. Though the public and private instructions of Mr. Newton would, from his well known views of Christian doctrine, incline him to exhibit to the awakened and trembling penitent the free and full forgiveness of the gospel, he would doubtless urge with equal solemnity and earnestness the necessity of ascertaining the sincerity of his repentance, the genuineness of his faith, and the stability of his resolutions of obedience to the divine precepts. That such was the general tenor of the counsel which was imparted upon these occasions, plainly appears from several succeeding letters of Mr. Buchanan; and though it is to be lamented that those of his pious correspondent to which he refers are not now to be found, it is evident, from various traces of their contents, that they were admirably calculated to relieve the distress, to remove the difficulties, and to direct the conduct of his new disciple.

Thus, in the venerable person to whom the providence of God had introduced him, Mr. Buchanan found an enlightened and experienced guide, a wise and faithful counsellor, and at length a steady and affectionate friend; while the latter discovered in the stranger who had been so remarkably made known to him, one who displayed talents and dispositions which appeared to him capable of being beneficially employed in the service of their common Lord and Master.

Before we proceed, however, with the narrative of their future intercourse, it may not be unnecessary to offer a few observations respecting the change in the religious and moral dispositions of Mr. Buchanan, which has been thus particularly described, for the purpose of obviating some probable objections and misapprehensions upon this subject.

It is possible, on the one hand, that some may perceive in Mr. Buchanan's ingenuous statement, little more than an example of that sudden and enthusiastic conversion, which it is so much the custom to ridicule and to decry; while, on the other, an equally numerous class of readers may be inclined to think that the circumstances thus related are easily to be accounted for, and little to be regarded. The one, in short, may be disposed to treat the whole as visionary and delusive; the other, as weak and unimportant.

In reply to the former of these objections, it may be observed, that even admitting the change in question to have been sudden, it does not necessarily follow that it was enthusiastic and visionary. "I do not in the smallest degree," says a peculiarly calm and cautious writer,* "mean to undervalue, or speak lightly of such changes, whenever, or in whomsoever they take place; nor to deny that they may be sudden, yet lasting: nay, I am rather inclined to think that it is in this manner that they frequently do take place." But in the present case, sudden as that impression appears to have been, which was the turning point in the mind of Mr. Buchanan between a life of sin and of religion, between the world and God, it was neither the first nor the last which he experienced; but one of many previous convictions, which had been comparatively ineffectual, and of many subsequent influences, which issued in the real conversion of his heart to God, and which continued through his future course to establish and edify him in christian faith and holiness. The substantial effects which followed sufficiently rescue the impressions which have been described from the imputation of enthusiasm, and vindicate their claim to a more legitimate and divine origin.

If the spiritual change, however, which has been thus explained, is acknowledged by some to have been devoid of any thing delusive or visionary, it may still perhaps be considered by others as neither extraordinary nor important. The reli-

* Dr. Paley, Sermons, p. 123.

gious education of Mr. Buchanan, it may be alleged, might naturally have been expected to lead, at some period of his life, to such a result; and the change in his character and conduct was only such as a regard to truth and propriety absolutely required.

The early associations and habits of Mr. Buchanan undoubtedly favoured the hope that he would eventually become a real christian: but their very inefficacy in restraining him during several years from a course of insincerity, vanity, and sin, is alone sufficient to prove that nothing short of that divine influence, to which he ascribed his conversion, could at once have convinced his understanding, and changed and purified his heart. With respect to the extent and importance of this change, it must not be estimated solely by the reformation of his external conduct, striking and decisive as it was: merely moral or prudential considerations might, perhaps, have been sufficiently powerful to have produced such an improvement. But how many, who either never deviated into what is grossly immoral, or whom inferior motives may have reclaimed from such a course, are, nevertheless, unconscious of the spirituality of that divine law, which reaches to the thoughts and intents of the heart, and consequently of those innumerable transgressions of its pure and extensive demands, and of that inward corruption and weakness, which lead the awakened mind to the deepest humiliation and repentance, and prepare it to embrace with lively gratitude the forgiveness and grace of the gospel! How many also, who are exemplary, perhaps, in social and relative duties, are yet destitute of any thing which can be justly called the love of God, and cannot be said to be actuated by any specific and prevailing desire of pleasing him, or of living to his glory!

It is, however, from considerations and comparisons such as these, that the nature and importance of the change which took place at this period in the character of Mr. Buchanan must be determined. It was initial, indeed, but it was radical; it was imperfect in degree, but universal as to its objects and influence. It not only redeemed him from a sinful and worldly course, but gradually introduced him to a state of "righteousness, and peace, and joy in the Holy Ghost." It rendered him, in short, "a new creature." He felt the powerful influence of the love of Christ; and cordially acquiescing in the unanswerable reasoning of the great Apostle, "that if one died for all, then were all "dead,"* he resolved no longer to

* 2 Cor. v. 14—16.

live unto himself, "but unto Him that died for him, and rose "again."

Such was the change, which by the effectual grace of God was produced in the subject of these memoirs; and such will be found to have been its practical results in his subsequent life and conduct. To the development, therefore, of these, as affording its most satisfactory vindication and illustration, let us next proceed.

CHAPTER II.

About a fortnight after the date of his first letter, Mr. Buchanan again wrote to Mr. Newton, for the purpose of communicating to him a strong inclination, which he had lately felt, to revert to the profession for which he was originally designed.

"Yesterday morning," he observes, "I went to hear Dr. S. Near the conclusion of the service, I was insensibly led to admire this passage of the prophet Isaiah, 'How beautiful are the feet of them that preach the gospel of peace!' It occurred to me, that that enviable office was once designed for *me*; that I was called to the ministry, as it were, from my infancy. For my pious grandfather chose me from among my mother's children to live with himself. He adopted me as his own child, and took great pleasure in forming my young mind to the love of God. He warmly encouraged my parents' design of bringing me up to the ministry. I particularly recollect the last memorable occasion of my seeing this good grandfather. The first season of my being at college, I paid him a visit. He lived but five miles from Glasgow. After asking me some particulars relating to my studies, he put the following question to me: 'What end I had in view in becoming a minister of the gospel?' I hesitated a moment, thinking, I suppose, of some temporal blessing. But he put an answer into my mouth. 'With a view, no doubt,' said he, 'to the glory of God.' I recollect no other particular of the conversation but this. It made a strong impression on my mind, and even often recurred to my thoughts in the midst of my unhappy years; and lastly, I thought of my present profession and prospect in life. It suddenly came into my mind, that I might yet be a preacher of the gospel. I began to consider the obstacles that had hitherto deterred me from attempting it; but they appeared to have vanished.

"These things passed rapidly through my mind. I wondered that I had not thought of them before. Your suggestion occurred to me, and I seemed clearly to perceive the hand of Providence in my not having been articled to the law. I now beheld it as an unkindly and unprofitable study, a profession I never cordially liked, and was thankful that I might shake it off when I pleased. These reflections filled me with delight, and as I walked home, the sensation increased; so that by the time I entered my chamber, my spirits were overpowered, and I fell on my knees before God, and wept. What shall I say to these things? At first I feared this change of sentiment might be some idle whim that would soon vanish. But when I began to deliberate calmly, reason pleaded that the plan was possible: and the wisdom and power of God, and my love to him, pleaded that it was probable. I thought that I, who had experienced so much of the divine mercy, was peculiarly engaged to declare it to others. After fervent prayer, I endeavoured to commit myself and my services into the hands of Him who alone is able to direct me.

"This day I still cherish the idea with delight. But I am much discouraged when I reflect on my weak abilities, my slender knowledge, my defective expression, and my advanced age. I am now four-and-twenty; and if I prosecute this new desire, I must return to the studies of fourteen."

At the close of this letter, Mr. Buchanan expresses the lively interest with which he had read Mr. Newton's narrative of his own life. "I am the person," he says, "out of ten thousand, who can read it aright; for I can read it with self-application. What a balm to a wounded conscience are your healing leaves! To-day I have felt a tranquillity of mind to which I have been long a stranger. I trust this peace has a right foundation."

It appears, that upon an early interview with Mr. Newton, in consequence of the preceding letter, he warmly approved the rising disposition of his young friend to change his profession, and to devote himself to the ministry of the gospel.

"He received me," says Mr. Buchanan, "with open arms, and in his family worship remembered me in a very affecting manner, and prayed for the divine direction in his counsels to me. We then passed a considerable time together. He observed, that this was a remarkable season with me; but that I must leave every thing with God; that I must use the means which he had appointed for those who aspire to his service; that I must devote the principal part of my leisure hours to meditation and prayer, and the remainder to the study of the languages; that I must persevere in this course for a considerable time; and then, if it pleased God, he would open a door to me. In the mean time," added Mr. Newton, "I would advise you to acquaint your mother with every circumstance of your situation, and to request, in the first instance, her advice and approbation."

To this suggestion Mr. Buchanan yielded without hesitation; and employed a great part of several nights in communicating to his affectionate parent an ingenuous narrative of his proceedings from the period of his departure from Scotland to the present time. At the close of this varied history, in which he strongly condemns himself for his past misconduct, he thus expresses himself.

"And now, my dear mother, how are you affected by this account? Is your heart ready to welcome the return of your long lost son, or does it reject with just indignation so much unworthiness? Whatever may be your emotions, I pray God, who has been so gracious to *me*, to bless this dispensation to *you*. The veil which was between us is at length rent, and I am now in peace; for believe me I have not enjoyed a day of peace since I left my father's house. I once thought I would rather suffer torture than betray my secret; but my 'sinews of iron' are now become like those of a child. Nothing less than what I have suffered could have softened so hard a heart as mine; and not even that, unless accompanied by the power of God."

Mr. Buchanan had no sooner made this disclosure to his excellent mother, than he communicated the result to Mr. Newton in a letter, which closes in the following terms:

"My desires of returning to my first pursuit, the ministry, still continue, and I think increase. Blackstone says somewhere, that to have a competent knowledge of the law requires 'the lucubrations of twenty years.' I once had the low ambition of being such a lawyer. But I am now so impressed with the dignity and importance of the office of the ministry, that I would with pleasure sit down to-morrow, and devote, not the lucubrations of twenty years alone, but all my life to it. But, alas! my present situation militates much against my wishes. O that He, who has led me thus far, would graciously direct my steps!"

During the three months which followed the date of this letter, Mr. Buchanan continued his employment in the law; diligently and devoutly cultivating the spirit of real religion, and anxiously revolving in his mind the practicability of accomplishing his wishes respecting the change of his profession. In the month of July, however, he addressed another letter to Mr. Newton, who was then absent from London, in which he laments, with much humility and feeling, the painful discoveries which he had been making in self-knowledge, and the slowness of his progress in his christian course. "I have but sipped," he modestly observes, "at Salem's spring—*Nec fonte labra prolui.*" He then informs his kind correspondent and friend, that his late letters from Scotland had afforded him much comfort. "My mother," he says, "writes thus:

"'The hint you gave me in your last, of your probably joining the Church of England, caused me, at first, some uneasiness. I hope you will forgive this. I find now that the difference between the two churches consists in discipline only, not in doctrine. I am, therefore, easy in mind, which ever way the providence of God may see fit to guide you. I am happy that you consulted your Bible, and sought the Lord's direction upon this occasion. If you cast your burden upon him, he will direct you aright. Since you were a boy, it was impressed upon my mind that some time or other you would be a good man. I own, of late years, I was beginning to lose my hope, particularly on the supposition of your going abroad. I thought with myself, this is not God's usual way of bringing sinners to himself. But the word of consolation often came in remembrance, that 'God is a God afar off.' O how merciful has he been to you, and how merciful to us, in concealing your miserable situation till grace brought it to light! I do believe the discovery a year ago would . . . . but these recollections are painful; therefore I forbear. What comforting letters have you sent us! Could a thousand pounds a-year have afforded an equal consolation? Impossible. It might, indeed, have tied us down faster to the earth, but it could not have set our hearts upon the unsearchable riches that are in Christ Jesus. Your friends in Glasgow are rejoicing with us: some of them saying, 'Had the good old people, (meaning his grandfather and mother) been alive, how would this have revived them!' Among your grandfather's papers, I find the enclosed letter, written by Mr. Maculloch to him, in a time of distress, when the sins of his youth oppressed him. Read it with care, and may God grant a blessing in the perusal."

It was surely with good reason that Mr. Buchanan added, "It is not the smallest of my comforts that I have such a mother as this;" who, though evidently grieved at his past misconduct, was, as he afterwards expressed it, "overwhelmed with joy, that her son, who was lost, had been found."

It appears, by the subsequent part of this letter, that Mr. Buchanan had a short time before been introduced, by the kindness of his friend, to the notice of a gentleman to whose munificent patronage he was afterwards indebted for the means of accomplishing the prevailing desire of his heart, in entering upon the ministry of the gospel in the Church of England. This was the late Mr. Henry Thornton; who, to talents of a superior order, and to various and extensive acquirements, devoted during a laborious and honourable course to the most important duties of public life, united a warm and enlightened attachment to genuine christianity; which, while it formed the basis of his religious character, not only supplied the rule and the motives of his general conduct, but prompted him, in an especial manner, to support with calm and steady zeal, whatever a remarkably sound and vigorous understanding deemed calculated to promote the glory of God, and the present and future happiness of his fellow-creatures. It was to this distinguished person that Mr. Buchanan, happily for himself and for others, was now made known and recommended. Mr. Newton had been largely indebted to the friendship and patronage of the excellent father of this gentleman; and justly thought, that he could not render a more important service to his young friend, or one which might eventually be more useful to the world, than by introducing him to the son; who, with higher mental powers, inherited that enlarged and generous spirit of benevolence, which had associated, in almost every mind, the name of Thornton,* with that of philanthropy and christian charity.

The liberal education which Mr. Buchanan had already received, and his advanced age as a student, naturally led his friends to wish that it might be practicable to obtain ordination for him without so long a preparation as a residence at an English University for a degree would require. The Bishop, however, to whom an application was made for this purpose, discouraged any such plan, and it was accordingly abandoned. It was afterwards thought, that holy orders might be procured for Mr. Buchanan at an early period, on the condition of his going abroad; and Mr. Thornton desired him to consider, whether his health would allow him to accept the chaplaincy of the colony at Sierra Leone. To this proposal Mr. Buchanan, after requesting Mr. Newton's advice, signified his cordial assent; but, for reasons which do not appear, this design was also relinquished. For a short time, the mind of Mr. Buchanan

* See Cowper's "Charity."

seems to have been somewhat depressed by the failure of these attempts.

"Notwithstanding," he says, at the close of the letter last quoted, "your endeavours in my behalf, I have little expectation that you will succeed. Providence, I think, has a few more trials and difficulties for me to encounter, before I am led into so pleasant a path; and I know that they are needful to make me more humble."

He felt, too, the absence of his paternal friend and guide, and looked around among his acquaintance for a companion, in vain. "I have but one serious friend," he observes, "and him I only see once in a week or fortnight. Next to the blessing of communion with God on earth, must surely be the society of his children. Yet I shall not complain, if I can enjoy the former privilege; for then, *Ille solus turba erit.*"

Amidst these discouraging circumstances, however, Mr. Buchanan assures his venerable correspondent, that he was never so truly happy in his life, having been guided into "the way of peace," relying on the direction of divine Providence, and being animated "by 'the hope set before him.'"

But it was not long before the kindness of the generous patron to whom he had been introduced, opened to him a prospect which his most sanguine expectations had never ventured to anticipate: instead of any further attempt to obtain ordination for him under his present circumstances, Mr. Thornton determined to send him to the University of Cambridge at his own expense; that he might thus enter the church with every possible advantage, and be prepared for a higher and more extensive sphere of usefulness than any for which he could otherwise be qualified. This resolution was scarcely less honourable to the character of Mr. Buchanan than to the liberality of his patron, whose discriminating judgment afforded no slight presumption in favour of any one to whom his protection was extended, and whose penetration was, in the present instance, amply justified by the event.

Early in the month of September, Mr. Buchanan communicated to his mother, and his friend, Mr. Newton, who was still in the country, the joyful news of Mr. Thornton's munificent intention. He had been so much depressed by the failure of former plans, and the present offer so far exceeded any hopes which he had indulged, that he was at first almost tempted to think it a delusion; but on Mr. Thornton's assuring him personally of the reality of the proposal, which he appears to have originally made to him by letter, he received it with those mingled feelings of gratitude and humility, which were the surest pledges that the benevolent exertions of his patron would not be made in vain.

"I was emancipated," he writes to Mr. Newton, "from the law a few days ago, and am now willing to enter into the eternal bonds of the gospel. I have been endeavouring to arrange my studies, in some measure, preparatory to my going to Cambridge; but I find so much to do, that I know not where to begin. I wish to devote my greatest attention to the Bible, and am desirous of adopting some regular plan in studying it; but I cannot please myself, and I am a perfect stranger to the system which is usually followed. The Bible appears to me like a confused heap of polished stones prepared for a building, which must be brought together, and each of them fitted to its place, before the proportion and symmetry of the temple appear. I would fain hope that the foundation-stone is laid with me; but the raising of the superstructure appears an arduous undertaking, and the pinnacle of the temple is quite out of sight, even in idea. I conjectured that probably the articles and creeds of the church contain the first principles of the oracles of God; and on this presumption I have begun to prove all the articles of my faith by scripture. Whether I am right in this mode of study I know not.

"I never felt myself in more need of divine direction than now. When I consider myself so evidently called forth on the Lord's side, my heart is faint; and I am apt to say, 'Who is sufficient for these things?' I find I am unable to go through the important studies before me, unless I am led every step. At present it appears to me, that my sole business at the University is contained in one line of St. Paul, 'to be enriched with all utterance, and all knowledge;' or in other words, 'to be eloquent, and mighty in the Scriptures;' which are said to have been the accomplishments of the preacher Apollos. But I find that I must attend to various branches of human learning, for which at present I have no relish. Alas! Sir, if St. Paul had sent Timothy and Titus to such a college as this, they would have complained to him of such a plan. But he would perhaps have answered, as he does somewhere, 'Till I come, give attendance to reading'—'that ye may know how ye ought to answer every man.'"

The sentiment expressed in the latter part of the preceding extract will not appear extraordinary to those who consider the state of Mr. Buchanan's mind at this period, and the one great object which he had in view in accepting Mr. Thornton's offer of an University education. The same train of thought occurs in his next letter to Mr. Newton; and although he afterwards acquiesced upon principle, in the usual course of University studies, it may not be without its use to develope somewhat more fully his present dispositions and feelings.

"Permit me," he observes to his first excellent friend, "to thank you for your letter. It is a mark of your regard, of which I am unworthy, and has affixed a seal to the truth of your interest in my welfare, which I hope will never be broken. Like Hezekiah, I spread it before the Lord, but with a different purpose; not to avert a curse, but to improve a blessing. The words in Hezekiah's letter were 'to reproach the living God;' but the words in my letter were to assure me that his name is *love*, that he is very gracious, and that I should serve him with a cheerful heart. I have prayed that I may be enabled to do so. Your letter is a silent monitor, which I hope at the University often to consult. It will, I trust, serve as a counterpoise to the parade of worldly wisdom, and teach me to reverse the motto of the schools, *Ubi philosophus cessat, illic incipit theologus.* Chrysostom was of your opinion; he says, Οπου σοφια Θεου, ουκετι χρεια ανθρωπινης. I think so too; but I also think, that the fault is not in the studies, but in the manner of pursuing them. If a student could wed himself to the Bible, and court the sciences merely as handmaids to her, I think this would do very well; but when we are seized by the *cacoethes philosophandi*, and devote ourselves to what Luther calls the *idola carnalium studiorum*, our taste becomes vitiated. Since I received your letter, I have seen something of this. I was introduced yesterday to the acquaintance of a clergyman's son, who has been two years at —— college, Cambridge. His father, I understand, sent him to that college that he might be under the care of religious tutors. From this account I hoped to find him a suitable companion; but I soon discovered that he had no inclination to talk of divinity, or of any thing that bore relation to it. His whole conversation turned on experimental philosophy and mathematics. I have not seen a young man so mathematic-mad in my life. During the whole evening I spent with him, his head was, (as Omicron expresses it,) continually wool-gathering after rhomboids and parallelograms. He assures me, that if I do not study mathematics very diligently, I shall have no chance at the end of my course of obtaining 'the honours.' I told him that I had heard college fame was very intoxicating; that perhaps it might be prudent to sip gently of it; and that as for myself, if I could pass my examination with a mediocrity of applause, I should be content. He observed, that *seven* hours a day studying mathematics would be sufficient for *that*.

"How much reason is there for that 'double guard of prayer and close walking with God' which you mention, in order that I may be enabled to pass through this fire unhurt! It is happy for me that I am not under my own guidance. It seems it is necessary for me to be somewhat 'learned in the wisdom of the Egyptians;' but I trust it is, that I may be able to see and set forth 'the wisdom that is from above' in a more transcendent light.

"The method you propose for my studying the Bible approves itself much to my judgment, and I desire to follow it. I have begun it this day in a solemn manner. O that my ardour for contemplating the truths of Scripture may never abate!

"What you say of a daily retrospect of my past life is an instructive lesson. Is it possible that for forty years it should have been so with you? I fear I shall come far short of this; and yet how much reason have I to sing of the mercies of the Lord all the day long? Is there any one of his children who is more indebted to him as the God of providence and of grace than I am? Who can 'sing of mercy and of judgment' as I can, when I remember him from the land of my nativity, all the way by which I have been led? How few are there who would believe that a man could be found capable of displaying so extraordinary an act of munificence as that with which Mr. Thornton is now honouring me? Were I possessed of both the Indies, I could scarcely do more for myself than he is now doing. And how unworthy I am of all this! When I think of these things, it is the grief of my heart that I cannot more admire and love that gracious Saviour, who has so highly favoured me. As yet, I have a very imperfect view of what I have passed through: but I trust these things will be shown me, as I shall be able to bear them.

"Mr. Thornton intends that I shall go to Queen's college; chiefly, I believe, because he is acquainted with the President,* and thinks that circumstance may be advantageous to me. I am happy to hear so favourable an account of Cambridge. It will be an encouragement for me to maintain my ground, when I see some around me who dare to be singular. It shall be my endeavour to attend to your advice with respect to my conduct to my superiors. I shall often pray to be endued with a meek and quiet spirit; and endeavour implicitly to comply with every rule and every injunction in the University, for the Lord's sake."

---

* The very reverend and learned Dr. Milner, Dean of Carlisle.

CHAPTER III.

Such were the views with which, in Michælmas term, 1791, Mr. Buchanan was admitted a member of Queen's college, Cambridge. "The day of my leaving London," he observes in a letter to his brother, "was very solemn. It was on Monday the 24th of October, exactly four years and two months since my entering that city. But with what a different spirit did I leave it, compared with that with which I had entered it! Had I seen at that time, in the book of Providence, all that I was about to do and to suffer in that city, I suppose I should hardly have dared to approach it: but God wisely conceals from us a knowledge of the future.

On the morning and evening preceding my leaving London, I was earnest in prayer for a blessing on my intended journey and its consequences. One request in particular was, that I might be favoured with the acquaintance of some pious companions in my studies. To this prayer I had an early answer. A gentleman set out with me from London in the same coach for Cambridge. He studied two seasons at Glasgow, as I did; then, like me, passed some years in vanity; and now comes to the University to qualify himself for preaching Christ, as I hope I do. This singular similarity in our circumstances occasioned a happiness of which none but ourselves could partake."

With a modesty and regard to frugality which reflect upon him much credit, Mr. Buchanan was at first disposed to enter as a Sizar; but upon the representations of the tutors, and of the friends to whom he had been recommended, he determined on being admitted as a pensioner. In a letter to Mr. Newton, written soon after his arrival at Cambridge, he very feelingly describes the perplexity which he had anticipated from the contrariety of the studies to which he was called, to the prevailing dispositions of his mind. Until he was actually at college he cherished the hope of being permitted to devote his chief attention to divinity, and to the mathematics only secondarily. But he found that the reverse was expected from him; and that the excellent friends, to whom his patron had introduced him, were quite as strenuous as his tutors in representing to him the necessity of complying with the established course of study in the University. Independently of the repugnance which Mr. Buchanan felt to this plan from the peculiarly serious frame of his mind at this period, he feared that by yielding to it he should disappoint the expectations of the friends who had sent him to Cambridge, and eventually frustrate the great object which he and they mutually had in view. The comparatively advanced age, too, at which he had entered the University, would naturally tend to strengthen this apprehension, and to dispose him to dedicate his time exclusively to theological pursuits. The state of doubt and uneasiness produced by these circumstances affected both his spirits and his health; but after stating the reasonings of his Cambridge friends, and his own feelings and inclinations, he expressed to his respected correspondent his resolution to follow that course of conduct, which, after mature deliberation, should appear to him to be the path of duty.

In the case of students in general, entering at the usual period at either University with a view to holy orders, however religiously they may be disposed, there can be no doubt either as to the duty or the wisdom of devoting their chief attention to the prescribed studies of the place. A competent acquaintance with the learned languages, and with the stores of historical and ethical knowledge which they contain; the principles of sound reasoning, and the elements, at least, of general science, are essential to the formation of an enlightened and able theologian. The basis of such a character must, indeed, be deeply laid in an experimental acquaintance with real religion; and it were devoutly to be wished, that this were more generally considered as an indispensable qualification in every candidate for the ministry, and that more effectual encouragements and facilities were afforded in our Universities for its attainment. But if to the spirit of piety be not added the advantages which are to be derived from the wise and temperate pursuit of human learning, there is great danger that religion itself will suffer in the hands of those who are thus unprepared to teach, to defend, and to adorn it. In the present instance, Mr. Buchanan was already possessed of such a share of learning as might have been sufficient to qualify him for the discharge of the ordinary duties of a Christian minister; but it was obviously desirable that this should be strengthened and enlarged by fresh accessions at the seat of science, to which the providence of God had so remarkably conducted him. Nor was it long before his judgment was convinced by the arguments of his friends, that the very honour of religion required his acquiescence in such a measure; and that, however the appointed studies of the University might appear to be foreign to the important purpose for which he had entered it, they would ultimately tend in the most effectual manner to promote it.

Among those who concurred in this salutary advice was Mr. Newton himself; and to him Mr. Buchanan early in the following year announced his disposition to yield to their suggestions.

"I think," he observes, "that my way is clearer than it was, and I hope soon to have little doubt of my path of duty at college. Your letter helped to pave the way for me. I have now taken up the study of the mathematics *ex animo*, that is, from a persuasion that God wills it. And for them I have made a sacrifice of some other studies truly dear to me. I tried for a time to continue them both, but I found it impossible; so that now, that portion of the day which I have set apart for divine things is extremely short, compared with what I once thought it would be; and yet I dare not tell some of my friends here that it is so long."

It will be readily imagined, that Mr. Buchanan had various difficulties to encounter on commencing his academical course. He had indeed been received by the Vice-President, in the absence of Dr. Milner, and by the tutors, with much attention and kindness; but having been entirely unacquainted with the mathematics before his entrance at college, it was only by hard study that he could contrive to keep pace with the lectures. "I once thought," he says, "that I should have been obliged to acknowledge my inability, and to have fallen behind, and was wishing for the last day of term as eagerly as ever truant did for a holiday. However, I was enabled to keep my ground, and my difficulties were never known, even to my tutor. This vacation will give me room to have some little beforehand; so that I hope to pass with more ease and credit through the succeeding terms."

From the time of his coming to college, according to the information of a contemporary friend, Mr. Buchanan was exceedingly regular and studious, keeping but little company, for the sake, he supposes, of economy, both as to expense and time.

His situation, too, was at first peculiarly unpleasant, from finding scarcely a single companion, whose sentiments and habits were congenial with his own. His indisposition to general visits even rendered him the subject of much animadversion. But from this trial he was shortly relieved by the praise which he received from his tutor for a Latin theme, the composition of which, thouth he had written nothing in that language for some years, was pronounced to be superior to that of any other student. He was in consequence treated with much additional respect by his fellow collegians, was allowed to visit them upon his own terms, and even received several applications to assist them in their studies, which served as a stimulus to his own exertions.

No sooner, however, had Mr. Buchanan determined on the diligent pursuit of his academical studies, than the wakeful spirit of piety, by which he was animated, made him anxious to guard against the possible dangers to which such a plan might expose him. For this purpose he cultivated the acquaintance of the more serious students at different colleges; and at his solicitation they agreed to meet regularly for the purpose of reading the New Testament, and conversing practically upon some chapter which had been selected. Their meetings were begun and ended with prayer. It is well known that such proceedings are regarded in our Universities, to say the least, with much jealousy, and are generally discouraged. Why meetings for religious improvement, when conducted as this at Cambridge appears by Mr. Buchanan's letters to his correspondents to have been, should be disapproved, more than debating, or other academical societies, for the purposes of conversation or even of festivity, it is not easy to discover. Young men, it is said, are incompetent to conduct with advantage discussions of a religious nature. But is their judgment at all better qualified to determine moral, or political questions; and is not the danger, whatever it may be, in the one case equal to that of the other? Both, it may be replied, are inexpedient. And if meetings of either kind are intended for the mere purpose of display, it is readily admitted, that the time consumed in them might be much more profitably employed. But in the case in question, the society met not so much for the purpose of discussion, as of raising a barrier against the undue influence of secular learning on the minds of those who were almost exclusively employed in its pursuit; and of cherishing that spirit of piety and devotion, the cultivation of which, in themselves and others, was to form the one great business of their lives. Meetings such as these may, indeed, and ever will be, objected to by those who perceive greater danger in the warmth of zeal, than in the coldness of indifference; but it may be permitted to those who, like Mr. Buchanan, have experienced not only their safety but their benefit, to vindicate, if not, under the regulation of that judgment which is seldom altogether wanting in our academical students, and in submission to academic discipline, to recommend them.

In addition to the society which has been just mentioned, Mr. Buchanan was invited to spend an hour on Sunday evenings at the rooms of one excellent person,* who has been distinguished during many years for his active and zealous support of religion in Cambridge, and to whom a numerous body of clerical and other students have been successively indebted, for the most important instruction and encouragement during their academical progress. Of the kindness of this gentleman, and of the benefit which he derived from his conversation and example, Mr. Buchanan wrote to more than one of his friends in terms of the highest respect and gratitude.

"These engagements," he says to one of them, "prove something of a counterbalance to the effects of human learning, and preserve my mind from being wholly absorbed in philosophy and metaphysics. Besides," and the remark affords a striking proof of the sobriety as well as fervour of his piety, "I have the opportunity every morning and evening of attending chapel prayers, which of itself I consider a great blessing."

Yet with all the encouragements with which he now began to be favoured, Mr. Buchanan expresses, at the close of the same letter, a deep, perhaps a melancholy, train of thought and feeling, which is not, however, uncommon with similar characters.

"I often meditate," he adds, "on the vanity of life, and the insufficiency of the world to confer happiness. Were I assured of my interest in the Redeemer, I should long for my departure. What is there to detain me here? I have no tie to this world, no earthly possession, no person, if I except my mother, for whose sake I desire to live, no idol of any kind. What then should induce me to linger here, groaning as I do daily with sin, and combating a powerful spiritual enemy? Nothing ought to urge me to stay, but a desire to promote the glory of God among men. But this desire is with me so weak at present, as scarcely to deserve the name. It is but a spark. This is my unhappiness. Yet the goodness of God may in his own time fan it into a flame."

Such was the resolution with which Mr. Buchanan engaged in the study of the mathematics, that at the close of his second term he found himself unequal to none in the lecture-room. He had at the same time, though contrary to the usual custom, paid equal attention to the classical and logical lectures; but very reasonably doubted whether he should be able to continue the same applicatipn to so many different objects.

"Indeed," he says to one of his correspondents, "I doubt

* Doubtless, the Rev. Charles Simeon.—Am. Ed.

much whether I ought to try it; and for this reason: I find that this great attention to study has made me exceedingly languid in my devotional duties. I feel not that delight in reading the Bible, nor that pleasure in thinking on divine things, which formerly animated me. On this account have many serious students in this University wholly abandoned the study of mathematics, and confined themselves to the classics, composition, and the like; for it seems they generally feel the same effects that I do. Now these effects were partly anticipated by my friends who advised the study of mathematics; yet they recommended perseverance by all means, and are seriously concerned for those young men who have rejected these studies, and have thus incurred the contempt of their respective colleges. Knowing now something of mathematics, I can form some opinion of them. I conceive that a course of them would be highly profitable to me; but I doubt whether I should run such hazards in completing this course, as you see I am exposed to.

"Your good sense will show you, when reflecting on my present situation, that I have much need of that wisdom which is profitable to direct. Weak in spirit, weak in body, and beset by hard study, which I know by experience to be a weariness to the flesh, what can I do but commit myself and all my cares to Him who hath hitherto cared for me, and will lead me, though blind, by a way I know not? By such a way is he now leading me: I know not whither his goodness is conducting me; I trust it is to his service: and yet there is such an ocean of mathematics and abstruse study which intervenes between me and usefulness in the ministry, that, like the Israelites, I stand on the sea-shore, thinking it impossible to get over: but I think also that I hear the Lord by his providence, which introduced me to the studies of this place, say, 'Go forward.' This I am resolved to do, till his goodness illuminate my mind, so that I shall be enabled to discover the errors (if any) of my path. If any, did I say? I know that there are many; but I need grace to abandon them, when I see them; I hope Cambridge University will prove a good school of Christ to me. I knew little of myself till I came here."

Notwithstanding the complaint which Mr. Buchanan expresses in the preceding letter, as to the unfavourable effect of his studies upon his devotional feelings, he occasionally experienced very different and more pleasing impressions.

"I ought," he observes, writing to Mr. Newton not long afterwards, "to thank you for your letter. There is an indescribable something which pervades the whole of it, and seems to intimate that all is peace and tranquillity within the mind of the writer. What an enviable frame of spirit does *he* possess who walks with God! About a fortnight ago, a dawn of that light, with which I suppose the Lord irradiates the souls of those that walk with him, shone upon my mind, and by its lustre showed me some things I had not seen before. I prayed often that this impression of love might not leave me. But, alas! it did leave me: no doubt it was my own fault. I would walk three times round the globe to attain it again: but no such great thing is required of me; I have only to believe; Πιστευω Κυριε, βοηθει μου τη απιστια.

"After what you have said on the subject of disappointment, I am resolved never to be disappointed. But it is a resolution which I fear I cannot keep. Let me pray for grace. If I possessed this fountain, all the streams would be mine; and among the rest, the christian grace of considering nothing in the providence of God a disappointment."

On the approach of the long vacation, Mr. Buchanan had some thoughts of spending a few weeks at Lynn, in Norfolk, for the benefit of his health, which had been impaired by his close application to study.

Mr. Newton had also invited him to pass a part of the vacation in London; and in the letter which conveyed this invitation, an extract from which Mr. Buchanan communicated to his brother, his kind friend expressed himself as follows.

"Our acquaintance was providential indeed! but it is a providence for which I hope ever to be thankful; and to account it one of the chief honours and pleasures of my life, to have been made instrumental in bringing you forward. May you be kept in the mind you express, to prefer 'a grain of humility to a mountain of gold;' and you will be like the tree described in the first Psalm, and Jer. xvii. when my head is laid in the dust. I hear well of you from all quarters."

The relaxation, however, thus proposed, both in Norfolk and London, as well as the offer of an excursion with a Cambridge friend, Mr. Buchanan, with commendable self-denial, thought it most expedient to decline, and determined on accepting the indulgence granted him of remaining in college during the whole vacation.

"It would be very pleasing," he says, "to make a short tour with a proper companion; but I think I could not do it without danger to myself. If I were somewhat advanced in the christian life, and more stable in the way of truth, I perhaps might; but at present I cannot, I dare not trust the deceitfulness of my own heart. In the retirement of a college,

I am unable to suppress evil thoughts and vain wishes; how then must it be abroad? Besides, I find that the art of study is difficult to attain. I must serve a long apprenticeship to it ere I am a good proficient. The greatest danger lies in breaking the thread of attention. On whatever study my mind is fixed, *that* study I can with pleasure resume: but if an interval of a day intervene, my attention is disengaged. I am conscious that I have lost a day as to that study, and find it irksome to begin *de novo*. But if instead of a day, an interval of a week or month should intervene, it would be a Herculean labour to resume it; and nothing could smooth the way, but a conviction that the interruption was from *necessity*; then, indeed, my duty would remove the obstacle.

"That you may have some idea of the nature of my present studies, I shall subjoin the calendar of a day.

½ bef. 5, 6, 7	Devotional Studies.
8	Breakfast and Recreation.
9, 10, 11, 12, 1	Mathematics.
2, 3	Dinner and Recreation.
4, 5	Classics.
6	Engagements or Recreation.
7, 8	Classics, or Logic, &c.
9	Devotional Studies.
10, 11, 12, 1, 2, 3, ½ after 4	Sleep.

Few persons would be disposed to think, on reviewing the preceding distribution of his time, that Mr. Buchanan had, at this early period of his academical course, assigned too small a portion to studies directly connected with his future profession. This is, however, the reflection which he immediately suggests to his friend; expressing his fears, which were certainly groundless, lest his patron should say, that he had not sent him to Cambridge to learn geometry; and, above all, lest the science which he was thus diligently pursuing should not ultimately reward him. It would, indeed, he says, be distressing to him to appear unqualified for his office as a preacher; "but then I hope," he adds, "I shall make more commendable proficiency in my divine studies when I undertake them. This hope alone enables me to persevere in my present course."

The observations which follow in the same letter are too valuable to be omitted.

"I apprehend," continues Mr. Buchanan, "that a student should *labour* as for his daily bread; not choosing the study he may like best, for then it would be no *labour*, but learning the great lesson of self-denial by taking up the study he likes least, if it be best for him. If I can by nine hours study a day serve my heavenly Master as faithfully as I served Mr. D. I think he will give me my hire. You cannot be surprised if sometimes I have my doubts, when I see the other serious students walking in a path directly contrary. All of them, I think, but one, (Mr. C.) have followed their own inclinations in this matter: and, in opposition to the advice of the experienced servants of God, have substituted divinity in lieu of mathematics. The reason they give is, that they do not *see* it to be so and so. Yet it is worthy of remark, that they do not appear to bring forth the fruits that might be expected in those very studies they love. I do not think that they live nearer to God for it, or make such proficiency as students earnest in their work should do. For myself, I know not what is best. Mr. C., the mathematical divine, has a more heavenly deportment than any of them. This they acknowledge, though it is somewhat of a paradox to them: but I think it will be solved to some of them ere long. I am inclined to believe, that were I an eminent saint, I should be a good mathematician, a good linguist, a good scripturist.

"I hope that the Lord is leading us *all* in the right path, and directing us individually to those studies which he sees necessary for the station he intends we shall fill; and if any of us undertake an improper study from improper motives, or a proper study at an improper time, like novices depending on our own judgment, I trust that we shall learn by it a lesson more useful than any study—a knowledge of ourselves, and of our inability to do any thing aright, much less to conduct such an important undertaking as the studies of a disciple of Christ.

"I should be exceedingly thankful for any hint that may

occasionally occur to you respecting the government of myself, and of my studies. The price which I have paid for the little wisdom I have obtained is very dear. Gladly then would I listen to the voice of experience."

"It might, perhaps, be expected, after such evident proofs of the enlarged, yet pious and temperate views which Mr. Buchanan entertained respecting the pursuit of human learning, that he would have been advised to continue his course patiently and uninterruptedly. The peculiar circumstances, however, of his case, and even the chastised ardour with which he appeared to be animated in his academical studies, excited some apprehensions in the mind of the venerable friend whose advice he had solicited, and induced him to suggest some modification of the plan which he had himself originally approved. The particular grounds of his opinion can only now be conjectured from the tenor of Mr. Buchanan's reply; which enters with so much judgment and feeling into this interesting subject, that the insertion of the greater part of it will scarcely be deemed superfluous.

"I was in earnest," he begins, "when in my last I solicited your advice and direction: and because I was in earnest, I think that your letter will be accompanied with a blessing to me.

"Your jealousy lest my heart might be gradually attached to our academical studies, awakened my fears, and I prayed for divine aid while I scrutinized myself and my views; and now I must candidly acknowledge, that I believe your doubts to be well founded: I believe that *you* are right, and that many of my friends here are wrong; I say I *believe* it, for as yet I am not sure: you and they view me in a different light; hence arises this difference of opinion relating to the plan of my studies. These gentlemen, not only bred at this University, but anxious for its fame, and still more for that of the religious students in it, are desirous that we should *excel* in the studies of the place, that we may, as it were, shed some lustre (in the eyes of men) on that gospel which the learned despise. The grand argument we use against infidels, who deride the truth as being only professed by men of weak judgment, is to point out some learned christian, (if such can be found,) and then say with St. Paul, ('Are you a Hebrew? so am I,') Are you a mathematician? so is he. Are you a classic, a historian? so is he. *What* are you? he is all that; but he is something more. Now it is natural to adopt such an argument when we can. On this account these gentlemen are eager to incline the serious young men to the studies of the University, which they therefore represent as being not only ornamental, but useful. Now this may be good advice to a young man who has many years before him, and expects to reside as a Fellow of a college, and preach occasionally at the University church. But I am not of this description; yet they look upon me as one who is to grow old in their own family; which is as improbable as I am averse to it. It was but the other day that one of my friends hinted to me, that it would be worth my while to change my college, that I might have a good Fellowship as a reward for my exertions. I am frequently addressed in such words as these—'Do pray persevere in your reading; devote your evening and morning hour to your closet, but give the rest of the day to the studies of the place. Nothing can redound more to the credit of the gospel. The most holy conduct will not here avail so much as that. Besides, you will be amply repaid by your rapid progress, when you begin your professional studies.' And now that my college has given me both an exhibition and a scholarship, they say, 'Did we not tell you so? You see that religion and diligence in academical study are mutual helps to each other.' If I have been allured by such speeches from those who are superior to myself in knowledge and experience, is it wonderful?

"This, then, is their mistake. They address me as if I were always to reside among them, and to remain an example either of learning or ignorance. As a young enthusiast, they consider themselves responsible for me to the University.

"On the other hand, you view me as having come to the University, not so much to qualify myself for the ministry, as to pave the way for my ordination, and think it of little import whether my name were ever heard in Cambridge or not. If this is right, their arguments are mostly out of place. Mr. —— approaches more nearly to your sentiments than any of them.

"I shall now give you the result of my own deliberations on the subject. Rather than you should have a moment's uneasiness lest the purity of my heart should be tainted by mathematics, I would throw every mathematical book I have into the fire, and make them a funeral pile to the manes of your jealousy. For compared with the word of truth, they are as dross to fine gold. In a certain degree they may be useful, and to that degree I would desire them; and I hope to be led so far, and no farther. At first I disliked them; but considering them as a nauseous medicine which might do me some good, I took them up. You, too, bade me. After a while, they became more palatable, and at length, a pleasing study. For this I was exceedingly thankful, as they were in the way of my duty. But now, as I have arrived at a certain length in them, and have in view very soon to enter on an important office which requires much preparation, I think it will be right—not to relinquish them wholly; I do not mean that: but so to circumscribe them, and my other academical exercises, as to afford me a considerable proportion of the day, (the half, if possible,) for 'the preparation of the gospel of peace.'

"I do not mean to put this sudden resolution into practice, till I know whether it be right. From some experience I know myself to be weak, injudicious, inconstant, changeable. I shall therefore prosecute my studies as usual, till I hear from you. Having acquired somewhat of a reputation for my attention to college studies, if I can preserve it, it will be a desirable thing. If not, I cannot help it; I willingly sacrifice it 'to a better name.'

"You do me great honour in the proposal you have made. I would rather serve you in your old age than a sceptre-bearing king. But I much fear that my services at so early a period will be weak and inadequate. It is like taking a babe out of his cradle to support the steps of his aged parent. But I am in God's hands: whatever he sees fit for me to do, I hope he will incline my heart, and enable me to do it. But as I cannot expect that he will work a miracle by qualifying me for his service at once, it is certainly my duty to resort to the means *now*, and pray for his blessing on his own studies. Surely I ought not to procrastinate.

"You ask me whether I would prefer preaching the gospel to the fame of learning? Ay, that would I, gladly. Were I convinced it was the will of God that I should depart this night for Nova Zembla, or the Antipodes, to testify of *Him*, I would not wait for an audit, or a college exit. There is nothing to be found *here* to satisfy my mind. There are indeed many gaudy vanities of specious appearance, pleasing to my fleshly eye; but if I know my own heart, the Lord Jesus is at this moment more lovely to me than the loveliest object which the eye can see, or fancy paint. And though I know him not as I could wish, yet is he precious. He is that pearl which I would willingly buy at the price of all the laurels which science ever bore. But I speak this in *his* strength. I wish not to be tried with wealth, honour, or the applause of men. A laurel even in preaching the gospel might intoxicate my brain, and drown my humble dependence on God, in Lethe. Then, like Lucifer, should I preach humility! Lord, my affections are *now* in thy possession. O, keep them there!

"You ask me what are my views? Dear sir, what views can *I* have? God has his views concerning me: I have none. *He* best knows why he brought me hither: I know not. Once I used to think, that as He had wrought so wondrously for me, he surely meant me for an eminent preacher of the gospel. Pride dictated this. I have now no such high thoughts of myself. I am in some degree sensible, that if I ever serve the Lord at all, I shall be one of his weakest servants. Nor are these mere disqualifying speeches. I have reason to fear that I am much more deficient than you apprehend. Nevertheless, with all my defects, I know the divine power. I have laid my hand to the plough; he can make me useful.

"You desire to know whether I would accept ordination before I take my degree, if it could be procured? Yes, without any hesitation, if I thought it was the will of God. Were I to submit it to our friends here, they would unanimously dissuade it; but I do not feel myself at liberty to consult them. In order to have it in my power to assist you as soon as possible, I would gladly receive ordination before the prescribed time; but in that case I should desire immediately to alter my plan of study, and prepare myself a little, who need so much preparation.

"If my purpose of beginning the studies of divinity be proper and practicable, could you give me the outline of what you conceive to be best worthy my attention *in primordio?* Mr. S., I know, will also be glad to lend me every assistance.

"A new desire of preaching the gospel has certainly sprung up in my heart, accompanied by ideas I do not recollect to have had before. I hope it is no delusion. As yet it has produced noble effects on my heart and views. But in a month's time I shall be better able to say, whether it be of God, or no."

The preceding letter is dated in August 1792, from which time till the October following, Mr. Buchanan appears to have continued the course of study which he had proposed at the commencement of the long vacation. The sentiments, however, expressed in that letter, combined with the suggestions of the venerable friend to whose advice he naturally paid much deference, prepare us to expect some alteration in his plan. The question as to the wisdom of such a step, may admit of some difference of opinion. Had Mr. Buchanan been a few years younger, it would obviously have been his duty to have persevered in his exertions to excel in the peculiar studies of the University. No conclusion, however, unfavourable to such a course in the case of the generality of students, ought to be drawn from his example. He had already proved both his ability and his diligence, and had the prospect of attaining, even with diminished application, an adequate share of scientific knowledge. Though it can scarcely be doubted, therefore, that continued and exclusive efforts would have rendered him successful in the competition for academical honours; there are but few, perhaps, who, under all the circumstances of his case, will not consider him as having piously, if not wisely judged, in abandoning that flattering pursuit; and in resolving to devote a larger proportion of his time to studies more congenial to his taste and feelings, and more directly subservient to his ultimate destination.

At the close of the long vacation, Mr. Buchanan accordingly communicated this determination both to Mr. Newton and to one of his friends in Cambridge; who, while he cordially approved it, recommended him at the same time not to announce it publicly, lest he should incur the imputation of being fickle or irresolute in his plans.

"I fear, however," he observes, in writing to the former of these friends, "that it will be difficult for me to conceal the change, as I must undergo two examinations next year, which will abundantly scrutinize my proficiency; besides, I have many competitors, who will exult when they see me halt. But I trust I shall be enabled to make every necessary sacrifice. What is *my* fame compared with that of the gospel? My desire is, that my light may so shine before men, that they seeing my good works may glorify my Father who is in heaven."

The continuation of this letter shows the sincerity of this profession, and the anxiety which Mr. Buchanan felt to fulfil it.

"How happy," he says, "should I be, did I always know what these good works are. It is strange that I should err when I have the Bible to direct me; but I find that it requires much of divine teaching to apply the general rules of scripture to particular cases. For instance, I would gladly know, whether it is the will of God that I should associate with my fellow students more than I do. Whether I ought to separate myself, or mingle with them, endeavour to obtain some weight among them, and correct their manners, and seek opportunities of speaking for God. Some of them, perhaps, never heard the terms of the gospel in their lives. If I were 'wise as a serpent,' I might possibly, under God, entwine some of them in the net of the gospel. Of late this subject has been much on my mind, and I have been earnest in prayer that I may be made useful to some of them. At my rooms they have always acted with the strictest decorum; scarcely a faulty word has been spoken; and I know not but I might have been a restraint upon them at their own. My principal reason for resisting their frequent invitations, is a fear lest I should lose time in idle conversation, or be unawares led into undue compliances. This latter operated much with me. I have been surprised that my conduct did not draw upon me their *open* reproach. But the Lord 'tempers the wind to the shorn lamb.' Last year I was extremely weak, ill-grounded in the truth, and perhaps should have sunk under much opposition. During this vacation, I trust I have obtained more spiritual strength; and perhaps I shall soon have occasion to exercise it."

Those who have experienced similar doubts and difficulties will be able to enter into the preceding expression of them. Mr. Buchanan appears to have steered that middle course, between absolute seclusion and indiscriminate association in college, which is dictated by enlightened piety and christian prudence; and the general respect in which he was evidently held, affords a sufficient assurance of the beneficial influence of his example.*

---

* The Christian Observer furnishes the following statement in relation to Dr. Buchanan's intercourse with his fellow students, from the pen of a "respected friend and correspondent:" "It is true," he observes, "that Dr. B. did not mix much in general society, while at college; but during his last year (when I went thither) he laid himself out a good deal to encourage younger men in keeping the right way. He called on me immediately on my arrival as a freshman, and watched over me while he continued at college with all the affection of a brother. There were several of us who used to look up to him as a Mentor; and he contrived to allot to us a portion of his time, either calling upon us at breakfast, or taking us with him when he walked out for exercise. In this way, his own time was not wasted; and he gained many opportunities of conveying to us both exhortation and encouragement."

"To this interesting statement," says the editor, "our friend, [by whom the circumstances are stated] subjoins a remark in which we very cordially concur, and indeed partly for the sake of which we have entered into this detail; 'What extensive good,' he observes, 'might be effected, if religious young men, while at college, and especially in their last year, would imitate in this respect the example of Buchanan. The youthful mind is then in a state to be influenced by the attentions of a superior: and although Dr. Buchanan might have had more weight with his fellow students, on account of his being a few years older than under gradutes generally are, yet it may be presumed that the well-timed kindness and counsel of a religious senior, especially of one who has distinguished himself by his academical attainments, will seldom fail to produce a favourable impression on his younger associates.'"—AM. ED.

In compliance with his request, Mr. Newton had recommended several books to Mr. Buchanan for the commencement of his theological studies. To this point he therefore next refers.

"I propose to confine myself to three branches of divinity during the following year; namely, the Bible, Bp. Pearson on the Creed, and Mr. Simeon's Lectures on Revealed Religion.* He went through a course of natural religion last year. My reason for beginning with Pearson is, because Dr. Hey gives public lectures on that author, which I wish to attend, if my college avocations permit."

In addition to the motives which have been already stated for relaxation in his mathematical studies, Mr. Buchanan again mentions in this letter the importance of *health*. "I see," he observes, "many around me whose usefulness is abridged by the want of it. Mr. L. and Mr. R., men of ability, are both *lying by*. I begin to think, that if at the expiration of my academic course, I have good health, some knowledge of the Bible, and some zeal, I may prove as useful as some who have great abilities, great eloquence, and—an asthma!"

The paragraph immediately following contains the first specific intimation of the important and interesting sphere of ministerial labour, to which the providence of God was conducting him.

"Mr. and Mrs. G. passed through Cambridge lately. Mr. S. and I dined and supped with them. I hope the conversation of that evening was useful to me. From hearing various accounts of the apostolic spirit of some missionaries to the Indies, and of the extensive field for preaching the gospel there, I was led to desire that I might be well qualified for such a department, in case God should intend me for it. Hence the origin of my three desiderata above mentioned—scripture knowledge, some zeal, and good health."

The subject of elocution is that to which Mr. Buchanan next adverts in this letter.

"I have read," he proceeds, "many codicils in my time, but I never read any one with such pleasure as that annexed to your letter. Do you think it possible that I ever shall be able to preach extempore from the pulpit? You know my defect in conversation. I scarcely know a person of any education who is so much at a loss in ordinary expression as I am. My fault is not that of Demosthenes, else there might

* Probably delivered in his church.

be hopes of amendment. I have no natural defect in the organs of speech; but I can never find apt words to express my ideas without much premeditation. I have a pretty large stock of words in my head, but they are seldom used: so that when I am able to draw some of them out, they appear quite strange to me. I fancy I have some hundreds which I never used in my life. This partly arises from our Scottish mode of education—reading much and speaking little; but chiefly, I suppose, from my being secluded from society for so many years. During my residence in London, I lived, like the Spectator, in silence. My business was to write, not to speak. Since my coming to Cambridge, I have passed most of my time in silent study. On an average I suppose I have not spoken half an hour a day, including both lectures and conversation. So you see that taciturnity is a disease in me; an evil habit of five years standing. When a boy I could *scold* well enough, but I do not think I could scold now. In conversation I am naturally cheerful, and therefore I must speak, whether I can do it well or ill: but I ascribe the patience of my company to my cheerfulness, not to my diction.

"Though I never mentioned it to you, there has scarcely been a subject more on my mind, since Providence opened to me a view of the pulpit, than this of public speaking. I was in hopes that I should have had some opportunity of improvement at Cambridge, but I have none. Mr. S. regrets that there is no person in Cambridge who teaches elocution, and he regrets it much on my account. He has kindly proposed to me to read to him once a fortnight. This is my only resource at present. I have little advantage from my college companions. Most of them speak ill, and read worse. All I can do is to read aloud by myself occasionally. I am persuaded that it would be worth a student's while to spend two or three hours a-day, for some years previous to his entering into the ministry, in the attainment of that accomplishment which distinguished the preacher Apollos. I have often thought how glad I should be if oratory were introduced into *my* college course instead of mathematics. Mr. Thornton's desires on this head should be an additional inducement to me to apply diligently to this study."

Though the peculiar circumstances of Mr. Buchanan's birth and education may account for his complaint and anxiety upon the subject of elocution, it is but too notorious, that those who do not labour under his disadvantages are frequently as deficient, and not seldom much more so, in this important accomplishment. To judge by its general neglect, at least among clerical students, it might almost be imagined, that to excel in it is deemed discreditable. The total absence of propriety, force, and dignity in the celebration of divine service, in the public reading of the holy scriptures, and in the delivery of discourses from the pulpit, which may so commonly be observed, can scarcely otherwise be accounted for. An affected and ostentatious display of artificial elocution in the performance of the sacred offices of the church, is, indeed, even more disgusting than rusticity and negligence. It is nothing of this kind which is intended to be recommended; and on this account it is by no means advisable to have recourse to any secular professors of the art of speaking. It is with elocution as with eloquence itself, that clear apprehensions of the subject, good taste, and deep feeling, will in all ordinary cases, and even under some natural disadvantages, secure the most important ends of public speaking. It is, however, a point which deserves much more attention than is usually given to it; and amongst other improvements in the present age, it must be confessed, that its importance is beginning to be more justly appreciated. The prize instituted in the University of Cambridge for the promotion of this accomplishment, by the late excellent Bishop Porteus, himself a striking example of forcible and dignified elocution, might be imitated with advantage in every seminary of learning; nor can those who are judges of good speaking perform a more important service to clerical students, than by freely suggesting to them hints for the correction of their errors, or the attainment of excellence in that art.*

Mr. Buchanan was probably led to the subject of elocution by an appointment to declaim in college in Latin, on the ensuing fifth of November. He expresses in the preceding letter his embarrassment in looking forward to this office; but instead of yielding to his fears, or shrinking from what may readily be believed to have been a trial to him, he applied vigorously to the duty which had been imposed upon him; and after frequent repetition of his composition in private, in one of which he enjoyed the advantage of the observations of a friend well qualified to advise him both as to the matter of his declamation and his manner of speaking, he succeeded in delivering it with more self-possession, propriety, and animation, than he had ever exhibited in his own room.

"This," he adds, "was a great victory over myself, and

---

* See Bishop Gibson's instructions to his clergy in the Clergyman's Instructor, p. 310, and Archbishop Hort's in the same volume.

was matter of much thankfulness. When I declaim on a more important subject, I trust I shall be equally assisted."

At the commencement of Michælmas term, Mr. Buchanan informed his friend Mr. Newton, that his health was much improved; but that in looking forward to five weeks of lectures, he feared that deference to his tutors, and his natural pride, might lead him to study them more closely than, after all that had now passed upon that subject, he felt he ought.

"I have been indulging myself a little," he observes, "in writing a sermon. It is for Mr. S.'s perusal; that he may be able to judge of my improvement, if I am spared to write another next year. It is on the matter and manner of a preacher of the gospel: 'And he spake *boldly* in the name of *Jesus;*' Acts ix. 29. I have just delivered it to Mr. S.; I fear he will think it a rhapsody: and what makes it worse, it is twenty-seven pages long. I fancy that youthful sermon-writers are generally at a loss how to *begin*, and when they do begin, they know not where to *stop*."

Of the manner in which Mr. Buchanan spent the term, the commencement of which he announced in the foregoing letter, some opinion may be formed by the following, dated the 26th of March 1793, in which he informed the same venerable correspondent of its close.

"Having finished the labours of a long term, I sit down with pleasure to inquire after your health, to beg your blessing, and to request the assistance of your prayers.

"I hope you will not desire me to show you the fruit of my labours. I am very unlike those geniuses who reap knowledge by *handsful*. My improvement is so slow, that it is scarcely visible; I seem only to vegetate in science. Though planted by the banks of the Cam, his stream waters my roots in vain. This is humiliating; but it may be useful, if it show me that I am more likely to flourish if planted on the banks of the stream of Zion. When I consider how Cambridge is favoured, I ought to look on myself as already there. This is indeed the case: but, hostile to my own growth, I *drink* of the Cam, and sip of Zion; whereas I ought to sip of the Cam, and drink deep of Zion.

"For some time past I have been making many discoveries in the kingdom of nature, but few in the kingdom of grace. Since I last saw you, I have in idea traced the planets in their courses, and soared through the regions of boundless space. Philosophy, I find, agrees with revelation in declaring, that the earth (compared with the universe) is but as an atom of the dust that cleaveth to the balance. It is indeed highly honoured in being called the footstool of the Most High. The eclipses of the sun, the labours of the moon, and the sweet influences of the Pleiades, have also engaged my attention.

"While thus viewing the things made, one would have thought that I should have turned my eyes to their Maker. But by a strange perverseness, I often found it easier to comprehend an abstruse problem, than to meditate on a simple truth. On the whole, however, I have met with no part of science which led me nearer to the source of true knowledge, than this of investigating the wisdom of God in the creation.

"In addition to my mathematical studies, I have had a classical task assigned me. The college gave out for my declamation the following thesis. *An in Civitate bene constitutâ, Ludi Scenici admitti debeant?* As I considered this to be in some measure the cause of religion, I thought it right to pay attention to it. For this purpose I employed myself in classical research, till I had found sufficient authorities from the Greeks, Romans, and Fathers, to condemn the stage, not only as immoral, but as impolitic. I adverted to the encouragement lately given it by the French, and argued thence its evil tendency.

"I have now done with all our lectures, and I am glad of it. Though I found some things here and there which flattered the earthly mind, and pleased vain-glorious reason, yet in all my researches have I found nothing like—'Come unto me all ye that labour and are heavy laden, and I will give you rest.' Perhaps your good memory will remind you that I stole this idea from Archbishop Leighton. Agreeably to your recommendation, I am now reading the Prælections of that good man: and I must say, that I have seldom met with such genuine Christianity in such a classical dress.

"The college have lately appointed me their librarian. This is an office rather of trust than of emolument. My business is easily done, as I am only required to give in an account of the state of the library once a year. Many good divines of the last century have found a place in it. Halyburton's life has engaged my attention for a few days past. His work on the Spirit" (which had probably been recommended to him by Mr. Newton) "I cannot find."

It may perhaps be objected, that the progress of this narrative is too much interrupted by the insertion of so many extracts from Mr. Buchanan's letters; more particularly as some of them relate only incidentally to himself. Such a suggestion may possibly arise on the perusal of the following; which, however, seemed to convey sentiments and consolation too interesting to be omitted. They occur in a letter to Mr. Newton, from Cambridge, dated May the 30th, 1793.

"It gives me great pleasure to hear that you are still supported in health and strength sufficient for the discharge of your ministerial labours. I hope that you will continue to be refreshed abundantly with the divine presence; and I pray, that as your body yields to weakness and the infirmities of age, your spirit may derive new strength from our Redeemer's fulness.

"I sometimes find myself indulging a wish, that your experience in your evening hour may be singularly joyful to you; and that your death may preach as powerfully as your life has done. But I believe self prompts us sometimes to too sanguine expectations respecting our friends. Let us not dictate, but wait and see the salvation of the Lord. He will conduct you in the path most suitable to his own glory, your good, and our edification.

"We have lately had an illustrious instance of God's goodness to his children at the hour of death. Mrs. ——, of this place, was a woman of eminent piety, cheerful in disposition, and of elegant manners. She was but twenty-five years of age. I was introduced to her family about a twelvemonth ago, and have diligently cultivated her acquaintance ever since. Soon after her rising from her confinement, she discovered that she was in a rapid consumption; and in a few weeks the strength of the malady seemed to forbid all hopes of life. Her bodily pains were extreme, so that she frequently expressed a desire to be with the Lord; but she had yet two ties to earth—her husband and her child. The child she was soon enabled to give up, but the husband—this she confessed to be a trial indeed. However, after strong cries and tears, she obtained a victory here also. She afterwards recovered from a trial of another kind with an animating faith in her Redeemer's love, and an assurance of the joy about to be revealed. This was on Sunday morning at five o'clock. In half an hour after, she intimated that her departure was at hand. It was now that she experienced the truth of the promise of dying strength for a dying hour. For though unable to speak, yet she discovered her inward joy by such animation of countenance as delighted her surrounding friends. And when her mother and sister spoke to her of her approaching happiness, her eyes seemed to glisten with new fire. 'What a joyful Sabbath you will have to-day,' said her sister. Her looks seemed to reply, 'A joyful Sabbath indeed; an eternal Sabbath!' In a few minutes afterwards, she waved her hand in token of her abundant entrance into the joy of her Lord. And like your dear E. C. she met death with a smile, which kept possession of her features, until she was consigned to the grave.

"I would not have dwelt so long on this subject, were it not that my esteem for the deceased was great.

"Perhaps you would call it affectation, if I did not tell you that the college have adjudged to me the first prize for the best Latin declamation on 'the stage.'

"I believe I must pass this summer out of Cambridge. I think of going to London about the beginning of July, that I may have a few lessons in English pronunciation, in compliance with Mr. Thornton's desire.

"I have been assaulted of late from various quarters, both from without and from within; but I bless God, that while I pray over the Bible, I am enabled to triumph over my enemies. I delight in the Bible. When my heart is melted within me, and my soul sick with the combat between the contempt of the ungodly, and the remains of my own pride, then the Bible affords a comfort no other book can give."

In a similar strain as to his increasing love of the holy scriptures, and in peculiarly strong and lively terms as to the general state of his mind concerning religion, he thus writes to the same correspondent in the month of June following.

"I see you still have a godly jealousy over me, respecting the bent of my studies. I must make you easy on that head. I can now inform you, that the attention I pay to the classics or mathematics is comparatively very little; so little, that I sometimes fear that (in my present place) I neglect them too much. And I can further inform you, and I thank God for enabling me, that the cause of my being thus lukewarm in these studies, is, that I may redeem time for studying the scriptures, the value of which knowledge I see more and more. At present I can read the Bible when I can read nothing else. Some of my other studies are truly a cross to me."

What an unquestionable proof of a spiritual mind in an academical student, is such a declaration as this! He thus continues.

"I dare not tell you what I am, but I can tell you what I pray for.

"I pray that I may be content to be of no reputation among men, knowing that if I am truly wise, I must become a fool among the ungodly; that I may patiently submit to indignity and reproach for Christ's sake, and that my whole life may be devoted to his service; that for this purpose I may diligently improve the talent committed to me, however little it may be;

and that when I go forth into the ministry, I may not seek self, but Christ; content to be unnoticed, dead to the censure or applause of men, alive to God and his concerns, and chiefly solicitous that my preaching (however rude I may be in speech) may be powerful in awakening souls.

"These are my prayers in 1793, as to the event of my studies. I trust the Lord, that he will keep me; that he will put his fear in my heart, that I may not depart from him.

"You talk to me of academical reputation and dignity. If I were Regius Professor of Divinity to-morrow, I would resign the dignity to any man for a little brokenness of heart. The summit of my ambition (if I know my own mind) is, to be daily more conformed to Christ, to be enabled to follow that great sufferer, and to rejoice to be counted worthy to suffer shame for his sake.

"As to my future situation in the ministry, to which you allude at the close of your letter, that subject is very little in my thoughts. God has done the greater; shall he not do the less? If he means me to preach his gospel, then is the pulpit prepared, and the flock which I must tend. At present I feel ready to go wherever he pleases to send me; whether to India, America, New Holland, or if there be any other land more remote. I have already seen life in various shapes; and if I have been enabled to bear with difficulties when without God in the world, much more, when engaged in his service, aided by his Spirit and supported by his presence.

"If the Lord will I should be well pleased to enter his service under your advice and example. I hope that the first year I stay with you, I shall learn humility; the second, humility; the third, humility.

"Mr. S. and Mrs. M. beg their love to you; and so does he, who is, with great respect and affection, your's."

The note inscribed by Mr. Newton on the preceding letter strongly attests the pleasure with which he had perused it; nor can it be generally read without a lively impression of the glowing and devoted piety of its author. Two months afterwards we find him in London, replying to a letter from Mr. Newton; then in the country, in which his aged friend, under the painful remembrance of the transitory nature of earthly enjoyments, though by no means in the spirit of disappointment and complaint, had declared that of a happiness which had subsisted forty years, nothing then remained but the recollection; that the years he had passed, blessed as they had been by the sunshine of providence and grace, might be numbered with the years before the flood. To this somewhat melancholy but admonitory observation Mr. Buchanan replied, that the estimate of human life which he had thus given was, he presumed, just, as it accorded with the language of scripture.

"Is it possible, then," he says, "that I can be so foolish, as to fix my heart on any thing under the sun, if I believe the testimony of all ages, that to do so is vanity and vexation of spirit? I *do* believe this testimony, and I would gladly refrain from every created idol, come it in what shape it may; but unhappily I feel myself invested with flesh and blood. Now I understand from scripture, that I am permitted, nay, commanded, to nourish this body, to clothe and adorn it, and be careful of its well being; only I must study to keep it in subjection. But this is a charge more difficult than the government of a kingdom. I am to *taste*, the Bible says, of the sweets of earthly happiness, but I am *only* to taste of them. But who is to ascertain the quantum? Spiritual self and carnal self are always at variance about it, and I suppose this contest is the christian's warfare. A good soldier, therefore, would naturally endeavour either to strengthen himself or weaken his adversary. Am I then to strengthen the spiritual, or to weaken the carnal principle? I may do both, you will say; but which of the two demands my more particular attention? As I may go to an extreme in weakening the body, but cannot go too far in strengthening the soul, it would seem wise to lay the greater stress on the latter. Communion with God in private prayer is, I conceive, the best strengthener of the soul; and communion with the world is its greatest weakener. The result then appears to be this. To dedicate as much time as possible to acts of communion with God. But Archbishop Leighton says, that the desire of this sacred communion grows with its exercise. Every encouragement, therefore, is held out to this mode of attack and defence, since pleasure and profit conspire to recommend it. Prayer, then, I must consider as the christian's palladium, and as a present reward.

"Surely an hour in the morning, and an hour in the evening, is not too much for communion with God. But as to the season of prayer, I do not think that some manage this well. They pray early in the morning, and *late* at night. This may be necessary in families engaged in business; but I speak of ministers. Do you not think that an hour of devotion before we engage in company in the afternoon, would have a tendency to correct and animate our evening's conversation?

"Pardon this dissertation on prayer. I really had no design to trouble you with it when I began the letter."

To reflections such as the preceding, as solid and judicious as they are spiritual and instructive, no serious reader will object. Nor will the following account of the death of one of Mr. Buchanan's sisters, which occurs in a letter to Mr. Newton from Cambridge, at the close of his second long vacation, be deemed uninteresting.

"It was about a year and a half ago," he observes, "on her return from boarding-school, that her piety first appeared, though on her death-bed she confessed that her heart had been inclining to God nearly two years before that time. About three months since she was seized by a consumption, which has now given her a happy release from all sin and all sorrow."

A letter still remains, written by Mr. Buchanan from Cambridge, to his dying sister, for the purpose of cheering and supporting her under her early departure from the world, the piety and fraternal affection of which will sufficiently recommend the following extracts.

"I rejoice to hear that you are about to enter into the joy of your Lord, to behold the Saviour whom you love, face to face; to be clothed by him in a spotless robe, and presented to the Father as an heir of everlasting glory.

"Let me encourage you to pass over Jordan's flood with a resolute step, undismayed; let me remind you of the promise of Him, to whom the death of his saints is precious. Let me enforce the immutable love of your God, and proclaim to you the truth of your Redeemer. You have already known him as *the way;* on your death-bed you will find him *the truth;* and he will quickly welcome you to the gate of Zion as the *eternal life.*

"My dear sister, be of good cheer: lay hold of Jesus as the anchor of your soul. Was it ever heard that any one who fled to him for refuge was deserted in a trying hour? Was it ever known that he suffered one of his sheep to be plucked out of his hand? Has he not said, 'I will never leave thee, nor forsake thee?' 'When thou passeth through the waters, I will be with thee;' 'Fear not, thou art mine.' These are exceeding great and precious promises, on which you may safely rest. If your faith be weak, yet waver not. The promise is to the weak as well as to the strong; yea, to all those who can say, 'Thou knowest, Lord, that I love thee.'

"While you have life, magnify the praises of Him who hath called you with such a holy calling. Evince to the world that the Bible is not a cunningly-devised fable. Seek to glorify God in your death, and assuredly he will give you faith to do it. Speak from your dying bed of the things of the kingdom to which you are hastening; impart your views of the vanities of life, for the benefit of those who survive you. Pray that a double portion of your spirit may rest upon your brother, that he may gladden your eyes at the last day with a view of many souls whom he has brought with him to glory. Leave him such exhortations, encouragements, and reproofs, as an immediate prospect of heaven may inspire you to give.

"And now let me conduct you as far as I can, even to the gates of Jerusalem. Many a song will be sung, many a harp be strung, on your entrance into the kingdom of heaven. Who is this that I see foremost to welcome you? Is it not your grandfather or your father? My dear sister, what joy is this! They, accompanied by a heavenly host, conduct you to your Saviour, your King, and your God. Then your glory begins; you are crowned with honour and immortality. You join in the never-ending song of 'Worthy the Lamb,' and drink of the pleasures which are at God's right hand for evermore."

The preceding pious and animated address did not arrive until the relative, for whose consolation it was intended, was beyond the reach of human joy or sorrow.

The account, however, which Mr. Buchanan, in the words of another sister, gives to Mr. Newton of the last trying scene, is peaceful and encouraging.

"She now," he says, "in faith looked forward to her rest, and spent much of her time in reading the scriptures, and in prayer.

"On the evening of the day she died, she said to her mother, 'I think that my hour is now come.' Her mother was surprised at this, as there appeared no visible change in her countenance. She immediately began to pray, and prayed long. Her mother overheard some of her words. She prayed 'that she might be found in Christ; that she might have a title to that covenant which is well-ordered and sure.' About the conclusion of her prayer, death appeared to be fast approaching. She begged that the family might come round her bed; and then she began to exhort them, and to speak to them of the kingdom of God. Her mother, observing that her last moment was now at hand, asked her if she had any thing to say to her brother at Cambridge. 'Yes,' said she; 'tell him, be sure you tell him,' (repeating it emphatically,) 'that I die trusting in the Lord Jesus Christ.' She then lifted up both her hands, and looking up to heaven, committed herself to the Lord, her eyes streaming with joy; which having done, she sunk on the pillow and expired."

"The manner of her death," continues Mr. Buchanan, "has given my mother a comfort inexpressible.

"I know nothing which has had a greater tendency to animate me in my christian course, than this triumph of my sister. O were the work done which my Father hath given me to do, how gladly should I accompany her!

"I hope you are at present a large partaker of the consolations of the Spirit. Though I am young, I know thus much, that without those consolations, there is no happiness. What a blessing, that the pleasures of holiness begin on this side the grave!"

On the fifth of November Mr. Buchanan again delivered a public Latin speech on the Revolution in 1688; and on the 15th a declamation in favour of modern learning. His relaxation in mathematical studies exposed him, he informs Mr. Newton, to frequent remonstrances from different friends; and amongst others, from the late excellent Mr. Robinson of Leicester, who was anxious that he should view academical honours with less indifference. "They are little aware," he adds, "that I need no spur on this head, were I conscious that my abilities warranted me success. In arguments of this kind I usually urge the plea of duty; though I must confess, that the other weighs more strongly with myself, which it ought not to do."

Mr. Buchanan, as it will presently appear, probably, and perhaps happily, underrated his talents in this particular. However this may be, he was unmoved by the representations of his friends, and persevered in the course of study, which, as we have seen, he had deliberately adopted.

Early in the year 1794, a letter occurs to his venerable friend, Mr. Newton, which affords a specimen of that union of playful remark with christian seriousness, by which his correspondence was occasionally enlivened.

"Mr. F. writes to me, that your recommendations have been of great service to him at Edinburgh. I am happy to find that his zeal increases. More of my friends err through too much prudence than too much zeal. I think I have observed that a man who is well acquainted with the world, cannot have too much zeal. If he is ignorant of men and manners, his zeal will injure his cause; and it is not till after repeated lessons that he is put right.

"Your aged domestics will wonder why I stay so long at Cambridge, when I have so much work to do in the ministry. I wish they could impart to me somewhat of their experience, self-knowledge, and humility; and in exchange I promise to give them on my return from college, all my mathematics, pure and mixed, geometry, algebra, fluxions containing the nature of pneumatics, hydraulics, hydrostatics, the doctrine of incommensurables, indivisibles, and infinities, parabolic and hyperbolic logarithms, summation of series, solution of quadratics containing impossible roots, together with the properties of parallelepipeds and dodecahedrons, not forgetting Sir Isaac Newton, his celebrated corollaries to the paradoxical lemma respecting *curvilinear straight* lines! together with other particulars, too many to be here enumerated.

"What a mercy, you will say, that Phœbe* has not to learn all this in order to get to heaven!

"I thank you for your dissertation on Cambridge learning. I hope I have passed the ordeal now, and that I shall be led to the study of those things by which I may be best able to promote the glory of God. I sigh for the sublime grace of self-denial. It is the preservative of the youthful christian from snares innumerable."

Not long after the date of the preceding letter, Mr. Newton made the first direct proposal to Mr. Buchanan of a voyage to India. His reply was as follows:

"I request you to accept my thanks for the affectionate letter which I have just now read. I have only time to say, that with respect to my going to India, I must decline giving any opinion. It would argue a mind ill-instructed in the school of Christ, to pretend to decide on an event so important and unexpected; an event, which will doubtless give a complexion to the happiness and usefulness of every hour of my future life.

"It is with great pleasure I submit this matter to the determination of yourself, Mr. Thornton, and Mr. Grant. All I wish to ascertain is the will of God. I hope that the result of your deliberations will prove to be his will. Were I required to say something, I should observe that I feel myself very ill qualified for the arduous situation in question. My intimate friends know that my plan of college study was, to attend more immediately to academical learning the two first years, and to preparation for the ministry in the third and last, upon which I am but now entering. I think that our regard for the glory of God requires us to endeavour to find a person of acknowledged ability in things both human and divine, who has already approved himself such an one as might successfully resist gainsayers, and prosecute his mission with energy. A beginner, particularly if he be of slender capacity and at-

* Alluding to an old and highly-valued domestic of Mr. Newton.

tainments, will naturally shrink from such a situation, fearing lest he should tarnish the honour of his embassy by an unskilful or ungraceful negotiation.

"On the contrary, if the Lord does with me as with Jeremiah, and bids a child go and teach a great nation, it would be vain to plead my incapacity, since, if he sends me, he will certainly 'touch my mouth.' Only I would observe, that in the present state of christianity, it would appear that as strict attention ought to be paid to human means in our endeavours to promote the success of the gospel, as if it were merely a human dispensation.

"I trust that every word of the above is dictated by a regard to God's honour, and not my own.

"That *his* honour may be greatly promoted by the result of your deliberations is the prayer of C. B."

The judgment as well as the piety of Mr. Buchanan's reply to this proposal deserves to be noticed, and affords a satisfactory indication of his qualifications for the important station to which it refers. The following sentiments expressed in a subsequent letter are equally pleasing.

"With respect to my going to India, I am still in a strait between two. Some considerations incline me to stay; others persuade me to go, as being far better. Being unable to judge for myself, I submit it to the divine direction with perfect resignation. So gracious is He who 'careth for me' in this respect, that your determination, whether for or against my going, will be alike agreeable to me. I am equally ready to preach the gospel in the next village, or at the ends of the earth."

Such was the elevated spirit of piety which actuated Mr. Buchanan early in this year. As it advanced, he wrote thus to Mr. Newton.

"We have had Mrs. U. and Mr. C.'s family at Cambridge for a few days. It gives me great pleasure to see piety gladden with its presence our learned walls. Pride and superstition have doubtless built most of our colleges; but I am inclined to think, that genuine piety founded some of them. A solitary walk in such places, has a tendency to excite elevated thoughts of God, and of his goodness to man, through successive ages.

"My purpose in troubling you with this letter was to say, that I bear that affection for you a child beareth to his father, a desire to conceal his faults, (if he has any,) and to magnify his virtues; that I hope to be preserved from the snares and cares of this world, and thereby enabled to adorn that gospel which you first wished me to profess."

In Mr. Buchanan's next letter to Mr. Newton, dated early in June, it will be observed that the ardour which he had formerly evinced to enter into the ministry, without much academical preparation, had yielded to those more correct and enlarged views concerning religion which he had been gradually acquiring; and which had at once rendered him more diffident, and better qualified for the office to which he aspired.

"I sit down," he says, "to acquaint you, that I have just finished another term, and with it I complete another year at the University. I hope that God will graciously overrule the evil he has seen in me; and that he will cause my past experience and my past studies, to bear fruit to his glory and my own good.

"I once thought myself prepared for the church! I shudder at my temerity. A zeal (if zeal it may be called) 'without knowledge' must have dictated this unhallowed confidence. In one sense, indeed, any one to whom God has given his grace may enter the church, however ignorant or unfit in other matters; inasmuch as all success in it comes from God. But in another sense, no man ought to enter upon the ministry, who is not qualified by nature and education to do justice to a public station, and claim respect from a gainsaying world. This is absolutely necessary, unless miracles have not ceased. And for want of attending to these circumstances, viz. the present state of christianity, and the progress of civilization, I see that the gospel suffers in every quarter. At the time of the Reformation, there was not so much ground for this complaint as now. I differ in opinion from many good men on these points. However, I seldom mention them, as I have learnt from past fluctuations of sentiment, that I may possibly think differently after further observation and more accurate scripture study. I think that too little attention is paid to the *manner* of preaching the gospel; and too little to the prejudices of the age against the illiterate methodist. I feel a good deal hurt at these neglects, at the same time that I despair of doing otherwise myself. In these, and in all other doubts, I must wait patiently on his teaching, who hath so often made 'darkness light before me.'"

After informing his correspondent that he had a few days since spoken his last Latin declamation, Mr. Buchanan thus beautifully concludes this letter.

"That you are blessed with health, and stayed by the comforts of the gospel in your declining years, is to me a frequent theme of praise. In philosophy and human science, the mind loses its vigour by old age; but in religion, in divine science, we are taught to believe that youth will be restored, and new attainments acquired. *Fortunatus ille senex, qui cœlicola vivit.*"

It is probable that Mr. Buchanan passed the greater part of the long vacation of this year also at Cambridge. No letter, indeed, occurs in his correspondence with Mr. Newton from the commencement to the close of that period; but the following interesting communication from one of his most valued friends and relatives seems to confirm this conjecture.

"I first became acquainted with him," observes this gentleman, "at Cambridge, in the summer of the year 1794. We were almost the only two residents in our respective colleges of Queen's and St. John's; he being engaged in studying for orders, and I in preparing for my bachelor's degree. I had often heard of him from a common friend, as being a very distinguished member of a debating society, called the Speculative, or quaintly the Spec. consisting of a number of undergraduates from different colleges, especially Trinity and Queen's, who used to meet at each other's rooms to discuss various moral, political, and sometimes religious questions. He was represented to me as eminent among the speakers for acuteness and fluency,* and for piety of sentiment; but as a retired character, who scarcely ever mixed with any other persons at such social meetings as were usual in the college.

"We met accidentally in our solitary walks, and entered into conversation; which brought on an interchange of visits. We often walked together during the short time after our first meeting that he continued at Cambridge. I well remember to this moment a particular conversation which took place in one of our walks on a fine summer's evening, and can trace in my recollection some of the fields through which we rambled, little thinking that we should ever be so closely united in the bonds of domestic affection, or that if I survived him, I should have to drop the tear of hallowed regret over the grave of a brother.

"He greatly surprised me on that occasion by strongly condemning the vanity of the pursuits of ambition, in which I was then hotly engaged, coveting too earnestly University honours. I defended my side, in which self was so deeply con-

* This observation is a proof either of the modest estimate which Mr. Buchanan formed of his own powers of speaking, in writing to Mr. Newton upon this subject, or of the proficiency which he had made since that period, partly, perhaps, in consequence of the exercise afforded him by this society.

cerned, with much warmth and positiveness ; but when I was left alone, I could not altogether shake off the impression which his serious, solemn, and scriptural mode of argumentation had left upon my mind."

The same learned and excellent person adds, with reference to this period of Mr. Buchanan's life ; "I remember, in a letter to a common friend, some remarks on the necessity and efficacy of faith in the blood of Christ ; and of his hopes that he had experienced something of it, which were in a great measure new to us both, and affected me considerably."

It is pleasing to reflect, that the writer of the preceding passages, after having succeeded in the attainment of the highest of those academical honours* of which he was then so ardently in pursuit, should at no distant period have been led to adopt the religious views which he once combated ; and after the lapse of many years, have been permitted again to hold "sweet converse" with him to whom he first become known under such interesting circumstances, and to contribute to do honour to his memory, as a friend and brother.

We are now approaching the termination of Mr. Buchanan's academical course. On the 30th of November in this year, he wrote to Mr. Newton as follows.

"I have just finished my mathematical career. Previous to taking our degrees, an examination is held in our respective colleges for the purpose of ascertaining our success in science, and a prize of five guineas awarded to the best proficient. This prize has been adjudged to me.

"I take no public honour in mathematics. As my admission to college was irregular, I must go out at a bye-term ; that is, at Midsummer next. Were I to stay till the regular time of conferring honours and degrees, it must be till Christmas twelvemonth. My tutors are very urgent with me to remain till that time, in order that I may acquire some mathematical reputation to myself, and some honour to the college ; but I have declined it, as being an unjustifiable sacrifice of my time and duty. My friends are a good deal surprised at this ; and are astonished when I tell them, that though I studied science with attention, I never had a public honour in view. The college examination I had determined should be my *ne plus ultra*."

The preceding information appears to have surprised Mr. Newton himself; who in common with his other friends seems, notwithstanding his discouragement of Mr. Buchanan's

* He was the Senior Wrangler of his year.

mathematical studies, to have expected that he would obtain some University distinction. Some were even disposed to think that he might have aimed at the highest. This was evidently unreasonable; and Mr. Buchanan accordingly thus replies to such a suggestion.

"You seem to think that my abdication of mathematics is in consequence of a *late* resolution; but it is not. It is agreeable to my original plan. Those who think that I might have been Senior Wrangler, are not well-informed. There are few instances, I believe, of any persons arriving at this eminence, who had not studied mathematics before they went to Cambridge."

Considering the circumstances which have been before related, it will perhaps be deemed sufficiently creditable to Mr. Buchanan, that the college prize for mathematical proficiency should have been adjudged to him. Some manuscripts made by him at Cambridge, on the four branches of natural philosophy, and on some parts of Newton's Principia, still remain. They indicate, in the opinión of the learned friend to whom an allusion has been lately made, a competent knowledge of his subjects, though they are not the work of one who would be called *a high* man, at Cambridge. He adds, however, that had Mr. Buchanan been a candidate for a public honour, he would doubtless have distinguished himself.

How entirely he was satisfied as to his determination upon this point, may be inferred from the total absence of any sentiment of regret respecting it in his correspondence at this period. He was evidently intent upon an object which he deemed of far higher importance, as the following conclusion of the letter in which he announced the close of his mathematical career, sufficiently testifies.

"It is said that those who travel heavenwards acquire new strength from the toil of the way; *Iter instaurabit vires.* I wish I found it so. I *clamber* up hill with difficulty. It may be, I have not laid aside every *weight;* or, perhaps, I have not used the proper 'lamp to my path.' If so, it is a great happiness that the weariness of the way reproves me.

"To . . . . . . I wish to be remembered, as to fellow-pilgrims; who in their journey to the holy land, have learned to sympathise with those whose knees are feeble, and who travel slowly. Perhaps to some of them, or to you, 'the delectable mountains' are already in view; if so, 'the shining ones' are at hand, to conduct you to the holy city; where, I hope, ere long, you will meet

Your very affectionate son, C. B."

Mr. Buchanan was so entirely occupied with the pursuits of learning and religion, that the politics of the day, though of a peculiarly alarming and interesting nature, seldom found a place in his correspondence. On one or two occasions, however, he shows that he was by no means indifferent upon the subject, and expresses that mixture of truth and error which might be expected from a pious and acute, but young and ardent mind, speculating upon points which baffled the penetration of the most able and experienced observers. Amidst a variety of other remarks, the following, however, from its singular correspondence with subsequent events, seems deserving of insertion.

"Perhaps," says Mr. Buchanan, "the opinion of Sir Isaac Newton is correct, that antichristian superstition is only to be eradicated by the strong hand of infidelity. It may be agreeable to Providence, to permit infidel armies to ravage the world, to destroy superstition, and then to strew with *Bibles* the vacant lands."

The history of the last twenty years has tended in a most striking manner to verify this conjecture. We have seen antichristian superstition checked and depressed, though not eradicated, by the strong arm of infidelity; while we behold many of the desolated lands upon the continent literally '*strewed with Bibles*,' by the pious charity of our own highly-favoured country; which, after raising an effectual barrier against the tyranny by which every other European nation was oppressed, has survived to be the instrument of continued, and, it may be hoped, of still greater blessings to the world.

Upon the general subject of politics, as well as upon that of patriotism, of which, as he thought, Mr. Buchanan had taken an erroneous view, Mr. Newton remonstrated with his less experienced correspondent. To the latter of these points he recurs in the following terms in his next letter.

"I scarcely recollect what I said in my last on the subject of the *amor patriæ;* but I am ready to unsay it, if I cannot otherwise subscribe to the general tenor of your answer. It is natural to expect some little difference in deciding on a speculative point, particularly if the parties judge for themselves, and if they be of different ages. The old man may have a stock of premises far superior to the young man's; and therefore their conclusions will differ, though each may argue correctly from his own data.

"There are some subjects of secondary importance, on which I do not expect to have a determined opinion, till forced perhaps by the impatience of hoary hairs; for though I *hope*, yet I do not expect, to show so little of dogmatic and narrative old age as you do; and for this reason, that nature has made some difference in the constitution of our minds, (which is as lasting as the different conformation of our bodies,) namely, to you she has given a placid, to me a sanguine, temper."

In the passage which follows, some acute observations occur on the nature of superstition and prejudice, which are not unworthy of being preserved.

"I have learned one lesson, I think, since I came to the University, viz. my own ignorance. On some disputable points, such as, the best method of preaching, the use of the world as not abusing it, the connexion of things civil and religious, forms of government, and the distinctions between the Jewish and Christian dispensations—on such points, I say, my opinions seem to derive a new complexion from every new year. In one view this is proper; for not to change in sentiment on such things, would argue a man to be stationary or retrograde in improvement, or at best to be the superstitious disciple of some pope or infallible pedagogue. In some measure I envy such persons: *certainty* is doubtless a happiness; and therefore the superstitious are generally so far happy. Many good christians are superstitious. Indeed, he must be a man of singular learning and piety, who is not superstitious in some degree. For instance, most men have a superstitious regard for their peculiar form of worship. An Englishman regards his Liturgy as superstitiously as a Roman Catholic his mass-book. Those who have less ceremony than the English church, have a superstitious reverence for what they have left: and I can easily conceive a man to have a superstitious regard for the *want* of ceremony.

"Nothing but a cultivated mind, and the constant perusal of the New Testament, seem capable of delivering men from unnecessary prejudices and prepossessions. Grace does not necessarily do it. Some wonder at this; but why should they? Grace converts the heart, but it does not teach the understanding what the understanding may learn without it; and therefore it does not remove prejudice. For prejudice is founded on ignorance; on an ignorance of *facts*. Till these facts then are communicated, prejudice remains; knowledge, therefore, i. e. learning, philosophy, or by what name soever it may be called, is necessary to remove prejudice."

It is obvious that the foregoing remarks, though substantially correct, require considerable judgment to apply them with safety to any important subject. Their influence on some opinions expressed by Mr. Buchanan in the subsequent part of this letter, on the politics of the day, forms no uninstructive comment upon the difficulty which attends such discussions. These opinions it is unnecessary now to produce. It is but just, however, to add the following modest and sensible acknowledgment of the hesitation with which he had adopted them.

"Since you wished me to write what I *thought* on these subjects, I have done so. I shall thank you now to burn these sheets, as they contain the effusion of an unripe judgment. Whether I shall ever attain to a correct estimate of the points I have handled, I know not; but if ever I do, it can only be by the concurrence of these three causes; the influence of the Holy Spirit, to preserve my affections pure before God; the knowledge of new facts; and the power of reasoning accurately. No two of them seem sufficient for judging in matters irrelevant to our salvation.

"I have not seen the mission of the Moravian Brethren. I am inclined to think these excel others, because evangelizing barbarians is their *trade*. Their children are inspired with dignified ideas of it at an early age, which co-operating with ordinary grace, produces these *mirabilia*."

There is no doubt much truth in this last remark. It must, however, at the same time, be acknowledged, that the very circumstance of inculcating an early reverence for the office of a missionary, is in itself a proof of the prevalence of that spirit of simple and devoted piety which is the earnest and pledge of the success with which the efforts of the United Brethren, in promoting christianity among the heathen, have been crowned.

In the month of May following the date of the preceding letter, Mr. Buchanan informed Mr. Newton, who was now anxiously looking forward to his ordination, that he was to take his degree at the ensuing commencement, that is, on the 8th of July; that his ordination studies would engage his attention for the next two months; and that early in September he purposed being in London. His venerable friend having complained of his increasing deafness, Mr. Buchanan, with his usual affectionate piety, endeavours to console him under this infirmity.

"Your deafness," he observes, "is no doubt an evil; but you have been afflicted with it for good. Your reflections upon it show this. Some are alarmed at the decays of age in their christian friends. Why should they? When I see the aged christian losing one faculty and then another, I only see him passing through various 'changes of untried being,' till at last he throws off this 'mortal coil' itself. Deafness, or blindness, or mental weakness, are but precursors of immortality; they announce that heaven is at hand.

"Nor are they without *present* use. The grateful and reasonable reflections your short indisposition produced, are perhaps of more value to your soul, considering it as struggling for heavenly purity, than new accessions of mental power, or new refinements in every sense.

"Were it agreeable to the will of God, the *youthful* christian might find it a happy experience to suffer the temporary loss of every faculty he possesses. Nothing but experience, it seems, can teach us the value of these common blessings; and until we learn the value of them, we cannot be grateful. But the Lord sends us our sufferings in the fulness of time. To us it is given to be made conformable to Christ. This great sufferer has sent us his Comforter, to wait on infirmity and declining age. What more noble object does the all-seeing sun behold, than the '*patient sufferer?*' It is *awful* to little minds, and makes them tremble at the thought of that purity of soul which heaven demands.

"If you wish for an epitaph couched in a single word, I hope it will not be *Fui*. Your *friends*, indeed, might expound it in the manner you mention, but the stranger would do it differently. When *I* say *Fui*, I mean to say my glory is *past*. *Ilium fuit*, 'Troy is fallen.' Rather write, *Futurus sum*, 'My glory is to come.' King Arthur's epitaph boasts both of glory past and glory to come:

'Hic jacet Arthurus
Rex quondam et Rex futurus.'

But I am persuaded *you* will only think of the glory to come, and let *kings* talk of their glory past."

Mr. Buchanan was now within a few months of his ordination; and to that important termination of his academical course he from this time more particularly directed his attention. Of his chastened ardour in the pursuit of mathematical science, and of his successful cultivation of classical literature, some account has been already given. A series of common-place books from the year 1793, afford also abundant and satisfactory proof of his diligence in the acquisition of general knowledge. Some years after he had left Cambridge, having occasion to refer to his employments there, Mr. Buchanan observed to a friend, that during his residence at the University "he had tasted of almost every science, and had endeavoured to bend all his acquirements to worthy ends." The memorials of his studies, which have been just alluded to, bear ample testimony to the truth of this statement. His commonplace books contain abridgments of lectures on anatomy, harmonics, manufactures, and experimental philosophy; abstracts of Locke, of Grotius, and Paley on the Evidences of Christianity, of part of Smith's Wealth of Nations, of Aristotle's Rhetoric, and of some historical works. References occur to Bacon, Cudworth, Stillingfleet, Chillingworth, and other great authors. Extracts from various writers, both ancient and modern, chiefly with reference to moral and theological subjects. Notes of sermons preached before the University. Important historical facts, with occasional reflections upon them; the meaning of remarkable words, phrases, and customs; observations, either altogether original, or digested from different authors, and expressed in his own words—on infidelity; on natural and revealed religion; on style and eloquence; on memory and imagination; on real and alleged enthusiasm, and on the use of reason in religion; on various branches of political economy; on the French revolution, and on war. One of the most useful and interesting portions, however, of these *adversaria*, comprises a series of remarks on different parts of scripture: on the best method of reading the Bible; on the spirit and design of the sacred writings, particularly with respect to their hortatory and practical style; on preaching, and in general on the ministerial office; on prayer; on personal piety; and on the christian warfare.

These multifarious observations afford evident marks of extensive reading, of a correct taste, and a sound judgment. They exhibit much acuteness and refinement, much enlargement and originality of thought,* much acquaintance with himself and with the human character; "a mind of large discourse," anxious to derive information from every quarter, ever on the wing to extract sweetness from every flower, and solicitous to employ the whole to some valuable purpose. What that purpose was, we may learn from his own words in one of the memoranda in question.

"Is not," he asks, "the grand, the only object of my life, to preach Christ to men? Let me, therefore, convert every species of mental food into spiritual nourishment; whether it be Homer or Milton, Gibbon or Hume, that I read; whether

* Amongst a great variety of other subjects, one of Mr. Buchanan's commonplace books contains some remarks which are strongly characteristic of a vein of humour and archness, joined with penetration in studying human nature, for which he was remarkable. An equally striking indication of his wakeful attention to practical utility, may be perceived in the insertion in another book of a list of anthems calculated to excite devotional affections.

it be with intelligent or unlearned men that I converse; or whether it be sitting or walking that I meditate."

Again observes Mr. Buchanan, 'If the cross be continually in view, there is, perhaps, no line we read, no object we see, no fact we hear, but may be improved, by applying it to Christ, to ourselves, or to those around us. Such exercise as this would give a holy fertility to the imagination."

It would not be difficult to select from the copious collections in question, a variety of useful and interesting observations upon the important subjects which they embrace, as well as many striking illustrations of the sentiments expressed in the preceding quotations. For the sake, however, of brevity, two or three passages only shall be extracted, as a specimen of many others which might be adduced.

The first is from some remarks on Paley's definition, in his View of the Evidences of the design of christianity as a divine revelation; that is, as he represents it, to acquaint mankind with the doctrine of a future state. To which Mr. Buchanan replies, "No. Because, although men had been acquainted with this by an extraordinary messenger, they could not obtain heaven in the way proposed, namely, by observing the precepts of christianity. No one can keep them. It would have been an unhappy, an unwelcome revelation indeed—'There *is* a future state. Do this, and live to enjoy it.' Is this christianity?

"The christian might then say, 'I wish we had not heard of this. I wish we could have been left to solace ourselves with the thought of future Elysian fields, and waters of Lethe, and a temporary punishment: we had then never heard of everlasting chains and penal fire.'"

"No. The news by Christ is not," (he evidently means, not merely,) "that there is a future heaven; but rather, how to attain it. Christianity is the solution of that celebrated question of Job, 'How shall man be just with God?' Were I, therefore, to describe, in very few words, the scope of christianity as a revelation, I should say, that it was to show 'how God could be just, and the justifier of him that believes in Jesus.' The particular information, (for we had the *general* before,) is merely collateral. It is a part of the gospel. The angel announced it to the shepherds, not as discovering a future state, but a Saviour. 'Unto you is born this day in the city of David, a *Saviour*, which is Christ the Lord.' And St. Paul speaks of the gospel as revealing 'the righteousness of God by faith of Jesus Christ.'" (Rom. iii. 22.)

It may perhaps be thought, that in these remarks Mr. Buchanan has interpreted Paley's definition of the design of christianity too strictly. It is certain, however, that the revelation of a future state is described by that admirable writer in the work in question, too exclusively as the object of the gospel; and that its grand message of salvation through a divine Redeemer ought, under the actual condition of mankind, to be upon all occasions more prominently exhibited.

The next extract is of a more general, but not less important nature.

"That man is unacquainted with the constitution of the human mind, who does not know that it stands in constant need of being *roused to action*. You will answer, *I* pass a very active life. But what principle has roused you to this activity? Is it the acquisition of wealth? love of fame? love of splendour? the gratification of a particular passion? Or is it a principle of piety towards God? a conviction of a future judgment? a view of the cross?

"We do not ask in what your activity consists, that is unnecessary; because, if we learn the motive, we learn the action. Christianity is properly a religion of motives: it teaches us that a good tree cannot but bring forth good fruit: that good principles will produce good actions. And therefore it is, that it is of little service to declaim against a particular vice; for though one be removed, another will spring up. How can the streams be pure, if the fountain be troubled? Hence, too, it is, that no spiritual tyranny can be compared to that of the preacher insisting that his hearers should practise particular virtues, without giving them a principle which can produce such. It is like saying to the leper, 'be clean,' without pointing to the purifying waters of Jordan.

"Here too failed the Pagan philosophers. They insisted on certain virtues, but they knew of no soul-subduing principle. When at last a principle was proposed to them from heaven, some received it; but the many rejected it, because it was too simple, too humbling, too inconsistent with human dogmas and human pride. So it is now. It is easy to descant in metaphor and trope on the beauties of virtue, the unseemliness of vice, and the fitness of things; but it is difficult to preach Christ crucified. It is easy to say what men ought to be; but it is difficult to say what scripture declares they are.

"If any one should deny this, we would ask one question. Why were the Apostles persecuted? Why were the preachers of holiness despised?"

The third extract from the memorials of Mr. Buchanan's academical reflections and studies contains some brief observations on several important points. The first, relating to enthusiasm in religion, is one only of a series of remarks, which prove how carefully he had studied that subject, and with what jealousy he viewed any approach to enthusiasm, justly so called.

"Fanaticism proves nothing against religion. It is one of its *diseases;* and implies no more that there is no such thing as religion, than madness that there is no reason, or distemper that there is no health.

"To detect Enthusiasm in one's self or others."

"When a rational account cannot be given of our actions. The truly religious man can always give a reason of the hope that is in him. The enthusiast contents himself with enveloping his views in some mysterious passage of scripture, inexplicable even to himself, though influencing his conduct."

"The enthusiasm sanctioned by scripture is innoxious. It is a lambent flame, which warms and animates the soul to heavenly converse. By reason it is sought, by reason directed in its operation. But that lawless principle of which we speak, like an *ignis fatuus*, leads the benighted soul into an abyss of error and absurdity."

"'The wicked cannot be eternally punished,' says the philosopher, 'for it is contrary to my reason.' 'Thy reason,' replies the Almighty, 'What reason hast thou to judge of my purposes? "As the heavens are higher than the earth, so are my thoughts higher than thy thoughts." The portion of reason which I have given thee, is sufficient, if rightly exercised, to teach thee to believe all that I declare, whether thou understandest it or not.'

"But the philosopher will not submit his reason to God: he chooses to be an infidel. He laughs at the ignorance and obstinacy of the rustic, who refuses to believe that the earth moves round the sun, because it contradicts the evidence of his sight; while he himself, more stupidly ignorant, more unpardonably obstinate, disbelieves 'the word of God!'"

"When you find yourself active and alert in body and mind, your spirits high, and your understanding clear and capable of great things, then betake yourself to prayer, be it noon or night. Give to God your best hours."

"Christianity was at first assisted in its propagation by the civilization and extent of the Roman empire.

"Thus our extensive commerce with the known world ought to aid it once more."

One other extract from Mr. Buchanan's collections will recall our attention to the progress of this memoir. It contains his practical inferences from a view of the office of deacons in the primitive church, apparently compiled from Irenæus.

"It is my business," he concludes from this view, "to keep in the background, considering myself as but a servant or under-worker; to try to endear my rector more to his people, little solicitous about my own fame; only anxious to promote his cause by exemplary conduct, and to fill up the blank spaces or intervals of his labours; for though blank places are supplied by an unskilful hand, it does not much disfigure the work. Mine, in short, I conceive, is to be, the humble office of performing the mechanical part of the sacerdotal function."

The singular humility of these reflections, combined with the preceding evidence of his piety, as well as of his literary and theological attainments, sufficiently testify the fidelity and success with which Mr. Buchanan had improved the period of his academical residence, and how fully he was qualified to engage in the sacred office to which he aspired. He took his degree of B. A. at the commencement, as he had proposed; and in pursuance of the intention which he had expressed in his last letter to Mr. Newton, he appears to have continued at Cambridge during the long vacation till the second week in September, when he wrote to his excellent friend, under whose experienced guidance he was about shortly to enter upon the important work of the ministry, in the following terms.

"I had a letter from the Bishop's secretary this morning. His lordship approves of my credentials. Thursday se'nnight (the 17th inst.) is appointed for the examination, and Sunday following for the ordination. I propose to leave Cambridge on Tuesday evening by the mail, which will be in town early next morning; and I shall proceed to Fulham without stopping, that I may have the remainder of the day and next morning to *myself*. So it is not probable that I shall see you till Monday following.

"I *demand* your prayers for one who is about to enter on the ministry. Pray, that when the bishop lays his hands upon my head, I may devote myself a martyr for Him, who hung upon the cross for me."

In this strong and affecting language did Mr. Buchanan express the feelings with which he was about to dedicate himself to the service of his Redeemer. It is not often, perhaps, that so deep an impression of the love of Christ is felt by the candidate for the sacred office; but, though the disposition of every one ought to be similar, the case of Mr. Buchanan was doubtless somewhat peculiar. The steps by which he had been led to the ministry of the gospel, and the hints which had more than once been given of his probable employment in a foreign country, tended to inspire him with the purpose and the resolution which he thus briefly but forcibly described. It can scarcely be doubted, that the diary in which he had been accustomed, from the year 1790, to record both the events of his life and his private reflections, contained a more detailed account of his feelings and sentiments upon this interesting occasion; but the loss of that valuable memorial deprives us of any farther particulars respecting it, and compels us to be contented with the simple fact, that after an examination, which appears to have been more than ordinarily satisfactory, Mr. Buchanan was ordained a deacon on Sunday the 20th of September, 1795, at Fulham, by the late pious and excellent Bishop Porteus. Immediately after this admission into holy orders, he entered upon his engagement as curate to Mr. Newton, and continued, during a few succeeding months, to discharge the humble and unobtrusive duties which he had previously so well described.

Early, however, in the year 1796, the friends by whose christian kindness and liberality he had been introduced into the church, conceiving that his talents might be more advantageously employed abroad, recurred to the plan which had for some time been more or less in their view, and resolved to endeavour to obtain for him the appointment of a chaplain in the service of the East India Company. Application was accordingly made to a distinguished Director, Charles Grant, Esq., accompanied by such testimonials as amply certified the qualifications of Mr. Buchanan for the office to which he was recommended. Of these it may be proper to insert copies, more particularly as they may tend to accredit the judgment as well as the zeal which led to the appointment in question. The first is from the President and Fellows of Queen's College, Cambridge, and is expressed in the following terms.

"Queen's College, Cambridge, March 8, 1796.

"We the undersigned, the President, Tutors, and Fellows of Queen's college, Cambridge, do certify that Claudius Buchanan has been a member of this college upwards of four years, during which time he regularly resided among us, and always conducted himself with the greatest propriety and decorum. His attention to discipline, his sobriety, and progress in learning, gave the greatest satisfaction to the governing part of the college; and, in general, we have no doubt but that he is well qualified by talents and good principles to undertake the offices in India, for which we are informed he is a candidate.

Isaac Milner, President.
J. Thos. Jordan, Vice-President.
P. Heaton.
Fras. Knipe, Tutor.
T. L. Hubbersty.
R. A. Ingram.
C. Farish, Dean.
Thos. Bourdillon, Lecturer."

The preceding certificate was transmitted to Mr. Grant by Dr. Milner with the following letter, in which the learned President took the opportunity of bearing a more particular and decisive testimony to the merits of Mr. Buchanan.

"Queen's College, Cambridge, March 8, 1796.

"Dear Sir,—I enclose you the college's testimonial of Mr. Buchanan's good behaviour, which is expressed in general terms: but if it were needful to be more particular, I could add a great deal. In my judgment, much may be expected from his ability, industry, and discretion. He has an uncommon zeal for every thing that is praiseworthy, and this zeal is tempered and directed by a sound and well-informed understanding. His good sense and attainments must procure him respect everywhere. He will be certainly on the watch for opportunities to do good. Mr. Buchanan obtained both classical and mathematical prizes at college.

"I am, dear Sir, yours, Isaac Milner.

"To Charles Grant, Esq., London."

The testimonial of the venerable Bishop Porteus is equally satisfactory as to that part of Mr. Buchanan's qualifications which came more immediately under his lordship's notice. It was as follows.

"London House, March 12, 1796.

"Being desired to bear my testimony to the character and ability of the Rev. Claudius Buchanan, I hereby certify that he was admitted to the holy order of Deacon by me on the 20th of September, 1795; that he brought with him the usual testimonials from college, and was highly spoken of to me by some gentlemen of very respectable character. His attainments in sacred literature, and particularly in the knowledge of the scriptures, I think superior to what I have found in most of those that I have examined for holy orders.

B. London."

In consequence of these various testimonies to his abilities as a scholar, his attainments as a divine, and his general character for temperate and well-directed zeal for the honour of God, and the welfare of mankind, Mr. Buchanan was appointed one of the chaplains to the East India Company on Wednesday, March 30, 1796. When introduced to the Court of Directors, for the purpose of taking the oaths usual upon similar occasions, he was addressed by the chairman, the late Sir Stephen Lushington, on the importance of his office, and on the duties imposed on a minister of religion in India; and so lively a recollection did he retain of this unexpected but very laudable charge, that he more than once referred to it in the course of his future life. He thus mentions the address of the honourable chairman many years after it had been delivered.

"The venerable Baronet observed, that French principles were sapping the foundation of christianity and of social order; and he earnestly inculcated on me the duty of defending and promoting the principles of the christian religion by every proper means. I was much affected by the solemnity of the occasion, and by the energy and feeling with which the address was delivered: and the subject of the charge itself made a great impression on my mind, particularly when meditating on it afterwards, during my voyage."

Soon after the appointment of Mr. Buchanan to India, he received priest's orders from the Bishop of London; and in the month of May went down to Scotland, in order at once to revisit his family, and again take leave of them previously to his approaching voyage to India.

The feelings of both parties upon this meeting were, it may be readily imagined, of a mixed but very interesting nature. Nearly nine years had elapsed since Mr. Buchanan, partly impelled by disappointed affection, and partly by the flattering visions of a youthful imagination, had left his native country, and sojourned in a strange land. During that long interval many remarkable events had occurred. One of his earthly parents was no more; but he had, like the prodigal, returned to his heavenly Father, and by him he had been distinguished by peculiar marks of kindness and favour. After having suffered many external hardships and much inward distress, he had been relieved in no ordinary manner from both, by the providence and grace of God. Opportunities had been afforded him, which he had diligently improved, of acquiring the treasures of human science and learning; and with a mind thus richly stored, and a heart deeply impressed with the inestimable value of the gospel, he had been called to the work of the ministry, and had now the prospect of being permitted "to preach among the Gentiles the unsearchable riches of Christ." The emotions of Mr. Buchanan during his journey to Scotland, under these remarkable circumstances, must have been peculiarly affecting. While a "new song" had been put into his mouth, of joy and thanksgiving, it would be somewhat damped by the recollection of past sorrows, the pain of his approaching departure from his kindred and country, and the anticipation of future labours and trials. The feelings of his widowed mother and surviving brethren would be scarcely less chequered by joy and sorrow. Delighted as they must have been by the return of their beloved relative, enriched with divine and human knowledge, and honoured by an appointment which more than realized their highest wishes and expectations, the pleasure of their intercourse with him would be not a little clouded by the the thought of its transient nature, and the prospect of a long, perhaps, as to this world, a final separation in a far distant land. Such, we may justly suppose, were the mutual feelings and reflections of Mr. Buchanan and his family during his short abode with them at this interesting period. He appears to have remained in Scotland till the first week in June, when he returned to London to complete the preparations for his voyage. On the 3rd of July, he preached for Mr. Newton at St. Mary Woolnoth; and terminated by a pious and affectionate farewell, his short connexion with the congregation of his dear and venerable friend.

Memoirs of the Rev. Dr. Buchanan.

PART II.

CHAPTER I.

AMONGST the various recommendations and introductions from his more immediate patrons and friends, by which Mr. Buchanan was accompanied to India, one occurs, from so respectable a quarter, and of so appropriate a nature, that it may be proper to insert it. This is a letter from the Rev. Dr. Gaskin, Secretary to the Society for promoting Christian Knowledge, to the Rev. David Brown, then one of the East India Company's chaplains, resident in Calcutta. That part of his letter which relates to Mr. Buchanan, is as follows:

"LONDON, July 3, 1796.

"Rev. and dear Sir,—It is with particular pleasure that I introduce to you the name of the Rev. Claudius Buchanan, who is appointed to be chaplain to the Hon. Company, and in whom I am persuaded you will find a most valuable colleague; as I have every reason to believe, from the intercourse I have had with him, and from the testimony chiefly of my Lord Bishop of London, that he is a man of sound learning, serious piety, and great steadiness. I was myself present, and assisted at his admission to priest's orders. The pleasure I have in communicating this information is increased considerably from the full expectation I entertain, that he will cheerfully, and to the utmost of his power, assist you at the mission church."

This was, however, by no means the only introduction which Mr. Buchanan carried with him to the pious and excellent person to whom the foregoing letter was addressed; who afterwards proved one of his most valued and intimate friends, and with whom he was long associated in the various labours which devolved upon him in India.

Thus recommended and accredited, Mr. Buchanan left London for Portsmouth on Saturday the 30th of July, and on the

11th of August following, he embarked on board the Busbridge East Indiaman, commanded by Captain Dobree, and sailed for Bengal. During the course of his extensive voyage, Mr. Buchanan was diligently employed in acquiring useful knowledge, and in endeavouring to promote the improvement of his various companions and fellow-passengers.

The principal subjects of his studies were probably such as bore an immediate reference to the work of the ministry, and to his peculiar destination in India; but the only traces of them which now remain, consist of some additional common-place books, one of which is dated at sea, in January, 1797, near the island of St. Paul, containing abridgments of chemistry from Lavoisier, of Botany, from Rousseau and Martin, of the history of Denmark and Sweden, and miscellaneous observations, chiefly of an historical nature.

Of his employments, views, and feelings in the early part of his voyage, the following letter to Mr. Newton presents an interesting account.

"Busbridge East-Indiaman,
At sea, off the Canaries, 27 Aug. 1796.

"My dear Sir,—I take the opportunity of writing to you by the Polyphemus, a 64 gun ship, which, after convoying us safely to this latitude, returns now to England. We have had a monsoon all the way. We took our departure from the Lizard, and in eight days made the island of Madeira; a shorter passage than the East India fleet has ever had. In two days we hope to arrive at the trade winds; indeed, the captain thinks we have them already. About the end of September we expect to reach the cape, from which place you will probably hear from me. I enjoy good health on board. I was sea-sick for about a week. Every body pays me much attention. I am instructing some in science, some in classical knowledge, some in the belles lettres, and all, I hope, in christian truth. I do not expect to be so useful in preaching sermons to them, as in conversation. The captain supports a very consistent character. He is the friend of virtue, and I doubt not but he will continue to arm my endeavours with his power. All his officers are in proper subjection to him, and exert their authority in the ship in accommodating me.

"We have more than a dozen officers of the army going out as passengers. I have some weight with them; but there are many divisions among themselves. They have been challenging already; and probably duels may follow.

"We are now about twenty sail. The frigate l'Oiseau

accompanies us to the Cape, and will probably carry home our letters.

"One day lately an enemy appeared in sight, and we began to think of an engagement. Then was the time for examining myself, and learning what was my object in a voyage to India. Indeed, unless we have some confidence that the Lord is with us, our hearts must sink in despair on such occasions. But where we can believe that He is leading us out *on his own service*, we have nothing to fear from an enemy, or from the dangers of the sea. On the contrary, the *faithful* servant must rejoice that his Lord will come *so soon*, and lead him to that rest which he seeks for in vain on earth.

"When the enemy came nearer, they discovered that we had a superior force, and bore away.

"I hope Miss C. and the rest of your house are happy. They have great advantages, which I trust they improve. They live in the house of peace and instruction. They, with you, will, I hope, shortly inherit your mansion in the skies.

"It is with me as I expected. I feel little difference in mind, whether navigating the ocean, or sitting quietly in Coleman-street. It would appear as if I had lost all relish for earthly pleasure. No novelty excites my attention. My countenance is acquiring a grave settled cast. I feel as if nothing could give joy to my soul, but freedom from the body. And yet being sensible that I may remain long on duty here, I often inquire of myself how I am to pass the heavy hours. Perhaps a closer walk with God, greater activity in his service, and some species of affliction hitherto unfelt, may at length unloose my bonds, and give me that enjoyment of life to which I have so long been a stranger. I have great hopes indeed from enterprising a little in my Master's service, and fighting with courage for his honour. I shall write to you from time to time, and acquaint you how it is with me.

"It will be a remarkable day when you and I meet in heaven. I dare not say, *Serò redeas;* because I trust that you are 'ready.' I fear you will have learnt many a song in heaven before I come. But let me not despond. What saith the scripture? *Ut dies, sic robur.*

"May you be preserved in your old age, so that your Lord may be glorified in the ending, as in the beginning of your christian life.

"Forgive me all my faults, and believe me to be, my dear Sir, your affectionate son, C. BUCHANAN."

The foregoing letter appears to contain the only memorial of Mr. Buchanan's voyage which now exists. His diary, the loss of which we must have frequent occasion to lament, doubtless recorded many particulars which might have gratified and instructed us. A few memoranda, however, only remain. On the 18th of November, some weeks later than he had expected, the fleet arrived at the Cape of Good Hope. On the 10th of December, it again sailed, and reached Madras on the 17th of February; and on the 10th of March, Mr. Buchanan landed at Calcutta, two days before the completion of the 31st year of his age.

On his arrival at the capital of the British possessions in India, he was hospitably received by the Rev. Mr. Brown, and resided for a short time in his family. He then took a house in Durrumlollah, where, however, he continued but two months, being at the end of that time appointed chaplain at Barrackpore, a military station about sixteen miles above Calcutta.

By this arrangement, which, however usual according to the rules of the East India service, he does not appear to have anticipated, Mr. Buchanan found himself placed in a situation by no means congenial with his taste and feelings, and affording but few opportunities for the exercise of his ministry. Barrackpore possessed no place for public worship; and divine service was never required by the military staff to which he was attached.

This unexpected seclusion from active duty, combined with the influence of an enervating climate, which he very soon began to feel, and of society for the most part unfriendly to religion, produced in Mr. Buchanan a considerable depression of spirits, and even gave occasion to some of his friends in Europe to attribute his comparative inactivity on his arrival in India to abatement of zeal rather than, as the truth required, to causes over which he could exercise no control.

When Mr. Buchanan arrived at Calcutta, Mr. Brown was one of the two chaplains of the presidency. He held also the chaplaincy of the garrison. Some of Mr. Buchanan's friends in England conceived that the latter appointment might have been transferred to him; or that he might have officiated at the mission church. As to the garrison, it appears that motives of delicacy and kindness towards Mr. Brown, with whom he lived from the first on the most friendly and affectionate terms, prevented him from soliciting such an arrangement; and the mission church was then occupied by the Rev. Mr. Ringeltaube, a clergyman of the Lutheran church, who had been sent to India under the patronage of the Society for promoting Christian Knowledge. No sooner, however, had Mr. Ringeltaube abandoned this post, as he shortly afterwards did, than Mr. Buchanan participated with Mr. Brown the gratuitous labour of the mission church. It appears also, that he occasionally performed divine service in his house at Barrackpore; probably as often as he could obtain an audience.

The following letter will explain the confidential nature of Mr. Buchanan's intercourse with Mr. Brown. The former part of it relates to a proposed measure respecting an evening lecture at one of the churches in Calcutta, and to the chaplaincy of Fort William: the latter will exhibit a most interesting and instructive picture of the mind of the writer, and will throw considerable light on some of the preceding observations.

"Barrackpore, 9th June, 1797.

"My dear Sir,—I have just received yours. I understood your last very well. I meant to say in answer, that to levy a contribution for the current expenses of the lecture, would be very painful to me; equally so as a contribution for personal support.

"When I mentioned my idea of gratuity for professional duties, it was to explain my delicacy about pecuniary subscription. I had no allusion to the sentiments of others. If I were in your situation, it is probable that I should do as you do.

"I think the justice you owe your family in an expensive situation, demands that you be very well satisfied with the propriety of giving up the chaplaincy of the Fort, as long as it is agreeable to the rules of the service that you should retain it; and as long as you can perform the service it requires as well as any other.

"Let us now talk on the subject of your former letter a little.

"I think you speak of yourself with more diffidence, or rather despondency, than you ought. How do you know that your Thursday evening lecture is not the most useful of all your ministrations? And with respect to industry, have you not much reason to be thankful, that, after a ten years' residence in this deteriorating country, you feel yourself so much alive to the ministry of Christ? And is it not another reason for thankfulness, that you have been preserved from seeking great things for yourself? I think you very happy indeed, that you have nothing to do with this world; but that your *chief* work is to make proof of your ministry, as the Lord shall prosper it. As splendid a crown awaits him who shall do a *little* in *this* country, as him who shall do much at home.

"It is not probable that you or I shall live long. What seek we then? There is no fame for us here. There is some reproach, whether we be *faithful* or not. So that we lose nothing by being faithful. I am so young in these things, that I do not know any thing about them. I have only entered the wilderness. But I apprehend *much*. I would gladly enter Canaan, without encountering 'the greatness of the way.' Were it the will of God, and were he to give me faith and strength for it, I would *to-morrow*, with great joy, leave this world, and all it offers. Were I sure it would not entangle and destroy me at last, I would rather stay and endeavour to do something for God; but I am not sure of that.

"I often compare myself, in my present exile, to John, in the island of Patmos. Would that, like him, I had finished my course, and had only to contemplate 'the new heavens!' But I am a stranger to suffering 'for the word of God, and the testimony of Jesus Christ.'

"I sigh much for that singleness of mind and purity of heart, and love to God, which distinguish the disciple of Christ. And I often wonder whether it is to be effected by keen affliction in body and spirit, or by the 'power of the word of God, dividing asunder like a two-edged sword,' or by long fighting and sorrowful experience slowly teaching, and ending with a doubt whether I am taught.

"Amidst the multitude of my thoughts, 'the Lamb that was slain' is my only hope!

"How frequent is the character of a semi-serious christian! There is a state, in which some have been held for many years: a state, whose nature was never rightly understood by those around them, nor by themselves; sometimes looking to the word of God, and sometimes to the world; sometimes animated by a zeal to live holily, and sometimes sinking under a particular sin. From such a state they have at length emerged; and shone, in the evening of life, with a splendour which has dazzled all around.

"I hope that Mrs. Brown is in good health and spirits. Buxtorf came safe up the river. I am sorry to find that

that silent critic, the White Ant, has perused almost every page.

"I remain, dear Sir, yours very affectionately,

C. BUCHANAN."

The preceding letter scarcely requires a comment. Who can avoid perceiving in it evident traces of a generous, a spiritual, and a heavenly mind? Who can help lamenting that such a man should for a time have been placed in circumstances so unfavourable to the attainment of the great object which he had in view in accepting an appointment in India; or indulging a hope, that a time would come, when the providence of God would open to him a way to greater exertions, and more extensive usefulness?

Though Mr. Buchanan's retirement at Barrackpore did not, however, admit of very active employment in the duties of his ministry, it afforded him a valuable opportunity for private study, which he diligently and successfully improved.

His commonplace books at this period evince the same laudable desire of increasing his store of useful knowledge, which we have already witnessed. Some remarks in one of them prove his anxiety to fortify himself against the dangers of worldly society, to which he was then considerably exposed, and to attain the important art of living "in and out of the world at the same time," of "using this world as not abusing it." Upon this point he quotes a passage from Mr. Addison, which appears to express the object he was himself endeavouring to attain. "We shall never be able," observes that sensible and elegant writer, "to live to our satisfaction in the deepest retirement, until we learn to live, in some measure, to our satisfaction, amidst the noise and business of life."

Other parts of the same book contain reflections on the Persian language, on the improvement of time, on the value of christian friendship, on purity of conscience, on the propagation of the gospel, and on the happiness of heaven.

The following extract from a letter to Mr. Henry Thornton, dated the 25th of July, 1797, gives a pleasing view of one important branch of Mr. Buchanan's studies at Barrackpore.

"As the friend of my *beginning* studies, you will naturally be desirous to know in what way they have been continued since my arrival in India. I am now proceeding in a work which I began when I last enjoyed retirement, namely, a serious, and, I may say, laborious examination of the scriptures in the original tongues. My inquiries are not so much philological, as practical. The meaning of the Holy Spirit in scripture is the 'one thing needful' for the student: and I hope it will be the subject of many a joyful ευρηκα to me. This severity of investigation reminds me of my mathematical vigils. Some have considered that interval at college as the most useful era in the history of the mind. It shows what powers of application the soul possesses on a subject it loves; even such application as Paul recommends to Timothy, who was engaged in my present studies—εν τυτοις ισθι. 'Exist, or live in them.'

"This, Sir, is a climate which tries the mind like a furnace. Deterioration seems inherent in Indian existence. Were God to grant me a peculiar blessing, it would be the habit of industry whilst I remain in this country. I have observed, in reading the lives of the good, that the most eminent were men famed for their industry. I have observed too, that few of them had to encounter what Boileau calls the dangerous career of wit and genius. The wisdom of God is shown in choosing for them that disposition of mind which is best suited to a sedulous and humble perusal of his eternal word; for genius hath ever been a foe to industry.

"I have a Moonshee in the house to instruct me in the Hindostanee and Persian languages. Not knowing what may be the purpose of God concerning me, I have thought it my duty to attend early to the languages of the country; and to the constitution, civil and religious, of the mixed people in it."

Amidst this diligent improvement of his retirement at Barrackpore, Mr. Buchanan, however, entered with lively interest into every thing around him connected with real religion, and embraced with much warmth of feeling every occasion which presented itself, either of kindness or of service.

Of this the following extract from a letter to a lady at Edinburgh, on the death of her son, is a pleasing and satisfactory proof. It is dated from Calcutta, December 4, 1797, and was enclosed in another, in which she was kindly requested, before she opened it, to prepare her mind for intelligence which would at first deeply affect her, but which she would afterwards acknowledge had given her such a theme for rejoicing as she had never before possessed.

"I had no thoughts," Mr. Buchanan begins, "of writing to you at this time; but I have news for you from heaven. Your beloved E. has 'fought the good fight, he has finished his course, he has kept the faith.' His spirit took its flight at twelve o'clock. About three weeks ago he visited me at Barrackpore, where he stayed a day or two. He was then in good health. Our conversation was much on spiritual subjects. He told me his heart felt the first powerful impression of religion when on his passage to this country; and that since his arrival, God had been very gracious to him. Finding this country not only unfavourable to health, but to holiness of life, he had long deliberated whether he ought not to return to Europe, and had at length resolved to do so, believing it to be the will of God. He anticipated the joy of conversing with those amongst his friends at Edinburgh who knew the Lord, and wondered that he had not 'made more of them,' while among them. But he has now a better society.

"Next day he returned to Calcutta, and on the Sabbath following I went down to preach. My subject was, 'The triumph of the christian in being able to submit his soul to the darkest dispensations of God.' On that day your son took the sacrament for the second time in this country. On the evening of the same day the Rev. Mr. Brown preached, 'On the consolations of the soul which cordially assents to being justified by faith.' This was the last sermon your beloved child ever heard; and he told me it was sweet to the ear, and inexpressibly rich to his soul. On the next day he was taken ill. Our most able physician here, Dr. Hare from Edinburgh, attended him. During that week we had no apprehensions of his fever being dangerous. Before my return to Barrackpore on Monday last, I passed the morning with him. We then conceived hopes of his soon being well. He sat by me on the sofa for an hour. We talked about his passage to his native country; for the ship was now ready to sail—But I perceived that his mind was dwelling on his passage to the *heavenly* country. He spoke much of the consolations arising from converse with God during sickness. 'How amazing is it,' said he, 'that the Lord should have called *me* to such knowledge and to such grace before I die! India has been a happy land to me.' When I left him, he said, he hoped he should be able to come to church next Sunday. Not hearing from his brother of his being worse, I did not return to Calcutta till yesterday. In the evening I preached, but did not see him in his usual seat. When I called this morning, I found that he had just entered into rest. His countenance is placid and serene in death, like the state of his mind before his dissolution.

"Such, my dear madam, has been the happy death of your son. You are a happy mother, to have had such a son! He has left a noble testimony to the gospel in this place; and his memory will be long cherished by many. His brother loved him affectionately, and is inconsolable at his loss. His conversation and example have been of use to many. He preached to them in his life, and he preached to them by his death.

Admire therefore the dispensation of God in leading him to this country. It was not for evil, but for much good."

"TUESDAY, Dec. 5.

"This morning, at eight o'clock, I committed to the earth the remains of your dear son. It was a solemn occasion. I was much affected at seeing so many persons attend it. Most of them were only acquainted with his character; but they wished to show some respect to the memory of one of those few who 'wear white garments in this Sardis.' The Rev. Mr. Brown was chief mourner; but yet he rejoiced that the Lord had lent your child so long to us, and that now 'he had taken him from the evil to come.'"

The strain of Christian piety and consolation which pervades the foregoing letter must be obvious to every one, but will be best appreciated by those who know experimentally the unspeakable value of well-grounded hopes concerning the future happiness of those who were dear to them; more particularly, if they have been taken from them in a distant land. The spirit of lively faith with which Mr. Buchanan speaks of the glorious hope of the gospel, is strongly characteristic of his mind; and may serve to counterbalance some less cheerful and animating views respecting himself, which he at this period occasionally expressed.

Thus, early in the ensuing year, he wrote to Mr. Grant in the following terms.

"CALCUTTA, 6th Feb. 1798.

"My dear Sir,—I have now been near a year in this country, and have not yet had the satisfaction of hearing from you. I wish to know what you think of my voyage to the East. I seem to have come out under rather unfavourable auspices. No feature of my mission is very agreeable. But I view the whole as the counsel of the Almighty; and I know that in his plan there is great beauty, though I may not pereeive it.

"I have passed this last year in military society, or in solitude. And as I shall shortly be stationed up the country, I cannot expect any material change during life. But if I rightly improve the opportunities I may have, I shall do well. What I lament most is the effect this inactive life has on my mind. You will not be surprised if both my moral and intellectual powers suffer by it. The climate no doubt has its effect in this hebetation of the soul; and I hope I shall recover from it in time.

"I suffered a long struggle before I could resign myself passively to my unexpected destination. But the struggle is now over; and I view myself as one who has run his race; to whom little more is left to do. I have known some, who, in such a case, would have extricated themselves with violence, and sought a new fortune in the gospel. But it will require a very evident interposition of God indeed to bring me out of this Egypt, now that he has placed me in it: I shall esteem myself highly favoured, if I be enabled to pass my days in it, with a pure conscience, endeavouring to do a little, where much cannot be done.

"I take the liberty of enclosing a bill for fifty pounds for my mother: which I request you will be so good as to send to her, after it is accepted.

"I beg to be remembered to all your family, and to Mr. and Mrs. Thornton, and remain, dear Sir,

"Yours, with much respect and gratitude,

C. BUCHANAN."

The desponding tenor of this letter, connected as it is with similar expressions in some others, may require a few explanatory observations. The unfavourable influence of the climate upon his health, to which Mr. Buchanan refers, must evidently be considered as the principal cause of the depression under which he laboured. He was, doubtless, disappointed in the silence and obscurity to which his station at Barrackpore had consigned him, and which he imagined would be shortly rendered still more hopeless, by his removal to a greater distance from Calcutta, in the interior of the country. It is certain, also, that he felt the want of sympathy and encouragement from some of his friends in England. They had very reasonably formed considerable expectations of his exertions to promote the cause of religion in India; and their distance from the scene prevented them from being fully aware of the circumstances which had hitherto retarded them. Yet amidst it all, his calm submission to what he believed to be the will of God, his refusal to step beyond the prescribed limits of his duty as a military chaplain, and his pious reference of himself and his services to the divine disposal, prove, that whatever might be his discouragements, his heart was "right with God;" and that he was faithfully employing the "talent" at that time committed to his trust.

The history of Mr. Buchanan's first appointment in India will not be in vain, if it serve to check in any who may be similarly situated, either abroad or at home, the too natural disposition to despondency or haste; and to lead them, in the conscientious improvement of present opportunities, to wait patiently for farther openings, and in the mean time to "hope in God;" and if it tend to abate in those who may be observing them any impatience of their backwardness in fulfilling even just expectations; and to teach them that charity, which, concerning the substantially pious and sincere, "hopeth all things."

In the month of July following, Mr. Buchanan wrote to several of his friends by the overland despatch. In one of these letters to Mr. Elliott, of Clapham, he informs him of the arrival of his son at Calcutta.

Of the talents and extensive acquirements, the splendid career in the college of Fort William, shortly afterwards established, and the premature and lamented death of this valuable and accomplished young man, the writer of these memoirs has on a former occasion recorded a brief account.* In again mentioning his name, he does it chiefly for the purpose of illustrating the character of Mr. Buchanan; to whose kindness, counsels, and example, he was eminently indebted. To his father Mr. Buchanan thus writes.

"Your son William is arrived. I had long looked for him, as for a brother. He resided with me at Barrackpore for two months, and then went up to Malda, where he now is. He has conducted himself with much propriety, and conciliated the favour and respect of many. In some of his anticipations he was sanguine and incorrect; but his good sense gradually removed the veil, and discovered things in the right point of view; and I think he has now formed a very tolerable estimate of India, and of his situation in it. Government was at first disposed to place him at Calcutta. This would have deranged all your and my plans concerning him. I do not live at Calcutta. He would have been obliged to keep house by himself; for there is no private family that would receive him; and the expense would have been so great, that all his prudence could not easily save him from debt. Another evil of that situation is the ensnaring society. The young men live by themselves, as at college. Such a society has proved instant death to the virtue of many. After two or three years, I shall have less objection to his residence in Calcutta. He will then have more fortitude and more money, worse health, and lower spirits.

"I was happy to observe that William's mind was not injured by the infidel conversation on board ship. It led him however to *inquire*. And he was a good deal surprised at the volume of evidence for the truth of christianity, which he

* See Dissertation on the Promotion of Christianity in India, p. 141.

found at Barrackpore. While with me he made rapid progress in Persian; and was laying deep plans for the attainment of general knowledge. I had a letter from him this morning. He is well and happy. I wished him to consider Malda as a retirement, to be consecrated, like college, to the improvement of his mind. As yet he is well pleased with the idea. He complains that *business* usurps much time. But so he attain the habit of industry in this indolent climate, I care not whether it be by business or study. *An active mind, if it be a virtuous one, finds time for every thing.*

"He speaks of his father with much affection. Write often to him. A father's letter is very seasonable in this country. He begins well; he far surpasses my sanguine expectations. But he has only begun. He was surprised to find eight weekly newspapers here, together with libraries and learned men. Unfortunately, there are no classical folks at Malda. William's Latin and Greek are therefore in danger. He is already sensible of this; and begins to think that I was right in proposing to *task* him. He is much attached to one mode of mental improvement,—the committing to writing useful observations. He has ransacked many of my commonplace books to enrich his own. The only annual investment of books you need send him, will be the Reviews; all of which will be acceptable. Adieu."

Were it consistent with the plan of this narrative, several letters might here be introduced from Mr. William Elliott, which illustrate in a very pleasing manner the advantages he derived from the advice and assistance of Mr. Buchanan in his classical and oriental studies; and above all, in cherishing those religious views which after no long interval he found to be alone supremely valuable. It is probable, from Mr. Buchanan's extensive correspondence with young men in India, that many others enjoyed similar benefits from his friendly counsel.

A few of the preceding observations may perhaps be no longer applicable to the circumstances of the junior servants of the East India Company in Calcutta, in consequence of the salutary changes introduced not long afterwards by the institution of the College of Fort William: but the almost paternal anxiety displayed by the writer for the welfare and improvement of his young friend, and the practical wisdom of his suggestions, will be not uninteresting to those who may be connected, like his correspondent, with India.

To Mr. Newton, Mr. Buchanan wrote by the same despatch as follows.

"I hope, my dear Sir, that you have received many letters

from me since my arrival here, for I have written many. You are the only person who has written regularly to me since I left England. Your last, dated 2d. Oct. 1797, gave me much information, pleasure, and comfort. I have now been a year and a half in India, and have not yet engaged in the ministry;* and I know not when I shall. At present, indeed, I should scarcely be able, were I called to it. The oppression on my chest is so great, and my breathing so quick, that I cannot speak audibly in conversation but with difficulty. And the total relaxation of my frame, and my inability to sit up long, admonish me that I am not intended for long service. Two fevers since my arrival have no doubt had some effect in weakening me. But I do not attribute my present illness to India. I can trace my pectoral weakness to midnight study at college. But I am thankful that I am without actual pain. I can think and write a little for two or three hours every morning. Perhaps I may be restored. Perhaps 'my mouth may yet be opened to speak his praise.'

"Will you write a note to Mr. Storry, of Colchester, mentioning the following particulars? John Gale, lately a private in the king's service, was executed here for the murder of a woman and her child. But though he suffered the death of a felon, he died in the faith of Christ. He was just twenty-two years of age, being executed on his birthday. He could not read, and had only three days' instruction from Mr. Brown and myself. It revived our spirits to behold the power of the gospel thus displayed in this barren land. On the morning of his execution, he requested me to acquaint Mr. Storry with the circumstances of his happy death. His parents are hearers of Mr. Storry; and he will be the fittest bearer of these tidings.

"How is Dr. Fearon? My dear Fearon, how are you? you cannot easily imagine how gratifying your letter was to me. I received it on a sick-bed; and had not seen the face of a christian for a month before. A Hindoo, who worships an idol with an elephant's head, read it to me three times. I suppose the French have not restored my answer to it. My frequent indispositions have prevented me hitherto from writing so much as I wish. But as I consider that all my letters to Mr. Newton are letters to you, I conceive myself to have written to you a great deal. Remember me, as you ought, to every member of your family; and write me such another letter as you wrote me last, *if you are able*."

The serious indisposition of Mr. Buchanan, as affecting his

* Evidently meaning, not statedly.

capacities of usefulness, is distinctly marked in this last letter, as well as the expression of his hope of future service.

The narrative respecting the unhappy soldier, though necessarily brief, from the narrow limits of an overland despatch, ought not, on that account, to be viewed with suspicion. The character both of Mr. Brown and Mr. Buchanan forbids the supposition that they had formed a hasty judgment of this remarkable case; and though false hopes have not unfrequently been cherished upon similar melancholy occasions, yet why should we limit the mercies of the Most High, or doubt the saving efficacy of faith in the Redeemer, even under circumstances apparently desperate? It seems probable, too, from the introduction of the late Mr. Storry's name, that the unfortunate young man in question had received in very early life some salutary instructions from the ministry of that excellent man; which, though long forgotten, might have been remembered and confirmed to his everlasting benefit, in the hour of extremity.

Under the same cover, Mr. Buchanan wrote shortly to Mr. Grant to the following effect.

"Lord Mornington has been here near six weeks. As yet, he maintains much dignity in his government. He goes regularly to church, and professes a regard for religion. He has been at Barrackpore for ten days past. He was surprised when I told him that we never had divine service there, or at any other station. He was still more surprised when he heard there were horse-races here on Sunday morning,

"The apostolic Obeck is well, and affectionately remembers all your family. He succeeds to Swartz in the title to our reverence and esteem. Remember me to Mr. Thornton, the friend of my studies."

Mr. Obeck, thus favourably introduced, and whose name frequently occurs in Mr. Buchanan's letters, was a native of Germany, for many years employed as steward in Mr. Grant's family, during his residence in India. The piety and fidelity of this good man were rewarded by the liberal support and friendly regard of his patron to the day of his death.

The packet from which the preceding extracts are taken, contained a fourth letter to Mr. Simeon, of Cambridge, part of which is as follows.

"I thought to have passed my life near you; but—thus it is. You first, I think, proposed a voyage to me. But you did not mean to consign me to silence, or to a camp! We may yet see the wisdom of God in showing me a path through the mighty waters. As my health returns, my services may be called for.

"Remember me to Mrs. B. She alone opposed my coming to India. Tell her not to triumph. She has not seen *to the end*."

Three months after the despatch just detailed, Mr. Buchanan again wrote at some length to Mr. Newton. In the former part of his letter, he repeats, with some additional circumstances, what he had before communicated respecting his situation and prospects, chiefly with a view to convince his friends in England, that however desirous he might be of more effective services in the ministry, the attempt was at that time impracticable. In proof of this he mentions, that before Sir John Shore, now Lord Teignmouth, left India, Mr. Brown procured an Order of Council, that the military in the garrison should attend at the Presidency church every Sunday morning at six o'clock, there being no chapel or service in the garrison itself. Strong opposition was made to this order, on the ground that the troops would suffer in their health by marching in the sun. They attended a few Sundays, but at last the clamour became so violent that the order was revoked, and the triumph over religion considered complete. Mr. Buchanan states this circumstance in order to show how unavailing any transfer of the chaplaincy of the garrison to himself, could it with propriety have been effected, would have proved as to the great object of his increased usefulness. He adds, however, that when he was in Calcutta on a Sunday, he usually performed service at the hospital; where, though there was no regular audience, there was always a succession of hearers. It appears also by this letter, that as Mr. Buchanan had no immediate prospect of being himself placed in Calcutta, he was endeavouring, and with some success, to improve the religious views of one of the chaplains of the Presidency, who seemed desirous of discharging his duty with fidelity.

"My health," he observes, "is somewhat improved since my last. I have been recommended to take much gentle exercise. I think I never can be *strong;* but regular and easy employment, and christian society, may do a great deal; first to my spirits, and then to my health."

Mr. Buchanan next adverts to the Baptist missionaries, Messrs. Thomas and Carey. Of the latter he speaks in terms of much commendation. His own expectations respecting the conversion of the Hindoos were, at this period, by no means sanguine. Of Mr. Carey, therefore, he remarks, that he was then chiefly employed in laying the foundation of future usefulness. "He is," says Mr. Buchanan, "translating the Bible into the Bengal tongue. This, like Wickliff's first translation, may prove the father of many versions." How extensively this anticipation has been realized, it would be unnecessary to interrupt this narrative particularly to state.

"But," continues Mr. Buchanan, "a rapid spread of the gospel is not to be expected in India. You have heard that Mr. Swartz was useful in the southern part of Hindostan. It is true. But Mr. Swartz entered upon the labours of others. The gospel has been preached in that quarter for near a hundred years past. We may begin here now, as the Danes began there a century ago. Zeal and labour, and the lapse of years, will no doubt produce the usual fruit. In the revolution of this century, 'the dawn' of the gospel has appeared in India. After many centuries have revolved, there may be a general light.

"But I wish not that any prudential considerations from what *has been*, or from what may *probably* be, should check the missionary ardour of the day. Nothing great since the beginning of the world has been done, it is said, without enthusiasm. I am, therefore, well pleased to see multitudes of serious persons,* big with hope, and apt to communicate; for I think it will further the gospel. Instead of thirty missionaries, I wish they could transport three hundred. They can do little harm, and may do some good. But let them send as many children as possible, or those who may have children. They will do more good by and by than their parents. No man turned of thirty can learn to speak a new language *well.* No Englishman turned of twenty, who is only acquainted with the labials and dentals of his mother-tongue, can ever acquire an easy and natural use of the nasals and gutturals of the Bengal language. Send, therefore, old men to take care of the morals of the young; and send the young to convert the heathen."

Though the progressive observations and experience of Mr. Buchanan in some measure modified his sentiments upon the important points noticed in the preceding extract, his remarks are perhaps substantially true. But this is a subject which will hereafter be more fully considered. A few other sentences from this letter seem to be worth adding.

"Mr. Elliott will be glad to hear that William is well. I have a letter from him almost every week. He sends me down presents of peacocks and monkies, silk coverlets, and fine cossahs. I hear that Mr. Udney reposes much confidence in him. Every body must like him, for he has what few here have, 'fine spirits and a good temper.'

* This probably referred to the London Missionary Society.

"Mr. Swartz, the apostle of the east, is dead. I wrote him a Latin letter a short time before his death. I wished to write his life, but they refuse to send me materials.* Have you heard of the ancient Obeck, in Calcutta? Mr. Grant will tell you about him. Mr. Obeck, in Calcutta, is like Lot in Sodom. I asked him one day if he could produce ten righteous to save the city? He said he was not sure he could produce ten, but thought he could produce five."

It cannot be doubted that both these excellent men partook too largely of the spirit of the prophet, who thought that he was the only true worshipper of Jehovah, in a corrupt and degenerate age. It is at least certain that Calcutta has added greatly, within the last few years, to the number of its 'righteous' inhabitants; and not a few in consequence of the labours and example of the subject of these memoirs.†

"My last fever," Mr. Buchanan continues, "produced a deafness, which is not yet gone. It is very inconvenient to

---

* Some years afterwards Mr. Buchanan procured the documents he at this time requested; though other circumstances prevented him from making use of them as he had intended.

† The improvement in the state of religion at Calcutta, as in many other parts of India, has been progressive. While the number of consistent christians is still small, compared with the merely nominal adherents to christianity, and the far larger and more appalling mass of idolaters, it is certain that there has been a great increase of good, a considerable diminution of evil ingredients, in the population of this great city. The following statements respecting its condition were made by Archdeacon Corrie, now Bishop of Madras, at the anniversary of the Church Missionary Society, in 1835.

"In 1806, there were only two places for religious worship of the Established Church; and beyond the confines of Calcutta there was no place of any kind: some of the troops used to have prayers read to them in their barracks; others were drawn up for that purpose on the parade, where the chaplain used to read a selection of prayers, and a short sermon; but the full service of the Church of England was not used. Now, however, happily the case is different: there are six places of worship belonging to the Established Church in Calcutta; besides which, divine service is performed in a chapel belonging to the Orphan school, where any person who chooses may attend. In addition to these, there are places of worship belonging to the Scottish Church, and others." * * *

"There are at present in Calcutta, four native youths, who have been converted to the christian faith, and are prepared to teach the truths of christianity to their Hindoo brethren. One of these, who is of the highest caste of Brahmins, was converted by the missionary labours of the Scottish Church; another by means of a military officer and a young merchant."

The following, from the same address, is deeply interesting, and shows, that if the number of the "righteous" at Calcutta in the first part of this century was small, it is ever true that "the effectual fervent prayer of a righteous man availeth much."

"The commencement of the diffusion of religious instruction in India may be dated from a concert among the christians at Calcutta, who had united in earnest prayer to God that He would send labourers into that vineyard. The skeptic may possibly smile at the statement, but it is nevertheless true, that it has pleased God to hear that prayer, and to bless the exertions of those who made it."—Am. Ed.

me; and Dr. Hare says that it may remain a long time. The schoolmen say, the loss of *all* the senses is *death*. By the loss of hearing, I certainly feel the loss of the fifth part of *life*. When nature takes away one sense, they say, she adds to the rest. But when disease takes away one, it injures the rest. At least I think so. I feel that a sense of infirmity cows the mental powers, and thereby hinders their exertion.

"When you see Mr. Thornton, tell him I often think that he has great need of faith to believe the scripture, which says, 'Cast thy bread upon the waters, and thou shalt find it after many days.' Many days have elapsed, and yet the bread he threw to me is not returned. Adieu.

C. Buchanan."

The admirable friend and patron to whom Mr. Buchanan thus alludes, was the reverse of any thing impatient or unreasonable in his expectations from others; and his habit of scattering his beneficence widely and liberally was combined with a spirit of faith which could wait long for the promised fruit, and in many cases be satisfied with leaving his various work with God. In the present instance, however, he lived to reap, after "not many days," a rich reward of his labour.

In writing to Mr. Grant, in January, 1799, the following passage occurs, which, though brief, shows both Mr. Buchanan's anxiety to promote the interests of religion in India, and his lively satisfaction at any public regulations which promised to be auxiliary to that important object.

"I wrote to Mr. H. Thornton by the Montrose, on the 8th instant. In that letter I ventured to say in what way you might probably be of service to us here. But you will be the best judge of the propriety of the measure; though perhaps circumstances have now a complexion rather different from what they had when you left the country.

"Your moral regulations, of May last, are come,* and not before they were wanted; they have been just published, and are well received. I ought not to say published. Lord M.'s delicacy induced him to communicate them by circular letter. They ought to have been proclaimed from the house-top."

The next paragraph refers to a melancholy scene which had then recently taken place in India.

"I suppose you have already heard of the massacre at Benares. Cherry, Graham, Hill, Evans, and Conway, are, I

* Referring chiefly to a proclamation against Sunday horse-racing, and to the erection of chapels at some of the military stations.

think, the names of the Europeans murdered. Vizier Ally, the perpetrator, is not yet taken. Mr. Davis defended himself for an hour in a narrow stair-case. Mrs. Davis loaded his pistols behind him. He killed two or three of the assassins, and the rest fled on the approach of the military. Mrs. Robinson and Miss D'Aguilar had hid themselves in an out-house."

Mr. Buchanan's acquaintance with some of the literary natives of India appears from the following introduction of one of them to Mr. Grant.

BARRACKPORE, 28th Jan. 1799.

"Dear Sir,—I wrote to you a few days ago by one of the regular ships. I now write to introduce to you Aboo Talib Khan. He is a mussulman of some consideration among his countrymen, and of some eminence among the Persian literati. You may possibly have seen him, as he was well known to Lord Cornwallis. He goes to England for the purpose of giving his son an English education. And he is in hope that he will be assisted by his India friends in promoting this purpose.

"He is desirous to inspect the Arabic and Persian MSS. in the Universities. I have given him letters of introduction to some gentlemen at Cambridge. He has written, in the Persian language, a geographical work, a critique on Persian poetry, and biographical sketches on eminent poets.

"He may probably be competent to superintend your new museum for Oriental Literature in Leadenhall-street. As his circumstances are slender, he may be induced to offer his services for a pecuniary consideration, in any way that may be proposed.

"I do not myself know Aboo, but I am intimately acquainted with some of his literary friends."

On the 1st of February following, Mr. Buchanan, after informing Mr. Elliott of the arrival of his eldest son in India, thus intimates the commencement of the system which the Governor General was now contemplating with respect to the junior servants of the company.

"Lord Mornington aids us here. He no longer leaves it at the option of the young men, whether they will study or not. An examination at the expiration of three years hence is to decide on all pretensions to new appointments.

"I hope you received the letter in which I expressed a wish that you would send out all the periodical works issued in the style of literary reviews. These are necessary for me. Without them I know not what books to order for this country. I am constantly applied to by families, religious, moral, and dissipated, to name books for them. I have already inundated them with Barruel, Paley, Watson, Wilberforce, and the Pursuits of Literature. I sit here in secret, and do what I can. A *few* of the reviews will not do; but *all* will tell me the truth. Watch the press for me. You cannot do me a greater favour, or perhaps your sons here more good. I want both annual reviews from 1789, the era of the new philosophy in *operation*. Taylor's sermons, supposed to be written or revised by Johnson, send me; though perhaps they are but '*nugæ canoræ*.' I have not seen them."

A few days after the date of the preceding letter, he wrote at considerable length to one of his Cambridge friends, upon a variety of topics connected with their mutual pursuits, and interspersed with remarks on India. This letter exhibits the impressive sense which the writer entertained of the paramount importance of christianity, and of the duty of active exertions to promote the moral and religious welfare of mankind on the part of himself, and such men as the college friends to whom he refers. Many of his observations display both acuteness and elevation of thought, and much knowledge of the world. A few of them relating to the state of religion both in India and England were, perhaps, even then somewhat harsh and dogmatical; but it is extremely difficult in the present day to appreciate the justness of such remarks, so great has been the moral change in both countries since that period. The tendency, however, of the whole is obviously useful.

"CALCUTTA, February 4, 1799."

After rallying his friend on his remaining at college instead of marrying, he expresses himself thus: "A man advances, perhaps, till he becomes Bachelor of Arts; but after that, he is retrograde for ever. Is not this generally true? You may perhaps continue to advance *in verbiage*, but you will go back in life. Your endeavours to fulfil the great purposes for which you were sent into the world will grow daily more feeble, and your view of those purposes will at length be utterly lost." * * * "But whither then shall we go, if you divorce us from our learned ease? Why, go to London. Take a curacy, or take a chapel. Call forth your learning and put your eloquence to use. Sluice the fountain so long embanked at college stagnant and green, and permit the waters to rush abroad, to fertilize many a plant and gladden the vale. Go forth and stem the torrent of infidelity with a resistless eloquence; and let me hear your voice on the banks of the Ganges. To what purpose have you laboured at Quinctilian, if you do not now lift up your voice and proclaim the glad tidings of the everlasting gospel? * * * At present I see you and D. lisping with pebbles in your mouths on the banks of the Cam. But I hope one day to hear your thunder from the rostrum. I hope to see you 'wielding at will' your awful assemblies, and exciting them with a more than Demosthenic power to resist the invading foe, the New Philosophy. I hope to see you do more. In the more grateful and copious manner of the Roman orator, you will, like scribes well instructed in the kingdom, bring forth things new and old to confirm the believing, convince the doubtful, and heal the wounded spirit; ever displaying this your great and endless theme, the power of grace in awakening to life the torpid soul; and, in your previous studies, ever sitting by the fountain of truth, πηγη ρεουσα πειθους, that 'fountain flowing with persuasives,' the Bible: so will your orations have less of the lamp, and more of that heavenly fire, which alone can make them profitable to your hearers.

"How astonished you will be that my first pages to you from Milton's 'remote Bengala' should be on such subjects as these! You, no doubt, expected to hear

> Of moving accident, by flood, and field;
> And of the cannibals that each other eat,
> The Anthropophagi———

But I have not patience with all these subjects. "You must send out some of those fellows, who can write a tour through Wales, or Gogmagog Hills. *They* will *so* astonish you! Besides I am not writing to freshmen. I am writing to the learned. And all the *mirabilia* I could describe to you are already described in Queen's college library. But I must make some allowance for the different effects of an absolute and a partial view of things. The truth is, that the traveller who sees new things every day, sees new things with indifference. The passion of curiosity is so constantly excited, that it loses its power. The '*nil admirari*' seizes us much sooner with respect to objects of *sense* than objects of reflection. Besides, where all is new, the mind knows not where to rest. It cannot embrace all, and it studies none. This is particularly the case with many young men just arrived in India. They are wonder-struck; they suffer a kind of mental paroxysm; they ask questions for a while; but they find there is no end of subjects of wonder; and at length they are tired with wondering. The man of reflection will examine these subjects at his leisure, but the οι πολλοι would no longer wonder, if the moon were to fall; they would suppose it was the way with the Bengal moons.

"The most useful lesson I have learnt from travel is, that the world, or all that is in it, cannot satisfy the soul of man. Many years ago, my chief ambition, as you know, was to make the tour of Europe. But how *little* does this idea appear! As a village is the world to a child, so Europe was the world to me. But Europe is now become a village; and the globe itself, which seems to have revolved under my eye, has no longer its former extent, novelty, or importance. My ambition seeks now to explore new worlds. And were the Deity to gratify my wish, and to permit me to traverse the planetary globes around us, yet how circumscribed would be my view, how limited my knowledge! The solar system is but a point in the universe! What then is natural knowledge? Like space it has no limit. Let us return then to our village, and view its inhabitant;

> His knowledge suited to his state and place,
> His time, a moment; and a point, his space.

And this is equally true, whether you live but a few years, confined to your native spot, or live three ages, and traverse the world around.

"This thought casts a transient gloom over science and all human knowledge. It is confined and uncertain, and therefore unsatisfying. It is now that the mind turns with pleasure from the works of God to his word. The works of God indeed declare his glory; but the mind cannot comprehend them, nor be satisfied with surveying them. But the word of God quenches the thirst. It is that fountain which can alone satisfy the capacious soul of man.

* * * * *

"Infidelity raged here with great violence formerly, but it is rather on the *defensive* now. It was fashionable for a time to allege that oriental research was not favourable to the truth of christianity; but the contrary is found to be the case. As far as my own inquiries have gone, I can truly say, 'I have seen the star, and worshipped in the East.' In the study of eastern history and learning, there is endless proof of the truth of both the Old and New Testaments.

* * * * *

"I suppose you have heard of the grandeur of English life in India. To live in the first circle in India is to live at court. There is nearly the same dignity of etiquette, elegance of equipage, and variety of entertainment. Every lady is handed to table according to her rank; and—no grace is said.

"What chiefly astonishes an Englishman (I should have said a Scotchman) is the profusion of meat on the tables. We sit down to hecatombæan feasts. But you will not wonder at this, when you hear that the price of a sheep is but half-a-crown. We have no *drinking* here; no Bacchanalian feasts. Wine is a drug. Wherever we go, we expect to find what we have at home, plenty of claret and madeira; and he who would think it a compliment to urge another to drink, would be accounted a vulgar fellow, just imported from a military mess-room, or a literary combination-room.

"Must I say something of the natives? Their general character is imbecility of body, and imbecility of mind. Their moral powers are and have been for ages in a profound stupor; and there is seldom an instance of their being awakened. A partial attempt, or rather experiment, is now making on them by some christian teachers. The Hindoo mind seems at present to be bound by a Satanic spell; and it will require the co-operation of a more than human power to break it. But divine co-operation implies human endeavour. Many ages must then elapse before the conversion of India is accomplished.

"With respect to moral action, the Hindoos pay as little attention to their own religion as a rule of life, as the English do to theirs. Your profession of the christian religion is a proverbial jest throughout the world.

* * * * *

"The Hindoo is born blind; but you put out your own eyes. Loose principles and sensual indulgence first dims them, and then the 'drop serene' of the new philosophy quenches the orb.

"A residence in this country adds much to the personal dignity of the European. Here the labour of a multitude is demanded for the comfort of one: and it is not so much demanded as voluntarily given. In no other country can we so well see the homage which matter gives to mind. Generally, however, it is but the homage which black pays to white. This is the grand argument for keeping the Hindoos in a state of mental depression. The hyperborean Scotchman, broiling under a perpendicular sun, needs some *levamina laborum;* and the state of the Hindoo *minds* is admirably calculated to take care of our *bodies*.

"You know the character of the Hindoo superstition. It is lascivious and bloody. I know no epithet that embraces so much of it as either of these two. Of the first I shall say nothing: I shall not pollute the page with a description of their caprine orgies in the interior of their temples, nor the emblems engraved on the exterior.

"Their scenes of blood are not less revolting to the human mind. Human sacrifice is not quite abolished. The burning of women is common; I have witnessed it more than once.

"This power of self-sacrifice is given them from insensibility of mind, and from that alone. Just as a child may be persuaded to plunge into danger which infant reason cannot see, so the Hindoo, of childish capacity, is persuaded to destroy his existence; he views neither death nor life in their true light.

"All comparison, therefore, between the fortitude of the christian martyr and the madness of the Hindoo is nugatory and absurd.

* * * * *

"What are your studies now? They have long been general; I hope they are now particular. I expect soon to see your name and D—'s to some useful publication. I pray you, support the author of the Pursuits of Literature in his work: you are both able. Only conceive some grand design, some *one* purpose; collect your powers to it, and you will execute it. You remember the Johnsonian aphorism: 'Whatever a man is able to conceive fully, he will by patience and labour execute well.'

* * * * *

"What is T— of Sidney doing? Does he reap the fruit of our Hebrew and Italian hours? Has he published any thing since his Academical Contributions? The metaphysical T—! I never knew so grave a speculatist have such fine affections: but they had no object then. I was once afraid that he would prove to be of Godwin's school. But I can easily believe that his marriage has prevented it. Marriage and its accompanying joys and sorrows have cured many a theorist.

"There is no harmony among the mental powers, no consistency of purpose, no solace in life, till the affections are moved. Some find another object to move them than marriage; but rarely. Plato says that there are not many such objects. St. Paul says that there is *one.*

* * * * *

"I wish not to see any of you engage in general or speculative subjects at this time; nor even in useful works, *slow in operation*. This is the moment for urgent and direct attack.

We have had too many books of late, addressed to the Infidels in the style of alterative. In your academical laboratory have you not some 'strong purgative drug to scour these French ?'

"The truth is, we have acted too long on the defensive : let us now act on the offensive. Infidelity cannot bear to be attacked. It can annoy by stratagem and Parthian dexterity ; but it cannot show a resolute front. 'Resist the devil, and he will flee from you !'—Keep close to the Greek originals of the Socratic and Apostolic school, and you may fight a host of these lank sickly giants, *forced* by the compost of this vapouring age.

* * * * *

"Have you no MSS. of your own composition to send me ? I am desirous to *see* you, and I can't see you in a letter. I am anxious for your fame. I have seen you run the circle of the sciences with eclat. And I now wish to know what you are going to *do*." * * *

Some hints in the preceding letter respecting marriage, as well as the general character of Mr. Buchanan, lead us to expect that he was by no means indifferent to that subject. He had hitherto been too much occupied with study, and with his entrance upon his professional career, to indulge any thoughts respecting it ; but his affectionate and social disposition, and the comparative solitude in which he was compelled to live, convinced him of the expediency of entering into the married state. This important change in his condition took place on the 3rd of April, 1799 ; on which day Mr. Buchanan married Miss Mary Whish, third daughter of the Rev. Richard Whish, then rector of Northwold in Norfolk.

Upon this interesting event, it may be best to allow Mr. Buchanan to speak, as usual, for himself. He thus writes to Mr. Newton about two months after his marriage.

"Miss Mary Whish, and her elder sister," (afterwards married to Major Prole,) "came out to India about five months ago, with their aunt, Mrs. Sandys, wife of Captain Sandys, commissary of stores in Calcutta. The younger of these ladies was so much disgusted with the dissipation of India, that she would gladly have returned single to England. I did not see her till two months after her arrival. But we had not been long acquainted before she confessed that she had found a friend who could reconcile her to India. I did not expect that I should have ever found in this country a young woman whom I could so much approve. Mrs. Buchanan is not yet nineteen. She has had a very proper education for my wife.

She has docility of disposition, sweetness of temper, and a strong passion for retired life.

"She is religious as far as her knowledge goes, and her knowledge is as great as I suppose yours or mine was at her age. Our marriage was sanctioned by the approbation of all who knew her, and who knew me.

"I have now been married two months, and every successive day adds something to confirm the felicity of my choice, and the goodness of God in directing it.

"Mrs. Buchanan has read many of your letters to me, and hopes you will mention her name in your next. She is now reading the 'Christian Character Exemplified,' published by you, and aspires to the spirit and piety of the lady whose character it is.

"I still reside at Barrackpore, where it is now probable I shall remain some years. But I must take no thought for to-morrow. Years, days, and hours are not mine. *Moments*, how sacred!"

In replying to some inquiries of his correspondent, Mr. Buchanan proceeds to mention, what in the prospect of continuing at Barrackpore must have been peculiarly painful to him, that it was thought no chapel would be built there, under the new arrangement relative to that subject, as no European regiment was at any time ordered to that station. Under these circumstances he mentions that he was anxious to take every opportunity of assisting Mr. Brown at Calcutta; and adds, that he had successfully laboured to promote a good understanding between him and his colleague, and to remove some prejudices which had previously existed against him and the ministrations at the mission church. He then continues as follows.

"You will have heard by this time the fate of the expedition to Otaheite. The missionaries, banished by the natives, fled to Botany Bay. One of them, I hear, is lately arrived in Calcutta, from Port Jackson. I hope this south-sea scheme will not *discourage* the missionary societies. They have done no harm: and if they send out their next mission with less carnal eclat, and more Moravian diffidence, they may perhaps do some good. Their chief fault was in the selection of the men. It appears, that most of them were weak, and most of them novices.

"Lord Mornington is taking measures to send home all Frenchmen and republicans. I was applied to lately in a kind of official way, to give some account of the Baptist missionaries. It was asked, What was their object? How supported? Whether they were not of republican principles? As I had some good data for speaking favourably of Mr. Carey, I confined myself to him. I stated the origin of the Tranquebar mission, and its success under Swartz, and I represented Carey as endeavouring to do in Bengal what Swartz did in the Deccan. He called upon me lately in his way to Calcutta. He considers himself as sowing a seed, which haply may grow up and bear fruit. He is prosecuting his translation of the scriptures. This is a good work. It will be useful to those Hindoos who are somewhat influenced by christian instruction, and particularly useful to Hindoo children brought up in christian schools. I told Mr. Carey, that I thought he could not employ his time better than in translating the scriptures. I explained to him, from sources with which he seemed unacquainted, the plan and progress of the Tamulian scriptures, and the circumstances attending the publication.

"And now, my dear Sir, pray for us. Under my Mary's care, I improve in health and spirits."

The hint which Mr. Buchanan suggested in the preceding letter, as to the too confident spirit with which some missionary plans had been undertaken, and as to one of the principal causes of their failure, will be generally acknowledged to have been dictated by the soundest judgment.

In the autumn of this year, Mr. Buchanan informed Mr. Grant that he had been recommended to accept a vacant chaplaincy at Bombay. "Being altogether ignorant," says he, "of the particulars, I wrote to Mr. Fawcett, the accountant general there, (who wishes me to go,) to explain fully to me the nature of the situation. If it be the first chaplaincy to the Presidency, I shall accept it." He adds: "There is to be a relief of staff this ensuing November. Whether I shall be included in it, I know not."

It is probable that Mr. Buchanan's inquiry respecting the chaplaincy at Bombay proved unsatisfactory. However this may have been, the providence of God shortly afterwards introduced him to a sphere of labour in Calcutta, which was equally adapted to his talents and his wishes. Towards the close of the year, Lord Mornington appointed him a third chaplain to the Presidency, and he immediately entered upon the duties of that office.

One of the earliest occasions of public service, to which Mr. Buchanan was called after this appointment, was in February 1800; when he preached a sermon at the new church, before Lord Mornington and the principal officers of the government, on the day appointed for "a general thanksgiving, for the late signal successes obtained by the naval and military forces of his Majesty and of his allies; and for the ultimate and happy establishment of the tranquillity and security of the British possessions in India."

This sermon was so highly approved, that Mr. Buchanan received the thanks of the Governor General in Council, with a direction that it should be printed; and it was undoubtedly a production which well deserved that honour. It was founded on the 11th verse of the 21st Psalm; "For they intended mischief against THEE; and imagined such a device, as they are not able to perform:" and contains a luminous and impressive view of the principles, progress, and effects of the new French philosophy, to which Mr. Buchanan justly attributed the awful struggle in which this country was then engaged. This important subject has since received such ample discussion and illustration, that it is happily no longer necessary to dwell upon it. The following passages from Mr. Buchanan's discourse may, however, with propriety be extracted, in proof of the ability and judgment, as well as the piety, of its author.

"The contest in which our country has been so long engaged hath, in one particular, been of essential service to her. It hath excited a greater respect for christian institutions and christian principles. A long period of internal tranquillity and security had induced an *indifference* about religion, which was rapidly gaining ground, and was making room for that infidelity which our enemies wished to substitute. But the critical situation in which the nation was placed, and the dangers that threatened her, led men to review their principles, and to consider seriously by what means she might be saved. Hence there is now a growing regard for christian ordinances. There is now a more general acknowledgment of the providence of God; more attention is paid to moral character; more care is taken in forming the minds of youth; and more ample means of instruction are afforded to the common people.

"In the anxiety that prevails in the mother-country about the principles of all who are connected with her, she will naturally be interested to know what is the state of religion amongst *us*. 'How,' she will ask, 'amidst all this revolution of opinion and practice which agitates the world, is that distant society affected? Are they altogether free from infidel principles? And does the public spirit of the people show itself in combating these principles, and in maintaining a respect for christian institutions?'

"However this subject might have been overlooked in the infancy of our settlements, it becomes now a matter of public consequence. The importance we are daily acquiring in the eyes of the world, and the destructive effects of irreligion in other countries, make it proper that we should show that we yet profess the faith of our country, and that we are yet willing to be accounted a christian community.

"On this subject we think there can be but one sentiment. Men of sense and of responsible situation, who love their country, and who know the danger of the new principles, will not, we are persuaded, be averse to show this countenance to the christian religion. Such example is of the more consequence, on account of the great number of young persons who are yearly added to our society. These persons are denied those opportunities of instruction they enjoyed at home; and they arrive at so early an age, that, in general, their principles are formed and fixed *here*. And when it is considered that they are hereafter to fill the offices in the government of the country, and are to be themselves the guardians of the public principles, it will certainly appear of consequence, that their minds should be impressed with a respect for those religious and moral observances, on which the future safety and happiness of the country depend."

"—Skepticism and infidelity are not now so well received in society as they once were. It was formerly thought a mark of superior understanding to profess infidelity. It was thought a proof of some learning to think differently from others on religious subjects.

"But we have now seen, that the most illiterate and most abandoned of the human race can be infidels.

"We have also seen, that there is no superstition more irrational in its effects, no fanaticism more degrading to the human mind, than the fanaticism of infidelity.

"We have further seen the *moral* effects of infidelity; effects flowing directly from it, acknowledging no other source. And after what we have seen of these effects, we think no man can add to his respectability in society, either for understanding or for moral character, by avowing himself to be an advocate for infidelity."

"—But we trust that the great body of our society is yet animated by christian principles, and that they are ready to make common cause with their country in defending these principles to the uttermost.

"Some will doubt, and some will disbelieve, but it is an eternal truth, that the christian religion is the rock on which rests our existence as a civilized nation; on which rest our social blessings, and our individual happiness. Take away this rock, and you give your country to convulsion and endless disgrace. Built on this rock, she hath withstood the violence of the storms that have so long assailed her. Secure and tranquil in the midst of the tempest, she stands at this hour firm and impregnable, while those who built on the 'sands of infidelity,' have been overthrown."

Copies of Mr. Buchanan's thanksgiving sermon were distributed by order of government in every part of British India, and sent home to the Directors of the East India Company.

"You may easily conceive," says Mr. Buchanan, writing to a friend in England, well acquainted with the prevalence of skeptical principles at that period in India, "the astonishment of men at these religious proceedings. However, all was silence and decent acquiescence. It became fashionable to say, that religion was a very proper thing, that no civilized state could subsist without it; and it was reckoned much the same thing to praise the French, as to praise infidelity."

The importance of this public recognition of christianity as the only basis of civil prosperity, was soon perceived in the increasing attention to personal religion.

"Our christian society," adds Mr. Buchanan to the same friend, "flourishes. Merit is patronized, immoral characters are marked; and young men of good inclinations have the best opportunities of improvement."

The same happy effects were thus distinctly stated by Mr. Brown, in a memorial on the general state of society in Calcutta, drawn up some years afterwards, for the information of the Society for promoting Christian Knowledge.

"These solemn acts," observes that excellent man, "and the public thanksgivings, which took place for the first time under Marquis Wellesley's government, awakened a religious sense of things in many; and led to an open and general acknowledgment of the divine Providence, which has been highly beneficial to the interests of true religion and virtue."

On Mr. Buchanan's removal to Calcutta, he thus resumed the account of his studies and proceedings, in a letter to Mr. Henry Thornton.

"The plan of study I formed about two years and a half ago has not suffered any material alteration since. I soon, however, discovered the small value of the Persian and Hindostanee languages to me, and was contented with a superficial acquaintance with them. My scriptural studies I pursue with my first purpose, and I hope I shall continue to pursue them to the day of my death. My general studies have been much diversified by correspondence in different parts of India, on subjects classical, mathematical, and theological. The latter has been the most laborious and generally the most pleasant. This subject is often forced upon me. But I have seldom permitted myself to *defend* christianity. I have usually acted on the offensive, and attacked infidelity. This is a very unpleasant mode to the infidel. During the last year I received many anonymous letters, particularly from young persons, on polemical divinity; but the correspondence has generally ended in real names. In consequence, I am often applied to for books, and have expended much in purchasing valuable works at our dear market. Small religious tracts are of little service to those with whom I have to do.

"My public ministrations have been rare, but perhaps not so rare as from my situation might be expected. Of the three years I have been in India, including the number of times I have officiated at the hospital in Calcutta, and in my own house at Barrackpore, I have preached on an average once a fortnight.

"My great affliction since I came to India has been *bad health*. I feel a languor of constitution, and a difficulty of respiration, which no medical aid has yet been able to remove. This I sometimes think has taken away one-half of the energy and usefulness I might have preserved or acquired in a cooler region. But this also is the dispensation of God; and it has added to me *that*, which elsewhere I might not have found."

In a letter, however, to Mr. Newton, about the same time, Mr. Buchanan observes, "I have enjoyed better health this year than in any former; and I trust that I shall be strengthened and spared for some service."

During the first six months of the year 1800, the plan of a collegiate institution had been formed by Lord Mornington, (who, in consequence of the splendid successes of his policy in the Mysore, had been created Marquis Wellesley,) for the purpose of promoting the literary improvement of the younger civil servants of the Company. This important measure, in the arrangement and conduct of which Mr. Buchanan was so essentially concerned, he thus mentioned in the month of June in a letter to Mr. Grant.

"Lord Wellesley is at present engaged in founding a college for the instruction of the young civil servants in eastern literature and general learning. He desired me to draw out a sketch of the constitution of the college, which I did. And now Mr. Barlow has instructed me to draw up a minute as a justification of the measure. Lord Wellesley proposes that Mr. Brown should be the Provost of the college; and he is certainly the fittest man in Calcutta for that office. I had him in my mind when drawing up the duties of Provost. There will be about eight or ten professors. No promotion in the service, but through the medium of this institution. The students to remain at college for three or five years. Prizes and honours to be proposed for those who distinguish themselves, and degrees to be taken to qualify for certain offices."

Some allusion is made to the subject introduced in the preceding extract in the two following letters from Mrs. Buchanan, which, as they exhibit a pleasing and faithful picture of a most amiable woman, very early removed from this world, it may not be uninteresting to insert, before we proceed to a more enlarged view of the college of Fort William.

The first is addressed to Mr. Newton, and is dated Calcutta, 24th June, 1800.

"Dear Sir,—Mr. Buchanan assures me that you will excuse the liberty I take in writing to you. I have long wished to acknowledge the debt I owe you for your valuable works. They have been blessed to many, and I trust will be also blessed to me. But I believe I am still more indebted to you as the friend, father, and instructor of my beloved husband; as such, I must consider you as the instrument, under God, of my present happiness.

You will be glad to hear that Mr. B.'s health is of late much improved; but I am alarmed lest his approaching labours should be too much for him. We have reason to believe that he will be appointed a professor in the new college. He himself wishes to decline it, but his friends do not see how it is possible, as he has taken an active part in the institution. It is supposed that he may have his choice of three professorships, classics, mathematics, or the belles-lettres. I believe his intention is to accept of a situation in college, if it be easy; but if not, to decline it on the plea of health.

"Dear sir, I cannot expect to see you in this world; may I therefore request you to send your blessing to me and my little girl.

"I desire my love to your niece, and remain, my dear sir, yours, with christian affection, MARY BUCHANAN."

The second of these letters is to Mr. Elliott; and while it expresses with equal simplicity the advancing piety of her own mind, it recognizes the support which Lord Wellesley was then affording to religion in Calcutta. It is of the same date with the former.

"Dear Sir,—Your letter to Mr. Buchanan, in which you mention our marriage, gave me real pleasure. And as you expressed a wish that I should write to you, I take this opportunity to thank you for your affectionate congratulations. You have reason indeed to congratulate *me*. It is the happiest circumstance in my life, that I ever came to India; where I have been united to one whose endeavours God has been pleased to bless, in leading me to some knowledge of the everlasting gospel. It is a new gospel to me, and I seem to live in a new world, differing far more from my old world, than India differs from England. May I request your prayers, that this good work may be carried on in my heart, and that it may issue in honour to my beloved husband, and to his ministry here? He has much to encourage him in the work of the gospel. There is an evident change in the face of the society here, even in the short time since I arrived in the country. Lord Wellesley seems inclined to support the christian religion by *every* means. Vital religion also is increasing. It seems to be fostered under the wing of that general sanction to christianity which has lately been given. This is the only place in India where religion is countenanced. We have now many respectable families here in which piety meets with real encouragement. I remain, dear sir, yours, with much esteem,

MARY BUCHANAN."

By the despatch which conveyed the two preceding letters, Mr. Buchanan sent another remittance to his mother, to the comfort of whose declining years he was afterwards enabled still more largely to contribute.

On the 18th of August, 1800, the college of Fort William, which had been virtually in operation since the 4th of May, was formally established by a minute in council,* in which the Governor General detailed at length his reasons for such an institution. The important part which Mr. Buchanan took in the formation and subsequent conduct of that establishment will sufficiently justify the following brief abstract of the able and interesting document referred to.

The British possessions in India, said his Lordship, now constitute one of the most extensive and populous empires in the world. The immediate administration of the government of the various provinces and nations composing this empire, is principally confided to the European civil servants of the East

---

* See "The College of Fort William, in Bengal," published by Mr. Buchanan in 1805.

India Company. Upon them, in consequence, devolve the duties of dispensing justice to millions of people of various languages, manners, usages, and religions; of administering a vast and complicated system of revenue throughout districts, equal in extent to some of the most considerable kingdoms in Europe; and of maintaining civil order in one of the most populous and litigous regions of the world. They can, therefore, no longer be considered as the agents of a commercial concern; they are, in fact, the ministers and officers of a powerful sovereign, and must be viewed in that capacity, with a reference, not to their nominal, but to their real occupations. Their education should consequently be founded in a general knowledge of those branches of literature and science which form the basis of the education of persons destined to similar offices in Europe. To this foundation should be added an intimate acquaintance with the history, languages, customs, and manners of the people of India, with the Mohammedan and Hindoo codes of law and religion, and with the political interests and relations of Great Britain in Asia. They should be regularly instructed in the principles and system which constitute the foundation of that wise code of regulations and laws enacted by the Governor General in council, for the purpose of securing to the people of this empire the benefit of the ancient and established laws of the country, administered in the spirit of the British constitution. Finally, their early habits should be so formed, as to establish in their minds such solid foundations of industry, prudence, integrity, and religion, as should effectually guard them against those temptations and corruptions with which the nature of the climate, and the peculiar depravity of the people of India, will surround and assail them in every station, especially upon their first arrival in India. The early discipline of the service should be calculated to counteract the defects of the climate and the vices of the people, and to form a natural barrier against habitual indolence, dissipation, and licentious indulgence: the spirit of emulation in honourable and useful pursuits should be kindled and kept alive by the continual prospect of distinction and reward, of profit and honour; nor should any precaution be relaxed in India which is deemed necessary in England, to furnish a sufficient supply of men, qualified to fill the high offices of the state, with credit to themselves, and with advantage to the public.

It would be unnecessary, continued Lord Wellesley, in the document referred to, to enter into any examination of facts, to prove that no system of education, study, or discipline now exists, either in Europe or in India, founded on the principles, or directed to the objects, before described. His Lordship, however, proceeded to review the course through which the junior civil servants of the East India Company then entered upon the important duties of their respective stations; and the result of this examination tended to prove, that the actual state of the Company's civil service in India was far removed from perfection or efficiency, and that the cause of this defect was to be found principally, if not exclusively, in the imperfect education of the junior civil servants, and in the insufficient discipline of the early stages of the service.

In reply to the general argument, which might be adduced to disprove the necessity of any new institution, on the ground that the service of the East India Company had, through a long period of years, always furnished men equal to the exigency of the occasion, it was contended, that extraordinary combinations of human affairs, wars, revolutions, and all those unusual events which form the marked features and prominent characters of the history of mankind, naturally bring to light talents and exertions adapted to such emergencies. But that it must never be forgotten, that the successive efforts of the personages thus raised up, and the final result of various revolutions and wars, had imposed upon the East India Company the arduous and sacred trust of governing a great empire; that duty, policy, and honour required that it should not be administered as a temporary and precarious acquisition, but as a permanent succession; and that in this view its internal government should not be left to depend on the success of individual or accidental merit, struggling against the defects of established institutions; but should be so ordered as to secure a constant, steady, and regular supply of able magistrates, wise and honest judges, and skilful statesmen, properly qualified to conduct the ordinary movements of its administration.

An additional motive for such an institution as was then meditated, was derived from the acknowledged fact, that at this period the erroneous and pestilent principles of the French revolutionary school had reached the minds of some individuals in the service of the company in India; and that the state, as well of political as religious opinions, had been in some degree unsettled. An institution, therefore, tending to fix and establish sound and correct principles of religion and government in the minds of the junior servants of the Company at an early period of life, was the best security that could be provided for the stability of the British power in India.

After discussing the practicability of forming any adequate

establishment in England for the purpose of duly educating such a body of men as had been described, and determining that it could not be obtained otherwise than in India, the Governor General concluded by declaring, that a college was by this minute in council founded at Fort William, for the better instruction of the junior civil servants of the Company in such branches of literature, science, and knowledge, as might be deemed necessary to qualify them for the discharge of the duties of the different offices constituted for the administration of the government of the British possessions in the East Indies.

The general reasons upon which the Marquis Wellesley proceeded in the formation of this important institution, must be admitted to be characterized by the soundest views of a liberal and enlightened policy. Whatever difference of opinion may exist as to the extent or detailed arrangement of the establishment, there can scarcely be any as to the principles upon which it was founded. The success, too, of the institution, as will be hereafter seen, fully justified the wisdom of the original plan, and reflects the highest honour on its distinguished author.

The immediate government of the college was vested in a Provost and Vice-Provost, and three other officers, to whose notice every part of the private conduct of the students, their expenses, their connexions, their manners, and morals, were to be subject. Professorships were established in the languages chiefly spoken and used in the different provinces of India, in Hindoo and Mohammedan law, in the regulations and laws enacted at the several presidencies for the civil government of the British territories, in political economy, and particularly the commercial institutions and interests of the East India Company, and in various branches of literature and science. There was also to be a considerable establishment of learned natives attached to the college; some of whom were to be employed in teaching the students, others in making translations, and others in composing original works in the oriental tongues.

The excitements to exertion in the college of Fort William were of the highest and most effective nature; and its moral, economical, and religious discipline, such as was admirably calculated to promote all that is virtuous, dignified, and useful in civil society. This latter most important branch of the institution was, in an especial manner, confided to the Provost and Vice-Provost, who were thus honourably introduced to the public notice by its noble founder.

"Fortunately," observes his lordship, "for the objects of the institution, the Governor General has found at Calcutta two clergymen of the Church of England, eminently qualified to discharge the duties of Provost and Vice-Provost. To the former office he has appointed Mr. Brown, the Company's first chaplain, and to the latter, Mr. Buchanan. Mr. Brown's character must be well known in England, and particularly so to some members of the Court of Directors; it is in every respect such as to satisfy the Governor General that his views, in this nomination, will not be disappointed. He has also formed the highest expectations from the abilities, learning, temper, and morals of Mr. Buchanan, whose character is also well known in England, and particularly to Dr. Porteus, Bishop of London, and to Dr. Milner, Master of Queen's College in the University of Cambridge."

A body of statutes was afterwards compiled and promulgated by Marquis Wellesley, which regulated the admission of students and professors, the lectures, exercises, examinations, and public disputations, and every other branch of the college business. The office of the Provost, and, virtually, of the Vice-Provost, was expressed in the following terms.

"It shall be the peculiar province and sacred duty of the Provost governing the college at Fort William, to guard the moral and religious interests of the institution, and vigilantly to superintend the conduct and principles of all its members.

"Divine service shall be performed in the college chapel at such times as the Provost shall appoint."

Provision was also made by the statutes for applying the internal authority of the superior officers of the college, to strengthen and confirm within our eastern possessions the attachment of the civil servants of the Company to the laws and constitution of Great Britain, and to maintain and uphold the christian religion in that quarter of the globe.

Of the formation of the preceding institution, and of several additional particulars respecting it, Mr. Buchanan wrote to Mr. Grant a few days after the date of Lord Wellesley's minute in council, on his way to Prince of Wales' Island, where he stayed about a month, for the benefit of Mrs. Buchanan's health, which was already beginning to be impaired.

"SAUGER ROADS, 23d Aug. 1800.

"Dear Sir,—We have no news at present but what relates to the new college, which is now founded. It consists of a Provost, Vice-Provost, and Professors. All the writers, and some of the cadets, (the learned and well-recommended,) are admitted to the benefits of the institution. A building for the college, to contain two hundred students, is to be immediately erected in Garden Reach, together with a chapel, hall, &c. Mr. Speke's house, and Mr. Cowper's, will form part of the college; being intended for the principal officers. In the meantime, a range of large houses in Calcutta is taken for present use, not far from the writers' buildings. Mr. Brown is appointed Provost of the college. His duties are to receive the young men on their arrival, and to be their official friend. I have been appointed Vice-Provost. His duties are very laborious. When I planned them, I little thought I should be called to execute them. He is the censor morum, and arbiter of official and personal proprieties in college."

Mr. Buchanan next inserts a list of the professors already appointed; in which his own name appears as Professor of Greek, Latin, and English classics. He then continues as follows:

"The college council, or caput, consists of Provost, Vice-Provost, and Messrs. Barlow, Kirkpatrick, and Edmonstone.

"A public table to be established for the students. Their moonshees to be attached to the college. No student *in debt* to be admitted to the college, or to have promotion in service afterwards. Means are to be taken to pay off the debts of many students, in the first instance. The discipline is to be most rigid. Rewards and honours to the deserving, very liberal. Notwithstanding the expense to government of supporting table, moonshees, &c. the students are to have their three hundred rupees a month, in full.

"By this institution, two hundred students, the whole generation of English India, will be put, in some degree, under the direction of Mr. Brown and myself.

"Lectures will probably commence on the first of November, 1800. Four terms in a year of two months, and four vacations of one month.

"I mention the foregoing particulars at this time, because they may, perhaps, have some influence on yourself or friends, who may be thinking of sending their sons to India."

This last observation of Mr. Buchanan, which evidently points at the security to be afforded by the new establishment to the moral and religious principles and habits of the students, derives strength from the following striking passage in the original minute of Lord Wellesley.

"This institution," said his lordship, "will be best appreciated by every affectionate parent in the hour of separation from his child, destined to the public service in India. Let any parent, (especially if he has himself passed through the Company's service in India,) declare whether the prospect of this institution has aggravated or mitigated the solicitude of that painful hour; whether it has raised additional doubts and fears, or inspired a more lively hope of the honourable and prosperous service, of the early and fortunate return of his child."

It may perhaps afford a still more clear and interesting view of the actual plan of the college of Fort William, if we subjoin the two following letters from Mr. Buchanan to the young friend who has been already mentioned as enjoying his confidential correspondence.

"CALCUTTA, 1st Nov. 1800.

"My dear Friend,—Yours of the 27th October I have just received. I dare not advise with respect to the college. Some gentlemen have taken advantage of the regulation, and some declined it. Some are satisfied that the college will promote their interests; and some are satisfied that it will hurt them. Unless you are sure that you ought to come, and therefore come with a good will and ardent hopes, I would rather you would *not* come; for unless you distinguish yourself in some degree for your attention, success in study, and moral conduct, it would have been better for you that you had never seen the college at all. Recollect there will be nearly one hundred and thirty students, fifty of whom are now in Calcutta applying themselves closely to their studies.

"With respect to your college life, it will be what you make it. To some it will be very irksome, to others perfect freedom. So large a body must be governed by statutes, and these statutes shall be strictly enforced; but the whole institution is built on liberal principles; intended for gentlemen, for grown gentlemen, for men who enter it with the purpose of attaining to a certain object; and who are therefore willing to sacrifice something to the general good, as well as their own ultimate advantage.

"Mrs. Buchanan joins me in best regards to you and Mr. Darell, and I am very sincerely yours, C. BUCHANAN."

"To W. P. ELLIOTT, Esq., Malda."

To the same.

"My dear Friend,—Your letter of the 7th, mentioning your purpose of coming to college, I have just received. Whether you have done right I shall be able to tell you in about a year hence; not sooner. So entirely does it depend on yourself.

"Before you obtain your qualifying degree in the college at Fort William to serve the Company, you must hold four public disputations in the Persian or Bengalee languages, once as respondent, and thrice as opponent. As respondent, you are to defend a proposition given by yourself on a moral, literary, or historical subject, or concerning oriental manners and customs, against the objections of any three opponents who may be appointed. You are first to pronounce an essay on your subject, and then begin to defend it extempore, in classical Persian, against the meditated objections of your opponents; and this in public, before all Calcutta, and before all the natives of rank and learning, rajahs, pundits, moulvies, and moonshees;—an august tribunal!

"You are also to recite in public, at six different times, six essays or declamations composed by yourself on subjects which shall be given you, in the English language. Every student who takes a degree at Fort William must give proofs of his being a classical English scholar; and a practical one.

"*Ex pede Herculem.* Here is a ploughshare or two of your college ordeal. Be not surprised, then, that I did not urge your coming. Here there is room for honour, and also for disgrace.

"As for the number of *horses* you wish to bring down,—'consider what hath been said.'

"You and all of your year will have quarters in the Writers' Buildings; two in a house. There is no choice. Mr. Barlow will place you where there is a vacancy on your arrival.

"You will not be called down for a considerable time; and I suppose will see little of cavalry exercise this year.

"Yours very sincerely, C. BUCHANAN."

"CALCUTTA, 17th Nov. 1800."

In order to complete the specimen which has just been given of the views with which the younger servants of the Company entered the college of Fort William, it may not be improper to add the following extract of a letter from Mr. W. Elliott to one of his friends, who was then deliberating as to his own determination.

"MALDA, December 14, 1800.

"—Not to detain you longer from the subject of your letter, I will state to you the reasons which induce me to enter the college.

"I must confess to you that I sacrifice considerable present advantages; but if I may judge from all that Lord Wellesley has hitherto done, he is far too generous to allow us to sustain any loss which he will not make up on our leaving college. I say this on the supposition that he will continue so long in the government. If he does not, I shall still have the satisfaction of knowing myself qualified for any situation whatever.

"As the opportunities of information now offered are many, the examination of those who decline them will be proportionably strict: nor do I think myself qualified, or that I could qualify myself in this jungle, for any situation other than that of a commercial resident.

"As it is not my present intention to accept any thing less than a good residency, you will not be surprised that I devote two years and a half to improve myself in the languages, and in whatever else is to be taught in the college; at the end of which time, I shall not have been more than five years and a half in the country. Besides, I think it a most dangerous experiment to decline entering the college. We have nothing so much to dread as the being set aside, or not thought of when any appointment of trust becomes vacant; which will in my opinion certainly be the case with those who thus act.

"I am, moreover, one of those eccentric beings, who think that knowledge and information cannot be purchased at too dear a rate; and I do expect, from the known abilities of my friend Mr. Buchanan, and some of the other professors, not only to attain the immediate object which I have in view, a knowledge of the languages, and of my duty as a servant of the Company, but also improvement in those political studies which no gentleman should be ignorant of. Our education has not left us wholly uninformed on these subjects; but the early age at which we left England must have prevented our obtaining that degree of knowledge requisite for sustaining with eclat the rank in life which we hope to fill on our return home. Mr. Brown, the Provost, wrote to me, that the advantages of the college were so palpable, and the danger in declining it so great, that I could not reasonably hesitate on the subject."

The appointment of the superior officers of the college was notified in a Calcutta gazette extraordinary on the 20th of September, 1800, though they were not formally admitted to their offices till the 24th of April following. Towards the close of the former year, an advertisement was published in different parts of India, announcing the establishment of the college, and inviting men of learning and knowledge, moulvies, pundits, and moonshees, to Calcutta, for the purpose of submitting to an examination with a view to the choice of some as teachers in the college. About fifty natives, and subsequently a larger number, were in consequence attached to it,

Lectures in the Arabic, Hindostanee, and Persian languages, commenced in the month of November, 1800; and the first regular term opened on the 6th of February following.

CHAPTER II.

With the commencement of the year 1801, Mr. Buchanan entered upon his important and laborious duties as Vice-Provost and Professor of Classics in the college of Fort William. His health and spirits had hitherto been more or less depressed; nor was the former likely to be improved by the various weighty engagements which now devolved upon him. A work, however, had at length been assigned to him, both in the college, and as one of the chaplains of the Presidency; which, while it demanded his utmost talents and exertions, deeply interested his feelings, and animated him with the hope of becoming extensively useful in India. Early in this year he thus wrote to Mr. Grant.

"Since my last to you, dated Kedgeree, when I was going to sea, nothing of importance has occurred here. The regulation concerning the college has been carried into effect, and the institution has already acquired energy and tranquillity. We have about an hundred students; the greater part of whom promise to distinguish themselves. There are as remarkable instances of application here, as I have known at Cambridge.

"Both the churches are generally full, particularly in the cold weather. The college chapel has punkas, which will probably draw a great number of the townspeople during the hot season. Lord Wellesley has fitted up a pew for himself in chapel.

"Mr. Obeck breakfasted with Mrs. Buchanan this morning, and pleased her much with the account he gave of you and your family for a series of years in this country. The old man still retains his faculties in vigour, and is strong in body. His office at present is the distribution of four or five hundred rupees a month to the poor. The cold meat of college supports a great number of poor Portuguese and English."

On the 16th and 18th of the same month, Mr. Buchanan again wrote to Mr. Grant. The following are extracts from his letters.

"While we remained at Penang, Sir George Leith, the Governor, stated to me the want of a chaplain on the island. I have since represented it to Lord Wellesley, who said he would mention the subject to the Court of Directors. Lord W. allows one hundred dollars a month for a lay-chaplain. Perhaps you might effect an appointment of a regular chaplain at two hundred dollars more.*

"Lord W. has had serious thoughts of building a larger church. But the college institution has deranged his plans a little. If you cannot give us a new church at present, we shall thank you for a clock and bell; and also for a singing man and organist. The charity boys sing in the two churches and in the college chapel every Sunday. And there are organs in each, but only one organist.

"Some of the college students have already made most distinguished proficiency in the oriental languages. By the statutes they must be able to hold public disputations in these languages on a given subject. Ten of the first proficients go out the first year, and twenty the second. The spirit of emulation, of interest, and of fame, is excited in a very remarkable degree. No impropriety of conduct is known. All is silence, and study, and decorum. They all dine in the college hall, in the presence of the professors.

"There are some instances of a serious spirit of religious inquiry among the students.

"Lord Wellesley wants some persons of distinguished ability in science and classics to superintend in college, and thinks, properly, that they should, if possible, be clerical men. He has asked me for names, and I have mentioned those of several wranglers and medallists, which, he says, he will send to Mr. Dundas. Two or three of them promised once to do honour to their profession.

"Mr. Brown is in a precarious state of health at present; and I have never been strong. No such field is any where to be found for learning and piety, as that which Calcutta at this time exhibits.

"Sir Alured Clarke has just left us. He is entitled to the thanks of your Court for his attention to divine service, and for the general good example he has set to your settlement here."

In his next letter to Mr. Grant, Mr. Buchanan had the pleasure of introducing to him one of his earliest friends, Mr. Alexander Campbell, the second officer of the Walsingham East Indiaman, and afterwards commander of the United Kingdom.

"He was once," says Mr. Buchanan, "a pupil of mine, when I was fourteen, and he was ten years of age. He is the son of a respectable family; and though he was formerly gay,

* A chaplain has since been appointed to the island.

he is now more steady, and has had opportunities lately of seeing great changes of heart in those around him. He was," and it was surely a singular coincidence, "fourth officer of the Busbridge, which brought me to India. I do not know what you can do for him, farther than by recommending him as an active and intelligent officer, which he is. He does not much like the sea, and would gladly retire to a quiet and certain situation. But I have advised him to continue in his present line, and to maintain his activity and integrity before all men.

"General Lake is just arrived. He and his family were at church yesterday."

In the month of June following, Mr. Buchanan thus resumes his account of the two subjects of Indian intelligence most interesting to himself, the church and the college, in a letter to Mr. Grant, and announces Mrs. Buchanan's approaching return to England.

"Our church continues in much the same state in which I described it to be in my last. We have had an addition of some communicants, chiefly from college. The church thins a little always in the hot months of May and June. Lord W. has proposed to use punkas and tatties; and it is probable that we shall have recourse to them next season.

"The college still goes on with spirit and energy. Some of the students will leave it, and enter on the service in December 1801 (this year.) I see clearly that all our future professors and examiners will be taken from among those who have been students. It is with the greatest difficulty that we can find in the whole service examiners in the various languages, who have confidence to face the students. So that we have been obliged to take our examiners from among the professors, which is rather contrary to the statutes."

Mr. Buchanan appears to have detained this letter till after the 3d of July, on which day the first public examination of the college students took place. The name of his young friend, Mr. William Elliott, appeared at the head of the first class in the Persian and Hindostanee languages, and in Nagree writing, and in the first class of Arabic. Mr. Buchanan speaks also of the good conduct and distinguished proficiency in the languages, of some other young men, as being above all praise. He then adverts to the health of Mrs. Buchanan, who since her return from Pulo Penang had experienced a return of her consumptive complaint, which made it necessary for her to try the effect of her native air. "Should her health," he adds, "be restored, she will return to India, after a short residence with her family."

Accordingly on the 25th of July, 1801, Mrs. Buchanan embarked for England, taking with her their eldest daughter, Charlotte, and leaving the youngest, Augusta, then not quite six months old, with Mr. Buchanan. Her voyage was stormy, and otherwise perilous and painful, but she reached her native country in safety on the 18th of February, 1802.

She was the bearer of a letter to one of Mr. Buchanan's friends, in which he mentions that the regular attendance of the greater number of the students on divine worship, and still more decisive proofs of serious impressions amongst them, had given him new ardour and new hopes, that the college of Fort William would prove a religious as well as a literary institution to many of them.

Mr. Buchanan then observes in reply to a suggestion of his correspondent, whether he might not have attempted to preach to the Hindoos, that independently of various other impediments, it was inconsistent with the rules prescribed to him as a chaplain of the Company;* but that, although he had not converted any natives, he had been honoured as the instrument of the conversion of souls in India, and had seen some of them die in the faith.

The friend to whom Mr. Buchanan was writing had also hinted that some of his English correspondents were disappointed at so seldom hearing from him. To this he thus satisfactorily replies.

"I had such a numerous body of friends and acquaintances, literary and religious, in Scotland and in England, that I found it was in vain to attempt a correspondence with them all in my infirm state of health. I have therefore scarcely written to any one, but to yourself, Mr. Newton, and Mr. Grant. I have less time now than ever; and even my letters to you will be less frequent. The chief labour of the churches is devolving fast upon me. My religious correspondence in India is greater than at any former time. The whole direction of the college lies with me; every paper is drawn up by me; and every thing that is printed is revised by me. In addition to this, I give Greek and Latin lectures four days in the week during term; and I must visit and receive visits on an average twice a day.

"You desired me to say something in self-defence, else I should not have given you the above. I am yet an unprofitable servant, very unworthy the lowest place in my Master's vineyard; and I am supported chiefly at times by the feeble hope

* It must be remembered, that a considerable change with respect to religion has taken place in India since the period to which this observation refers, and that what was then a subject of the most jealous suspicion, is now regarded with more liberal and christian feelings.

that the Lord, who works by any means, will be pleased to work even by me."

From the time that Mr. Buchanan removed to the Presidency, he generally preached at one or other of the churches in Calcutta once, and sometimes twice, on the Sunday. It appears also from a book of memoranda, in which he briefly noticed his engagements during the five most active years of his residence in India, that he occasionally preached the weekly evening lecture, which had been established by Mr. Brown. In writing to a friend at Cambridge, Mr. Buchanan observed, that the congregations at the new church were more numerous* than those at St. Mary's, more elegant, equally critical, and perhaps not less intelligent. To address such audiences with acceptance and effect must consequently have demanded much laborious preparation. At the mission church the congregations were chiefly composed of those who simply sought christian instruction and edification.

Of the general tenor of his discourses at both places, some idea may be formed from the preceding view of his character and sentiments. A few notices of the subjects of his preaching occur amongst the memoranda just referred to. The following are some of them. "The inward witness to christianity," from 1 John v. 10. "The barren fig-tree," at the close of the year 1801. "In Adam all die," on the Easter following. "The second Adam." "Jairus." "On Knowledge." "We preach Christ crucified." "The second advent." "Abraham seeking a country." "St. Paul at Athens." "If then ye be risen with Christ, seek those things which are above." These are but scanty memorials of Mr. Buchanan's labours in Calcutta as a preacher. Some specimens, however, of his sermons will hereafter be adduced.

Scarcely more numerous or detailed traces remain of the other great branch of his employment, as Vice-Provost and Classical Professor in the college of Fort William. Although Mr. Brown, as the senior chaplain of the Presidency, accepted the office of Provost, and in both capacities was zealous and indefatigable in his endeavours to promote the interests of religion in Calcutta, the superintendence and practical government of the college rested upon Mr. Buchanan. Occasional notices occur in these imperfect records, of the books in which he lectured during different terms, as well as of his

* Some estimate may be formed of their numbers by a note of Mr. Buchanan's on Christmas day 1801, from which it appears, that two hundred communicants had attended that day at the administration of the Lord's supper.

sermons. Homer and Virgil, Longinus and Demosthenes, Terence and Juvenal, Livy, Horace, and Xenophon, are amongst the authors enumerated as occupying the attention of the students of Fort William. Independently of his lectures in these and other classical writers, Mr. Buchanan's memoranda notice frequent communications with Lord Wellesley, and the council of the college, upon points of internal discipline and arrangement, the composition of various public orders, letters, and other papers and documents, the revision of college essays, and books connected with the institution, and attendances at the terminal examinations, disputations, and subsequent distribution into classes, of the students.

The time necessarily employed in these multiplied labours, in maintaining a correspondence in India and Europe, and in visits of ceremony, friendship, or charity, and amongst the latter some are mentioned to the orphan and other schools in and near Calcutta, will suffice to prove, that no sooner were these opportunities of active service and usefulness presented to Mr. Buchanan, than he embraced them with a degree of ardour, diligence, and perseverance, which reflects the highest honour on his principles and his practice.

It will not, however, be a subject of surprise to those who are aware of the high standard by which such men as Mr. Brown and Mr. Buchanan are accustomed to measure their obligations, to find that neither of them was satisfied with his endeavours to fulfil them. We have already noticed one proof of their mutual anxiety upon these important points.* And we have now to witness another of a still more interesting nature, in a reply of Mr. Buchanan to a communication from Mr. Brown, who was then at Chandernagore, where he had been residing some months for the benefit of his health. This valuable testimony to the pastoral feelings of both is as follows.

"Calcutta, 29th November, 1801.

"My dear Sir,—I received your letter last night. I envy much the zealous affection which animates your mind, and would gladly go up to Chandernagore also, to obtain the same. Old Mr. Newton, when in the country, used to think that London was Sardis; but when he came up to town, he found there a great assembly walking in white; and so he joined them. I have thought more seriously in Calcutta than ever I did at Barrackpore. But what I have been (at any period of my

* See p. 77.

life) is so little like what I would wish to be, that I cannot contemplate it without remorse. I do not know that I ever had what christians call 'zeal.' I recollect that I expected it would grow, when I entered the ministry; but I had scarcely entered the ministry, and preached a few times, when I was sent to this country.

"I never knew, as you do, what it was to preach profitably and zealously for a season. That is a work I have to begin; and how to begin it I know not. I need an unction from on high, which I anxiously look for; and yet in looking for this, I look for that which I never knew, as most have known it.

"One thing urges me sometimes to press forward with hope; and that is, that all I hear and all I say appears to me to be so very unlike what it ought to be, that I imagine something better might be attempted. And yet were the Spirit indeed to descend, we cannot expect that God, who worketh by natural means, should suddenly add the eloquent mouth, and new powers of memory and understanding. The holy skill of preaching appears to be the fruit of long experience and converse among God's people. And in Calcutta, as in every other place, the able minister of the New Testament can only be made, by nightly and wakeful meditation, patient study, and prayer producing self-denial.

"It appears to me that it was never intended that the gospel should flourish in the heart and mouth of any minister, who did not make it the 'one thing,' the sole point of heartfelt recurrence. But when it is made so, I can easily conceive how the tender plant grows a great tree with spreading branches and refreshing fruit. Then, no doubt, even a mind naturally barren bears exuberant ideas, and is constantly forming lively images; and, though the mouth be rude in speech, the full heart becomes vocal, and utters the 'word in season.'

"Whether either of us will be able thus to make the gospel the 'one thing,' time will show. 'He that warreth,' ought not to 'entangle himself with the affairs of this life.' But do we *war?* Time enough for the soldier to disencumber himself when he begins to fight. It is easy to throw off a college; but it is very difficult to take up the church. But when the church spirit appears, it will soon conquer the college.

"The grand question is, ought not *means* to be used to mature that spirit which we desire? We read 'that a good soldier of Jesus Christ entangleth himself not with the affairs of this life, that he may please him who hath chosen him to be a soldier;' or, as Guyse explains it, 'he must not follow any civil calling, unprofitable reading, or unnecessary relaxation, to entangle his thoughts, and swallow up his time;' (superintending a college is a civil calling; Latin and Greek is unprofitable reading, and lying in bed after five in the morning is unnecessary relaxation;) 'but his whole time, words, thoughts, and actions must be employed, like a soldier's, on his calling, that he may please Him who hath chosen and authorized him to fight.'

"How far, in what manner and in what particulars, St. Paul would obey the spirit of this passage, were he in your situation or mine, I really cannot tell. Were he here, he would be *warring*. After *we* have warred for some time, we also shall know. 'O that I knew the will of God in this matter,' saith Augustine; 'but I am not worthy to know his will. This ignorance is the fruit of my backsliding.'

"One thing seems probable, that no *sudden* success will appear from any sudden change of our style of address, or manner of preaching. It arises usually from the impression of private character and manner of life. Private character alone will confirm the public sermon. The holy life of the minister is the good alterative among men.

"As to myself, it is my only desire to be of some service to the church of Christ before I die; and I would gladly seize any means, by change of situation or otherwise, which would enable me to do so. As to this world, there is no object (if I know my own heart at all) which I have in view; neither of family, of fortune, of situation, of leaving this country, or continuing in it. I have chiefly to complain of a languid and heartless constitution, both in body and mind, which makes me to bear easily with all things, and to have little pleasure in any thing. This loss of energy and life has been occasioned partly by a continued course of ill health, partly by the untoward circumstances in my situation since I arrived in the country, but chiefly by the natural contagion of unchristian manners.

"I am, however, at this time more independent of society I dislike, than at any former period since my arrival in India; and I hope to be yet more so. Whether by resigning college appointments, secluding myself from the world, and preaching twice a week, I should be of more service, than by maintaining a public situation, is a question I cannot answer. What may be impossible and improper now, may be possible and proper hereafter.

"However, the chief consideration at present is the state of the heart. How is the soul with God? I endeavour by prayer to restore it daily, relying (though feebly) on the aid of the Mediator, wondering sometimes that I am not worse, oppressed in spirit at a review of the past, and hoping for better days.

"I shall ever be ready to accede to any plan you can suggest, for the furtherance of our ministry. You say you 'long to launch out into the fulness of Christ.' So do I. But these words are too apostolic for me at present. In order to launch forth like * * * I should need not only a new effusion of the Holy Spirit; but those natural abilities which generally accompany such an effusion, in order to make it useful. Circumstances seem to admonish me, that the 'still small voice,' and not 'the rushing mighty wind,' is my province in the gospel. What another school than Calcutta would have produced, I know not. But I shall be blessed, if grace be given unto me, to do what good I can, consistently and steadily in my various situations. Unhappily, collegiate avocations usurp much of my time. But let us beware of repining at the necessity of spending time in this way, till we become *confident*, that were all our time at our own disposal, we should spend it in a better.

"I earnestly pray that we may both be rightly directed in our labours in this vineyard, that we may see some fruit in others, and enjoy the comfort ourselves of faithful ministers of the gospel. I think better days are at hand.

"In this hope I remain, my dear Sir, very affectionately yours, C. BUCHANAN.

"To the Rev. D. BROWN, Chandernagore.

"*Sunday evening.*"

It is not amongst the least interesting circumstances relative to this exquisite letter, that it exhibits both its author, and the friend to whom it was addressed, in a country which at that time possessed no ecclesiastical superior, amidst multiplied engagements of the most honourable and useful nature, and under the pressure of infirm health in an enervating climate, earnestly occupied, not in devising some method of relieving themselves from the burthen of their employments, in framing plausible apologies for the indulgence of ease and indolence, or in schemes for the attainment of wealth; but affording mutual examples of self-inquiry, reproaching themselves with the lukewarmness of exertions which some, perhaps, had already accounted excessive; and exciting each other to more animated and abundant labours in the service of their Lord and Master. Yet such is the impressive sense which every faithful minister of the gospel entertains of his obligations and his duties, of the love of Christ and the value of souls, of the uncertainty of opportunity and life, and the approach of an eternal world, that while many who observe him may imagine that he is indulging in self-complacency and satisfaction in the review of his exertions, he is in fact humbling himself before God, and in the confidence of private friendship, at the recollection of his numerous deficiencies.

How well Mr. Buchanan understood the nature of true pastoral zeal, together with what he justly calls 'the holy skill of preaching;' how highly he estimated both, and how perfectly he was acquainted with the means by which they may be cultivated and beneficially exercised, is evident from his dignified and eloquent observations upon those important points. They can scarcely be read without producing a powerful conviction, that personal piety, of a vigorous and exalted character, must form the basis of any reasonable hope of success as a preacher of the gospel; that it is "*the heart* of the wise," which must communicate persuasion to his lips; and that it is the "doctrine and the life coincident," which can alone be expected to constitute the divine art of winning souls to God.

The humility which breathes throughout the whole letter, the disinterestedness of the writer's views, the ardent desire which he expresses of more decisive usefulness, and the obscure intimation of a purpose, which was gradually becoming more definite and mature, of endeavouring more effectually to promote the extension of the Redeemer's kingdom in the East, cannot fail to be observed by every thoughtful reader; and while they serve to illustrate the character of Mr. Buchanan, and the principles which he professed, are well calculated to excite others to the imitation of such an example.

A few days after the date of the preceding letter, Mr. Buchanan wrote to Mr. Grant as follows.

"Mr. Brown and his family have been on the river for their health, for five or six weeks past. Our churches during this cold season are more crowded than I ever saw them before. Even on Wednesday evening there are a great number, and good is done. Some of the students attend on that evening. Their presence warms the heart of old Mr. Obeck. They know and visit him. 'How would Mr. Grant rejoice,'* he sometimes says, 'to see these things!' The pillars are removed, and a number of additional seats made, to accommodate the many who come."

* For the history of the Mission Church, and of the peculiar interest which Mr. Grant would feel in its propriety, the reader is referred to the "Memorial Sketches" of Mr. Brown, lately published.

On the 20th of January, 1802, it appears by a brief memorandum, that Mr. Buchanan, in taking his usual evening's exercise, suffered a severe fall from his horse. "He came down," he says, "at full gallop, and I was thrown over his head, and stunned. He seemed to tumble over me. Mercy! mercy!" The sense which he thus emphatically expressed of the divine goodness which had preserved him from any fatal injury, was probably heightened by his recollection of the death of a Mr. M'Intyre, in consequence of a similar accident about two months before, which he had also recorded, from the singular circumstance that this gentleman had lived some time at Carradell, in Kintyre, when he was himself there, in the year 1785. It was scarcely less remarkable, that Mr. Buchanan should have occasion, a few months afterwards, to notice the death of a Mr. Mackay, in Calcutta, whom he had succeeded, about the same period, as tutor in the family of Captain Campbell, of Carradell. Though Mr. Buchanan complained for several weeks of the effects of his fall, he was sufficiently recovered to preach, yet not without much weakness and pain, the next evening.

During the whole of this month Mr. Buchanan was employed in making various arrangements preparatory to the anniversary of the commencement of the college on the 6th of February On that day public disputations* were held in the Persian, Bengalee, and Hindostanee languages, in the presence of the supreme council, and many other distinguished persons; the prizes and honorary rewards adjudged at the preceding examinations were distributed, and a speech was delivered by Sir George Barlow, the acting visiter, in the absence of Marquis Wellesley; in which, after expressing his satisfaction at the zeal and ability of the officers and professors of the college in the discharge of their public duties, and at the distinguished proficiency of many of the students, as well as their exemplary conduct, he observed, that the establishment of the college had already excited a general and most beneficial attention to oriental languages, literature, and knowledge; and avowed his conviction, that by diligently availing themselves of the advantages afforded by the institution, the students would enjoy the animating prospect of being eminently useful to their country, by aiding it in fulfilling the high moral obligations attendant on the possession of its Indian empire; on the discharge of which the prosperity and permanence of that empire must equally depend.

* See "The College of Fort William," p. 58.

The various occupations, however, of Mr. Buchanan, did not induce him to forget his friends in Europe. Early in the year 1802, his income being now considerably augmented, he, with that filial piety which marked his character, authorized his mother to draw upon his agents for the sum of three hundred pounds annually.

With Mrs. Buchanan, whose arrival in England has been mentioned, he maintained a frequent correspondence. In one of his letters he gave her an interesting sketch of his early life, some circumstances of which he does not appear to have previously communicated to her, and which he observed might form a good commentary on Isaiah xlii. 16.—"I will bring the blind by a way that they knew not, I will lead them in paths that they have not known: I will make darkness light before them, and crooked things straight. These things will I do unto them, and not forsake them."

Having brought down his history to the time at which he was writing, he concludes with the following reflections on his present views and purposes, the piety, beauty, and affection of which cannot but be generally admired.

"Such, my dearest Mary, has been my varied life, and such the wonderful providence which has watched over me during so long a period. I pray that now I am settled, I may be enabled to show a heart fixed on my Saviour, and on the ministration of his word. I feel that nothing in this world can afford me any delight equal to what I hope to find in the labour of the everlasting gospel. No fortune, or rank in life, can ever, I think, give any solid comfort to my soul: nothing but heavenly draughts can quench my thirst.

"My infirm constitution admonishes me not to expect to enjoy life, as some speak, and I am thankful for every barrier which God erects against my taking up my rest in this wilderness. Let us then, my dear Mary, live for the day, seeking that heavenly peace which is always attainable. We have learnt from our past experience, that 'our times are in HIS hands,' and we shall confess at the end that 'He hath done all things well.'

"I feel a deep sense of the importance of my present situation, and of the necessity of using the talent committed to my charge; the uncertainty of having such an useful sphere of action much longer, or my health continued, or my reputation supported; these things excite me to greater exertions while it is called 'to-day.'

"The society of religious people here pray that I may be enabled to do something for the gospel. I am now in better health than formerly. My spirits are more alive. My desires after a regular life increase, and I trust my hopes in the gospel will be fulfilled. You, my beloved wife, can now pray in *faith:* a sense of religion has visited you. Cherish it as the life of your soul. Esteem it the pearl of great price, far exceeding in value the joys of your family, or the wealth of the Indies. I know that gay society at home will impede your progress for awhile, but these difficulties are useful in proving and trying us, and bringing us forth like gold purified in the fire. It is not preciseness of external conduct, but communion with God in prayer which forms the christian's character. If you continue to approach the throne of grace with as much earnestness as you used when on the great waters, you will gradually arrive at a holy state of mind, pure satisfaction of soul, and inexpressible delight in the contemplation of the gos pel. Christ will be formed in you, and you will begin to learn the breadth, and length, and height, and depth of his unsearchable riches.

"All you have to do is to give your testimony to the truth of *real* religion, when opportunities shall be afforded, in modesty and simplicity; alleging that the gospel is not in *form*, but in *power;* and that we must all suffer a change of heart, before we can enter the kingdom of God. This is the truth which I maintain in my preaching, and it is found to be the only effectual doctrine to reach the hearts of men."

The close of this truly interesting letter affords a most substantial proof of the practical influence of Mr. Buchanan's principles, and of the sincerity of the religious professions and purposes which precede it.

"By the last ships I sent four hundred pounds to Mr. H. Thornton, being the amount of his expense on my own account at college for four years, at one hundred pounds per annum. He never expected that I should repay him, but God has put it in my power, and therefore it is my duty.

"I told him I only sent it back to the fountain from whence it would probably soon flow again in some act of benevolence.

"I also told him that I meant to devote five hundred pounds for the support of a young man at the University, of religious character and good ability, who might be in poor circumstances, and whom he, or Mr. Newton, or Dr. Milner, President of Queen's college, should select. At the same time I remitted an order on Messrs. Boehm and Co. to Mr. T. for paying the sum of one hundred and twenty-five pounds per annum, by half yearly instalments, for this purpose: and I expressed a wish that the young man might prove an honour to the gospel, and become an useful labourer in his Master's vineyard.

"While it is in my power, I wish to do some good thing for the gospel of my blessed Lord. I may soon be called hence. May I be able to devote my heart to his glory while I stay!

"May we be grateful stewards of God's blessings, so abundant and unlooked for! And may we continue daily to remember the wonderful way in which we have been led from our early years to this day!"

Various motives might have suggested to many men, possessed of lucrative appointments, the propriety of restoring to a patron the sum which might have been expended in preparing them for their stations. Such a step, however, might not have been distinguished by promptness, and still less by any act of spontaneous liberality. In both these respects, the conduct of Mr. Buchanan was of a very elevated and generous character. It was but a short time that he had enjoyed an abundant income; he had already two children, for whom he could as yet have made but very little provision; he was affording a liberal allowance to his mother; his own health was precarious, and that of his wife was subjecting him to the expense of a voyage to England, with a view to her return to India; the principal source of his emoluments was of an uncertain nature, and had, in fact, though then unknown to him, been already considerably diminished. Gratitude, however, to his earthly benefactor, and love to his divine Lord and Master, induced him, notwithstanding many plausible motives at least to defer his purpose, at once to discharge a debt of kindness, and to fulfil a truly christian design; and under these impressions he communicated to Mr. Thornton the arrangement which has been already detailed. The sense which that gentleman entertained of Mr. Buchanan's conduct was probably expressed in a letter to himself: but the only memorial of it which remains is in the following letter to a mutual friend.

London, Dec. 24, 1802.

"Dear Sir,—I called at your house the other day, and if I had met with you, I should have informed you of the letter which I have received from Mr. Buchanan. He remits in it five hundred and twenty pounds; of which four hundred is intended as a repayment to myself of the four years' allowance which I made to him at college, and the remaining sum is to be applied in a manner which he directs. He moreover gives me a letter to a house in London, desiring them to pay me an annual sum for four years, for the education of such young man for the ministry as I, Mr. Newton, and Dr. Milner may select.

"I am not quite clear whether Mr. Buchanan, at the time of writing the letter, was apprized of all that diminution of his income which the orders sent out from hence for suspending the institution of the college will produce: and I feel some doubt, on this account, whether either to take or to keep the four hundred pounds. I shall thank you for any information on this point which you may possess; as well as for the mention of any promising young man for education at college, with a view to the ministry of the church. I would also request you to take some occasion of expressing to Mr. Buchanan the satisfaction which I felt at this mark of integrity, or of something more than integrity, as I ought to term it, in his conduct. It has raised him in the opinion both of myself and others, and it will not, as I am persuaded, be one of the acts of which he will repent whenever he may come to die. For my own part, I shall always hold that his children will have some claim upon me in consequence of the return of this money, in the event of their falling into pecuniary difficulties; and Providence, I am well persuaded, is wont to provide for those who, without robbing or neglecting their own household, avoid the common eagerness to lay up for them.

"I am, dear sir, yours sincerely, H. Thornton."

It may be satisfactory to add to the preceding letter, that Mr. Buchanan's liberal offer was accepted; and that a young man, approved by the three friends to whom the selection was referred, was afterwards supported during the usual term of residence at the University of Cambridge; who is now filling with ability and credit a very useful station in the church.

While the members of the college of Fort William were zealously and successfully occupied in the prosecution of their labours, the Governor General in council, on the 15th of June, 1802, received with the utmost concern the commands of the Court of Directors for the immediate abolition of that important institution. On the 22d following, Lord Wellesley communicated this despatch to Mr. Buchanan, who, in common with every other friend of the college, deeply lamented this unexpected determination; and directed him to consider of a reply to the reasons upon which it was professedly grounded. Concerning the share which he might have had in that which was shortly afterwards produced, it is unnecessary to inquire. The Governor General was at all times fully competent to the defence of his own measures, though he might, and probably did, avail himself of the talents and information of those around him, upon every great question. It is sufficient to observe that, in a letter* to the chairman of the Court of Directors, dated the 5th of August, 1802, characterized by the same ability which had distinguished his minute in council, Marquis Wellesley submitted to the Court a general view of the principles by which his conduct had been regulated relative to the establishment of the college, and of the measures which he had pursued on, what his lordship termed, the present "most painful and afflicting occasion."

In directing the immediate abolition of the college of Fort William, the Governor General observed, the letter of the honourable Court appeared to acknowledge with approbation the liberal and enlightened spirit of the institution, the just principles on which it was founded, and the important ends to which it was directed. The objections stated by the Court against the continuance of the establishment were apparently confined to its expense, and to the pressure of that charge on the present circumstances of the Company's finances in India. The first object, therefore, of Lord Wellesley was, by a minute detail of facts, to convince the Court that the expenses already incurred on account of the college had not been more considerable than was required by the magnitude of the objects proposed by the institution; that those expenses had been actually defrayed by new resources destined to that express purpose; and that provision had been secured for defraying the future current expenses of the college, without interfering with any other branch of the public service, and without diminishing the scale of their commercial investments.

It appeared, however, to be manifestly the intention of the Court of Directors that *some* establishment for the better instruction of the civil servants at each of the Presidencies should subsist in India; the outlines of which had been traced in their letter to the Governor General. His lordship, therefore, next proceeded to compare the actual expense and ascertained benefit of the institution then subsisting at Fort William, with the probable expense and probable benefit of the seminaries by which the Court intended to supersede that institution. The result of this comparison was stated to be, that the necessary effect of the latter plan would be to involve the expense of a triple establishment for every branch of study, alike requisite at each of the three Presidencies, which must equal, and

* See "The College of Fort William," p. 65.

would probably exceed, the total current charges, on the highest estimate, of the college of Fort William.

The Court of Directors had instructed the Governor General to supersede that institution by the revival of a seminary of Mr. Gilchrist, the learned and meritorious Professor of the Hindostanee language, which had existed previously to the establishment of the college. But no modification or extension of that plan could, as the Governor General contended, embrace the objects proposed to be secured by the collegiate establishment of Fort William; the fundamental defects of that limited plan having, in fact, furnished rules for his lordship's guidance in founding a comprehensive and liberal institution on the ground of practical experience. These defects related especially to the want of any means of enforcing a due system of discipline and study, in regulating private economy and moral conduct, in precluding temptation to expense, and in guarding against every vicious excess; without which, great mischief would be infused into the students at its very source, by establishing any seminary of instruction which should require the whole body of the junior civil servants to continue assembled for any considerable period of time in any part of India, and, above all, at the seats of the respective Presidencies. Lord Wellesley, therefore, expressed his decided conviction that, in addition to the necessary teachers and professors in the seminary proposed by the Court of Directors, some authority of the nature of that exercised in colleges in Europe, and of that then existing in the college of Fort William, must be established for the purpose of maintaining and promoting order and discipline, good morals and religion. Under these circumstances, the final result of the plan proposed by the Court of Directors, of dividing the college of Fort William into three seminaries, to be established separately at each Presidency, would either be to render each and all those seminaries inefficient and dangerous, or to aggravate the collective expense of this triple institution to an amount greatly exceeding the charges of the united establishment then existing.

After this comparison of the expenses and advantages of these several institutions, the Governor General directed the particular attention of the Court to the benefits already derived to their civil service, from the operation and effect of the system of study and discipline constituted and enforced by the college of Fort William. The general progress of the students, his lordship declared, in the oriental languages and literature, had exceeded the most sanguine expectations of the examiners, who had always been selected from the ablest oriental scholars actually at Calcutta, and whose voluntary aid had been afforded to support the discipline, and to improve the course of study, and the mode of instruction pursued in the institution. A spirit of emulation had been excited among the students, as unexampled in its scope and ardour, as it was propitious to the future government of India. The institution had already corrected many of the defects which Lord Wellesley had found in the younger branches of the civil service upon his arrival in India, and had reclaimed to industrious and laborious pursuits many of the junior servants, who were disposed to pursue courses of a contrary tendency. That a general disposition to economy and regularity then prevailed among the students; that principles of due subordination had also been established among them with the happiest success; and that the young men then composing the body of the students at Fort William afforded the most auspicious hope, that the local administration of India for several years to come would be amply provided with instruments properly qualified to accomplish all the purposes of a wise, just, and benevolent government.

Though these and other considerations might have induced the Governer General to suspend the execution of the order for the abolition of the college, and to refer the question to the further pleasure of the Court, the peculiar character and spirit of its commands, and the nature of the institution, seemed to require their immediate execution. To this his lordship accordingly proceeded; but in fulfilling this painful duty, a most serious and difficult question arose with regard to the time when the abolition of the college should take effect. The determination of this question involved principles so deeply affecting the welfare, future prospects, and just expectations of the students, and also the consideration due to the situation of the professors and teachers, and of the numerous learned natives attached to the institution, that Lord Wellesley felt himself compelled to declare, that the abolition of the college of Fort William must be gradual; and that the institution should not terminate previously to the 31st of December, 1803, when the great body of the students then attached to the college would have completed the course which they had so successfully commenced. His lordship finally observed, that he had been partly induced to protract the existence of the institution, from the hope that his preceding representation might prove the means of inducing the Court of Directors to review their late orders, and to restore to their civil service in India the inestimable advantages which must be destroyed by the destruction of the college, and to suffer it to remain unaltered until he should have the opportunity of reporting in person to the Court the condition and effects of the institution, and of submitting to them such details as might enable them to exercise their final judgment on the whole plan.

The foregoing abstract of Marquis Wellesley's defence of the college of Fort William will not be deemed irrelevant to the subject of these memoirs, when it is considered how prominent a station Mr. Buchanan held in that institution. It is by no means necessary for his biographer to express any opinion upon the merits of the question between the Governor General and the Court of Directors. That of Mr. Buchanan, as will hereafter frequently appear, was certainly uniform and decided; and the subsequent conduct of the Directors themselves sufficiently proves, that however they might differ from Lord Wellesley, and those who thought with him, as to the detail of its form and circumstances, they considered the institution of the college as a measure of substantial wisdom and necessity.

For the present it was to remain, as we have seen, unaltered; and on the 30th of June, 1802, a volume was published under the superintendance of the Vice-Provost, entitled, "Primitiæ Orientales; containing Essays by the students of the college of Fort William; to which are added, the Theses pronounced at the public disputations in the oriental languages, on the 6th of February, 1802." The subjects of the disputations contained in this volume are the three following. First, "An academical institution in India is advantageous to the natives and to the British nation; sustained in Persian by Messrs. Lovett, Lloyd, and Guthrie. Secondly, "The Hindostanee language is the most generally useful in India;" supported in Hindostanee by Messrs. Bayley, Lovett, and Lloyd. Thirdly, "The Asiatics are capable of as high degrees of civilization as the Europeans;" maintained in Bengalee by Messrs. Martin, Bayley, and Hodgson. The English essays comprised in the same volume were, first, "On the advantages to be expected from an academical institution in India; considered in a moral, literary, and political point of view;" by Messrs. Martin, Elliott, and Bayley. Secondly, "On the best means of acquiring a knowledge of the manners and customs of the natives of India;" by Messrs. Hamilton, Martin, and Metcalfe. Thirdly, "On the character and capacity of the Asiatics; and particularly of the natives of Hindostan;" by Messrs. Wood, Martin, and Newnham. Many of these compositions are highly creditable to the talents, information, principles, and taste of their authors, and would bear a comparison with similar productions in our English Universities.

Early in the year 1803, Marquis Wellesley presided at the second annual disputations of the students of the college of Fort William. The subjects were the advantages of the British Government to the natives of India, the burning of Hindoo widows, and the distribution of Hindoos into castes. Declamations were also pronounced for the first time in the Arabic language. After the degrees of honour had been conferred, and the prizes and rewards for proficiency both in oriental and classical learning had been distributed, the noble visitor delivered a very dignified and eloquent speech, in which he declared, in the most public and solemn manner, that the institution had answered his most sanguine hopes and expectations; that its beneficial operation had justified the principles of its original foundation; and that the administration and discipline of the college had been conducted with honour and credit to the character and spirit of the institution, and with great advantage to the public service. Essays on the Mohammedan conquests and government in India, and on the restoration of learning in the East, by several of the students, were afterwards published, together with the preceding disputations and declamations, in the second volume of the "Primitiæ Orientales."

In the spring of this year Mr. Buchanan received letters from his wife, whose health appeared to be considerably restored by her visit to her native country, announcing her intention of leaving England in the month of January. "This," said he, in a letter to the friend, in whose family she had resided some months during her visit, "was joyful intelligence to me. In two or three months hence, I may be blessed with seeing her again. When she mentions her affectionate intimacy with your family, she writes in tears. But I see evidently that it is the gospel union which so powerfully awakens her heart in speaking of the happiness of her residing with you. I expect that she will do good in the Carmarthen, and I hope she will do good in Calcutta. She comes out to a promising scene of joy; to see her little Augusta, now grown up a healthy and talkative girl; calling out for mamma for two years past in vain. And she comes out to many, who love and respect her, and to some who have learnt during her absence to love 'the excellent of the earth.'

"I have now a house in the country, about three miles from Calcutta, on the banks of the river, where she may sleep occasionally, and retire from company. I spend three or four solitary evenings every week in Garden Reach. The change of place and air refreshes me for the labours of the succeeding day. Augusta and I play together in the groves, and then return by water to Calcutta. A gentleman leaving India sent me his boat as a present to Mary when she comes out. I find the river air very salutary and renovating, and perhaps she will find it so too. But our pleasures at Clapham or on the Ganges are transitory. May they be so tempered with prayer, as to prepare us both for the pleasures of that 'other country,' where there will be no separation, and where the inhabitants will never say, 'I am sick!' Mrs. B. mentions the circumstances of your illness with a lively concern, mingled with a sensation of pleasure. Her hours passed by your sick couch were delightful. Providence hath well ordered her steps. It may be, indeed, that I shall never see her; or that I shall contemplate her departing spirit for a short time, in her emaciated frame. But then God hath made with her a covenant well-ordered and sure! Thus it is with my house. And this is my joy. Thus God hath blessed our short sojourn together; and the end will be an eternal song of glory to his redeeming love."

Though the fears, which Mr. Buchanan expresses with so much tenderness and piety as to the probably short period of his reunion with his wife, were but too well founded, it is pleasing to reflect, that he was gratified by again seeing her in India. She embarked on board the Carmarthen in the month of February; and, as Mr. Buchanan had anticipated, the piety of her mind was displayed during the voyage by her endeavours to promote the religious improvement of two young ladies, one of whom had been placed under her protection. Mrs. Buchanan had a more favourable voyage than in returning to Europe, and arrived safely at Calcutta on the 24th of August.

The remainder of the letter from which an interesting passage respecting Mrs. Buchanan has just been extracted, is occupied with the important subject of the college of Fort William; in which, though some things occur similar to those which have been already stated from the public letter of Lord Wellesley, many additional facts and sentiments are contained, more particularly with reference to Mr. Buchanan himself, which it may be proper to insert.

"You say," he continues, "that you hear the college is abolished. It has been long abolished in London, but it still exists here, in greater spirit and utility than ever; and it must continue to exist, (though perhaps under a different name,) as long as the British empire reigns in India. To send a young man adrift in the upper provinces, without any knowledge of the languages, and without any official preparation, is now utterly impossible. The good sense of young men themselves would deprecate it. Every one here sees that the body of civil servants educated these three years in the college of Fort William will by and by govern India. Many of them are already approaching to the most responsible situations. The body of juniors that follow, if left in their native ignorance, will be held in comparative contempt, and must ever feel the injustice done to them.

"The Directors wish the institution to be called a *seminary*, and then they will support it. I have no objection to the name, provided that the young men are taught; and they must be taught in future. You might as well think of abolishing the schools in London, as abolishing schools in Calcutta. Thus much then has been effected by the institution of the college. Education has been proved to be useful in India. Of the students who have just left college, only eight out of thirty have contracted any debt. Many of them have saved money; a thing unheard of in India, and by the old civil servants accounted impossible. This is the point to which the public attention is turned. The reign of native money lenders is now at an end. But a school or *seminary* directed by native moonshees, and destitute of the high and respectable jurisdiction of learned and religious men, would never be able to effect this desirable purpose. The authority and the honours of a college are alone competent to restrain a body of young men of good families and flattering prospects in this luxurious and deteriorating country. That ever such an objection as that of expense should have been urged by the Directors appears to me unaccountable. The expense, whatever it has been, is now amply liquidated; and in a manner more favourable to the interests of the Company than if the sum had been paid into their treasury; with some advantage of health, of morals, and of learning, and with some coercion of the native ascendancy, which has ever been deemed the bane of the British administration in India.

"Satisfied, however, with the good which *has* been done by the institution, we wait submissively for the period of its regular dissolution; which will be in December next. Even were it to continue in its present state, or in one yet more improved and respectable, I should not desire to bear a part in it. I have weak health. My heart seeks to be disengaged from collegiate labours, and to find rest and refreshment in the *one* spiritual work of the everlasting gospel. Fortune or fame cannot add an hour's happiness to my present existence; but they may interrupt it. I feel a secret pleasure in the purpose of the Directors to abolish the college, as it respects *myself;* but I feel at the same time that its continuance under other men would be favourable to my evangelical labours in this country.

"In perfect confidence, therefore, that God will order all things aright, in time, manner, and event, I implore the direction of his Spirit to improve 'the passing day.' My chief source of despondency at times is the want of fellow-labourers, of learned and serious men, in this vineyard, where there is so numerous a body of well-educated young men.

"I would willingly at this moment give 50,000 rupees for two religious and respectable young men established in the church of Calcutta, and capable of conducting the studies of the college. Foreseeing where we were likely to fail, I took early measures to procure such from home; both by addressing Lord Wellesley, and by writing myself. But we have not succeeded. But this also is directed by an all-wise Providence; and he will accomplish his glory by any means."

The following letter to Mr. Grant enters still more fully into the interesting subject of the college, and contains some particulars respecting Mr. Buchanan's lectures as classical professor, which have not been before mentioned. Whatever may have been the sentiments of the distinguished Director to whom this letter was addressed, it cannot but be considered most honourable to the talents and principles of its author.

"CALCUTTA, 22d August, 1803.

"Dear Sir,—Your letter of January last, introducing your nephews, I have received. You may be assured of my rendering them every service in my power, both in the superintendance of their moral conduct, and of their progress in learning.

"Circumstances are not so favourable at present to a well disposed youth newly arrived, as at an earlier era of the college.

"The repeated shocks the institution has sustained from home, and its often predicted dissolution here, have been injurious to its religious and moral influence. On the arrival of the Court's letter, abolishing the college, the students found that religion and morality formed no part of the plan proposed as a substitute. And so absolutely did they consider the Court's opinion to be favourable to the old system of relaxed morals and contracting debt, that they circulated a placard in college, containing a parody of Henry the Fourth's speech to his son; beginning with these lines:

"Pluck down my officers; break my decrees;
For now a time is come to mock at form.
Have you a ruffian (a writer) that will swear, drink, dance,
England (the Court) shall double gild his treble guilt," &c.

"The religious people here perceived the bad consequences immediately. Old Mr. Obeck, whose hopes of the good effects of the institution had ever been sanguine, sighed from his heart, and exclaimed, 'Cruel, cruel!' while the black banians and the old leaven in the service grinned their ghastly exultation.

"Order and discipline were nevertheless preserved in the exterior. But the wound inflicted by that letter on the growing honour of religion and exemplary morals is not healed to this day. The first symptoms appeared in the gradual secession of the students from the mission church in the evening.

"At the present time the regular and well disposed youths attend church either morning or evening; but in small proportion, compared to the former number.

"As to general good order, attention to lectures, success in study, and dread of debt, there cannot be a college in Europe in a better state. If a young man is faulty in these points, he is sent up the country on the *old system*, in the character of an 'ignorant assistant,' to, it may be, an ignorant judge. The frequent letters sent in of late to government by these expelled members petitioning to be restored to college, will appear to you some argument in favour of the institution; when you consider that at this moment we know nothing of the Court's intentions on the subject, and think the abolition of the college as likely as not.

"Your nephews have been now attached to the college for two weeks. The report made to me yesterday by their professor is favourable to their diligence. But they have to contend with some formidable rivals, who commence their studies with them. Of these two or three have not a single friend here, except their official friends in college. And this circumstance sometimes makes a rival formidable; his hope of promotion depending on the college alone.

"The appointments continue to be made according to merit. Of the eleven students belonging to the Presidency of Bengal, who entered on the public service this year, the two highest in proficiency, Messrs. Bayley and Martin, had their choice of situations; and are in the diplomatic department in the Governor General's office. The next four were appointed to registerships; and the five lowest to assistantships.

"Letters of recommendation from England are of no avail. Lord Wellesley once observed, that, of those young men who had brought him letters from the king's ministers and others, the greater part had been expelled from college, or were in the lowest classes.

"I doubt not but you and the whole Court are by this time satisfied of the vast accession to the interests of the Company, derived from the juniors of the last two years entering their service, unincumbered by debt.

"The extent of this good, either as referring to the morals and fortune of the individual, or to his fidelity and exertion for the public service, cannot be calculated here. It is admitted, as if by acclamation, throughout the British territories in India.

"You must also have heard of the good effects of the institution on the general health of the students; resulting from their regular habits of study, in a climate, where exposure to the sun is so baneful to youth on their first arrival.

"Never, perhaps, was there an institution in any age or country raised so rapidly on so doubtful a foundation, or which flourished so extensively under such severe assaults, or which produced so much of public and of private benefit, in so short a space of time, as the college of Fort William in Bengal.

"The Gazette you will receive herewith, though published in course, is amplified at this time, in anticipation of the dissolution of the college by the court; and is intended as a monument of what the college *was*.

"Many a parent in Great Britain and Ireland, who reads this gazette, will lament that it should be the *last*.

"Those gratifying half-yearly reports of the health and studies of their sons in this distant country (where sons are so negligent in writing to their parents) will now be withheld; one of the chains of affection will be broken, and one of the chief incentives to good conduct, destroyed.

"Of your own good wishes for the success of this institution, I never entertained a doubt. And I even believe that your influence in the direction will induce them to qualify their late letter of abolition. But it is not probable that any thing less than the ample support of the first principles and first establishment of the institution will restore it to its first dignity, or maintain its present effect.

"In the midst of this uncertainty we 'are sure that the Lord reigneth;' and that his gracious providence hath ordered all things aright; hath produced the good already done, and will overrule the evil, past and to come, to his own glory, and the good of his faithful church on earth.

"It is now upwards of three years since I was appointed to offices in this college; and, as I before mentioned to you, every collegiate object of a private nature is extinct in my breast; and I would gladly resign my situation to some other person of more ability, health, and spirits, even in the event of the Court's increasing the first dignity and importance of the institution. What I write to you comes really from an indifferent person.

"If God were pleased to give me my heart's desire, he would give me more grace and a greater sense of the value of souls; with a measure of better health and more undisturbed leisure to make known the glory of his gospel among his people here, during the short period that may be allotted to my ministry.

"But I may add, for your consideration, in the event of your continuing a clergyman to govern the college, that his establishment must be made equal to that of a senior civil servant in the higher departments. If the church had dignity in India, that might suffice. But in present circumstances, the governor of the whole body of the junior civil servants cannot possibly be inferior in rank and establishment to a senior civil servant. If he be inferior, he will never be able to preserve the necessary authority and respect, whatever his character, his ability, or acquirements may be.

"And this has been hitherto the most material defect in the institution.

"One other point I may mention, as for the last time, and which is of equal importance: and that is, that the union of the three Presidencies in one institution has been now demonstrated to be the best and perhaps the only mode of effecting the purposes intended; in promoting a rapid knowledge of the languages, and a knowledge of public business, in encouraging honourable and temperate conduct under the eye of the supreme authority, and in facilitating the future administration of the country by a concert of principles and a personal knowledge of character.

"Whatever good the private schools, proposed by the Court at the different Presidencies, may do, (and they will do a little,) they can never produce some of the effects to which I allude *at all*; and none of them in a degree equal to what has been already done at this college.

"Five students have lately proceeded to Madras, who will in a short time be qualified to govern the country; whether you require great talents, oriental knowledge, classical learning, prudent and upright conduct, or (I can add of two of them) a just sense of religion.

"Now the local position of these five young men for the last three years at Madras, rather than at Calcutta, would not have answered any important purpose that I can conceive; or, as they often told me, that they could ever conceive. And the evidence of the young men's letters after their return to their respective Presidencies is conclusive on this subject.

"I began this letter with the mention of your nephews. They have the happiness of being placed where exemplary morals will be encouraged if they have a disposition to profess them. The daily inspection of their conduct will fall to the lot of the individual families with whom they reside, Mr. Udny and Major Fraser. In my present situation I can seldom see the students but when they require admonition or deserve praise.

"Of those indeed who attend the classical lectures I gain a more intimate knowledge.

"Continuance in my class can only be maintained by exemplary conduct, and by honourable progress in the oriental languages. And these qualifications have characterized my pupils to this time, almost without exception.

"In many cases a personal friendship has been formed, which has proved of much service to me in regulating the manners of the other students. Of these my young friends, some have now proceeded to Bombay, some to Madras, and some to the provinces attached to this Presidency. And they seem to value our acquaintance now as much as formerly; and frequently favour me with letters on the subject of their studies, or on the state of affairs at their respective stations.

"But it is not always that a well disposed young man can attend my lectures. His previous knowledge of classics may be so inconsiderable, that he is incompetent to join a class; and I have no time for individual instruction. Or it may happen that his progress in the oriental languages is very slow and unsatisfactory to his professor; in which case he is not permitted to expend time on the classics. At all events it is not till after a term or two, when his acquirements and talents are known, that he is admitted. So that your nephews cannot resume the study of their European learning for some months. And this makes it doubtful whether they will ever be my pupils, as I wish to exonerate myself from the classical department immediately on the arrival of your letter to the Governor General, whether that letter confirm the institution or not.

" I shall, however, feel warmly interested in young men so nearly related to you, and whose welfare you have so much at heart.

" Mrs. Buchanan is not yet arrived. I have heard of her good health at St. Helena, and of her pious care of two young ladies whom she found on board ship. One of them comes out to her father, who was once commander of a country ship; but she comes out to disappointment, for he is now reduced to beggary, and banished from society by his worthless character; so that I suppose Mrs. B. will not think it right to resign her charge. The young lady bears an amiable character, and is well educated. And from 'her attending prayers in Mrs. B.'s cabin morning and evening, and reading the scriptures with much interest and affection,' (a circumstance which Mrs. B. mentions in her letters to me,) we may look for the best fruits, and hope that she is acquiring a consolation that will triumph over her misfortune.

" Mr. Brown is in his usual state of doubtful health; doubtful also whether he shall go home or stay in India; but he is constant and faithful in his charge over his faithful people.

" I have written to you a long letter; and, according to my dawk book, it is the thirteenth within the last eighteen months. You will not expect frequent letters from me for the future. I consider this as my winding up letter; like that of a merchant who is about to retire from business, and wishes to settle his accounts.

To Mr. Newton I wrote lately, and I could wish you to communicate to him this letter, if he be able to read it.

" To his pious affection and fatherly counsel it has been owing, under the wonder-working providence of God, that the junior servants of the East India Company have been placed for the last three years under my superintendence.

" By Mr. Thornton's means also, and by yours, this dispensation has been directed.

" I remain, dear sir, with much regard, very sincerely yours,

C. Buchanan."

The number of Mr. Buchanan's correspondents was this year increased by the return to Europe of Major Sandys, who, in a season of severe domestic affliction, had been led to search the scriptures for consolation; and to whom the preaching of Brown and Mr. Buchanan had been blessed as the means of bringing him to the knowledge of the gospel, from the proud holds of philosophical infidelity. To this gentleman, with whom Mr. Buchanan afterwards maintained an uninterrupted and affectionate intercourse, he wrote, in the month of June, as follows:

"I suppose you will have seen all your friends by this time, and settled your plans. I am anxious to know how you find yourself after a year's residence in England. We do as usual in Calcutta. Serious religion appears to increase. Mr. Obeck is yet alive, but declining fast. He begs his blessing on you, whom he calls a 'young man,' and wishes you a long christian life. You are quite forgotten by the gay world here, even by those who used to *feast* with you sometimes. Those who are always asking me about you are the poor people who knew you but half a year.

" . . . . and . . . . are labouring at their docks and accounts, thinking often of England, and sometimes of another world.

"Since you and Prole left me, I have had no hooka. I do not yet find the abstinence of much service, farther than it saves time, now and then. The advantage of the hooka was, that I could easily compose myself for *composition* by its help.

"The whole settlement is at present in agitation, giving Lord W. a public entertainment. The hawk as usual on the steeple looks down in amazement at the bustle. It costs sixty thousand rupees.

" . . . . is sick. He has had many attacks. *She* seeks comfort at church; and he begins to think, perhaps, that he can obtain it no where else.

"But your interest in all these Calcutta matters will weaken every month. That the gospel is honoured will be to you the most welcome and the most interesting news. Adieu, my dear Sandys."

The following is an extract from a second letter of Mr. Buchanan to Major Sandys, dated early in September.

"Your letter from St. Helana I have just received by Mrs. Buchanan, who arrived there the day after you had sailed. Mary is much improved in health, and greatly matured in spiritual knowledge, strength, and grace, which is the chief theme of my happiness. Her missing you was a keen disappointment at the moment. But she soon reflected that God had ordered it for wise and gracious purposes, and then she submitted. She opened your letters to me which she found at Major Greentree's. These letters astonished her beyond measure. She thought that you had yet been a man of the world, (for she had not heard that your affliction had been sanctified to you,) but behold she found you to be a child of

God; your understanding illuminated with knowledge, and your heart expanding with love, hope, joy, zeal, and all the charities. She lamented that she had no christian near her to whom she might, in pious confidence, communicate these happy news. So she disburdened her heart by writing a letter to me.

"I was rejoiced to find by your letters that the gospel is still glorious in your view, and that the world and its vanities had not obscured the heavenly vision. May this happy state be ever yours without alloy or reverse, but such as may be necessary to confirm, and strengthen, and perfect you in the inner man."

By a letter of the same date as the preceding, Mr. Buchanan communicated to Mr. Elliott an affecting but consoling account of the death of his son, who, in consequence of his distinguished proficiency in oriental learning, had been appointed by Marquis Wellesley secretary to an embassy to Arabia; but who, after having fulfilled with great ability the duties of his mission, fell a victim to a fever in that country, and as a mark of peculir honour, was interred in the garden of the Imam of Senna.

To the same friend Mr. Buchanan again wrote in the course of the month, as follows:

"Your letter by Mrs. Buchanan I received about a month ago, since which time no ship for Europe has sailed. I thank you for the 'Christian Observer.' You wish me to furnish some papers for it. Mr. Thornton wrote to me on the same subject; but I answered him that my present avocations will not permit it. A period of leisure may perhaps soon be granted to me. But this is not the only objection to my furnishing you with the life of Mr. Swartz. He left no papers; and those persons are now removed who could give the best information. He also deprecated posthumous praise; and was in constant dread of fame. He concealed often from Mr. Obeck, (his only friend at one time,) his favoured seasons from on high.

"Mrs. Buchanan is quite surprised to find so much vital religion amongst us. My responsibility in college is greater at present than formerly; but the answer of the court will determine many points; and as far as relates to myself, they cannot help determining them to my satisfaction.

"We are carrying on a successful war against the Mahrattas, fighting against them in three different quarters, and obtaining three victories at the same time. The Hindoos are happy that Juggernaut, their famous place of worship, has fallen into our hands, for our imposts will not be so great as those of the former possessors of the adjoining district."

The occasional notices which have occurred in Mr. Buchanan's letters respecting the pious and excellent Mr. Obeck, have probably excited a wish in the minds of most readers, to know something of the closing scene of his life, as well as some farther particulars of his character. In the month of May, Mr. Buchanan thus wrote to Mr. Grant:

"The departure of the aged Obeck appears to be at hand. At least he thinks so, and bids me impart to you his blessing while his understanding remains. He was carried into church last night, (Wednesday's lecture,) but was so much revived by the service and view of his brethren, that he walked out, with assistance. His only food at present is bread dipped in wine.

"Under this decay of body his mind is more vigorous than ever. He has, within this last year, assumed a very intrepid tone in rebuking sin, and remonstrating with the lukewarm, and in defining a holy life in India. But he has great joy among the true disciples, and his spiritual comforts have of late been abundant."

Towards the end of the month of August following, Mr. Buchanan thus describes to the same friend the progress of Mr. Obeck's decline:

"The good Obeck is yet alive; but his loins are girt for the heavenly journey. He is confined to his room, and cannot attend church. But the church attends him. He listens with delight to the voice of praise in the adjoining building on the Sunday and Thursday evenings.

"We have arranged all his temporal affairs to his satisfaction. He has given us his text for his funeral sermon; in preaching which, I fear my spirits will fail me. It is difficult to speak of the deceased father to the surviving children."

This venerable man was now very fast approaching his end. Early in September he felt a presentiment that he should not live to the close of that month; and accordingly, on the 24th, Mr. Buchanan thus announced his death to his respected friend and benefactor:

"The aged Obeck has at last departed. For some weeks before he almost daily expected his dismission. He had no spiritual conflict at his last hour, but manifested constantly peace, joy, and high assurance. He was sensible to the last; and when he could not speak, he testified his exultation of soul by pressing ardently to his breast his fellow saints. He left to you and your family his solemn blessing. I send you a paper containing some notice of his death.

"Just before Mr. Obeck's death, I preached his dying sermon in the mission church from these words; 'The time of my departure is at hand. I have fought a good fight, I have finished my course, I have kept the faith. Henceforth there is laid up for me a crown of righteousness, which the Lord the righteous Judge shall give me at that day; and not to me only, but unto all them also who love his appearing.'

"Mr. Brown will preach his funeral sermon next Sunday evening."

Of what Mr. Buchanan styles Mr. Obeck's dying sermon it may not be uninteresting to many readers to insert an extract; both as it contains a pleasing and animated sketch of the life and character of that exemplary christian, and as it may afford a specimen of the spirit of Mr. Buchanan's preaching upon such occasions.

"These are the words of the Apostle Paul, in the view of his approaching death. They are words which manifest the triumph of faith; and which the Spirit of God enabled him to utter; to be adopted by every faithful christian in after ages. By these words he sets a seal to his doctrine, that it was *true*; that it was really the life of the soul at the dissolution of the body: that the assurance of the christian in the view of death is strong and sensible; manifesting a power denied to others in like circumstances; and anticipating the joys to be revealed in the kingdom of God.

"In the records of every age of the church, we read of those who were enabled to testify their faith and hope in the words of the apostle; and wherever the gospel is faithfully declared, and its power is felt, there will be frequent instances of this triumph in death.

"God hath been graciously pleased to honour this church with such an instance at this time; exemplified in his aged and faithful servant, the venerable John Obeck; who has for many years been a member of this congregation, and is now supposed to be at the point of death.

"This good man has ever been distinguished for his genuine piety, for his ardent faith in the gospel, for his singular benevolence, and for his unremitted labours of love among the poor and needy. He has been long known in this place, as one who was always 'going about doing good;' exhibiting an affecting and amiable example of that 'pure religion and undefiled,' taught by the precepts and doctrine of our Saviour.

"But his chief labour was in inculcating the sacred truths of the gospel whenever he had opportunity; and such opportunities he often enjoyed. Many persons have for some years attended his prayers in his own family, which was indeed a church in his own house, where they enjoyed the inestimable advantage of hearing his spiritual instruction, and listening to the counsels of age and experince.

"His temperate and pure life has now carried him to his seventy-third year. And from his fifteenth year (as I think he once mentioned) he has endeavoured to serve God. Since that period he has had a sense of religion in his heart, and has been enabled to 'keep himself unspotted from the world.'

"All serious persons who knew him had reason to expect that God would honour the death of so faithful a servant; and this honour hath been conferred on him in an abundant manner. During the two last months of his illness, the praise of his Redeemer has been his constant theme. Surrounded daily by his numerous family, his pleasure has been to talk of the things of God, and of the glories of the kingdom to which he is hastening. And his ability has been as great as his pleasure. For even at this time, when it is doubtful whether he will survive another day, and when his bodily frame is in the last stage of debility; even now, his understanding is clear and unclouded; his perception of divine truths is undoubtedly stronger than at a former period of his illness; his soul seems to swell with exultation when he recounts the past mercies of God; and his admonitions and exhortations to others have an earnestness and emphasis, united with a force of reasoning and firmness of persuasion, which is nowhere to be seen but on the death-bed of the christian; and which nothing can inspire but a power from on high.

"It will not be necessary to apologize for exhibiting to you such an instance of the truth and divine power of the christian religion. It is of great importance that such instances should be exhibited; for the knowledge of them is oftentimes blessed in a peculiar manner to the hearers. And this excellent man is himself fully sensible of the inexpressible goodness of God to him, in enabling him to bear this blessed testimony at his dying hour.

"He does not speak of manifestations and visions of glory, which have sometimes attended the death of good men; but he manifests a calm, rational, and placid spirit, founded on the basis of an immoveable faith, yet accompanied by such ardour of expression, and by such an assurance of hope, as would abash philosophy itself.

"He has none of those doubts which are often found on a death-bed. He has not those fears and misgivings of conscience which the unstable and careless christian often experiences. He has none of those fearful forebodings which harass the soul of the despiser of religion in his last hour. He is a stranger to that gloomy despair which often haunts the soul of the man who hath passed through life the slave of ambition, or the votary of pleasure. No, *his* last moments are the happiest of his life. *His* ambition through life has been to obtain 'that honour which cometh from God;' and *his* pleasure has been, in serving God with his whole heart; in loving his neighbour as himself; in forgiving his enemies; and in praying for those who persecute and despitefully use the professor of the gospel of Christ.

"Do you inquire on what *faith* these good works and this holy disposition were founded? Let me express to you his faith, collected chiefly from his own words:

"'I am a sinner saved by the mercy of God in Christ. By nature I am impure and unholy. Nothing in me, no merit of mine, could make me the object of God's distinguishing grace. But I believed the word of God, and I was enabled to offer up my prayers at an early age, that he would open my understanding, and lead me to a knowledge of his truth. And his promise was fulfilled to me, (as it is fulfilled to every serious inquirer,) 'Ask, and it shall be given unto you; seek, and ye shall find.' By degrees the mysteries of the gospel were opened to my view. I beheld myself a lost and undone soul, lying with a multitude in a world of wickedness; subject to the just wrath of God. But I at the same time heard of the offer made to a perishing world by the Saviour Christ. I beheld the whole world overwhelmed by a flood of sin and misery, and the ark of redemption floating on the waters. Every page of the gospel showed me that there was no salvation, but by the ark Christ; that his atonement on the cross was the only atonement for my past and future sins; that his gracious Spirit influencing my soul was the only preservative from my evil passions and from an ensnaring world; and that his mediation alone procures our access to God, and warrants an answer to our prayers.

"'Thus,' said he, 'the perusal of the word of God was blessed to my soul. I received it in its plain and obvious meaning; and I have had a constant experience of its truth through my past life. It has been a light to my steps, and a lantern to my paths. Its peculiar doctrines appear now all light and glory to my soul. I know that the denunciations of God against the despisers of his gospel will be expressly executed; and I know that his promises of glory to the righteous will be fulfilled in a way that 'eye hath not seen, or ear heard, or hath entered into the heart of man to conceive;' and the anticipation of this glory is to me *unutterable*. My prayer at my last moments is, that this power of the gospel may be felt more and more at this place; that the blessing of God may rest on this church; that the ministers may labour in the word with zeal and faithfulness; and that the hearers may receive the word preached with meekness and affection; that so the testimony of the gospel may prevail, and the church of Christ may begin to flourish in this dark corner of the world.

"'I leave,' said he, 'my blessing on this church.

"'As to my numerous family, I leave them with scarcely the means of subsistence; but I leave them dependant on that gracious Providence, which has supported me from youth to age, in a state of apparent poverty and yet possessing abundance. I leave my children to God as to a surviving Father, who will care for them as he hath cared for me, and will, I trust, bless my instructions to the salvation of their souls.

"'As to *myself*, my hope is in heaven. The promises of God are in a manner already fulfilled to me. His truth and faithfulness are demonstrated to my soul. By his mercy "I have fought the good fight, I have finished my course, I have kept the faith. Henceforth there is laid up for me a crown of righteousness, which the Lord the righteous Judge shall give me at that day; and not to me only, but unto all them also who love his appearing."'"

"Such, my brethren, are the sentiments, the expressions, and the heavenly hope of this good man. He now lies on his death-bed in the house adjoining this church; and endeavours to join the praises of the congregation with his feeble voice. He could even now confirm every sentiment respecting him which I have uttered; and he could confirm them with an energy and eloquence of which I am incapable.

"Who is there in this assembly who is not ready to say, 'Let *me* also die the death of the righteous; and let my last end be like *his*?'"

In the same month in which the preceding sermon was preached, Mr. Buchanan was called to perform a similar office on occasion of the death of Mr. Archibald Edmonstone, of the Board of Trade, who left behind him a noble testimony to his faith in the gospel. "His last words," says Mr. Buchanan, in mentioning the event in a letter to a friend, "were these, 'Blessed be the God and Father of our Lord Jesus Christ, who through his abundant mercy hath begotten me again unto a lively hope, through the resurrection of his Son Jesus Christ from the dead, to an inheritance incorruptible, undefiled, and that fadeth not away.' These words his brother has directed to be engraven on his tomb."

The manner in which Mr. Edmonstone, who then filled one of the most confidential situations under the Presidency of Bengal, and is celebrated for his oriental learning, classical taste, and cultivated understanding, described Mr. Buchanan's funeral sermon on his brother, is too honourable to him to be omitted. It occurs in a note from Mr. Edmonstone to his friend Captain Baillie, professor of the Arabic language and of Mohammedan law in the college of Fort William, and is as follows:

"My dear B.—I am returned from hearing a most affecting and impressive discourse delivered by Mr. Buchanan with a degree of feeling that does honour to his heart, on the occurrence of last week. I am anxious that Mr. B. should know how grateful I feel for this high tribute of respect to the memory and virtues of a beloved brother, and I therefore entreat you to express to Mr. B. my sincere gratitude for this distinguished mark of his regard for him. Tell him that he has afforded to my mind a real consolation, and that I trust I shall ever after be the better for the affecting and forcible manner in which he has held forth to imitation the example of a life of true piety and virtue. Further, I request that you will convey to Mr. B. my earnest wish (if it be not improper) that he will allow me to transcribe his discourse, both for the purpose of retaining it for my own use and benefit, and of transmitting a copy of it to those in Europe who will indeed need the consolation for such an irreparable loss, which so distinguished a testimony to the merits of a son and a brother is calculated to afford. Never does a clergyman appear more conspicuously respectable, than when he combines with the public duties of his calling the offices of humanity and consolation; and never while I live will the memory of Mr. B.'s solemn and eloquent discourse on this melancholy occasion, nor the gratitude and respect for him which it has excited, be obliterated from the mind of your ever affectionate

N. B. Edmonstone.

"Sunday, 11th September, 1803.

"To Captain Baillie."

It was in the summer of this year that Mr. Buchanan first thought of proposing certain subjects of prize composition, connected with the civilization and moral improvement of India to the Universities of the United Kingdom. With this laudable intention he waited on the Governor General, and having obtained his lordship's approbation of the plan, he on the 20th of October despatched letters to the Vice-Chancellors and Principals of the Universities of Oxford and Cambridge, of Edinburgh, Glasgow, St. Andrew's, and Aberdeen, to the Provost of Trinity College, Dublin, and to the head masters of Eton, Westminster, and the Charter-House Schools, containing the following proposals. For the best essay in English prose on "the best means of extending the blessings of civilization and true religion among the sixty millions, inhabitants of Hindostan, subject to British authority;" in each University, one hundred pounds. For the best English poem on "the revival of letters in the East," sixty pounds. For the best Latin ode or poem on "Collegium Bengalense," twenty-five pounds; and the same sum for the best Greek ode on "Γενεσθω φως." The sum of fifty pounds each for the best Latin and Greek poems was offered to the successful candidate at each of the public schools. No less a sum than sixteen hundred and fifty pounds was thus appropriated by Mr. Buchanan to this benevolent and patriotic purpose. The unusual nature and munificent extent of his offers induced some to suppose, either that they were not made simply at his own suggestion and responsibility, or that he must have been actuated by motives of ostentation and vanity. With respect to the proposals themselves, they undoubtedly originated solely with Mr. Buchanan, and were supported exclusively by his own liberality. He was ever a man of a large and generous mind, fertile in devising plans of usefulness, and prompt in seizing the first opportunity of executing them. He was anxious to extend in this country the knowledge of the character and effects of the great collegiate institution which he had been called to superintend; and the recent victories of our armies in the peninsula having enlarged and confirmed our eastern empire, he was desirous of awakening and directing the minds of his countrymen at home to the duty and the opportunity of promoting the moral and political welfare of our fellow subjects in India. Publicity and inquiry were therefore his great objects; publicity, not as to his own character or fame, for this he knew might have been far more certainly obtained by more obvious and less costly means, but as to the great and philanthropic design which he had in view; and this induced him to endeavour to interest in his plan even the higher forms in our public schools. The *result* of his liberal proposals must be reserved to the period of their reception and success in this country.

In the month of November following, Mr. Buchanan first

communicated his thoughts on the expediency of an ecclesiastical establishment for British India, in letters to the Archbishop of Canterbury, and to the rest of the episcopal bench, having previously submitted them to Marquis Wellesley. The reply which he received from the late Bishop Porteus confirmed and encouraged him in his determination to bring that important subject fully before the public.

It was in the course of this year also, that Mr. Buchanan obtained the sanction of the Governor-General to the building of a new church in Calcutta. But the extensive plans of Lord Wellesley respecting the college, and other political concerns, prevented the execution of this design.

A few circumstances which occur in Mr. Buchanan's letters to Mr. Grant and Major Sandys towards the end of this year, may here be added. To the former he thus wrote in October and December:

"The venerable Obeck had not been dead many weeks, when his old friend Mr. Gerické, that valuable man, took his departure also. The church at Madras is in great affliction; for there is no one to fill his place. Letters have come to us for help. But we can give none. I do not know what acquaintance you may have with that mission; but attention to it appears to me highly important in the present state of things. If there were any missionary like-minded with Gerické within your reach, we could from Calcutta add something to his salary, if that be desirable."

To Major Sandys, Mr. Buchanan wrote as follows:

"We are passing through an eventful season in India. The order of the day is victory, and the Mahratta power is at length destroyed. The whole peninsula is now under British dominion. I have taken advantage of the crisis, in endeavouring to excite our Universities at home to plead the cause of eastern civilization.

"Mary improves in health daily. She has no sanguine wish to return to England; and it is a subject on which I never think. My health continually bids it, but nothing else. Providence will in due time unlock every difficulty, and make our purpose and duty clear.

"The young lady who came out with Mrs. B. in the Carmarthen appears to be dying of a consumption. If her strength permit, we mean to send her to sea in a few days. She will go first to Madras, where Lady Sinclair will receive her. She has a serious impression of religion, and is preparing for her great change.

"Mr. Brown lives generally at Serampore. He is well,

and begs his christian love to you, solicitous for your welfare amidst the trials to which you will be exposed.

"* * * * and I are on our usual footing. I certainly give him a great deal of trouble; but it is on important subjects. I suffer sometimes a repulse; then I wait for a favourable moment, anxious, during the little time that may be spared, to do all I can for the church of Christ in India; for that is the chief subject of my late endeavours."

The character of the audience usually assembling at the Presidency church has been already noticed. It has also been observed, that a few years previous to this period, the spirit of infidelity or of religious indifference was lamentably general in our eastern capital; and the infection still remained amongst some, who, from neglected education, or the influence of circumstances and habits, peculiarly unfriendly to christianity, were scarcely aware of the nature of religious sentiment and feeling. Amongst other subjects, therefore, of discourse, more directly suited to those who acknowledged the great truths of the gospel, Mr. Buchanan occasionally addressed those who doubted of its divine authority; and the perspicuity and force, with which he stated its various evidences, tended materially to extend and confirm the conviction of its truth. The importance of such discourses is much heightened from the consideration of their probable effect on the minds of the numerous young men, who as yet continued to be assembled from the three Presidencies at the college of Fort William; and who might be justly expected to carry with them to their different stations throughout India, those sound principles of christian faith and practice which they had heard thus ably and eloquently inculcated. The memorial of the year 1803 cannot, perhaps, be better closed than by a short extract or two from a sermon of this class preached by Mr. Buchanan on Christmas-day, from the confession of the Samaritans, John iv. 42. "Now we believe—and know that this is indeed the Christ, the Saviour of the world."

The discourse opens with a brief review of the origin and prevalence of christianity by the preaching of a few unlearned men in a remote age, at a period when learning and science flourished in the surrounding nations; and closing with the following striking observation:

"Long before that period, a prophecy had gone forth concerning the advent of the Messiah, in these remarkable words: 'The nation and kingdom that will not serve thee shall perish.' (Isaiah lx. 12.) If we look back to the history of the world, we shall accordingly find that every nation which embraced the christian religion, emerged from ignorance and obscurity to knowledge and light. If we consider the condition of mankind at this day, we shall perceive that those nations alone which have been educated in the christian religion, are in a state of civilization. .Every other nation is in comparative ignorance and barbarism.

"Of those who do not support christianity," continued Mr. Buchanan, "there are some men of talents and learning, who allege that they do not believe it, and a great number, possessing neither talents nor learning, would sanction a denial of it by their authority. We shall, however, suppose that such persons would be accounted good members of society; and, supposing this, we shall make some concessions in the way of argument, in order to lead to our conclusion as to their public conduct."

These concessions, which are as follow, form, in fact, an indirect but powerful series of proofs in favour of the divine origin of christianity:

"We shall suppose for a moment that the evidence for the truth of our religion is not sufficient for human conviction. We shall even suppose, a miracle, (as it will appear to some,) that the principles which exalt our nation in the present zenith of human refinement, were taught, not divinely, but by a few fishermen of Judea, who imposed them forcibly on mankind, and bade every nation bow to their authority; who, being illiterate themselves, subjugated the learning, good sense, and piety of future ages to the excellence of *their* precepts, and the sublime purity of *their* conceptions.

"We shall even imagine that the system of *prophecy* from the earliest ages is not divine, and that the prophecies were not fulfilled by miracle, but by *chance:* that the Jewish church, with all its predictions, types, and figures of things to come; and the Christian church, with all its fulfilments of these predictions, types, and figures, are but the result of uncertain tradition; that the scriptures themselves, not accounted a work either of learning or science, were yet handed down to us with a purity of which no classical record can boast, and whose antiquity and durability appear to the minds of some like that of the works of nature, which God hath created incorruptible; we shall farther suppose that some other book has been found, or may be found in some future age, bearing some analogy to *this*. All these, and a thousand other collateral evidences, we shall suppose not to be sufficient for conviction; that although our religion has urged its way through every age, and hath acquired, in these latter days, the sanction of the highest degree of learning and science which the world has ever known, yet that its evidence is not sufficient for certain men of superior minds, or of purer hearts.

"We shall now inquire, what rule of conduct respecting this religion such an one ought to observe at this day; one who would be accounted a man of humane and honourable principles, a friend of his country and of social order.

"In the first place, his country *professes* the christian religion. This of itself might inspire him with some delicacy in speaking disrespectfully of it. Again, we suppose that our country has been *defending* this religion for many years past; that she has been accounted its representative amidst the desolation of other christian nations, and that she is now again called forth in that character.

"Now, supposing this to be true, would it be proper to weaken this sentiment? Would it add any thing to the spirit and energy of the nation, to believe that its religion is nothing concerned in the event?

"But leaving the consideration of the *religion* of our country, let us advert to its *principles*. The moral principles of our country, whencesoever they have been derived, whether from an improved barbarism, from the relics of learned antiquity, or from a yet higher source, are at this time called *christian* principles. Their excellence is acknowledged by the friends and foes of the christian religion. In the degree in which they are practised, they promote the happiness of individuals, of communities, and of nations; and the general practice of them would keep the world in peace.

"It will be granted, that if our country be defending any thing, she is defending her principles. Even those who deny her religion will consider the defence of her principles a sacred duty. Now let such persons consider how they are fulfilling this duty. 'The principles of our country,' you will say, 'are good; but the religion which taught them is not true, at least we are inclined to think so; and, therefore, we may be permitted to express our doubt on the subject, and to indulge in occasional levity at the expense of the belief of others.'

"Now, in the first place, do you think that it is a likely way to preserve these principles in the minds of men to insinuate that they are not *divine?* Do you think it a likely way to preserve moral principles in your children, or in young persons under your direction, to take away all religious sanction?

"But you will say, that you mean not to do any harm; that your casual reflections on religion cannot be supposed to have much effect, and that you only indulge your passion for displaying your talents in your own circle, by asserting what you think liberal sentiments among young people, and by retailing the wit of learned infidels.

"But in doing this, do you assume the character of a good member of society? If all men were such as you are, our constitution and liberties would not survive another day. They have not hitherto been maintained by such defenders! It was not this levity of principle which conducted us through our late dangers, and gave vigour to our fleets and armies in the awful contest. Nor is it this principle which at this eventful moment animates our nation with such a holy enthusiasm for the preservation of their country, their laws, and their religion.

"If it please the providence of God that success should still attend us in the deliverance of our country, you will yet have to reflect that *you* have not contributed to its preservation; that you have neither supported its religion nor its principles; but will have to fear that, in the degree of your influence, you have injured both. You will have to reflect that you have not done *your* part as a good member of society; that however obscure your situation, or small your ability, you have put no mite into the treasury of the public good; that, on the contrary, you have lived a mere inactive pensioner on the bounty of your country, which grants you the blessing of a tranquil life, and grants you also that liberty of opinion which is abused to her injury."

The preceding passages form a brief abstract only of the train of reasoning pursued in this able sermon. Towards the close of it Mr. Buchanan observes, that great as is the benefit of the christian religion to nations, and irresistible as are the arguments for maintaining it for the good of society, its importance to the happiness of the individual is still greater.

"Had not its eternal sanctions awakened the consciences of men in every age, and its spirit sunk deep into their hearts, its *national* importance would never have preserved it, and the solemnity of this day would not now have been observed. But there are those now who pronounce the confession of the text with the same confidence and in the same spirit with which it was pronounced at first. 'We believe and know that this is indeed the Christ, the Saviour of the world.'"

After referring to the practical illustrations of this assertion which had been lately afforded amongst themselves,* Mr. Buchanan thus conludes:

---

* Probably alluding to the deaths of Mr. Obeck and Mr. Edmonstone.

"'That which was prophesied of the christian religion has been fulfilled in every age; 'that it should be in a state of conflict, but that the spirit of some would preserve it unto the end of the world.' 'Ye,' saith the Lord, 'are the salt of the earth.' Ye are they, who, having an impression of the eternal truth of my gospel, will maintain its doctrines and principles for your own salvation, and for the advantage of an evil world.

"'But if at any time this salt shall lose its savour;' if at any time your profession of religion should degenerate into a mere form, it then only serveth to be cast out, and 'to be trodden under the feet of men;' under the feet of your present enemies, and by a vain philosophy.

"We, my brethren, may be accounted the representatives of the christian religion in this remote country. A duty is imposed on us from which some societies may think themselves exonerated. And however little many of us may think of this duty, it is one which *must* and *will* be performed by some, zealously and faithfully, as a duty to God and to their country.

"And living in the observance of this duty, they will wait the event of that awful commotion which begins again to agitate the world, in humble acquiescence in the righteous dispensations of God, not trusting to the merits of our nation for deliverance, but firmly believing that, since it hath pleased his providence to honour us, in time past, with the defence of his religion, it is his will that it should yet be established by our means."

It is a gratifying reflection, that the high duty and privilege of maintaining inviolate the purity of the christian religion has been faithfully fulfilled by the British empire at large; and that we have emerged out of that great conflict which had then lately recommenced, with augmented strength and glory, a monument of the truth of the divine declaration, that the steady profession, and the undaunted defence of truth and righteousness, are the surest means of protecting and exalting a nation.

It may not be improper to add, that, at the close of the preceding sermon, a collection was made to the amount of 6,000 rupees, a sum highly creditable to the liberality of the congregation, for the benefit of "the Calcutta Charitable Fund," instituted in the year 1800, by the Rev. David Brown, under the auspices of Marquis Wellesley, for the relief of distressed Europeans, Mohammedans, and Hindoos, of which Mr. Buchanan some years afterwards observed, that it had been a fountain of mercy to thousands.

CHAPTER III.

The college of Fort William, according to the regulation of Lord Wellesley, in obedience to the decision of the Court of Directors, was to close on the 31st of December, 1803. It was, however, a very gratifying circumstance to the friends of that institution, that on the 3d of January, 1804, a despatch announced to the Governor General the determination of the court, that the college should for the present continue on its original footing. The business and examinations of the students accordingly proceeded in their usual train, or rather, with additional spirit.

"An example of idleness," says Mr. Buchanan in a letter to a friend, "is a rare thing. The appointments to the service continue to be made according to the college list, that is, according to merit."

* The annual disputations in the oriental languages were held this year on the 20th of September, in the presence of the Governor General, accompanied, as usual, by the principal officers of the Presidency, with the addition, on this occasion, of Soliman Aga, the envoy from Bagdad. The subjects of the disputations were, "the Shanscrit, as the parent language of India," in Hindostanee; "the figurative sense of the poems of Hafiz," in Persian; "the utility of translations of the best works extant in the Shanscrit into the popular languages of India," in Bengalee; and, in Arabic, "the importance of the Arabic to a grammatical knowledge of the Persian language." A declamation was afterwards pronounced in Shanscrit, for the first time, by one of the students, which was followed by a speech in the same language by the Rev. Mr. Carey,† the Moderator and Professor.

Prizes were at the same time awarded for the best English essays on "the utility of the Persian language in India," on "the progress of civilization in India under the British government," and on "the decline and fall of the Mohammedan empire in India." Honorary rewards of books were also adjudg-

---

* See "The College of Fort William," page 124.

† For a translation of this eloquent and interesting speech, see "The College of Fort William," page 168.

ed to the best proficients in the Greek and Latin classics, and in the French language.

The several compositions of this year were afterwards published in the third volume of the "Primitiæ Orientales."

In the speech with which Marquis Wellesley closed the proceedings of the day, his lordship declared, that in each successive year the standard of comparative merit had been progressive in the highest classes of the college, and expressed his cordial satisfaction at the proficiency and good conduct of the students.

"The observance of all the statutes," said his lordship, "is equally essential to the interests and honour of the students; nor is their duty confined merely to the diligent pursuit of the prescribed course of study. The intention of the statutes is not only to provide instruction in the oriental languages, and in the several branches of study immediately connected with the performance of official functions, but to prescribe habits of regularity and good order. My principal purpose in founding this institution was, to secure the junior servants of the Company from all undue influence in the discharge of their official functions, and to introduce them into the public service in perfect freedom and independence, exempt from every restraint, excepting the high and sacred obligations of their civil, moral, and religious duty."

In the course of the year 1804, several circumstances occurred, connected with Mr. Buchanan and the college of Fort William, which will be best introduced by a few extracts from his letters. He thus wrote to Major Sandys in the month of February:

"We are much the same in church, state, and college, as when you left us; only in respect to myself my various abours have increased, are increasing, and, I fear, will not be diminished.

"I am literally left alone in many matters of a public nature, particularly in a battle now fighting, (the worst I have yet had,) with Mussulman and Hindoo prejudices against translations of the Scriptures. Their clamour has assailed the government. Lord Wellesley and Mr. Barlow are neuter; but the old civil servants fan the flame. A folio volume would not detail the particulars; but I trust you will soon hear of the good effect. In the mean time, I am growing infirm in body, and long for more holy employ than that of hewing wood only for our future sanctuary in India. I know that what is doing is useful; but spiritual comforts do not accompany the occupation, in the degree I desire, and look forward to, when I have peace from public conflict."

The particular circumstance to which Mr. Buchanan probably referred in the preceding extract was a memorial which about this time was addressed to the Governor General, in consequence of the following subject having been proposed, among others, for discussion by the students of the college, at the annual disputations which have been just mentioned; viz. "The advantage which the natives of this country might derive from translations, in the vernacular tongues, of the books containing the principles of their respective religions, and those of the christian faith."

There certainly appears to be no ground of offence to the natives of India in the foregoing thesis. A christian might rather have objected to it as placing his most holy faith too much upon a level with heathen and Mohammedan error. A memorial was, however, addressed to the Governor General on the part of the Mohammedan moonshees, and of a number of the Mussulman inhabitants of Calcutta, remonstrating against this supposed infringement of the toleration afforded to them by the British government. In reply, Marquis Wellesley signified to the memorialists, that although he perceived no principle of an objectionable tendency in the foregoing thesis, yet, with a view to prevent all apprehension on the part of the natives, he had prohibited the intended disputation upon that subject.

Some years afterwards this incident was appealed to on the part of the Bengal government in support of some measures tending to discourage or suppress the exertions of missionaries. Upon which occasion Mr. Buchanan observed,* that the memorial probably originated in the suggestions of some individuals at that time connected with the government and the college, who appeared to entertain a degree of morbid tenderness for the religious feelings of the natives.

These gentlemen had from the beginning been hostile to a most important work which had been carrying on in the college; viz. the translation of the Scriptures into the oriental languages by natives and Europeans. So great was their jealousy on this subject, that there existed a kind of compromise between the friends and the opponents of this salutary measure, that if the Bible were printed for christians, the Koran should be printed for Mohammedans. It is to this honourable contest that Mr. Buchanan refers in the letter last quoted; and, happily for the interests of christianity, he was decidedly successful. So early

* See his "Apology for promoting Christianity in India," p. 102.

as the year after the present period of these memoirs, a commencement had been made in the translation of the Scriptures into several languages.* The first versions of any of the gospels in Persian and Hindostanee, which were printed in India, issued from the press of the college of Fort William. The Persian was superintended by Lieut. Colonel Colebrooke, and the Hindostanee by William Hunter, Esq. The gospels were translated into the Malay by Thomas Jarrett, Esq., of the civil service.

Of these and other translations of the Scriptures then projected and undertaken, only a very inconsiderable part was executed at the public expense. The sole charge incurred by the college in the department of sacred translation, was for the gospel of St. Matthew in Persian and Hindostanee; with this exception, the extensive Biblical works successively announced from this institution were carried on at the private expense of those members of the college, amongst whom the Provost and Vice-Provost held the first rank, and others who deemed it to be of the highest importance to promote the diffusion of sacred literature in Asia.

A second occurrence in this year marked an improved state of moral feeling in Calcutta, and particularly illustrates the salutary influence of the college of Fort William. It is thus mentioned by Mr. Buchanan in a letter to Major Sandys, in the month of August:

"The institution of a civil fund for widows and orphans agitates this service at present. The old gentlemen wish to include black illegitimate children. The junior servants, who are now or have been in college, almost with one voice exclaim against a measure which they conceive would have a tendency to sanction vice, and to countenance an illicit connexion with native women. The question is now referred to the vote of every individual in the service. In the meantime, one of my old scholars has written a letter to the service; in which he complains of their violation of the divine law, and requests them to revert to the principles of honour and chastity. Mr. M. is in the Governor General's office, and is supported by the young school, by all the college, by the Governor General, and by all the friends of revealed religion. Caricatura prints, exhibiting the mover of the subject, with a black child in his arms, pleading its cause in full assembly, while a black dye behind urges him forward; and various other devices mark the popular question, and promise to brand the immoral practice.

* See the "Christian Researches," introduct. p. 2.

It is said, that the affliction and shame of the old service are extreme; and that they execrate the college and its fruits, and hope that the Court of Directors will now see, how unfriendly it is to ancient institutions!

"What the result as to the fund will be, I know not."

This, however, Mr. Buchanan stated to the public in the following year, in some remarks on the college of Fort William.* "The contest," he observes, "was maintained for a considerable time, by printed correspondence, and the fund was at length established *without* the opprobrious clause. But a few years ago," adds Mr. Buchanan, "any man who should have ventured to resist such a measure on the ground of religious or moral propriety, would have become the jest of the whole service. He must be an entire stranger to what is passing in Bengal, who does not perceive that the college of Fort William is sensibly promoting an amelioration of the European character, as well as the civilization of India."

The activity of Mr. Buchanan's mind respecting objects which he deemed important to the interests of morals and religion, may be collected, not only from the preceding circumstances, but from various hints in his correspondence and diary.

Thus at the close of the letter from which the foregoing extract was made, he says, "I have always some plans relating to church or college in his excellency's hands; and generally in arrear. But when he does take them up, it is with the proper attention." A memorandum also occurs in the same year, in which Mr. Buchanan notices a consultation which he had lately held with Sir George Barlow on a public thanksgiving, probably on account of the victorious termination of the Mahratta war, on the subject of a cenotaph for those who had fallen in battle, and respecting an order for the better observance of the Sunday.

Amidst his various labours, however, the domestic trial, with which Mr. Buchanan had been already exercised, was renewed by the reappearance, early in the summer of this year, of alarming consumptive symptoms in Mrs. Buchanan. In the course of the autumn she became so ill, that her life was for a short time despaired of; and on her partial recovery, being strongly urged to proceed a second time to Europe, she at length very reluctantly consented.

Preparations were accordingly made for this purpose, and in October Mr. Buchanan briefly mentions in his diary, that he had been on board the Lady Jane Dundas to look at Mrs.

---

* See "The College of Fort William," p. 163.

B.'s cabin. She did not, however, leave Calcutta till the 22d of January following, when Mr. Buchanan accompanied her and her youngest daughter to the ship at Kedgeree; and on the 25th the fleet sailed for Madras, leaving him once more to return to a solitary home, full of tender but melancholy musings; hoping almost "against hope," for some favourable effect from her voyage, but rather endeavouring to prepare his mind for a contrary result. His memoranda testify the warmth of affection with which he again followed Mrs. Buchanan, by frequent notices of the letters which he wrote to her weekly, and sometimes almost daily, and of which it is much to be regretted that not a vestige remains.

It was at the anxious period, which immediately preceded her departure from India, that Mr. Buchanan resolved to employ a part of the very limited leisure which his ministerial and collegiate duties allowed, to prepare a work which had long been the subject of his thoughts, and the importance of which is now universally acknowledged. This was what he afterwards entitled, "A Memoir of the Expediency of an Ecclesiastical Establishment for British India."

During the century in which they had been gradually acquiring their oriental empire, the East India Company, intent on the pursuits of commerce and ambition, and contending frequently not merely for aggrandizement but for existence, were but little at leisure to attend to the moral and religious claims even of their own servants; much less to consider those of their native subjects to any thing beyond general protection, and the administration of justice; and even to these, till of late years, but partially and imperfectly. Some provision, but of a very scanty and inadequate kind, was made for the supply of the spiritual wants of their European servants, by the establishment of a few chaplains at each of the three Presidencies; the number of whom was gradually increased as the Company progressively extended its Indian territories.

To those who from principles of infidelity, whether speculative or practical, or from the absorbing influence of worldly pursuits, were disposed to treat religion as a subordinate concern, to consider the most distant and transient attention to it as amply fulfilling its demands, and who, in the acquisition or consolidation of power amidst the half-civilized votaries of idolatry and imposture, were tremblingly alive to the danger of offending or alarming them, by the too prominent profession of a purer faith, it may be easily imagined, that the ecclesiastical appointments in India were deemed sufficiently numerous and effective. But to the eye of christian observation, and even of enlightened policy, they had long been considered unworthy of our public profession as a Protestant and religious empire, inadequate to the necessities of the European population, and inconsistent both with our interest and our duty as the almost undisputed sovereigns of India. The immense distance which separates Great Britain and Hindostan, the comparatively small number of those who are either acquainted with Indian affairs, or interested in their management, the peculiar nature of their direction by a commercial company, and the lateness of the period at which they assumed the aspect of political and territorial importance, all tended to involve the religious consideration of India in obscurity and neglect. The providence of God had, however, within the space of a few years, not only given to Great Britain a decided predominance over every other European nation, but by the extinction of the Mohammedan, and the subjection of the Mahratta power, had in fact bestowed upon us the empire of India. An enlarged attention to the religious welfare of an augmented body of European servants, and to the political and moral improvement of fifty millions of native subjects, was one of the necessary consequences of our Indian sovereignty—a result, however, which those whose views are principally directed to political aggrandizement, would, for the reasons already assigned, be naturally slow to perceive and acknowledge; but which the christian patriot and philosopher would be eager to anticipate and assert. It cannot, therefore, be a matter of surprise, that a subject so important in itself, and so intimately connected with his own profession and local situation, should have early occurred to the mind of such a diligent and wakeful observer as Mr. Buchanan. The design of his "Memoir" was indeed, as he afterwards declared, first suggested to him by the late excellent Bishop Porteus;* who had, he said, "attentively surveyed the state of our dominions in Asia," and had expressed his "conviction of the indispensable necessity of an ecclesiastical establishment for our Indian empire." He was encouraged also, as he added, "by subsequent communications with Marquis Wellesley, to endeavour to lead the attention of the nation to this subject." The manuscript of this work was transmitted to England in the spring, and published in the autumn of the year 1805.

Before we proceed, however, with the consideration of his "Memoir," it will be proper to recur to the prizes proposed

* See his "Christian Researches," p. 273, and the first Dedication of his "Memoir," p. iv.

by Mr. Buchanan to the Universities, and some of the public schools, of the United Kingdom. They were accepted in the summer of 1804, by the several bodies to which they were offered, with the exception of the University of Oxford; by which they were declined, on the ground of certain objections in point of form. The prize compositions were directed to be delivered to the respective judges towards the end of the year; and early in the following spring, the prizes were awarded to the successful candidates. Of the compositions which were thus honoured, the greater number were afterwards published, as well as a few others, which had proved unsuccessful. In the University of Cambridge, the prize for the Greek ode was adjudged to Mr. Pryme, of Trinity college; and at Eton to Mr. Rennell, afterwards Fellow of King's college. At the same distinguished school Mr. Richards obtained the prize for the best Latin verses on the college of Fort William.

In Scotland, three Latin poems were also published, by Mr. Mac Arthur, Mr. Adamson, and Dr. Brown, of which the two former were thought worthy of the prize by the Universities of Glasgow and Aberdeen. The composition, however, which reflected the highest honour on its author, and on the occasion which called it forth, was the English poem on "the restoration of learning in the East," by Charles Grant, Esq., then Fellow of Magdalen college, Cambridge. The poetical talents, the classical and oriental learning, the elevated sentiments, and the rich and varied command of language, displayed in this prize composition, attracted general admiration; and tended materially to promote the design which the proposer of the subject had in view, by directing the public attention to the revival of learning on the banks of the Ganges, and by exciting it to the duty and the privilege of improving the condition of the degraded natives of Hindostan, and of spreading throughout our oriental empire the blessings of literature and religion. A second poem on this subject was published at the request of the examiners, by the Rev. Francis Wrangham, of Trinity College.

Essays on "the best means of civilizing the subjects of the British empire in India, and of diffusing the light of the christian religion throughout the eastern world," were published by the Rev. William Cockburn, Fellow of St. John's College, and Christian Advocate in the University of Cambridge, to whom the prize was assigned; by Mr. Wrangham, who with laudable zeal engaged in the prose as well as in the poetical competition; by Dr. Tennant, then lately returned as a military chaplain from India; and by Messrs. Mitchell and Bryce, to whom the prize was respectively adjudged by the Universities of Edinburgh, Glasgow, and Aberdeen.

These essays were, with one exception, the production of studious and speculative men, whose attention was probably first directed to the subject by Mr. Buchanan's proposal to the learned bodies of which they were members. Whilst it could scarcely, therefore, be expected that they should suggest any detailed practical arrangements for the civilization and instruction of the natives of Hindostan, they exhibited considerable historical and political research, together with enlightened and benevolent views of the duty of Great Britain to promote the important objects submitted to their discussion, and concurred in recommending the adoption of certain direct means for diffusing the blessings of christianity in India. They possessed the additional merit of contributing to bring before the public inquiries tending to ameliorate the moral and religious condition of our oriental empire.

The utility of the labours of missionaries, and the establishment of schools, was recognized by several of the writers last mentioned. The consideration, however, of an ecclesiastical establishment was reserved for Mr. Buchanan himself; whose "Memoir" upon that subject was intended to point out the expediency of such a measure, "both as the means of perpetuating the christian religion among our own countrymen, and as a foundation for the ultimate civilization of the natives."

After the extensive circulation of the work itself, and the ample discussion of its subject, which we have witnessed; more especially after the ecclesiastical appointments which have lately taken place, and which must be attributed chiefly to the original proposal and the persevering efforts of Mr. Buchanan, it will not now be necessary to enter much at large into the statements and reasonings of his able and interesting memoir. It will be sufficient to observe, that the first part of it exhibited the very inadequate state of the clerical establishment in India at that period, for the great purposes of the instruction and religious communion of our resident countrymen. Upon this point, the facts and arguments adduced by Mr. Buchanan were conclusive as to the obligation and the policy of a more suitable provision for the due performance of the ordinances of the established religion.

In the second part, he supposed such an establishment to have been given to India, and proceeded to consider the result with respect to the civilization of the natives. After describing in just and forcible terms their actual condition—the pride, immorality, and bigotry of the Mohammedans, and the vices, enormities, and barbarities of Hindoo superstition and idolatry, Mr. Buchanan discussed at some length the practicability and the policy of attempting to civilize and improve them. In this part of his work he exhibited the character of the Hindoos in a different point of view from that in which they had been generally regarded. He asserted that their apathy is extreme, and that no efforts to instruct them, except such as partook of a compulsory nature, ought to be considered as attended with danger to the British government; that their prejudices are daily weakening in every European settlement; that they are a divided people; that they are less tenacious of opinion than of custom; and that to disseminate new principles among them is by no means so difficult as it is frequently represented.

In support of the *policy* of the measure which he proposed, the arguments of Mr. Buchanan were irresistible. The single consideration, that the attachment of a people separated from their governors by a variety of moral and physical distinctions, without any mutual bond of union, must necessarily be precarious, and that such a connecting link can only be afforded by means of our religion, is a sufficient proof of this point. In obviating objections founded on the supposed impolicy of civilizing our Indian subjects, Mr. Buchanan, however, advanced to higher ground.

"The progressive civilization of India," he observes, "will never injure the interests of the East India Company. But shall a christian people, acknowledging a Providence in the rise and fall of empire, regulate the policy of future times, and neglect a present duty, a solemn and imperious duty, exacted by their religion, by their public principles, and by the opinion of the christian nations around them? Or can it be gratifying to the English nation to reflect that they receive the riches of the East on the terms of chartering immoral superstition?" Memoir, p. 40.

The appeal was unanswerable, and produced a corresponding impression upon the public mind.

The third part of Mr. Buchanan's memoir strongly confirmed his arguments as to the practicability of his proposed plan, by a view of the progress already made in civilizing the nations of Hindostan. Many interesting facts were here stated relative to the existence of christianity in India from the earliest ages, and particularly respecting the native christians on the coast of Malabar, who, notwithstanding the accounts given of them by a few learned men, were now, for the first time, prominently introduced to the knowledge of the English public. The labours of the Danish missionaries, Ziegenbalg and Grundler, and of the apostolic Swartz, were also commemorated; and the laudable and truly christian addresses of King George the First and Archbishop Wake to the former excellent men, were exhibited as models of imitation to political and ecclesiastical governors of the present day.

The memoir itself was with great propriety, and in a strain of dignified and impressive eloquence, dedicated to his Grace, the late Archbishop of Canterbury, having been transmitted to this country before the death of that most reverend prelate was known in Bengal.

An appendix to the memoir contained a variety of important information on the superstitions of the Hindoos, tending powerfully to correct the erroneous opinion so commonly entertained of them at this period, as a mild, humane, and inoffensive race.

In advocating the expediency of an ecclesiastical establishment as a foundation for the ultimate civilization of the natives of India, Mr. Buchanan did not state at length the reasonings upon which he grounded his expectation of that important result.

"No immediate effect," he observes, "is to be expected from it in the way of revolution; but it may be demonstrated by a deduction from facts, that the most beneficial consequences will follow in the way of ordinary effect from an adequate cause." P. 21.

A detailed view of the intermediate steps between the cause and its supposed consequences, would, doubtless, as it was afterwards suggested, have been a desirable addition to the arguments of his memoir. Mr. Buchanan, however, probably thought, that the concurring testimony of history as to the connexion between the profession and establishment of a religion by the governing power in a state, and its progressive influence among the people, was sufficiently known and acknowledged to authorize the general assertion just quoted; and it was not, perhaps, absolutely necessary to the conclusiveness of his proofs as to the expediency of an ecclesiastical establishment in India for both the important purposes stated in his memoir.

Such was briefly the nature of the novel and interesting work which Mr. Buchanan transmitted to England in the year 1805, for publication. It was calculated, from the peculiar subjects of which it treated, to excite general attention, and to provoke both discussion and animadversion. The consideration, however, of its reception and effect, must be suspended, while we revert to the intermediate course of this narrative.

It had long been an object of anxiety to the superintendents of the college of Fort William to obtain a version of the scriptures in the Chinese language. After many fruitless inquiries, they in this year succeeded in procuring the assistance of Mr. Lassar, a native of China, and an Arminian christian, whose name is now well known as a learned professor of that language. Mr. Lassar arrived at Calcutta in a commercial capacity, and having met with some difficulties, he became known to Mr. Buchanan, who, appreciating his talents, generously liberated him from his embarrassments, and engaged him at a stipend of three hundred rupees per month to devote himself to the translation of the scriptures, and to the instruction of a Chinese class, formed of one of the elder, and three of the junior members of the missionary establishment at Serampore. The expected reduction of the college rendering it inexpedient that Mr. Lassar should be attached to that institution, this stipend was afforded for about three years at the sole expense of Mr. Buchanan. To his liberality, therefore,* must be chiefly ascribed the progress which has been made in that quarter towards supplying the vast empire of China with a translation of the sacred volume into its own extraordinary language.

The name of Mr. Buchanan appears in the year 1805 in the list of members of the Asiatic Society. He had probably been elected previously to that period, and if he did not contribute to the curious and valuable "researches" of that learned body, it was not so much from any want of interest in their labours, as from the pressure of his various employments, which allowed him only to devote his leisure to inquiries which were exclusively of an ecclesiastical and religious nature.

Two letters to one of his friends in this year contain proofs of the paternal anxiety with which Mr. Buchanan watched over the progress of the students of Fort William. The weekly reports of the different professors as to the proficiency of their classes were delivered to him every Saturday. Their representations, whether favourable or otherwise, were by him communicated to the college council, and ultimately, through them, or himself, as their organ, to the Governor General. Mr. Buchanan mentions several instances of the beneficial effects of this watchful superintendence in stimulating even those who would otherwise have remained incorrigibly indolent to diligence and exertion. In a few cases the discipline which had been originally announced was firmly and impartially enforced; sometimes, but very rarely, by absolute removal from college, and the consequent loss of promotion in the service;

* See the "Christian Researches," p. 11; Christian Observer for 1809, p. 601; and Dr. Marshman's Clavis Sinica, Preface, p. ii.

at others, by the kind intervention of Mr. Buchanan with the Governor General, in cases which admitted of apology or excuse, by permission to retire, and an appointment which sufficiently marked the circumstances of inferiority in which the neglect of college duties had issued. Upon one such occasion Mr. Buchanan thus writes:

"It would have given me great satisfaction to have been able to send you such gratifying letters as I have often written, and am now writing, to various families in England, Scotland, and Ireland, respecting their sons who have passed a long period in diligent study, acquired honours, and then lucrative appointments. But it has been ordered otherwise. Perhaps all will be well. Poor . . . ." (speaking of a student who had lately died,) "had certainly been cherishing solemn and serious purposes the fortnight before his death; and he no doubt died the child of many prayers . . . . may yet prove himself to be the child of religious parents. Their case, however, speaks loudly to us who are fathers, teaching us to walk with humility and fear before God, committing our children to him in prayer and tears, and with much wrestling for a blessing on them when they depart from us. The world says, 'He who hath children, hath given pledges to fortune.' The christian knows how this is to be translated."

Upon the general subject of religion in Calcutta, Mr. Buchanan gave the following encouraging accounts to one of his correspondents:

"We have had divine service at the mission church, lately, for the settlement. The punkas make it very pleasant; but it was found to be too small for the auditory, many families going away every Sunday morning, seats being in general occupied an hour before service.

"You will be glad to hear that ——— still perseveres in listening to sacred things, as do many other young political servants whom you do not know. The demand for religious books, particularly of evangelical principles, has been very great these two last years. Messrs. Dring told me they had sold an investment of fifty 8vo. Bibles in the course of three months."

In a subsequent letter Mr. Buchanan thus continued his account of ecclesiastical affairs, after prefacing it with an act of kindness to a clerical brother:

"The bearer of this, the Rev. Mr. ———, requests me to state to you his hope that you will peruse his memorial referred by this government to the Court of Directors. He has been twenty-five years a chaplain here, and is now old and infirm. I assured him that every justice would be done by you in relation to his memorial, and that you would direct such an investigation of the circumstances as might be proper.

"On account of the increase of our congregations we are about to have two morning services on Sunday, the first at seven o'clock, in the old church, and the second at the usual hour of ten, at the new. This is very agreeable to a great majority. Only Mr. Brown and myself will officiate at the old church. We shall, of course, (at least I shall,) continue to officiate as usual at the new."

About this time Mr. Buchanan thus mentions to a friend and relative the mixed nature of the congregations in Calcutta:

"We have some of all sects in our congregations; Presbyterians, Independants, Baptists, Armenians, Greeks, and Nestorians. And some of these are part of my audience at the English church. But a *name* or a *sect* is never mentioned from the pulpit; and thus the word preached becomes profitable to all.

"Even among the writers in the college there are Presbyterians, Independants, and Methodists. Their chief difficulty at first is from the ceremonies of the English church, which few of them ever witnessed till they came here.

"I must lie down awhile and dictate to an amanuensis, for it is very hot. The thermometer is to-day near 110.

"· · · · · · used in former life to prosecute all he took in hand with enthusiasm. He thought nothing done right, if not done with all his might. So, perhaps, it is in his religion and private life. He is actuated by a pure, genuine enthusiasm. Eternity, he says, has opened to his view, and he would save the souls of men. We shall judge him by *his works* a few years hence. * * * *

"When the Hindoo had laid down the pen, and I had got up from my couch, he asked me what kind of a thing a *Methodist* was. I told him that it was a christian man in the little Isle of Britain, who prayed too much, and was 'righteous overmuch.' The lad stared, and said, How can that be? So it is, said I; behold that man, (pointing to ——'s picture,) who is reputed a Methodist in England, and is a subject of ridicule, on account of his excessive godliness. 'Among us,' replied the Hindoo, 'he would thereby acquire the more reverence and veneration.'"

At the close of one of the preceding letters, Mr. Buchanan expressed his fears as to the result of some public measures, concerning which he had formed sanguine expectations; but not long afterwards he wrote in a more animated, and, as before, in a prophetic strain.

"The war seems to be now near its close; and it will probably be followed by a long reign of peace in India. Having obtained complete dominion over it, we shall then bless it with the Word of Life; and Christ will be once more glorified in the East."

* The fourth annual disputations in the oriental languages in the college of Fort William were held this year in the month of February, in the presence of Marquis Wellesley and the superior members of the government. Upon this occasion it was maintained in Hindostanee, that "the oriental languages are studied with more advantage in India than in England, and with greater advantage to the public service." And in Persian, that that language is of more utility in the general administration of the British empire in India than the Hindostanee." In addition to declamations in Bengalee and Arabic, one was pronounced for the first time in the Mahratta language. In the speech which Lord Wellesley delivered after the distribution of the prizes and honorary rewards, his lordship observed, that the general zeal, industry, and spirit of study in the college had not declined, notwithstanding the contraction of the sphere of emulation and competition by the separation which had now taken place of the gentlemen of the establishments of Fort St. George and Bombay.

"Since the last meeting," continued his lordship, "the promotion of oriental knowledge in the British service in India has proceeded with increased success, by the progress of the studies and labours of the gentlemen of this college.

"The attention also of the officers and students of the college appears to have been successfully directed to those important objects of discipline, regularity, and good order, which formed an essential part of my recent admonitions from this place.

"The most eminent and brilliant success in the highest objects of study, will prove an inadequate qualification for the service of the Company, and of our country in India, if the just application of those happy attainments be not secured by a solid foundation of virtuous principles and correct conduct."

The remainder of this elaborate address is occupied with a strong recommendation of the study of the laws and regulations enacted by the Governor General in Council, introduced by "that great and worthy statesman," as Lord Wellesley

* See "The College of Fort William," p. 139.

justly styles him, "the Marquis Cornwallis, and improved and extended by succeeding governments, with the aid of the talents, knowledge, and virtues of Sir George Barlow," for the administration of the British territories subject to the Presidency of Bengal.

In consequence of the reduction in the extent of the college of Fort William, referred to in the preceding speech, the Governor General thought it expedient, by a minute in council, dated the 30th of April, 1805, to declare, that the duties at present committed to the Provost and Vice-Provost of the college might be performed in future by one officer only, with the designation of Provost. His excellency, however, deemed it to be proper, in consideration, as he was pleased to express it, "of the highly meritorious and useful services rendered to the college by the present Provost and Vice-Provost, Mr. Brown and Mr. Buchanan," to postpone the adoption of this arrangement until a vacancy should occur in one of those offices, provided that the Honourable the Court of Directors should be pleased to sanction the continuance of the allowances to the Provost and Vice-Provost until that time.

By the same minute, the Governor General rescinded that part of the original regulation of the college, by which pensions were to be eventually granted to certain of its officers, including the Provost and Vice-Provost, until the farther pleasure of the Court of Directors should have been received.

The extensive plan of the college of Fort William had never been approved by one distinguished correspondent of Mr. Buchanan, to whom he had been in the habit of communicating his own views upon that subject. This disapprobation, it appears, had been plainly expressed to him; in consequence of which, early in this year, he briefly notices it in the following reply:

"I have forborne saying any thing to you respecting the college, its founder, and his Indian policy, since my sentiments on these subjects can afford you no pleasure, as you observe in your last. It appears, in fact, that, since the commencement of the institution, I have been looking to one object, and you to another. In its dignity and extent, I perceived a radical revolution in the European character, the future civilization of India, and the foundation of an Ecclesiastical Establishment. And these results appear to be in a course of accomplishment.

"Good men in England are yet in ignorance respecting the purpose or effects of this institution. I mean therefore to publish shortly all the official papers relating to this college, with some account of its first four years. This will be acceptable to many, and useful to all. In the mean time I have written a short Memoir on an Ecclesiastical Establishment and Indian Civilization, a copy of which I have directed the bookseller to send to you."

The work thus announced by Mr. Buchanan respecting the college, was accordingly compiled in the spring of 1805, and transmitted, together with his Ecclesiastical Memoir, to this country, where it was published towards the end of the year. It was entitled, "The College of Fort William in Bengal." Mr. Buchanan did not affix his name to this publication; but it was well known to have proceeded from him, and he afterwards acknowledged it. A short prefatory note states, that the volume contains the official papers and the literary proceedings of the college during its first four years; and it was intended to form a record of the nature and operations of that institution during the period in which alone its founder could be considered as answerable for its success; an important reduction of its original plan having then taken place. It is to this volume that reference has been frequently made in the preceding pages, in noticing the rise and progress of the Eastern college. Besides the documents which have been already mentioned relative to the foundation, the statutes, and the defence of the college, and the disputations of the first four years, it contains the public examinations in regular series, with a list of the students who had entered on service, and a register of those who had obtained degrees of honour; a catalogue of works in the oriental languages and literature, published by members of the college since its commencement; the names and offices of those who had borne any part in the conduct of the institution; and some remarks by the Editor on the primary establishment of the college, and on the operation of its first four years.

In these remarks, Mr. Buchanan, after noticing the necessity and importance of such an institution, which had been proved by its triumph over the most powerful and systematic opposition, observes, that the publication of an hundred original volumes in the oriental languages and literature in the term of four years, is no inconsiderable proof of the flourishing state of the college, as a literary institution. That was, however, but one of its subordinate objects.

"The distinguished proficiency of the students in the oriental languages," says Mr. Buchanan, "is the proof we would propose of the efficiency, utility, and undoubted success of the college of Fort William. That proficiency is great, perhaps beyond example. Gentlemen who have been at different Universities in Europe, acknowledge that they never witnessed at any of them more numerous instances of ardent application to study, than at the college of Fort William. The mathematical vigils of Cambridge are perhaps more severe than ours; (though even with us there have been instances of sixteen hours a day reading, and a voyage to sea in consequence for recovery of health;) but the instances of close application at Cambridge are not so general as at Fort William, in proportion to the number of students."

The two chief excellencies of this institution upon which Mr. Buchanan insists in his remarks, are, that it afforded to young men the opportunity of completing the usual course of an English education, as well as of learning the oriental languages; and that it gave to all the civil servants in India equal advantages of instruction, and of consequent promotion in the service.

In a series of farther remarks, Mr. Buchanan points out the moral and economical benefits of the college, which have been already alluded to; particularly its influence in preventing the junior servants of the Company from incurring a load of debt, by which they had been formerly oppressed. He mentions also the remarkable fact, that during the period of four years there had not been one duel, and but one death, among the students of this oriental college. It appears, indeed, as if these indefatigable young men, like a great military commander of a former age, had never been sufficiently at leisure to be vicious.

The work from which this sketch of the institution to which they belonged, and of the labours of all its officers and members has been derived, will be perused with high gratification by those who feel the importance, and are interested in the perpetuity, and the just and beneficial administration of our Indian empire.*

---

* In passing from the history of the College of Fort William, it will not be inappropriate to notice the establishment of another literary institution at Calcutta, which promises to accomplish more for the cause of Christianity than the plan of the former would have permitted. In the year 1818, Bishop Middleton addressed the Society for the "Propagation of the Gospel in Foreign Parts," in relation to the establishment of a *Mission College*, near Calcutta. The purposes which he proposed, were the instruction of Mussulmans and Hindoos in the English language and in useful knowledge, the education of native and European christians in the doctrines of the Church of England, so as to fit them for the offices of schoolmasters, catechists, and ministers, and the reception of missionaries sent from England before they were appointed to their respective stations. It was also proposed that the Scriptures and the Book of Common Prayer should be translated into the Eastern languages by the learned

Towards the end of the year 1804, and the commencement of the following year, a considerable degree of opposition to the doctrines inculcated by Messrs. Brown and Buchanan had been manifested by two or three of the other chaplains of the Presidency. Mr. Buchanan was in consequence induced to preach a series of discourses on the doctrinal Articles of the Church of England. These sermons were of a very superior order, and were productive of a corresponding effect, in checking the clamour which had given birth to them. In an introductory discourse, from the direction of St. Paul to Titus, to "speak the things which become sound doctrine," Mr. Buchanan took occasion to state the importance of that digest of the principal points of christian faith exhibited in the Articles, Homilies, and Liturgy of our Church. He afterwards introduced some admirable remarks on the new complexion which some of her doctrines have derived from the spirit of

---

men who should be connected with the College, and the versions be published under its auspices.

This proposal was cordially received by the Society, and measures were taken to establish a College on the plan proposed by Bishop Middleton. Collections were authorized for the promotion of the object, in the churches throughout England, and such was the zeal manifested on the occasion, that upwards of £50,000 was collected. The Society for Promoting Christian Knowledge, and the Church Missionary Society, contributed £5,000 each, for the College buildings, and the latter commenced in 1822, an annual appropriation of £1000, which was continued for many years afterwards. The College has at present a permanent endowment of upwards of £100,000.

The corner-stone of the College edifice was laid by Bishop Middleton on the 15th of December, 1820. It was designated by him in this act as "the Episcopal Mission College of the Incorporated Society for the Propagation of the Gospel in Foreign parts, to be commonly known as Bishop's College, near Calcutta."

The College has since been completed upon the tract of land on the Hoogly granted by the government. It is of the Gothic order of architecture, and is of sufficient extent for the accommodation of the Professors and seventy students. It has connected with it a printing press for the purposes previously specified, and a handsome chapel and library.

In January, 1824, Mr. Mill, the principal Professor, with his family, took up his residence in the College. In 1827, its inmates were three professers with their families, two missionaries and eleven students, one of whom was an Armenian Deacon.

In the year 1834, Bishop Wilson states the number of students to be only eight, with two professors, one of whom has since been recalled, but writes of the College in one of his letters in the following terms:

"Bishop's College is capable of becoming the centre of missionary proceedings in India. The temporary delays and embarrassments attending its first ten or twenty years, I think nothing of. A College is of slow growth: confidence and efficiency are the offspring of many circumstances and many benedictions, which no human means can command. It is a grand thing to have the College at all. There it stands—erected by the piety of England—complete in all its parts—and entirely successful, as a design and platform for future good."

This passage is quoted from the London Missionary Register, from which work and from the life of Bishop Heber, the foregoing particulars are derived.

AM. ED.

the times, from inattention to the religion of Christ, and the ignorance and prejudice consequent upon it, and upon the necessity of caution in expressing those points which are repugnant to human pride, or which may be thought by some to be at variance with human reason. He exemplified this in the manner of stating the doctrine of justification by faith, and of the use of the moral law under the dispensation of the gospel. The following practical observation upon this part of his subject is particularly excellent:

"Now if any one should say, 'I cannot yet understand this argument of the apostle, or see how faith can thus work by love, and establish the law;' we can only answer, that must be because you have not sought or known the justifying righteousness of Christ; which the apostle saith is previously necessary to your having any sense of that love and gratitude, of which he speaks. Perhaps you have not come to God and his word with the disposition required. Perhaps to this moment the scriptures are to you a dead letter; and you have never prayed for the aid of that Spirit which giveth them life, with any hope or serious expectation of obtaining it. Perhaps in your inquiry after the truth you have not maintained that purity of heart and practice which is required by the precept of our Saviour: 'If any man will do the will of God, he shall know of the doctrine, whether it be of God.'"

At the close of this sermon, Mr. Buchanan thus announced his intention as to the subject of some succeeding discourses:

"My brethren, you cannot be indifferent as to what kind of doctrines are delivered to you. Your regular attendance on the worship of God demonstrates that you are serious; and if there be seriousness on your part, it becomes us to show some zeal on ours.

"If at any time you perceive a discrepancy of opinion regarding doctrine, let it excite you to inquire into the truth for yourselves; and it will have a happy consequence."

Adverting to the tendency there was at that day to withdraw from the principles of our forefathers both in religion and morals, he added, "I purpose to preach a series of discourses on the chief doctrines of our Church, as contained in her Articles, Liturgy, and Homilies; and to illustrate them from the lives and writings of our first Reformers, and of our most learned and pious divines. The object will be to show, what that religion was, which enabled our bishops to become martyrs to the faith, and to contrast its genuine principles with the doctrines frequently set forth at this day.

"Every thing spoken from this place ought to be spoken

for edification. We are accounted the stewards of the mysteries of God; and we shall soon be called to give an account of our stewardship.

"To obtain your approbation is desirable; but the great object of our ministry ought to be, to lead you to the exercise of every christian grace and virtue; to unfold to you the beauty and harmony of the gospel, its power, influence, consolations, and reward; and to obtain your testimony after we are gone, that we have not 'shunned to declare unto you the whole counsel of God.'"

In the second of this valuable series of discourses, from the words of the prophet Isaiah, chap. lx. 2, "For, behold, the darkness shall cover the earth, and gross darkness the people," Mr. Buchanan thought it necessary to consider the state of the church previously to the Reformation, in order that the magnitude of the blessing then vouchsafed to our country might be more justly estimated. He described in striking terms the mental bondage of the people under the dominion of the Romish church, and the means employed to perpetuate that bondage, by withholding the scriptures from them. He farther stated the grand doctrine of antichrist on which the whole fabric of his superstition was built; namely, "that a man could justify himself in the sight of God by his own merits and observances;" thereby dishonouring the sacrifice, and depreciating the merits of our Saviour; and showed that the chief article of the Reformation, properly so called, was our justification by the sole merits of Christ; and that this doctrine was declared by our Reformers to be the symbol of the true church, and the corner-stone of our redemption.

The succeeding sermon contained an animated view of the reformation from popery in this country; of the translation of the scriptures into our native languuge, and the eagerness with which they were read by all ranks of the people; and of the first great labour of our venerable Reformers in setting forth in the Articles the chief doctrines of scripture, in elucidating them clearly to the people by the Homilies, and in establishing by the Liturgy an unity of faith and worship. A sketch was then given of the temporary revival of popery and the persecution of protestantism, under the reign of Queen Mary, of the happy restoration of the Reformed Faith, and the long period of peace and tranquillity which followed; of the triumph of fanaticism in the subsequent age, and finally of the rise and progress of infidelity in our own. Upon these two last topics some admirable observations were made; and as at the time when Mr. Buchanan delivered these discourses, it was impossible to foresee how far the reign of infidelity might extend, he occupied the remainder of his third sermon in warning his distinguished auditory against its snares, and in exhorting them to diligent examination and inquiry.

"Wherever we may suspect a deviation from rectitude of opinion, let us look in general to the first principles of our church, which have been engrafted in our laws and constitution, which have been honoured and acknowledged of God, proved in the day of trial, and found perfect. Let us examine ourselves, whether, after making every allowance for the different state of society, there be any correspondence between our religious principles, and those of the fathers of our church. These principles are unalterable in their importance; they suffer no diminution by civil improvement, or by the expansion of knowledge. The doctrines of God respect the state of the soul, and the condition of man by nature; and 'are the same yesterday, to-day, and for ever.' The reasons which urged our forefathers to lay down their lives for the truth, ought to be known and felt by us. Since their time, the same truth has been confirmed by additional testimonies; if we obey it not, we sin against our own souls; and God hath said, that he will not urge his proofs and evidences on us beyond a certain limit. When the conscience and understanding of a man condemn him, he has no reason to expect any additional evidence of the truth; but rather a diminution of its weight, by his habit of neglecting it."

This able and interesting sermon closed with a faithful appeal to the consciences of his hearers as to various points of religious declension and neglect, and with a series of devout aspirations for the progress and permanence of religion in our own country.

"Let us pray," said Mr. Buchanan, "that our country may ever continue to be, in this sense, a light to the world, and an example to the nations; and that God may continue to send the light of his truth into the hearts of kings and of all that be in authority, that the kingdom may ever be governed according to his will; and that in particular, we, in this place, who are in an especial manner the light of the nations around us, and whose example must pervade so many of our countrymen, may never want a succession of wise and good men, in respectable stations, to uphold the interests of true religion and virtue; so shall the circumstances of our residence in this country be improved as much as may be; we shall be grateful for the benefits we enjoy, and we shall know better how to enjoy them, at the same time that we shall have more reason to expect a continuance of the divine blessing amongst us."

The fourth discourse in this series on the words of St. Paul, "In Adam all die," contained an elaborate statement of the doctrine of the fall, and consequent corruption of mankind, as the groundwork of the christian dispensation. "Unless we have a distinct knowledge," observed Mr. Buchanan, "of what we are by nature, that is, of the state of the soul in the sight of God, as born of Adam, we shall never be able to appreciate the blessing of the great atonement. Without a just view of this primary doctrine, the other doctrines of the New Testament will appear to be inconsistent, or without foundation. Our justification by Christ, the second Adam, and the influence of the Holy Spirit in renewing the corrupt heart, will be accounted doctrines of a mystical nature, or they will be interpreted in a sense suited to the prejudices or passions of men."

The method adopted by Mr. Buchanan in this sermon, after previously adverting to the knowledge of the subject attainable by the light of nature, was first, to state those passages of scripture on which the doctrine of original sin is founded, and to which our church refers; to set forth the terms in which the church expresses herself on the subject, both in the letter of the article, and in her illustrations of it; and, lastly, to declare the deviations from the original sense which have taken place, and also the arguments of the recent philosophy in their favour. He afterwards took occasion to confirm his own representations by an extract from the Bishop of Lincoln's "Elements of Christian Theology," upon which he founded the following brief improvement of the whole subject:

"If we are indeed in a lost and fallen state, exposed to the displeasure of God, (as is testified even by the miseries of this life,) how much doth it become us to consider how we are to be restored to his favour and mercy.

"It is no mark of our penitence, or of a right disposition, to allege that we are not liable to judgment for the sin of our nature. The accumulation of guilt by *actual* sin is sufficient to condemn every man; it condemns him now at the bar of conscience, and ought to urge him to the most serious reflection on the state of his soul in the sight of God. The delusion of many is this: they suppose that the expressions of scripture concerning a renovation of heart relate merely to some moral reformation, independent of the Spirit of God. But the renovation there intended is not independent of the Spirit of God. The expressions alluded to are founded on the *present ruined* state of the soul; and they constitute the great realities of revealed truth. If it be true that our nature is vitiated by the taint of Adam's sin, it is true also that the heart must be sanctified by the Spirit of God before it can be restored to his image or favour.

"We must be renewed, (saith the apostle,) in the spirit of our minds, and be transformed into the 'image and likeness' of the second Adam, our Lord Jesus Christ, who came to seek and to save that which was lost."

The next sermon was on the redemption and restoration of mankind by Jesus Christ, from Romans iii. 23—31. In the discussion of this most important subject, Mr. Buchanan first inquired what method God was pleased to adopt for the salvation of guilty man, in consistency with his own justice; and then stated the objections which are sometimes made to that mode of salvation.

After describing the plan of redemption which unbelievers and Socinians allege to be alone consistent with our natural ideas of divine justice and mercy, Mr. Buchanan decisively replied, that this method of salvation was not adopted, because in the first place, man could not, as they propose, "keep the moral law;" and in the next, because he is already in a state of condemnation. Justification by the grace of God, through the redemption which is in Christ Jesus, and by faith in his blood, is the "wholesome and comfortable doctrine" which was then established. In replying to the denial of this doctrine by the Socinians, Mr. Buchanan added the following important observation:

"This doctrine of justification by *works* is in substance also the doctrine of the Romish church; and it will always be the popular doctrine among christians who have little true religion, by whatever denomination they may be called. For it is the doctrine of the *world;* it is found where the name of Christ is not known; and it is the spirit of every false religion and superstition upon earth."

The succeeding passage, which concluded the sermon on the nature of justifying faith, and on the security afforded by that doctrine to the interests of morality, is in a strain of scriptural and elevated piety, which cannot but be acceptable to the reader.

"It is true that some who hold this doctrine of justification by works, use the expressions of scripture, and will perhaps allow that faith is necessary to salvation. But what kind of faith is by them intended? If a man believe in the general truth of the christian religion, he is said by them to have *faith*. If his understanding be convinced by its evidences, he is accounted by them to have *faith*. And this faith also, saith the apostle James, 'have the devils, for they also believe.' All men, whose understandings are not obscured by pride or evil passion, must believe the evidence of the christian religion, but they have not, therefore, that faith in the blood of Christ which justifies the guilty soul. *The faith which so justifies* is the 'gift of God;' it is a reliance on the propitiation of Christ, wrought in the soul of the penitent sinner by the operation of God's Holy Spirit.

"It is a faith which cannot be understood by any one who has passed through life a stranger 'to the tears of repentance.' If he cannot recollect any interval of contrition of heart for his past sins, any season of earnest prayer to be accepted in Christ, and to obtain an interest in his atonement, it is not probable that he can have any knowledge of a saving faith. Such an one will not understand our church when she saith, 'that a man is justified by his faith in Christ only,' and 'that works are shut out from the office of justifying.' The language of the scriptures and of our church must ever continue to be equally doubtful to him; some casual notice of their doctrines may be taken, but he will never enter with delight or with confidence into the spirit and elucidation of them.

"We shall conclude with showing that the interests of morality are best secured by a true faith in our Redeemer.

"It is worthy of observation, that though our church teaches that the sinner is justified by faith *only*, she has never been accused of neglecting good works; and though the apostle Paul teaches that the sinner is justified by faith only, he has never been charged with overlooking moral duties. It is probable, then, that the doctrine of both is favourable to virtuous practice. Both insist fully on moral duties, and both deduce the right performance of these duties from a justifying faith; they show that the right performance springs from it, and that without it we cannot please God in any duty.

"The true doctrine of our church is, that every man's person must be accepted in Christ before he can do any thing pleasing and acceptable to God; that is, he must be considered as a friend, and not as an enemy; as one reconciled to God through the death of his Son, and not 'as far off and alienated from him;' as an adopted child of God, and not as of the world.

"The doctrine of our church maintains, that no man can glorify God by his works until he be restored to the favour of God through that faith which justifies his person; that until the heart be purified by the grace of God, and the motives of action be under the influence of his Spirit, we can neither glorify God in our business nor in our devotions, neither in solitude nor in a tumult, neither by abstinence nor by festivity. Our works, however, will ever testify of our faith, of what sort it is; whether it be a general belief in christianity, which is common to good and bad men, or a true and lively faith wrought in the heart by the Spirit of God, and 'leading the soul captive to the obedience of Christ.'

"Many who, for a time, resisted the doctrine of 'justification by faith,' have at last embraced it as the only hope of salvation. Oftentimes, in the season of sickness or of affliction, when the soul is humbled, and begins to take a review of her past sins, and to look out earnestly for a right foundation of her hope, the pride of moral merit is abandoned, and she is enabled, through the grace of God, to view the great propitiation for her sins, and to exercise a lively faith in its efficacy.

"Then it is that the doctrine will be perceived to be, what our church calls it, 'a most wholesome doctrine, and very full of comfort.' It is *wholesome*, because it will urge the soul to good works, from a principle of love to the Redeemer who has justified her, from a sense of that unmerited mercy by which she is saved, and from a gratitude which will ever render her duties not a task, but a labour of love, in which she is willingly engaged.

"This doctrine is also 'full of *comfort;*' for now the soul hath peace with God. In her former state, while she depended on a righteousness of her own, there was no peace; but doubt, and fear, and misgivings of conscience. But now there is peace, because there is *acceptance;* and there is acceptance, because the soul appears in a righteousness not her own, even in the complete righteousness of Christ, by which she is restored in a measure to the image of God, reconciled to his favour, and thus becomes an heir of the promises, and of eternal life."

The last of these admirable discourses was on the nature and necessity of the operation of the Spirit of God to lead the soul to accept of the redemption which had been previously described.

"Our church teaches," observed Mr. Buchanan, "that the grace of God is necessary to produce in us repentance from dead works to a life of righteousness, to enlighten our minds in all necessary truth, and to inspire the soul with a steadfast faith in the word of God."

This view of the doctrine of our church was next confirmed

by the tenth article, and elucidated by a second quotation from the "Elements of Christian Theology." The transforming effects produced by the operation of the Spirit on the hearts of men, which are sometimes denominated "repentance unto life," sometimes "conversion of the heart," and sometimes "the being born again," were then considered; after which, the following objection to the doctrine of divine grace was thus noticed, and satisfactorily answered:

"It is alleged," observed Mr. Buchanan, "that the grace of God, if it operate at all, must be irresistible, and if irresistible, then is free-will destroyed, and man can no longer act as a voluntary agent, and an accountable being. It is indeed difficult for us to comprehend how the foreknowledge of God can be consistent with the free-will of man; but then this is a difficulty which is common to all systems of religion and philosophy, and it ought not to be once mentioned as being peculiar to the christian religion, or as invalidating any doctrine which it teaches. It is one of those difficulties which are equally obvious to all, even to the meanest capacities, and whose solution is equally remote from all. It is left unnoticed in scripture, as if to humble the pride of human understanding, and to baffle the reason of man 'attempting to find out his Maker to perfection.' But at the same time it seems to assure us of another state of being, where higher degrees of knowledge and of intellect shall be bestowed. As to man's freedom of will in acting the part of a rational and accountable creature, it is constantly testified in scripture. The whole word of God seems to be addressed to men who have perfect freedom of will to use the *means* of salvation. In reply to what is alleged by some of the *irresistible* effects of grace, we are warned 'not to receive the grace of God *in vain*,' 'not to *quench* the Spirit, nor to do *despite* to the Spirit of grace.' And our church plainly declares the same thing in the following words: 'After we have received the Holy Ghost, we may depart from grace given, and fall into sin, and by the grace of God we may arise again and amend our lives.' This doctrine will discover itself to the humble inquirer, (who will put its efficacy to the proof,) as being perfectly consistent with his most rational ideas of the communication of the divine assistance. It is moreover the very fountain of life to the soul; for without the aid of God's Spirit, a christian will make no nearer approaches to heaven by his learning, labours, and works than a heathen. Until the Spirit of God regenerate the heart, all hearts must remain in their natural state in the sight of God. Some men may be more civilized than others; some more learned, more humane, more benevolent, more virtuous; as it was in the heathen world, in different ranks, families, and individuals. But spiritual life there is none. They are still children of the first Adam, and will continue to be such till they are renewed in their minds by the power of the divine Spirit, and are made to 'bear the image of the heavenly.'"

Here Mr. Buchanan closed his elaborate and eloquent exposition of the leading doctrines of our church. The conclusion of the whole is, however, so important, and exhibits the character of the author of these sermons, as a preacher, and as an able and faithful minister of the gospel, in so just and elevated a point of view, that his biographer could not consider himself as doing justice to his subject, were he to omit it; though to some it may appear, that this, as well as a former extract, is scarcely within the appropriate limits of these memoirs.

"I have now, my brethren, set before you those important doctrines of our church, which are certainly too much neglected at this day. The purpose I had in view will be answered, if it excite in those who doubt or misapprehend them, a serious inquiry into their truth and importance. The sources of knowledge are open to all. It is always an advantage to the truth to be fully tried, examined, and compared. The very *doubts* of men are useful to it, in putting it upon its defence, and leading to its better confirmation. Let us not then supinely suffer any innovation in the doctrines of our church, since we are able to judge for ourselves, and can refer 'to the law and to the testimony.'

"The doctrines which we have discussed are commonly called the doctrines of grace; and with propriety, for they are the peculiar doctrines of the gospel. They exalt and glorify the Creator, and humble the creature; they are at unity with themselves, and harmonize with each other; he who receives one of them, will receive them all; and he who rejects one, will reject them all.

"The preaching the doctrines of grace differs from preaching morality on merely human motives, as light from darkness. The preachers among the heathen around us, and the teachers of philosophy without religion, can say, 'Thou shalt not kill, thou shalt not steal, thou shalt not bear false witness;' they can inculcate justice, prudence, and temperance, from very strong and very persuasive motives; but they cannot teach those good works which flow from the christian doctrines of grace. They cannot teach a hatred of sin, or a contrition of heart for offending God; they cannot teach us 'to bless them which persecute us, and to pray for them who despitefully use us.' They cannot suppress envies, secret resentments, and evil speakings against those who differ from us in opinion. They cannot produce love to God, a lively gratitude for his daily mercies, and delight in his service. They cannot urge us to labour in the word and doctrine according to our profession, our ability, or our means; and to be anxiously concerned about the salvation of the souls of men. Finally, they cannot teach us patience in affliction, joy in tribulation, and a well-founded hope in death.

"The grand test of the truth of the doctrines of grace is their influence at the hour of death. This is a proof which is ever present with the church of Christ, and which will in every place distinguish the true doctrine from the false.

"No sinner ever yet departed this life with a lively hope in God, and with confidence of salvation by his Redeemer, who was a stranger to the doctrines of grace. No christian, who denies these doctrines, can have any hope that he will be enabled to triumph at his last hour, 'desiring to depart as being far better;' and thus leave to his family behind him a testimony to the truth by his steadfast faith.

"By some, such a dissolution is not expected in any circumstances; such a testimony is not looked for. They hear, indeed, of such instances among others, but they are willing to believe that they are not true, for if they be, they know that their own hope cannot rest on the right foundation.

"All preaching ought to have reference to the sinner's hope in death; for whatever is short of this, is doing nothing for eternity. We must all soon come to that state when the doctrines which we have individually received will be put to the proof, and their efficacy manifested to others; we must soon be in those circumstances, when every vain refuge shall be swept away, and the truth of God shall alone prevail.

"I have discharged a duty, my brethren, in setting plainly before you those doctrines of our religion, which I am myself fully convinced can alone produce the fruits of righteousness and the good works of the New Testament. I am further convinced that they alone can give peace to the soul, and comfort in death. They are the doctrines of the Church of England, the good old religion of our ancestors, without taint of Romish corruption, of Socinianism, or of modern philosophy. Nor am I conscious of having used a single expression or sentiment which does not accord with the language and spirit of our church and of the holy scriptures; and I must continue to believe this, till I am convinced of the contrary by well-ordered proof.

"These are the doctrines which I have ever maintained, and which I ever desire to uphold in my ministry; and on whatever other subjects I may occasionally dwell, the truth and admission of these doctrines is always to be understood.

"It is easy to discourse on more pleasing and popular subjects, but it is not so profitable to you. Some may not approve, but to others 'the word preached may be made the power of God unto salvation.' If our doctrine give no offence to the world in general, ye know that it can be no longer the doctrine of Christ. It is 'another gospel.' It is a doctrine which may confirm our hearers in error, and lead them onward to old age with no better view of heavenly things than that of the infidel.

"It is a view of our lost estate by nature, and actual guilt in the sight of God, and then a view of the great propitiation on the cross, which alone can open to our understandings the transcendant and ineffable glory of the gospel of Christ. Nor can such a view be exhibited, even in the lowest degree, but by the influence of the divine grace, co-operating with our prayers, by enlightening the judgment and purifying the heart.

"But the aid of the Holy Spirit 'is promised to them who ask it.' Thus are we encouraged to begin the work of our salvation in the most rational manner, and by the most natural means. And those who can prevail on themselves to begin thus seriously, will find the truth of God's promises confirmed to them in every progressive stage of religious knowledge and practical virtue.

"The life of such persons is thus described in one of the articles of the church, commencing from the period of their first seeking the aid of the divine Spirit, unto the end of their course.

"'Wherefore they be called, according to God's purpose, by his Spirit working in due season;

"'They, through grace, obey the calling;

"'They be justified freely;

"'They be made sons of God by adoption;

"'They be made like the image of his only begotten Son, Jesus Christ;

"'They walk religiously in good works, and at length, by God's mercy,

"'They attain to everlasting felicity.'"

The impression of these sermons upon his audience was, as we have already observed, considerable. There were probably some whose prejudices or whose passions would render them proof against both the reasonings and the exhortations of their author, though the one were unquestionably sound and scriptural, and the other powerful and persuasive. There were doubtless, however, others who were instructed, confirmed, and edified by his labours; while these, whether accepted or refused, afford an evidence of his fidelity as a minister and ambassador of Christ, which will hereafter "testify for him before his glorious throne."

CHAPTER IV.

In prosecution of the design which Mr. Buchanan had conceived of effectually exciting the public attention in this country to the obligations of Great Britain to promote the religious welfare of its oriental dominions, and which he had already partially executed by the proposal of his first series of prizes, and the publication of his own "Memoir;" he on the 4th of June, 1805, addressed to the Vice-Chancellors of the Universities of Oxford and Cambridge, the proposal of the following subjects of prize composition.

"For the best work in English prose, embracing the following subjects:

"I. The probable design of the Divine Providence in subjecting so large a portion of Asia to the British dominion.

"II. The duty, the means, and the consequences of translating the scriptures into the oriental tongues, and of promoting christian knowledge in Asia.

"III. A brief historic view of the progress of the gospel in different nations, since its first promulgation; illustrated by maps, showing its luminous tract throughout the world; with chronological notices of its duration in particular places."

The candidates were permitted to prefix such title to the proposed work as they might think proper; and the munificent prize offered by Mr. Buchanan upon this occasion to each University was the sum of five hundred pounds. He directed, that the prizes should be determined on the 4th of June, 1807, being the anniversary of the birth of our venerable sovereign; "whose religious example," Mr. Buchanan added, "had extended its influence to that remote part of his empire."

The letters conveying intelligence of these very liberal offers were received towards the close of the year. They were soon afterwards accepted by both Universities; and the spring of the year 1807 was appointed as the period for the delivery of the prize compositions to the judges who were to determine their merits.

A few days subsequent to the date of these proposals to the English Universities, and not long before the departure of Marquis Wellesley from Bengal, Mr. Buchanan communicated to his lordship his wish to be absent from Calcutta during four months, for the benefit of his health, which his residence and labours in India had considerably impaired; and for the purpose of proceeding to the coast of Malabar, with a view of obtaining information relative to certain religious objects, which were particularly specified in his letter, and will be hereafter fully detailed.

With this request the Governor General signified officially his ready compliance, together with his entire approbation of Mr. Buchanan's intended journey. It was added, that the governments of Fort St. George and Bombay would be requested to afford him every assistance, as well in the progress of his journey, by the accommodation of the dawk bearers, or other conveyances of government, as in the prosecution of his inquiries on the coast of Malabar.

While Mr. Buchanan was preparing for this important and interesting journey, he was, for the present, prevented from fulfilling his intentions by a serious illness, the approach of which he first perceived on the 13th of August. He was well enough to meet Lord Wellesley at dinner the next day, and on the two following complained only of weakness and languor. On the 17th, a decided attack of fever came on; and on the 19th, danger was apprehended by his physician.

Of this alarming illness, a brief but remarkable memorial has been preserved in the hand-writing of Mr. Brown, who appears to have attended and watched over his valued friend and coadjutor with fraternal anxiety and affection. The feelings and sentiments of Mr. Buchanan at this trying season, as described in the paper alluded to, are such as, while they may surprise a certain class of readers, will appear to better judges to be the genuine effusions of a pious mind, alive to the apprehended solemnities of a dying hour.

On the evening of the 20th of August, Mr. Buchanan spoke much to his friend of his state and views; said that he had been looking for his hope in the Bible, and that he had found it in the 51st psalm, and in the history of the penitent thief upon the cross. He at the same time gave directions to Mr. Brown respecting the college, his papers, and his affairs. The next day Mr. Buchanan was still more strongly impressed with the idea that he should not recover. Under this persuasion, he mentioned the place in which he wished to be interred, made some observations respecting his books, and desired that his sermons might be published after the arrival of his "Memoir" in India.

Mr. Buchanan next adverted to his experience and views as a christian; declared his entire renunciation of his own merits as any ground of acceptance with God, lamented his unprofitableness, and spoke of himself in terms of the deepest humility. He then again referred to the church and to the college, and suggested various hints respecting both. After this he recurred to his present feelings and circumstances. He expressed his fear of living, and his desire of being received as the least and lowest of the servants of God. He was anxious to glorify him by his death, and prayed to be preserved from the enemy at the last hour, that he might not do or say any thing to weaken the testimony he had borne to the truth in that place. There was nothing, he said, upon earth, for which he had a wish, besides his wife and children; that she was much before him in experimental knowledge, and had been twice on the wing to leave the world; (he knew not, alas! that she had in fact already taken her flight!) that his children would be brought up in the nurture and admonition of the Lord; that if sent to Scotland, they would be in the heart of Sunday-schools and of true religion; or that in England, the . . .'s, and other friends who feared God, would take care of them. After thus speaking of his children, Mr. Buchanan alluded to a painful letter which he had lately received from one of his correspondents; and lamented what he considered his unkindness, in forbearing to encourage him during the labours of the last five years. He then expressed a hope, that his death would prove useful to two persons whom he particularly named.

On the morning of the 22d, Mr. Brown, on entering his sick chamber, found him still fixed in his opinion that he should die, and opening his spiritual state to another christian friend. He then took a review of the way in which the providence of God had led him from his earliest years; and gave his friends a brief sketch of his history: the romantic project of his youth; his residence in London; his conversion to the faith and practice of a real christian; his career at Cambridge; his voyage to India; and his comparative banishment during the first three years of his residence in that country. At this critical period, Mr. Buchanan observed, his call by Lord Wellesley to the chaplaincy of the Presidency, and the subsequent establishment of the college, had given him an important work to perform; that his preaching, indeed, (notwithstanding the specimens which have been before given of its ability and excellence, such was the high standard to which he aspired,) had been unsatisfactory to himself; but that his spiritual labours and opportunities in college, though desultory, had often afforded him comfort. He added, says Mr. Brown, "that I must preach, probably intending his funeral sermon, "though he felt himself unworthy to choose a text; yet that it must be from these words, 'Being justified by faith, we have peace with God.'"

"After praying earnestly," continues Mr. Brown, "for some time, he lay quite still, and then with great tranquillity and satisfaction said, 'What a happy moment! Now I am resigned; now I desire not to live. I am unworthy of this.' He then spoke of his hope, and said that he could only be saved by grace."

After this conversation, Mr. Buchanan mentioned his wishes concerning his funeral and monument, and spoke of his departure from the world as a happy deliverance from the evils which he foresaw he should have to encounter, if he were to return to Europe. Alluding to his intended journey, which his present illness had prevented, he said, "I am now about to travel not an earthly journey, but still to 'unknown regions of the gospel.' I shall now pass over the heads of old men labouring usefully for Christ; and at this early period be advanced to see what 'eye hath not seen, nor ear heard, nor hath entered into the heart of man to conceive,' and behold discoveries of the glory of Christ, 'God manifest in the flesh,' who hath come to us, and kindly taken us by the hand. He will lift us out of the deep waters, and set us at his own right hand. I once saw not the things I now see; I knew not the gospel. Now I pray, that the little I have known may be perfected, and that God would complete his work on my soul."

Mr. Brown adds, that his apparently dying friend was almost continually praying, in a humble, submissive, patient, and fervent tone, for mercy and grace through Jesus Christ; and, with the apostle, that God might be glorified by his life or death.

Such is the interesting and instructive memorial which remains of this alarming illness of Mr. Buchanan. While it demonstrates the excellence and the solidity of the principles which could thus support him, it must surely excite in the mind of every reader a conviction of their value, and an earnest desire to possess the same consolation in a season of similar trial.

Of the progress of his recovery nothing is particularly recorded. The fever appears gradually to have subsided; and on the 4th of September he was so far restored as to be able to remove to Barrackpore for change of air, and afterwards to Sooksagur, about forty miles above Calcutta. The remembrance, however, of his illness, and the impressions which an anticipated death-bed had made upon his mind, instead of being obliterated, as in too many instances, by returning health, were ever afterwards cherished and retained. The scene was, perhaps, intended to prepare him for the painful trial which was approaching; and both, as we shall shortly perceive, produced the happy effect of quickening him in his christian course, and of rendering him even more zealous and unwearied in the service of his heavenly Master.

One of Mr. Buchanan's first exertions of recovered health was in writing the following reply to a pious man, who appears to have been known to him during the early part of his residence in England, and to have been employed as a humble preacher of the gospel. It was found amongst the papers of the late Mr. Henry Thornton, to whom it had probably been sent by the person to whom it was addressed, for the purpose which the letter itself will explain. The christian kindness and humility which it breathes sufficiently authorize its insertion.

"Calcutta, 3d Sept. 1805.

"My dear Friend,—I received your letter by Mr. B— about five years ago, and in consequence took him into my house for some time. The young man is in the army, and conducts himself, I hear, with propriety. I am sorry to find that my answer to your letter on that occasion has never reached you.

"A few days ago I received your letter of the 4th of November, 1804, by Mr. Taylor, a missionary to India. In that letter you mention that you are still poor; and, what is better, that you preach the gospel to the poor. After so long an interval, it gives me great pleasure to learn that you are yet found faithful, and that in the midst of your poverty you have found the 'unsearchable riches.' Your heavenly Father knoweth best what is good for you; and he hath, no doubt, led you hitherto in that narrow and peculiar path which was suited to your state, and necessary for the advancement of his glory.

"I have, on the other hand, been led in a broader road, and a more dangerous way. If I have been preserved, if I am yet, in my measure, faithful in dispensing the gospel, and in promoting by various means the interests of Christ's kingdom, it is mercy; far more distinguished mercy, as it appears to me, than that which has been manifested in you. The gospel is not without its witness even in this place. The company of the faithful is increasing, and the opportunities of publishing the good tidings are multiplying.

"I enclose to you a note on my agents in London for fifty pounds. I should send you more, if I thought it would do you any good. If you should want more, ask Mr. Henry Thornton for it, and I will repay him.

"I was much pleased with your account of your aged father. I think on the whole you have reason to be thankful that your family are so well disposed of in the course of years and worldly revolution. It seemeth good to Providence to keep you all in a strait estate; and that is the general dispensation to God's favoured people.

"That you may be blessed yourself, and continue to be a blessing to others, is the prayer of,

Dear sir, your sincere friend, C. Buchanan."

During the temporary retreat of Mr. Buchanan at Sooksagur, for the re-establishment of his health, he was diligently employed in Hebrew, Syriac, and Chaldaic studies, with various accompaniments of Rabbinical and other commentators. In the midst, however, of this occupation, he was interrupted by the afflicting intelligence of the death of Mrs. Buchanan. This distressing, though in some measure expected, event had taken place on the 18th of June, on board the East India ship, in which she was returning to England, off the Island of St. Helena. Of Mr. Buchanan's feelings upon this mournful occasion, as well as respecting his own late illness, the two following letters will afford an affecting and truly interesting picture. The first is to his friend Colonel Sandys.

"Sooksagur, near Calcutta, 22d Oct. 1805.

"My dear Sandys,—I have been at this place for some time past, in the hope of getting a little strength. I was visited by a fever about two months ago, and was despaired of for a day or two. But the prayers of the righteous were offered up, and my days have been prolonged. It was with a kind of reluctance I felt myself carried back by the refluent waves to encounter again the storms of this life: for I had hoped the fight was done. Although unprofitable has been my life, and feeble my exertions; yet I was more afraid of the trials to come, if I should survive, than of departing to my rest, if it was the will of God. I had made a disposition of my fortune to Mary, and her pious purposes; (for she too had undertakings in view;) believing that she would be much more useful than I could. My first care on my convalescence was to write to *her* an account of that event. In a few days afterwards the Calcutta Indiaman arrived from St. Helena, and brought me the news of my dear Mary's decease! Before she went away I perceived that her affections were nearly weaned from this world; and she often said, that she thought God was preparing her for his presence in glory. She was greatly favoured in her near access to God in prayer; and she delighted in retirement and sacred meditation. She was jealous of herself latterly, when she anticipated the happiness of our all meeting in England; and endeavoured to chastise the thought.

"Her sufferings were great, but she accounted her consolations greater; and she used to admire the goodness of God to her, in bringing her to a knowledge of the truth at so early an age. It was her intention, had she lived to reach England, to have gone down with her two little girls to visit you; saying, 'we shall behold each other as two new creatures.' You had been accused to her of being too peculiar, and she wished to see what was amiss.

"When she found her dissolution drawing near, she solemnly devoted her two little girls to God; and prayed that he would be their Father, and bring them up in his holy fear, and preserve them from the vanities of this evil world. She said she could willingly die for the souls of her children; and she did die, in the confident hope of seeing them both in glory.

"Having had it in contemplation to have followed my dear Mary to England next year, I had let my house at Garden Reach to Sir John D'Oyly. I had also sold my furniture, horses, &c., previously to my proceeding to Malabar. But in the meantime I fell sick; and now that I have recovered, I mean to defer my journey to the coast till the new government be settled. Sir George Barlow is at present up the country; Mr. Udny is Deputy Governor. Both of them are warm supporters of religious improvement in India, and I trust they will do good. They know nothing of my "Memoir," nor any one else but Mr. Brown.

"The B.'s here are affectionately concerned in my recovery, and pay me every attention in their power. I do not know whether I shall go to England next year or not; I am now a desolate old man, though young in years. But my path will, I doubt not, be made 'clear as the noon day.'

"By your late letters I see that you are 'flourishing like a palm tree.' How often have you passed the palm tree in India, without comparing it to the righteous man!

"My dear Mary's name and character was latterly well known among the excellent of the earth; and her memory has left a fragrance for years to come."

Mr. Buchanan then mentions the lamented and unexpected death of the Marquis Cornwallis; who had lately arrived to resume the government of the country, which had been already so signally benefited by his former administration.

"The body," he observes, of this illustrious nobleman, "had no honourable interment; neither a clergyman to read the office, nor a coffin to put it in. Thus ended his earthly name and greatness. God promised to Jacob, as a temporal blessing, that his son Joseph 'should close his eyes.' It is indeed a blessing to have a righteous son or daughter to hallow our remains in death. May you have that son, and I that daughter!

Yours affectionately, C. BUCHANAN."

The second of the two letters relative to the death of Mrs. Buchanan is to another friend, who well knew her worth, and sincerely sympathized with Mr. Buchanan under his loss. The somewhat varied expression of his feelings upon this painful subject will not, perhaps, be unacceptable.

"SOOKSAGUR, 24th Oct. 1805.

"My dear Sir.—Your letter of March 18th, of this year, addressed to my dear Mary, arrived here about a month ago. A few days afterwards I received the account of her death.

"You will rejoice to hear that, when she was preparing to leave India, she considered herself as preparing for another and better country than England.

"She enjoyed latterly much communion with God in prayer; and often, when she came out of her closet, the gleam on her countenance evinced her peace and acceptance. The words of some hymn to her Redeemer were often on her lips. You I believe knew enough of her to make you consider this portrait of her last days to be true. She died at the age of twenty-five. She considered that the period of her sufferings (only, she said, three or four years) was very short, and wondered at the goodness of God in so early calling her to his glory. She lamented that she could never be 'made perfect by suffering;' and therefore viewed the end of her probation with great comfort, and latterly with joyful anticipation. She expressed and felt strong affection towards you and your family. In the last page of your letter to Mrs. Buchanan, you remind her of the promise, 'Be thou faithful unto death, and I will give the a crown of life.' These words were prophetic. You wrote them on the 18th of March; and on the 18th of June, three months after, she, I trust, received the crown.

"I have been at this place for some weeks past, in the hope of acquiring a little strength after my late illness. I am now perfectly well, and propose to return to Calcutta to resume my public duties in a few days.

"During the period of my retirement I have been chiefly employed in researches in the Hebrew and Syriac scriptures. I happily met with some valuable Syriac volumes on my way up hither. While I was thus engaged, the news of Mrs. Buchanan's death arrived! I found some consolation in writing a few lines to her memory in the Hebrew, Syriac, Greek, and Latin languages; which I inscribed on a leaf of her own Bible: the best monument that I could erect; for her body was buried in the deep.

"I sometimes think that, had I my two little girls to play with, I should be happy, even in this dreary land. My chief solace is in a mind constantly occupied; and this is the greatest temporal blessing I can expect, even unto the end. I could relate to you scenes of tribulation and keen persecution in regard to others and to myself: but these could give you no pleasure, and I wish not to think of them.

"How little do you all know of Calcutta, or of what is doing or has been done here; as little even as of the court of Pekin!

"Of the many letters you wrote to us during the two last years, I think we received only two. My next to you, if I live to write another, will probably be from *Taprobane*.

I remain, my dear sir, very affectionately yours,

C. BUCHANAN."

On the day on which the preceding letter is dated, Mr. Buchanan addressed the following to Mr. Grant:

"SOOKSAGUR, 24th Oct. 1805.

"Dear Sir,—I was favoured with your letter by the last fleet, enclosing a copy of the prospectus of the new college. I was much pleased with the perusal, and have no doubt of its becoming an useful institution.

"About three years ago I sent you a memorial on the necessity of having some regulations passed for the instruction of writers and cadets on board ship. The ship is often the bane of young men who leave home. Alter they are committed by their parents to the care of the Company, it is doubtless the Company's duty to look to their morals, and the employment of their time, on board their own ships. I suggested to you the easy method by which this might be effected.

"Your son's poem is much admired here. It certainly does him great honour as a man, a scholar, and a poet; and it must be highly gratifying to you that he should, at so early an age, have established his fame. I trust that his health is improved, and that he will be long preserved to you and to his country.

"What you mention of the prose dissertation is interesting. One of the Cambridge judges wrote me a letter, in which he observes, that of the unsuccessful dissertations, one was excellent; but he did not mention the name of the writer. I hope you will publish it. At all events it must be creditable to your son; and it will probably do good, as it is, I doubt not, founded on just sentiments.

"I remain, dear sir, very sincerely yours,

C. BUCHANAN."

Having derived much benefit from the change of air, and the retirement which he had enjoyed during two months at Sooksagur, Mr. Buchanan, on the 4th of November, returned to Calcutta. A few weeks afterwards he addressed a letter of considerable length to his grace, the Archbishbop of Canterbury, npon the great and important subject of the promotion of christian knowledge in India, which had of late so much occupied his mind, chiefly with reference to an ecclesiastical establishment, and the translation of the scriptures into the oriental languages. Much of Mr. Buchanan's fervid reasoning in his address to the Metropolitan of England proceeds upon the comparative indifference which then prevailed in this country, relative to the religious interests of India.

This circumstance being borne in mind, the following extracts will afford another proof of the devoted, yet enlarged and disinterested attachment of the writer to the important work which he was pursuing. After noticing the Archbishop's recent elevation to the highest dignity in the church, Mr. Buchanan thus proceeds:

"Permit me, my lord, in the name of the few representatives of the English church in Asia, to offer to your grace the tribute of affectionate congratulation, and to express our hope that the glory of the Messiah's kingdom may be manifested to all nations of the earth during the period of your administration.

"Our hope of evangelizing Asia was once founded on the

college of Fort William. But a rude hand hath already touched it, and unless the Imperial Parliament interpore, it will soon be said of this great and useful institution, which enlightened a hemisphere of the globe, 'Fuit Ilium et ingens gloria.' Its name, however, will remain, for its record is in many languages, and the good it hath done will never die, for it hath taught many the way to heaven. Had the college of Fort William been cherished at home with the same ardour with which it was opposed, it might, in the period of ten years, have produced translations of the scriptures into all the languages from the borders of the Caspian to the sea of Japan.

"An idea seems to have gone forth in England that Lord Wellesley founded his college merely to instruct the Company's writers. Lord Wellesley founded the college of Fort William to enlighten the oriental world; to give science, religion, and pure morals to Asia; and to confirm in it the British power and dominion.

". . . . It is the opinion of intelligent men in India, that the formation of an extensive ecclesiastical establishment is a measure which, during the present revolutions of Europe, will tend greatly to confirm our dominion. It is certain that nothing would more alarm the portentous invader of nations, than our taking a 'religious possession' of Hindostan. Five hundred respectable clergy of the English church, established in our Gentoo cities, would more perplex his views of conquest than an army of fifty thousand British soldiers. The army of fifty thousand would melt away in seven years, but the influence of an upright clergyman among the natives of his district would be permanent. He would be to them in time their mouth and mind, and speak for them peace or war. Friendly, admonitory, social intercourse, is what is wanting to enchain the hearts of the people of Hindostan, and to make them *our* people.

". . . . The toleration of all religions, and the zealous extension of our own, is the way to rule and preserve a conquered kingdom. It is certain that men are ruled virtually by the church, though ostensibly by the state, in every country. The seeds of moral obedience and social order are all in the church.

"How India is to be preserved in time to come must be submitted to the wisdom of the Imperial Parliament. If the scriptures be from God, our nation does not deserve at his hand to retain the possession of this 'paradise of nations' a year longer, so greatly have we abused our sacred trust. We have, in one word, 'withheld the revelation of God, and permitted the libation to Moloch of human blood.' In the course of the two last months, the Rev. Mr. Brown, the senior of the English clergy now in India, has witnessed the burning alive of eight women at the place of sacrifice, in the suburbs of Calcutta, as he passed casually on his way from his country-house to the church in town. How can the minister of the altar approach without trembling to his holy office, when he reflects on such scences, and on their connexion with the sin of his country!

"I said a little on these subjects in my memoir, but had I said all I could say, I should have exposed to severe censure the national character. I have since been visited by a dangerous illness; and when I considered myself at the point of death, I repented that I had not spoken more loudly and more faithfully to my christian country.

"In the hope of atoning for a mistaken tenderness, I would now impress the mind of your grace with a just sentiment of our present state in India, in order that your grace may deliberate on the means of promoting the welfare of the hundred million of souls which Providence has committed to our charge.

"One observation I would make on the proposed ecclesiastical establishment. A partial or half measure will have no useful effect. A few additional chaplains can do nothing towards the attainment of the great objects in view.

"An archbishop is wanted for India; a sacred and exalted character, surrounded by his bishops, of ample revenue and extensive sway; a venerable personage, whose name shall be greater than that of the transitory governors of the land, and whose fame for piety, and for the will and power to do good, may pass throughout every region.

"We want something royal, in a spiritual or temporal sense, for the abject subjects of this great eastern empire to look up to. They cannot conceive themselves in a settled state without a Sultan or Maha Rajah. They are incapable of freedom, for superstition keeps men in childhood. And yet they have neither king nor emperor; they have neither national temple nor high priest. They are a mixed multitude, who have no common sentiment of truth or falsehood, of right or wrong. Every man contradicts his neighbour, and the European tells them they are all right!

"Spiritual power, with means of instruction, is wanting, to awaken to life this sluggish and inert race. Vegetating in ignorance and passive misery, they want a sacred guide, who shall take them by the hand, and lift them up, and look them in the face, and express some interest in their happiness. The success of the solitary missionary demonstrates what would be the powerful effect of the whole church.

"I feel a solicitude that your grace should not consider me as adverting to subjects unnecessary or unimportant in themselves, or such as it is not becoming in me to allude to. My apology for noticing the political state of our Indian empire, is this: The existence of it is involved in *religious* considerations. The men whose business it is to know this will not believe it. But where is the truth to be found, if not from those who are at the fountain of information; who, if they fulfil their sacred character, are not careless 'observers of the signs of the times,' and who stand, as it were, on an eminence, and behold their own country and India distinctly in one view? I would not, without reason, urge this subject on the attention of good men at home. India is nothing to me, in the sense in which some value it. I am about to leave it. But truth and the honour of the nation are something. There is a yet more solemn sanction. The word of God is everlasting, but our dominion in India is temporary. That dominion has been exercised in succession by the other powers of Europe. But Providence did not intend that the Romish faith should be given to Asia. Now we reign. But we do not fulfil the purpose for which the sceptre was given. Why then should Providence withhold the country from a new invader? If we ultimately lose it, let us acknowledge the justice of God in the dispensation.

"It will be a satisfaction to your grace, to know that the translation of the scriptures into the oriental languages still proceeds with spirit, though many do not smile on our labours. A few individuals have devoted their slender means to the furtherance of this great work. But these private resources will soon fail. A *commencement*, however, in the translations is of vast importance. They are 'begun in faith;' and we trust to the divine Author to bring to a happy termination (though not perhaps in our time) the versions of his own most holy word.

"We have it in contemplation to bring the great question of giving the scriptures to the heathen before the public in a few weeks, and to move the subject at all the Presidencies in India at the same time. The protestant mission here must be used as the engine to effect this design, (wielded by the power of the college,) seeing we have no church of our own as a corporate body, and the duration of the college is uncertain. If the public voice shall favour the proposal, an immense sum will be subscribed, and the translations will be carried on under happy auspices.

"Britain will acquire by these works a lasting renown among 'the churches which are in Asia,' planted in a new age. She is indebted for it (under the divine counsel) to the honest purpose of Marquis Wellesley to do good in India. And I consider that the success which has hitherto attended the translations of the scriptures is a 'token for good,' and the best 'sign' we have in present circumstances that Providence means to preserve to us this country.

"I have the honour to present to your grace, for the archiepiscopal library at Lambeth Palace, in the name of the college of Fort William, and with the permission of the Marquis Wellesley, a valuable copy of the Mohammedan Koran in folio, beautifully ornamented with paintings and oriental enamel, and written by the pen of the Sultaun Allavuddeen Siljuky, about four hundred years ago. It has descended to these times in the line of emperors; and was found in the library of Tippoo Sultan at Seringapatam, after the reduction of that capital by the British armies.

"By depositing the most valuable Koran of Asia in the ancient library of the Archbishop of Canterbury, the college of Fort William would intimate, that the sway of the East, once usurped by the Arabian imposter, has now reverted to a christian power; and would express the hope, that, in return for this volume of emblazoned delusion, the Church of England will exhibit to all nations the dutiful act so long expected, and send forth to the inhabitants of Asia the true revelation of God."

The reply which the archbishop was pleased to make to the preceding letter will prove, that his grace duly appreciated the importance of the subject of which it treated; nor can it be doubted that the representations of Mr. Buchanan contributed to the accomplishment of the great purpose to which his labours had been long directed.

Within a few days after the date of this able and eloquent address, a second attack of ague and fever again laid Mr. Buchanan aside for a fortnight. On his recovery, he was informed, by Mr. Udny, that Sir George Barlow, now Governor General, had appointed him Provost of the college, under the new regulation, which admitted only of one superintending officer. This honourable distinction afforded Mr. Buchanan an opportunity, which he immediately embraced, of manifesting both his disinterestedness and his friendship for his valuable associate Mr. Brown. On the very next day he intimated to the government his wish to resign the appointment to the provostship in favour of Mr. Brown, in consideration not only of his long and meritorious services as a chaplain of the Company, but of the extent of his family, and the slender provision which in consequence of that circumstance, and of his liberal and charitable disposition, he had as yet been able to make for their support. No decisive arrangement, however, appears to have been made, until the arrival of final orders upon the subject from England.

Mr. Buchanan closed his ministerial labours this year by a sermon on Christmas-day, on the appropriate subject of the diffusion of that evangelical light in India, the dawn of which they were commemorating on that festival.

The usual college examinations first occupied the attention of Mr. Buchanan in the following year. At their close, towards the end of January, in writing to Mr. Grant respecting one of the students who had distinguished himself by his talents and assiduity, he mentions an idea which had occurred to him relative to the new establishment at Hertford, and which may serve to show the activity of his mind upon every subject connected with the improvement of India.

"I have encouraged a few native moonshees to think of proceeding to England, to aid the students of Hertford college in their pronunciation of the oriental tongues. It appears to me that it would greatly subserve the cause of christian knowledge in Asia, if the Company were to invite to England a few respectable and learned natives every year. They would see us to advantage at home; but they see us at a great disadvantage here.

"I forgot to say in my last how much I was gratified by your mention of the Chinese language in the printed prospectus of the new college which you sent me. That passage was highly valuable and important."

It is, however, to be regretted, that the Chinese language has not yet been cultivated by the servants of the Company, either in India or in England, notwithstanding the facilities afforded by the Chinese class, the establishment of which by Mr. Buchanan has been already mentioned.

On the 12th of February, Mr. Buchanan again wrote to Mr. Grant, on the return of some of his friends to England, and thus expresses his sentiments on the political state of Europe, respecting which, though the period was then distant to which he looked forward, his view was remarkably just, as well as religious.

"It is now nearly six months since we had any ships from

England; and few private letters since April, 1805. By the overland packet, however, we learn the state of public affairs in Europe. If the combined nations should not be able to make much impression on Buonaparte, then may we believe that a remarkable period, spoken of in the prophets, is at hand. But if (as is most natural to suppose from the common course of things) he is to be shorn of his power, then will another nation (that is, Britain) be triumphant in the world; and another great event spoken of by the prophets may be expected, even that to which our Lord alludes, 'And the gospel must first be published among all nations.' For what other people can begin this work like us? It would require three centuries, judging by past history, for any other nation to be so matured by power and will to evangelize the heathen, as we now are, or rather as we shall be when the usurper of many crowns shall fall like Lucifer, and we shall be delivered from the fear of that dreaded event, his expedition to the East; for with infinitely more ease than ever Alexander did may he march through eastern countries, if he could once get his army to the south of the Hellespont."

Mr. Buchanan's next letter to the same highly esteemed correspondent displays, in a striking yet unaffected point of view, the piety, tenderness, and humility of his mind, together with his unremitting anxiety, amidst infirm and languid health, for the great interests of religion. The hint of ecclesiastical preferment to which he alludes, was very natural. It occurred to many in England and in India; and amongst others to his excellent colleague, Mr. Brown; who, as he had the best opportunities of knowing his talents and qualifications, wrote expressly to a distinguished person connected with India in this country, recommending in the strongest terms the elevation of Mr. Buchanan to the episcopal dignity in the East, whenever it should happily be determined to make such an appointment for our oriental dominions. For the present, however, let us hear Mr. Buchanan himself.

"Calcutta, 1st March, 1806.

"Dear Sir,—I was favoured to-day with your letter by the Thalia of the 25th of September last; and I am greatly obliged to you for your notice of the decease of Mrs. Buchanan, and for the tenderness of your expressions in relation to that event. She was indeed a model of humility; so framed by a spiritual power, and richly adorned by the grace of God. I was not worthy of her; but she has left two little daughters to read her history, who I trust will be chosen to follow her high example.

"The subject in your letter, which you will wish me to notice, is that of my return to England. You desire I would stay beyond this year. I would with pleasure, if I thought it would be attended with good. But I must inform you, that since my late illness I am become infirm in body and mind; and I am scarcely fit for those public duties in this place, which require the heart of a lion, and a countenance of brass. I trust my excursion to the Deccan, which I meditate next month, will be beneficial to me. The circumstance I communicate to you is not as yet, perhaps, very evident from my appearance, but it is so in fact.

"The good to be expected now will flow from other sources than Calcutta; so I am less anxious about maintaining this strong post any longer. But if Providence think fit, I will, or rather I shall.

"As to returning in order to receive episcopal dignity, my soul sinks at the thought of it. I trust my lines will rather be cast in a curacy.

"Place the mitre on any head. Never fear; it will do good among the Hindoos. A spiritual bishop will appear in due time.

"My thoughts pass not beyond next month, or that following. But I say thus much, that if I return this year, you may hope that it has been rightly ordered.

"I am sorry you should trouble yourself in noticing my difference of opinion with you on some points. I do not know that there is a right and a wrong in them. They are varying shades of a picture we both love. If any thing I have ever said or done give you uneasiness, I pray you to pardon me. I have no opinion on any thing, at least I desire not to maintain any, but what concerns the gospel of Christ. Had I been brought up in your school, and sat in your chair, I should probably think as you do. But we are both scholars in the school of Christ, where all are taught 'the same words.' And we shall wonder hereafter, (if it be given us to look on from above,) that our right and wrong, our truth and error in India and England, should be overruled to harmonize for the glory of God.

"I preach to-morrow a discourse before the government; 'And the gospel must first be preached among all nations.' Mark xiii. 10. My last effort, I suppose, on these subjects. On Monday, the next day, the Governor General delivers his annual speech before the college; for which I have furnished him, at his desire, with some notes. Much depends, very much, which I have not time now to explain to you, on the complexion of his discourse. And many are waiting with solicitude the result; many on both sides.

"If he admit the word 'civilization' into his speech this year, you may expect to hear the word 'religion' next year. For thus by slow degrees we must proceed.

"If I were nearer to you, communication in present circumstances would be useful. As it is, little can be done.

"May your sun continue long to give its light in your present sphere. Your work that remains, may it be wrought in humility of soul, that heavenly frame! and your decease, like that of Jacob, may it be attended with blessings; blessing your own family, and embalming your memory among the righteous that remain.

"I am, dear sir, very sincerely yours, C. BUCHANAN."

"P. S. I read sometimes with tears (which flow more commonly than usual) the two last pages of your son's poem.

"I hope the prose composition of the other will be published. With the helps of the two last years he may enlarge and improve it; and I shall be obliged to him if he will permit it to be published at my expense."

The annual disputations in the oriental languages, to which Mr. Buchanan refers in the preceding letter, were held on the 3d of March; on which occasion Sir George Barlow, the new Governor General, presided as Visitor.* In the speech with which his excellency closed the proceedings, after paying a merited tribute of respect to the great and venerable nobleman of whom they had been so lately deprived, and of applause to the illustrious founder of the college, he alluded to the conviction which he had expressed at a very early period of the beneficial consequences of its establishment; and added, that the correctness of that judgment had been confirmed by the experience of every successive year. Those branches of the projected education, he observed, which they had the means of prosecuting, had been cultivated beyond the limits of their most sanguine expectations. The Governor General proceeded to declare, that those students of the college who had been distinguished for their proficiency in its prescribed studies, and had been employed in public situations, more particularly in the diplomatic service, had maintained the credit, and demon-

* Calcutta Gazette Extraordinary, March 8, 1806.

strated the advantages of the institution, by the distinguished merit of their general conduct, and by their peculiar ability, industry, and judgment in the execution of the important duties committed to their charge. Sir George Barlow next referred to the new establishment at Hertford.

"An opinion has, I understand, prevailed, that the oriental seminary established in England under the authority of the honourable the Court of Directors, is calculated ultimately to supersede the existing institution of the college of Fort William.

"I deem it proper therefore to take this opportunity of stating, that the oriental seminary founded in England is not intended to supersede the college of Fort William; and it is my deliberate opinion, that the system of oriental study projected in England will tend to support the efficiency of this institution, and to accelerate its operation, by affording to the youth who are destined for this country the advantages of an earlier proficiency in those branches of knowledge which are considered to be peculiarly adapted to the nature of their future duties, and of an early acquisition of the rudiments of the oriental languages."

After complimenting the professors and officers of the college on their persevering and zealous activity in the discharge of their various duties, the Governor General concluded a long and able speech by thus expressing, as Mr. Buchanan had hoped, his conviction of the benefits which might justly be expected to be derived, both by the natives of India and by the British government, from the literary branch of the college of Fort William.

"The numerous works which have been published under the auspices of the college in the course of the last six years, will not only open to the learned in Europe ample sources of information on all subjects of oriental history and science, but will afford to the various nations and tribes of India, and especially to those which compose the body of our Indian subjects, a more favourable view, and a more just and accurate conception of the British character, principles, and laws, than they have hitherto been enabled to form; and may be expected gradually to diffuse among them a spirit of civilization, and an improved sense of those genuine principles of morality and virtue, which are equally calculated to promote their happiness, and to contribute to the stability of the British dominion in India."

The disapprobation, with which the extensive nature of the college of Fort William had been viewed by the Court of Directors, had long prepared its superintendents to expect a reduction of its establishment. Anticipating, therefore, the suspension of that department in it which had hitherto been instrumental in promoting translations of the scriptures into the oriental languages, they were anxious to make some provision for the continuation of these important works. With this view, they resolved to encourage individuals to proceed with versions of the scriptures, by such means as they could command; purposing, at the same time, not to confine this encouragement to Bengal, but to extend it to every part of the East, where fit instruments could be found. Mr. Buchanan particularly determined to devote his influence, as Vice-Provost of the college, in aid of the translations then in the hands of the missionaries at Serampore, and to endeavour to excite the public interest in their favour. For this purpose, early in the year 1806, he drew up "proposals for a subscription for translating the holy scriptures" into fifteen oriental languages; containing a prospectus of Indian versions, and observations on the practicability of the general design. To these proposals, thus composed by Mr. Buchanan from materials partly furnished by the missionaries, their names were subscribed; and in the month of March, copies were distributed liberally in India and in England; in this country to the Court of Directors, to the Bench of Bishops, to the Universities, to Lord Teignmouth, as President of the British and Foreign Bible Society, and to some other public bodies, as well as to many private gentlemen. In India, copies were transmitted to nearly the whole of the principal civil, and to many of the military officers, in the Company's service, from Delhi to Travancore; to many of whom the mission at Serampore was previously unknown. Mr. Buchanan obtained permission, at the same time, to send the proposals, in his official character as Vice-Provost of the college, free of expense, to all parts of the empire; and he accompanied them in most instances with letters, which amounted to about one hundred, from himself.

In two of those letters to friends in England, Mr. Buchanan informed them it had been at first intended that they should issue from the college, under the sanction of government. It appears, that he communicated the manuscript to the Governor General; but, although he was personally disposed to favour the undertaking, he declined authorizing a measure which might appear to identify the government too closely and prominently with an extensive plan for promoting christian knowledge amongst our native subjects. Whatever may be conceded, as to the cautious policy of this conduct, it cannot but be regretted, that the noble and extensive work thus projected could not have been placed under the immediate superintendence and control of the college of Fort William; possessing as it did, in the assemblage of oriental scholars collected around it, such superior facilities for their execution, connected as it was with the Church of England, and consequently affording a pledge, both as to soundness of principle and unity of design, which could be expected from no other quarter.

It was, however, plainly implied in the proposals, that the undertaking would enjoy the countenance and support of the college; and it was doubtless on this ground that the concurrence of the public was principally obtained. That expectation was accordingly expressed in the following terms:

"Our hope of success in this great undertaking depends chiefly on the patronage of the college of Fort William. To that institution we are much indebted for the progress we have already made. Oriental translation has become comparatively easy, in consequence of our having the aid of those learned men from distant provinces in Asia, who have assembled, during the period of the last six years, at that great emporium of eastern letters. These intelligent strangers voluntarily engage with us in translating the scriptures into their respective languages; and they do not conceal their admiration of the sublime doctrine, pure precept, and divine eloquence of the word of God. The plan of these translations was sanctioned at an early period by the most noble the Marquis Wellesley, the great patron of useful learning. To give the christian scriptures to the inhabitants of Asia is indeed a work which every man, who believes these scriptures to be from God, will approve. In Hindostan alone there is a great variety of religions; and there are some tribes which have no certain cast or religion at all. To render the revealed religion accessible to men who 'desire' it, to open its eternal sanctions, and display its pure morals to those who 'seek a religion,' is to fulfil the sacred duty of a christian people, and accords well with the humane and generous spirit of the English nation."

Another passage of the document, from which the preceding extract is taken, announced in India the formation and the proffered friendship of the British and Foreign Bible Society, as furnishing material encouragement to the proposed undertaking. Thus accredited and patronized, the address from the missionaries at Serampore was advertised in the government gazettes, and published throughout India; and such was the approbation with which it was received, that in a short time the sum of sixteen hundred pounds was subscribed in aid of the intended translations.

The communication of the proposals in question to the British and Foreign Bible Society was made by Mr. Buchanan in the month of March. He at the same time recommended, that a sermon should be preached before the Society, "on the subject of oriental translations;" and with the zeal and liberality which had now so frequently marked all his proceedings, requested, "that the reverend preacher would do him the honour to accept the sum of fifty pounds on delivery of a printed copy of the sermon to his agents in London, for the college of Fort William in Bengal." This proposition was at first acceded to by the committee of the society; and the Rev. John Owen, one of its able and indefatigable secretaries, was requested to become the preacher.* It was, however, upon reconsideration, unanimously agreed, that, as the measure did not fall strictly within the professed object of the society, and might open a door to practical irregularities, it would not be expedient to sanction its adoption. The generous offer of Mr. Buchanan was, in consequence of this decision, respectfully declined.

A similar proposal was transmitted by Mr. Buchanan to the Vice-Chancellors of the Universities of Oxford and Cambridge, that two sermons should be preached before each of those learned bodies, on the translation of the scriptures into the oriental languages, by such persons as the Universities should appoint; accompanied by a request, that each of the four preachers would accept the sum of thirty guineas, on the similar condition of the delivery to his agents of a printed copy of the sermon for the college of Fort William. These additional offers to the Universities were in each case accepted.

In the course of the preceding year, Mr. Buchanan received from the University of Glasgow, of which he had been formerly a member, a diploma conferring upon him the degree of Doctor in Divinity. By this title, confirmed as it afterwards was by a similar honour from the University to which he more immediately belonged, he will accordingly be designated in the continuation of these memoirs.

---

* History of the British and Foreign Bible Society, vol. i. p. 281.

CHAPTER V.

Dr. Buchanan was now again looking forward to his long projected journey to the south of the peninsula. On the 12th of March, 1806, he thus wrote to a friend in England:

"I proceed to Malabar in a few weeks. My delay has been chiefly occasioned by the difficulty of my resigning appointments and offices here, where there is no one to receive them. And even now, if I get off fairly, I shall wonder.

"I still continue in my purpose of going home about the end of this year. So that I shall possibly see you and your family once more."

On the 22d of March, Dr. Buchanan obtained leave of absence from the government for six months, together with renewed assurances of the countenance and assistance formerly promised; but his preparations for his journey were again interrupted by a return of ague and fever. This attack was, however, less serious, and of shorter duration than the former; so that at the end of the month he was able to wait upon the Governor General, who kindly offered to accommodate him with one of his tents for his intended journey to the coast. During the month of April, Dr. Buchanan continued his preparations for his approaching absence; attended an examination of the Chinese class at Serampore, and made arrangements for the performance of his clerical duties. His last sermon, previously to his departure, was from the beautiful address in the Revelation of St. John, (chap. iii. 7—13,) to the church at Philadelphia, which he probably considered as in some respects appropriate to that at Calcutta. Dr. Buchanan spent several of the days immediately preceding his journey, with Mr. Udny, who appears to have entered with much interest into his views for the promotion of christianity in India. The late learned and lamented Dr. Leyden had at one time proposed to accompany Dr. Buchanan in his tour; but this plan, though it would doubtless have proved mutually agreeable and beneficial, was finally abandoned.

The design of this extensive and laborious journey cannot be better explained than in the following quotation from the account which Dr. Buchanan afterwards published of his researches:

"*In order to obtain a distinct view of the state of christianity and of superstition in Asia, the superintendents of the college had, before this period, entered into correspondence with intelligent persons in different countries, and from every quarter, (even from the confines of China,) they received encouragement to proceed. But, as contradictory accounts were given by different writers concerning the real state of the numerous tribes in India, both of christians and natives, the author conceived the design of devoting the last year or two of his residence in the east to purposes of local examination and inquiry.

"The principal objects of this tour were to investigate the state of superstition at the most celebrated temples of the Hindoos; to examine the churches and libraries of the Romish, Syrian, and Protestant christians; to ascertain the present state and recent history of the eastern Jews; and to discover what persons might be fit instruments for the promotion of learning in their respective countries, and for maintaining a future correspondence on the subject of disseminating the scriptures in India."

Such were the important views with which Dr. Buchanan entered upon his intended journey. It is no disparagement to travels undertaken from motives either of personal curiosity or of public utility, to assert, that the tour which Dr. Buchanan was meditating, derived, from its disinterested and sacred objects, a peculiar degree of dignity and value. If our great philanthropist, Howard, was justly eulogized by a late celebrated statesman for his indefatigable and self-denying exertions in "travelling over land and sea," not to gratify his taste, or to extend his fame, but "to remember the forgotten, to attend the neglected, and to visit the forsaken," it is not too much to say, that although the labours of that eminent person were more various and continued, it required, in a man of infirm and precarious health, like Dr. Buchanan, a degree of zeal and resolution to enter upon his projected journey, which reflects upon him the highest honour. And although in each case the love of God and of man was the prevailing motive, the object of the one was, in proportion to its extent, as much more important than the other, as inquiries into spiritual wants with a view to their relief are more weighty than those which concern temporal necessities, and as interests of eternal duration are more momentous than any which are bounded by the narrow limits of time. It must be remembered, too, that, with

* Christian Researches, Introduct. p. 7, 8.

the exception of the accommodations afforded him by the kindness of the Governor General, and the hospitality of the British residing at the different stations through which he passed, Dr. Buchanan's extensive tour was undertaken exclusively at his own expense.

On the 3d of May Dr. Buchanan left Calcutta on his way to the south; and on his arrival the same day at Fulta, forty miles below that city, he wrote to Colonel Sandys as follows:

"My dear Sandys,—I am thus far on my journey to Malabar. I propose to visit Juggernaut first, and hope to be there early in June, when the grand festival of the Rutt Jattra takes place. Sir George Barlow has been so good as to lend me some of the Governor General's small tents, so that I shall travel very comfortably. My inquiries, you know, have a threefold aspect, Hindoos, Jews, and Christians. The bands of infidelity and superstition are loosening fast, and Calcutta is by no means the place it was when you were here.

"I have heard this morning that the fleet from England, which went to the Cape, is expected at Madras every day, as one of the ships is already arrived. In this fleet, your friend, Mr. Martyn, is passenger. Mr. Jeffries has been appointed to act as my substitute in the new church in my absence, which will be about six or eight months, if, indeed, I should ever return; for my route is full of danger and difficulty to one infirm as I am. With some view, I trust, to the glory of God, I have purposed; but it is He who must dispose of me and my objects as shall seem to him best.

"I remain, my dear Sandys, very affectionately yours,

C. Buchanan."

Dr. Buchanan, from the time of his arrival at Juggernaut, kept a regular journal of his tour, parts of which, it is well known, he afterwards published on his return to this country. He maintained also a constant correspondence during his journey with the Rev. Dr. Brown, and from these letters a series of extracts shall now be given, which, avoiding, for the most part, the repetition of what Dr. Buchanan himself communicated to the public, will afford a connected view of his whole tour, and contain some additional information, as well as some instructive and interesting reflections on the various scenes through which he passed in this original and enterprising journey. A few letters which Dr. Buchanan wrote to his friends in Europe in the course of his tour will also be inserted in their order.

The first letter to Mr. Brown, dated the 10th of May, from Fulta, informs him, that Dr. Buchanan continued in good health, and that his servants and travelling equipage were all well appointed. On the 13th he thus wrote from Contai:

"I arrived here the day before yesterday in good health and fine spirits. My tents were first hoisted on the backs of elephants, belonging to a Hindoo Rajah, in my journey to the south. I ought always to speak well of the Hindoo people.

"Mr. Mason's kindness and attention are very remarkable; and I am in danger of being detained in my way, like Abraham's servant, by hospitality, before the business be done. But I see there is much to be done by the way which I thought not of.

"I shall leave this place to-morrow, perhaps, or next day, and hope to arrive at Balasore on the 20th, where I propose to stay two days, and then proceed with the pilgrims (who now cover the roads) to Juggernaut.

"I am in haste to pass over the marshy lands of the salt districts, lest fever should come. If it should come here, or before I arrive at my journey's end, and you should not see me again, I pray you to consider it as the hand of God, giving glory to his own cause in his own way, leading our feeble resolves in triumph to a certain stage, and then calling another servant. I leave all my temporal affairs in perfect order. I have no papers, literary or religious; so that no trouble awaits my executors, except those in England, to whom I have consigned the religious education of my two little girls."

The concluding observations of this letter point out in a simple yet solemn manner the entire resignation of its author to the divine will, and evidently imply his preparation for every event of his journey. The spirit of calm yet devoted piety which they breathe, is at once to be admired and imitated.

In a letter on the 17th, from Jellasore, where he waited for his elephant and horse, the following passage occurs:

"At Mohunpore, between Contai and this place, I stopped a night. Juggernaut is to be found there in miniature; having the same name and service. The Hindoo Zemindar gave me a feast, and presented me with a sword, a piece of fine cloth, and ten rupees at parting. When I began to eat, Juggernaut's bells began to ring. I asked the reason, and was told that Juggernaut had begun his supper. So we ate together for near half an hour, during which time the gongs and bells continued a horrid clangor.

"This temple is falling into decay for want of revenue."

On the 25th and 27th, Mr. Buchanan thus describes from

Balasore his mode of travelling, and the conjectures of the natives concerning the object of his journey:

"The commanding officer here has given me a guard of seven seapoys all the way to Cuttack, which is seven days' march. I passed through a jungle where tigers abound. One sprung on a large bullock last week, but he could not carry him off, and the bullock escaped. The tiger hunters showed me their manner of shooting tigers with arrows.

"I leave this place to-morrow; and on the 4th of June, I expect to be at Cuttack. Juggernaut is only three or four days from Cuttack.

"I find it inconvenient to have many followers. I have therefore discharged some servants from this place, and also a supernumerary tent. I have but few wants on a march, as to eating and drinking; and I cannot be troubled with table-cloths. I enjoy refreshing tea after my ride in the morning; for I generally ride one half of the march on horseback, and sometimes on an elephant. I sometimes use my gun, at which I was formerly as expert as any of the writers. But I feel a repugnance in killing harmless animals which I did not feel formerly. Tell H—— that during the two last days' march, I saw beautiful peacocks sitting on the lofty trees by the road side, and monkeys leaping from branch to branch, holding their young ones in their arms.

"You may direct to me to the care of the postmaster at Cuttack until further notice. I am very well known now in this country, so that all letters will easily come to hand. Indeed there has been a singular spirit of inquiry among the natives on the subject of the march of a company's Padre; and I learn from them, that I am a rich man, proceeding on a pilgrimage, to worship the God of the christians, not far from Singhul Deep."

Dr. Buchanan's next letter is dated May 31st, from Buddruck in Orissa, from which he began to anticipate his approach to Juggernaut, and the frightful impression of which, from the bones of pilgrims with which the road in its neighbourhood was strewed, he has painted in such striking colours in the first published extract from his Journal.* The following account of a rencontre with a Hindoo Rajah, is from his letter to Mr. Brown:

"Juggernaut's temples begin to multiply as I move on. The common huts are decorated by his horrid face. The

* Christian Researches, p. 19.

Sanyasses (holy men) are now more naked; and the talk and manners of the Byraggies more licentious.

The Kunka or Kannaka Rajah paid me a visit at my tent last night. I had heard he had formerly murdered some English sailors who were wrecked on his coast, between Balasore and Juggernaut, and therefore resolved not to acknowledge him as a gentleman. I accordingly desired a table to be placed on the lawn before the tent, and one chair, in which I sat with a book before me. The Rajah came up with much ceremony, and presented a nuzzur. I did not rise from my seat, nor offer him one. He was much embarrassed. I spoke to him civilly; and presently rose up and made salam to him as a signal to depart. The crowd of Faquirs and Sanyasses could not understand this. After he was gone I told them the reason, and that I could not, as a christian Padre, bow to vice, whether in a Rajah or in a Priest. This seemed something new to them; but one of them, a very old man, said it was very proper.

"I believe I mentioned to you that it was my purpose to move rapidly *by dawk* along the coast from Juggernaut to Cochin, staying a few days at Madras. Hitherto I have suffered no inconveniences from heat or fatigue. I am therefore encouraged to try a flying course for a few weeks.

"At Jagepoor, my next stage, the names of all the pilgrims are registered. Illustrious names, for four hundred years back, are found on giving a small fee."

On the 6th of June, Dr. Buchanan reached Cuttack, from whence he wrote the two next amusing and interesting letters:

"I arrived here yesterday after eight days' march without seeing a white face; aboriginal Uriahs, Burgahs, that is, Mahrattas, and Loll Jattris, being all my society. I hear I am expected at Juggernaut, fame having travelled before, and informed him that a Company's Padre is on a progress. No unworthy suspicion is yet entertained, I believe; and I am received at the Bhur or Banian tree of each Munzil with a hurrebol by my fellow Padres and their flocks. The scene is rather comic; but so it is. Notes tragic I sound not; and thus we travel onward harmoniously together.

"I dine to day with Mr. Hartwell, register, and to-morrow with Colonel Marley. Next day, Sunday, is sacred; and next day to it, Monday, I dine with the judge of the province, Mr. Ker, who has offered me every aid in the prosecution of my journey. On Tuesday I proceed for Juggernaut.

"The novel scenes of this place occupy my attention, but meet with nothing worthy of description. It is just as I told you; I have not yet had pen or pencil in my hand since I left Calcutta. I have lived too long for natural history. What are called manners and customs of a people, are nearly as futile to him who is inquiring in what state a people are in relation to the Almighty, and to the purpose of their creation."

"CUTTACK, 8th June, 1806.

"The tigers abound in the vicinity of Juggernaut, and kill the pilgrims. A hunting party of eight elephants have lately proceeded from this place to kill them.

"It is supposed that eight lacks of pilgrims are already arrived at Juggernaut.

"The Kunka Rajah, alarmed at my reception of him, and fearing lest I should give an unfavourable character of him at this place, followed me, and overtook me in two marches. He requested moolaqat. I explained to him the cause of my conduct towards him. He said he repented of his former sins, and hoped the British government would pardon him. I told him that on condition of his learning English *principles* I would befriend him, if I could. He is at present under the displeasure of our government, having defended his fort after the conquest of the country, which cost us blood and money. His first request was, that I would intercede for him with the judge of the province, that he should be permitted to visit Juggernaut, which was formerly refused. I mentioned the circumstance to Mr. Ker last night, who has given him permission. The Rajah is now here, with an immense Sowarree; and I suppose we shall proceed together to Juggernaut.

"Much attention is paid to me by all ranks of people here, attention undeserved and unnecessary. The tone is favourable to civilization, and the language conciliating and decorous on all grave subjects.

"In the meantime, this world, like the wilderness through which I am passing, has nothing interesting to my hopes or fears. And I have more comfort in reading a hymn of Watts, than in contemplating plans of improvement for India. I look to no resting place but in a close walk with God. To find that, is a more valuable ευρηκα than to find manuscripts at Cochin.

"The commander of the troops in this province has ordered a guard of seven seapoys for me to the Madras frontier, Ganjam. I am glad I shall have them around me among the priests at Juggernaut.

"Tell H—— that there is a fort here built by a proud king, having the following inscription in Persian on the gate. 'My walls are of iron, and my ditch is full of alligators. I shall never be taken.' And so, because he trusted not in God, but in his iron walls, his fort was taken by Colonel H——."

Of Juggernaut,* one of the principal objects of Dr. Buchanan's journey, of his stupendous temple and countless worshippers, of the impure rites and ceremonies exhibited by his priests, and of the cruel sacrifices by which this Moloch of the East is propitiated, the public has been so fully informed by Dr. Buchanan himself, that it is unnecessary to repeat his dreadfully interesting narrative of the whole scene.† His letters to Mr. Brown, though in a somewhat varied form, contain substantially the same details; and, like the extracts from his Journal, to which any who are desirous of farther information are referred, cannot be read without the deepest emotions of horror and pity, and without exciting in every benevolent and christian mind an ardent prayer, that the time may not be far distant when these abominations shall cease, and the horrid tower of Juggernaut be replaced by the temple of the God of purity and love. A few circumstances, however, which did not appear in the Journal, shall be added from the letters to Mr. Brown, from the 14th to the 21st of June.

"I shall not enter into farther detail of the state of superstition here. Suffice it to say, that all you have heard is true. A short record of facts may be committed to paper; but I have no design of disclosing the philosophy of Juggernaut at this time; and I hope that it will never be necessary."

Such was Dr. Buchanan's intention at this period; but the time at length came when an imperious sense of duty compelled him to publish it.

"Tell H.," continues Dr. Buchanan, "(who gets all my natural history and political remarks,) that the temple of Juggernaut is so high, that men appear on the top of it like crows; and that it is surrounded by a square area of great extent, in each side of which there is a gateway larger than the pagoda near your house.

"A chief object of my journey is perhaps accomplished by my having seen Juggernaut. Nothing has been, I believe, concealed from me. Every question is answered, and I scarcely wish to know more. I shall continue to mix with the people two days more, and then I proceed to Ganjam. Mr. Hunter is desirous that I should prolong my visit; but my spirit of inquiry is exhausted, and my body is fatigued with

* The popular orthography of this word is here adopted, as more familiar to the English reader. For an account of the origin of this idol and his worship, see the eighth volume of the Asiatic Researches.

† Christian Researches, pp. 19—32.

my spirits; so that I look forward to my journey for relief from this twofold oppression.

"I write this from the plain of sculls, near the sea; and it so happens that a scull is under my chair, half buried in the sand."

"JUGGERNAUT, Saturday, 21st June, 1806.

"I propose to proceed on my journey this evening, that I may find a place of rest for my Sabbath, to-morrow, far off from Juggernaut. My best Sabbaths are generally in the wilderness.

"The number of pilgrims here is uncertain. Mr. Hunter has no means of probable calculation. From the nature of the place, we perhaps did not see more than two or three hundred thousand persons at the same time. But I cannot judge, any more than I could say how many grains there are in a handful of sand.

"Can it be that the true seed of Abraham shall be 'as the sand upon the sea shore for multitude?' Doubtless it is true; and with this faith I conclude my last line to you from Juggernaut."*

Dr. Buchanan himself published his reflections on viewing the distant towers of Juggernaut from an eminence on the delightful banks of the Chilka Lake, and the design which he then conceived of some "christian institution," which might gradually undermine the frightful idolatry he had been contemplating, and blot out its memory for ever. This was on Sunday, the 22d. On the 29th he dates from Ganjam, and thus continues his correspondence with Mr. Brown:

"I write to you from a new Presidency. I am happy I did not die at Juggernaut, (the danger was imminent.) My record is engraved in strong legible characters, and it is of less importance where I shall die; I mean in reference to my testimony against the empire of Moloch, 'whose seat in the whole earth is Juggernaut.' His horrors have awakened me a little, and I have committed to paper some notices of my route from Bengal.

"On my entrance into the Madras territory, I have experienced great civility and attention. Here I leave my tents, servants, and equipage, and I proceed by dawk to Fort St. George. Mr. Cherry, the judge, being doubtful whether I shall not feel inconvenience in having no servant at all, has issued orders for a dooly to be prepared for my steward, and

* Christian Researches, p. 31.

has provided means of carrying him close to my own palanquin to the extremity of this province.

"I encounter now a new mode of travelling. How I shall bear it I cannot tell. The chief suffering is the want of a bed, which I have already sometimes experienced. But I am anxious to get to the capital. On the other side I shall take my time."

"GANJAM, 1st July, 1806.

"I proceed this evening on my journey to Visagapatam by dawk. I dine first with Captain E. He has been planting one lack and fifty thousand cocoanut trees, and has made a barren land like the garden of Eden.

"I have been among the mountains for some days, and visited Rumbo, the famous villa on the Chilka Lake. I *look* at what is wonderful or great in the eyes of men.

"My residence at each of my stations is a history, if it were written. New places, new characters, new politics. Truth alone is the same."

"VISAGAPATAM, 6th July, 1806.

"Before this reaches you, I shall probably be at Madras.

"I found travelling by dawk very pleasant. It affords me more time to stop at places of importance.

"The families here pay me much attention, and have made a party for me to go out to see a celebrated pagoda, (not yet noticed by any writer, because not seen,) about sixteen miles in the interior among the mountains.

"I have no news for H., except that I live among lofty mountains, from which I see ships far off at sea, and hear the roar of the billows on the rocky shore."

"VISAGAPATAM, 12th July, 1806.

"The pagoda at Seemachalum is in many respects more interesting than Juggernaut. No scene of nature I have yet beheld is so romantic as the site and vicinity of this temple, which is built on a rocky mountain. You ascend nearly a quarter of a mile by steps of hewn stone and of live rock. A stream of pure water issues from the mount, and this is the sacred fountain, and the origin of the temple. Here the idolatry of Juggernaut is exhibited in another form; but the substance is the same.

"I have not been able to disengage myself from this society till the present hour. I proceed on my journey this morning. I have passed the last two days with Mr. C., the collector here, at his beautiful mansion on the top of a hill, from which we look down on the deck of the St. Fiorenzo and the Albatross, which appear like two *little boats* below."

"SAMULCOTTA, 15th July, 1806.

"I intended to have passed this place without stopping, but Colonel O'Reilly, who commands the troops here, came to the bazar for me himself, and prevailed on me to stay a night.

"I am in great danger of being detained frequently in my future progress through these territories.

"I have this evening visited the botanic garden, over which Dr. R. formerly presided."

From this point no letter to Mr. Brown occurs till Dr. Buchanan's arrival at Madras. In a memorandum book which remains, he notices a sail on the Godavery; and that at Ellore, where he hired bearers for Madras, he passed through a flat country, bounded by the horizon.

On the 3d of August Dr. Buchanan thus resumes his correspondence:

"MADRAS, 3d August, 1805.

"I arrived here on the 31st July, and am now hospitably lodged in the house of Mr. H. I was retarded in my journey by a fever, which seized me between Rajamundry and Ongole, far off from medical aid. It was accompanied by the same symptoms as my former. I found a great difference between this last illness in a palanquin in a jungle, and the former, when I was surrounded by the skilful and the good. On my arrival at Ongole, I obtained some medicine from a native, which was useful. I am now well again.

"Tell H. that all my way from the Chilka Lake to Madras I did not see one scull; that the people on the sea-coast are generally without cast; that they are humane to strangers; and that the women used to make broths and congee for me when I was sick of the fever. They eat pork and all meats. The Telinga missionaries will have a fine harvest if they labour among them. No rain has fallen since I left Juggernaut. The weather has been temperate and very favourable to my journey. I shall now meet with rains in Tanjore, Mr. R. tells me."

"MADRAS, 6th August, 1806.

"I have letters for every station to the south, and letters from almost every station inviting me to call. There has indeed been so much blood shed at Vellore, and so many gentlemen murdered, that an attack on *me* would not be thought strange.

"In the meantime government have *authorized* me to proceed, and desired me to communicate my observations on the state of the christians in the south. I trust, therefore, that my way is not of myself, but of Providence directing me.

"I visited yesterday the deputy Bishop at St. Thomé, and the ancient Portuguese library. Mr. T., the Gentoo scholar, goes to see it to-morrow. It contains, among other valuable books, the Bullarium Magnum Romanum, or the Pope's Statutes at large during the dark ages.

"At Tritchinopoly is another famous library, and a Syrian church.

"Tell H. that I saw yesterday St. Thomas' bones, preserved as a relic, in a gold shrine; and that I saw his grave, whence the Roman Catholic pilgrims carry the dust."

"Pondicherry, 13th Aug. 1806.

"I have travelled these two days with Mr. E., the orientalist, and Mr. S., Judge of Tinavelley. Mr. E. is extremely attentive to me, and wishes to oblige me by every information in his power.

"It is impossible for me to conceal my name, as was proposed. The christians have heard of it, and I am greeted by them as one who comes in the name of government to do them good. I already know what is to be done at the missionary stations. Dr. R. and others informed me fully. From every quarter there is a cry of the sheep for a shepherd. They meet and pray under a tree, and the Brahmins mock."

Dr. Buchanan's next letter is dated from Ziegenbalg's church, in Tranquebar, August 25th. Of the visit which he paid to this spot, consecrated by the memory of the first christian missionaries to India, and of his subsequent arrival at Tanjore, he has given an account in the work which has been already referred to.* This was, however, so interesting a part of his tour, that it appears desirable to give a sketch of it from his correspondence, together with a few particulars, which were either wholly omitted, or but partially detailed in his journal.

"I have just visited the tomb of Ziegenbalg, which is on the side of the altar in the church he built. It was consecrated on

---

* Christian Researches, p. 65—81.

the 2d of October, 1718, and he died on the 23d of February, 1719. I heard divine service performed in the Tamul tongue, and about two hundred natives sung the hundredth psalm. During the sermon some of them wrote on an olla or Palmyra leaf. The missionary told me that the catechists sometimes take down a whole sermon in this manner, and repeat it to the children in the evening.

"I also visited Ziegenbalg's dwelling-house, built by himself, and not altered since his time. I inspected the records of baptism commencing in May, 1706. Mr. C., a missionary here, told me they had some thoughts of celebrating the hundredth anniversary this year, but they had no money.

"I then visited the library in which Ziegenbalg first preached; and afterwards a small chapel on the sea-shore, in which he sometimes exhorted. The library is extensive and valuable, but in a perishing state. Here I found the Hindostanee Psalter; and I am informed that at Tanjore I shall find a Hindostanee Grammar, published about sixty years ago.

"The Jesuits at Pondicherry have a fine collection of ancient Indian history. They very politely gave me all the books I wanted, and letters of introduction to their brethren in the south. They also furnished me with a late statement of their churches in India; and Padre B. requested leave to correspond with me in Latin.

"Dr. John is at Tanjore, where I expect to see him and Mr. Kolhoff in two or three days.

"The most pious man I have yet found is Mr. S., a young missionary, lately arrived. He assured me that there are some real christians among the Hindoo converts. At Cuddalore I passed a night with Mr. H. At that place the Cadet Company (one hundred and twenty strong) is now established on account of the salubrity of the situation.

"At the celebrated pagoda of Chillumbrum, near Porto Novo, I was admitted (I know not why) into the interior, while the priests made Pooja. I never had such a clear revelation of this idolatry before. The dancing girls were present. The Judge of the place, Mr. R., had introduced me to the Brahmins the evening before in the outer court. During the ceremony two immense bells were rung and drums were beat. My heart began to palpitate a little, from fear I believe; and I hastily retired. This is a remarkable scene. I could easily pass a month at every stage This is more illustrious than classic ground. For here Ziegenbalg and Grundler preached the gospel to men, whose descendants I have conversed with, and who can justly appreciate the heavenly gift. The Danish Governor here invited the missionaries to meet me. Tanjore is the grand theatre of the gospel in late years, and to that place I proceed this afternoon; but I shall stay one day at Combeconum, where the oriental E. is Judge. He is very anxious to see some pages of a Portuguese book which I procured from the Jesuits at Pondicherry. It is about three hundred years old. He is a great admirer of the genius of Xavier, and thinks that a Protestant missionary of such powers might convert Hindostan."

"COMBECONUM, near TANJORE, Aug. 27, 1806.

"In the midst of some horrible looking bloodred idols, I shall write a few lines. Mr. E. is not yet arrived here, having supposed that I should have staid longer at Tranquebar; which I should have done, had I not been afraid of a number of entertainments. These are sometimes useful, for the best information I generally obtain is from the chief people. They were all much surprised at the interest I took in the ancient mission of Ziegenbalg. The missionaries themselves were ignorant of many subjects of my inquiry; and were a good deal ashamed, I believe, at my notice of the former glory of the mission compared with its present state. I have reason to believe that the three London missionaries, Desgranges, Cran, and Mr. Palm,* are three holy men; and it appears as if the glory had now departed from Germany, and was given to England. So Mr. S. speaks. He is a promising young man; and as his society gives him only three hundred rupees a year, I gave him a half year's salary to buy some clothes and books. Though he has been but two years in India, he pronounced a very good sermon in the Tamul tongue, which the native catechist told me was perfectly intelligible to all the congregation.

"It is a pleasant thing to see an assembly of natives listening most earnestly to a sermon. Every one of them can read the Bible; and Luther's first Psalter (the German Gesang Buch) is very familiar with them. They sing a great variety of tunes with much propriety."

"TANJORE, 1st Sept. 1806.

"This is the grand scene of all. This is the garden of the gospel.

"Some days before my arrival here, the Resident, Major Blackburne, wrote to me, inviting me to reside at his house.

* Mrs. P. is a help meet in the gospel. She learns the languages faster than her husband, and devotes herself to the real object of the mission. Mr. P. is at Jaffnapatam.

This was unexpected, for as yet I had no communication with Tanjore. On my arrival there, I first waited on Mr. Kolhoff, and he showed me two rooms, which he had prepared for my reception. He told me that the Rajah (Serfogee) was impatient to see me, and had directed the Resident to let him know when I came. I asked how the Rajah came to know me. He said that the Resident had a copy of my memoir, and of Mr. Mitchell's essay.

"Mr. Kolhoff is first in piety, in ardour, in meekness, and in knowledge of the Tamul; for he has been brought up chiefly in India. His countenance is more expressive of amiable qualities of mind than that of any man I ever saw. Major Blackburne admires him much."

"Tanjore, 2d Sept. 1806.

"On my arrival here on Friday last, the 29th of August, great numbers of christians came to visit me; and Mr. Kolhoff introduced some particularly to me, as being truly godly and intelligent men. He gave me also an account of many triumphant deaths lately, both of men and women, young and old.

"As I went to the Resident's house I passed through a long street inhabited by christians only. They stood in rows as we passed, and bowed affectionately to their pastor, the young women coming forward with lively confidence, and soliciting his benediction. The infants also form themselves in little rows, and waiting his approach make the customary salutation, 'God be praised.'

"When we arrived at the Resident's, he told me that the Rajah had appointed next day (Saturday) at noon to receive me. I proceeded accordingly to the palace, accompanied by the Resident: the Rajah arose on our entrance, and taking me by the hand led me to a seat on his right. He spoke English very well, and intimated that he knew me very well. After some conversation, he carried me up to his splendid apartments, which are ornamented with the portraits of the Tanjore kings. All around there is a display of gold, silver, and mirrors, English paintings, libraries, musical instruments, orreries, portfolios of oriental drawings, and many curiosities in art and nature. Finding that I wished to hear the music of the *vina*,* he ordered up the chief musician. He has a band of twenty performers, of whom twelve play on the vina, and one on the harp. The whole black band can read English music. In the

* Described by Sir William Jones in the third volume of the Asiatic Researches.

evening his highness sent the band to Major B., where I dined. Six vinas and six singers played 'God save the King,' in Tamul words, applied to the Maha Rajah. They played also a variety of English overtures and Indian airs, the master of the band sitting by and keeping time.

"My visit to the Rajah was very long. Our chief conversation related to Mr. Swartz. When I first mentioned his name, his highness led me up to the picture of the reverend apostle. He then showed me the design for the groupe for the marble monument, now executing by Mr. Bacon in England. It represents the Rajah coming to the bed of the dying Swartz, and taking him affectionately by the hand, while a number of boys are weeping at his feet.

"When I was about to depart, the Rajah presented me, to my great surprise, with a picture of himself, a miniature about six inches in length, elegantly set in a gold and silver frame, and glazed. We then went down stairs and resumed our seats. I took this opportunity (having previously acquainted the Resident with my purpose, who communicated it to the Rajah) of thanking his highness, in the name of the society at home, and of all Mr. Swartz's friends in India, for the remarkable kindness shown by the Rajah to that worthy man, and to his successors, and for the munificent support granted lately by the Rajah to the body of christians in his dominions.

"To this he replied in suitable terms, declaring it to be his purpose to befriend the christians *for ever*. He then called for pawn; and immediately afterwards a servant came up with four pieces of gold cloth of different kinds, which the Rajah taking into his hands presented to me. He then put a chaplet of flowers round my neck, (this is the usual etiquette,) and a bracelet of flowers on my arms, and, leading me and the Resident, one in each hand, to the steps of the hall, he bowed and retired.

"The Rajah has lately erected a college for Hindoos, Mohammedans, and Christians. Fifty christian boys are admitted, and taught by schoolmasters provided by the missionaries. The expense of this institution is (according to the account of the Resident) about five lacks of rupees. But this includes the expense of buildings. It is also a charitable asylum for the aged, and a choultry for travellers, there being an apartment for every denomination. His highness wished me to visit his college. It is about fifteen miles from Tanjore. He is now constructing a brass orrery to represent the Tychonic system; which he wishes to believe rather than the Copernican, as it is the system of the Brahmins. He is still a heathen; but Dr.

John says he is a Cornelius. The Brahmins fear him for his learning, and dread the result.

"Last Sunday (the 30th August,) was a great day among the christians at Tanjore. It being rumoured that a friend of Mr. Swartz was arrived, the christians flocked together from all quarters. Divine service was performed three times. In the morning we all proceeded to Mr. Swartz's church in the fort. It is a large, commodious building, not inferior to your Calcutta church. Mr. Kolhoff read prayers in English, and I preached. When I came to the mention of the faithful ministers whom God had sent to his people in this place, there was a general commotion, and Mr. Kolhoff's tears flowed fast, which not a little affected his flock. Having understood that the missionaries seldom prayed for the reigning prince of the country, I thought it expedient to say, (in enumerating the themes of gratitude of the church here,) 'and it is their bounden duty to pray for the long life, peace, and prosperity of the present most excellent prince, who hath manifested by many munificent acts his regard for their happiness and welfare.'

"At eleven o'clock, the Tamul congregation assembled, filling the whole church, and Dr. John preached a powerful and eloquent sermon in the Tamul language.

"In the vestry all the native teachers and preachers came to make their speeches to me; and among others the celebrated Sattianaden, the Hindoo preacher. He is now stricken in years and infirm. His black hair is grown grey. He is rather stout, and has a placid look, which is rendered more pleasing by his wrinkles and age. He said to me, alluding to some part of my sermon, 'This news from a far country, is refreshing to our souls.'

"We dined at Mr. Kolhoff's at one o'clock, and at five we went to the small church out of the fort, in which Mr. Swartz first preached, and where now his body lies. It is close by the schools and Mr. K.'s house and mission garden. Here Mr. Horst preached in the Portuguese tougue from these words: 'Ye who were once afar off,' &c. This was a solemn service. The organ was drowned by the human voices, which sung a tune of Luther's in a noble manner. I was sitting with my feet on the granite stone which covers Swartz's grave. Upon the stone is an English epitaph in verse, written by the present Rajah. In the evening, Mr. K. catechised (or superintended the exercise) in the schools; and the sermon of the morning was read over by one of the short-hand writers, and every boy's olla was examined to see how much he had written.

"Having expressed a wish to hear Sattianaden preach, the same was intimated to the people, and they were desired to assemble at the little church next morning (Monday) at nine o'clock. Accordingly a great number came together, and the venerable minister delivered a sermon full of fire. His natural eloquence and various intonation were truly calculated to command attention. Both Mr. Kolhoff and Dr. John were affected by the discourse. It had reference to the former darkness in India, the light of Ziegenbalg and Swartz, the present endeavour to spread the gospel, and lastly the light of heaven. He addressed the young generation chiefly, and they responded* as usual to many of his sentences. He made great use of the Bible; but in quoting a passage, he called upon a lower minister to read it with a distinct voice, to which he himself listened as to a record, and then proceeded to expound. His prayer for the Church of England at the end was full of fervour; and the psalm which concluded the service was sung with an ardent devotion.

"I went up to Sattianaden in the presence of the people, and addressed him in a few words, hoping he would be faithful unto death, like his old master Swartz. The women and aged men crowded round, and shed tears. The whole multitude came after the sermon to Mr. Kolhoff's house and garden. The catechists and aged christians came into the verandahs, and while Mr. Kolhoff and myself were engaged up stairs, Dr. John addressed them in an affectionate and impressive manner.

"Mr. Kolhoff had been praying that there might be an outpouring of the Spirit in these days at Tanjore, and circumstances made him believe that it was coming. His success is indeed great. The congregation is doubled since Mr. Swartz's death.

"Not wishing to leave this people without some mark of my regard, I have given Mr. Kolhoff fifty pounds sterling as a 'donation to the native catechists of the protestant mission,' to be distributed according to Mr. K.'s pleasure.

"The Resident requested that I would dine with him on Monday evening, and invited all the missionaries to meet me.

"Mr. Kolhoff has presented me with a gold and agate snuff-box, which belonged to the late Rev. Mr. Swartz; and the mission here has given me from the library a Hebrew

---

* Referring to an interesting custom, which Dr. Buchanan has fully detailed in his Christian Researches, p. 71.

Psalter, which he constantly used; and also his Greek Testament. You shall have the latter if you like.

"I proceed to-morrow to Tritchinopoly to Mr. Pohlé, an aged missionary, and a good Hebrew and Syriac scholar. I procured here a beautiful gilt Syriac Testament, and some tracts in Syriac, translated from the German by Mr. Swartz. There is in the library a copy of Schultz's Hindostanee Grammar, published at Halle, in 1745. Nor is that the first; for Schultz mentions one printed some years before by the Dutch ambassador at Agra, Johannes Josua Ketelaer, and edited by David Millius at Utrecht.

"I am now going to inspect Mr. Swartz's correspondence, which fills two boxes, He kept the letters of his friends, and destroyed his own. I could stay a month at Tanjore, but I must be gone. No fear of Vellore Brahmins or Mussulmans in this land. The christians form a firm phalanx around me. But if I should not be permitted to proceed farther, I may be thankful that something is done here.

"Tell H. that I have seen many wonderful things of late, but that I cease to wonder at any thing; and that I should be glad to have her, or some other little girl like Augusta, along with me, that I might enjoy the pleasure of seeing her *astonished* now and then.

"The interesting scenes of the christian missions have lately obliterated from my mind the poor Syrians and Jews, although I am just on their borders; and, being on the borders, I can get no information about them from any European. Every body refers me to Colonel Macaulay.

"Mr. Pohlé told me, that a Romish priest, who was lately in the vicinity of Tritchinopoly, preached the atonement with great clearness and force, to the astonishment of the people; and that he had been removed by his superiors in consequence. I shall endeavour to find him out. If I could make a confidant of a Jesuit, he would be an admirable companion in my tour.

"I have just read the orders of the Madras government passed last year, excluding the French and Italian Jesuits from ecclesiastical authority in the Deccan, and granting the whole to the Archbishop of Goa, and his ignorant native priests. This circumstance renders my approaches to the Jesuits more facile. I must look into Goa. I have read in French, since I left Pondicherry, La Croze's Christianity in India, a most admirable classical work. His chief subject is the inquisition at Goa, and the Syrian christians; and his last pages are devoted to Ziegenbalg. He expresses a hope that some persons will be sent from Europe on an embassy to the Syrian christians, to inquire concerning their state, learning, and religion, after so long an interval.

"Joachim at Aughoor told me I should find them in five days' march through the woods from Travancore palace; he called them *schismatiques*, whom no European or Romish priest had ever visited."

During his stay at Tanjore, Dr. Buchanan wrote at considerable length to his venerable friend, Mr. Newton. His letter contained a sketch of his journey up to that time, with a full account of the gratifying scenes which he had lately witnessed among the christians in that quarter. The publicity which has been already given to this narrative renders the repetition of it in these memoirs superfluous. Two circumstances only hitherto unnoticed may be mentioned as occurring in the letter to Mr. Newton. One is, that Dr. Buchanan, having heard much of the sculptures at Vellore, had intended to have been there on the 8th of July, which was two days before the dreadful massacre took place. "But the providence of God," he adds, "retarded my steps. I was visited by a fever, which confined me for some time at a caravansera." This temporary detention was probably the means of preserving his life!

The other additional circumstance relates to the newly converted christians; "some of whom," observes Dr. Buchanan, "have suffered persecution. This has, however, been so far useful, that it shows the serious change of mind in the Hindoo who can bear it. For it is often alleged in India, that the Hindoo can never be so much attached to Christ, as the Brahmin to his idol." The constancy of the native christians in any instances of persecution for the faith is therefore a sufficient refutation of this calumny.

On the same day on which Dr. Buchanan addressed Mr. Newton at such length, and on so many important topics, he wrote a short letter to his two little girls, then only four and five years old, the affectionate simplicity of which will render it interesting, at least to parental readers.

"Tanjore, in India, 1st September, 1806.

"My dearest little girls, Charlotte and Augusta,—I hope you are very well. Whenever you can both read the Bible, let me know, and I shall go home. I want little girls who can say to papa at breakfast, 'Papa, we will read the newspapers to you, while you take tea.' I want little girls who can read when papa writes to them *so;** and who do not oblige him to draw little letters till his fingers ache.

"I am happy, my dear children, to hear so good an account of you. Be very good, and I shall come to you soon.

"I saw the two little daughters of the king of Tanjore today. They are covered with pearls and diamonds; but their skins are black; and they cannot read one word, although they are about eight years of age. Therefore my own two little girls are more dear to their affectionate father than the princesses at Tanjore. C. BUCHANAN."

On the 4th of September, Dr. Buchanan addressed the following letter to Mr. Henry Thornton, which is particularly valuable from the contemporaneous and almost local testimony which it contains respecting the cause of the unhappy massacre at Vellore, which was afterwards so invidiously brought forward to injure the interests of christianity in India.

"SERINGHAM PAGODA, near Tritchinopoly,
"4th Sept. 1806.

"Dear Sir,—I had the pleasure of receiving at this place your letter of the 16th February, 1806. I am concerned to hear of your frequent indisposition. You mention particularly that sedentary employment is inconvenient to you; and you notice this as a cause for not writing to me. I do not expect that you should write, as you may perceive by my never entering fully into any particular subject. You have other and more important avocations to employ your pen, when you are able to sit down. I write to you sometimes, because I feel it natural that I should inform you from year to year that I am alive.

"In mentioning Mrs. Buchanan's happy death, you express a hope that my last end may be like hers. And what can I better wish for you, that when your hour cometh, you may die like your father, blessing your children?

"It is now four months since I left Calcutta, having travelled by land all the way, looking into Hindoo superstitions, and English manners in India. The officers of government, civil and military, English and native, have everywhere shown

* This refers to the first six lines of his letter, which Dr. Buchanan had taken the pains to write, or, to express it more plainly, *to print* in Roman characters.

me civilities, and aided my inquiries; and everywhere there have been many and serious subjects of inquiry.

"At most of the stations between Calcutta and Madras there is an evident disposition to favour the establishment of a christian ministry. But they have no clergy of any kind. Two Presbyterian ministers arrived at Visagapatam last year, and the inhabitants have now built a house for them. They insisted on their reading the Episcopal liturgy, which they had the good sense to do; and in return they are allowed to preach an extempore sermon.

"At Cuttack, Balasore, Juggernaut, Ganjam, Rajahmundry, Nellore, and the intervening stations, there is 'total eclipse.' And yet in all these places the residents would probably support a minister, if he were on the spot. 'We are indeed very bad,' they say; 'but if we had some encouragement we should be better.'

"Lord W. Bentinck desired I would report my opinion on the best mode of ameliorating the state of the newly converted, in my progress through the Deccan. And indeed their state demands the attention of government; for I find that the Company's servants in some districts consider the christian as the lowest cast.

"The success of the Protestant mission during the last century has been very great. Something more perhaps will be done during the present. The Jesuits have hewed wood and drawn water for us. I am as yet on good terms with them, and their information is generally more important than that of the Protestant missionaries. Schisms and dissensions at present disturb both Protestants and Catholics.

"A rumour has for some months pervaded India, that all casts are to be made christians. I know the alleged causes of the rumour, but I consider them as inadequate to produce the present effect, without a concurring Providence. This strange rumour of conversion is perhaps auspicious to the event itself; as the shaking of an old building announces its approaching fall.

"It was attempted to be shown, that the massacre at Vellore, which happened when I was in the neighbourhood, was in some measure caused by this rumour. But it has been proved by the evidence of the conspirators, that the design of resuming the Mohammedan dynasty in Mysore was planned by the princes immediately on their hearing the joyful news that the tiger Wellesley, as they styled him, had been recalled from India.

"I have just been conversing with the Brahmins of this celebrated Pagoda, (which, according to Orme, once maintained 40,000,) and they have been inquiring about Bonaparte. They have heard that on his arrival they are all to be made christians.

"I remain, dear sir, very sincerely yours,

C. BUCHANAN."

"P. S. I have just measured the length of the granite stones of the Pagoda gate, which Orme says are five feet square, and thirty-three in length. But they are exactly forty-one in length."

The next letter of Dr. Buchanan is addressed to Mr. Grant, and is chiefly occupied with the state of the missions supported by the Society for Promoting Christian Knowledge. The testimony at the close to the character of the native christians, when compared with that of the unconverted Hindoo, is particularly gratifying.

"MADURA, 14th Sept. 1806.

"Dear Sir,—I was lately favoured with a letter from Mr. Thornton, in which he mentions that you were yet well, and actively engaged in useful labours.

"Having been for upwards of four months past travelling in the interior of the country, I have heard but little of public affairs, and I do not desire at present to think of them. In consequence of my uncertain route, I am cut off from all correspondence, except that of the stations through which I have passed. This correspondence, however, is very interesting, as it usually refers to the suppression of idolatry, and the promotion of the knowledge of the only true God.

"As I suppose you are still connected with the Society for Promoting Christian Knowledge, I shall notice some particulars of their missions in these parts. I have now visited all the stations, and conversed with all the missionaries. At Tanjore I sat in conclave with three of them on the subject of the general mission, when they proposed that I should make a report to the society of their present state. But this will not be necessary till I know what the society has the power to do.

"I did not observe that the gospel flourished anywhere but in Tanjore. In Tranquebar a holy remnant is left; perhaps also at Madras; but I heard not of many recent conversions. But from Tanjore streams will flow, like its own fertilizing rivers, throughout the neighbouring lands.

"Of all the missionaries, Mr. Kolhoff, at Tanjore, is the

first and best; a man of meek spirit, but of ardent faith, and a worthy successor of the illustrious Swartz.

"Mr. Horst and Mr. Shveiffvogel appear to be zealous men, pure in their life and doctrine.

"Messrs. Pohlé, John, and Rottler, are now old men, and incapable of labour in the proper duties of the mission. Dr. John and Dr. Rottler are conversant in natural history, which is often fascinating enough to become a study. Dr. Rottler is an amiable man, but seems to want energy.

"Mr. Pohlé, at Tritchinopoly, the senior missionary, is a learned man, but now stricken in years, He devotes himself chiefly to the *English* church at Tritchinopoly, which of itself demands the whole labours of one minister.

"Three men of learning and piety are wanted to fill up the places of Swartz, Jœnické, and Gerické. But it seems that such are now to be found in Germany.

"There is a great cry for Bibles throughout the Tamul land. The poor funds of the mission here cannot supply them. I have visited several christian villages where there were but two Bible-houses. Mr. Kolhoff wishes this to be immediately represented. As the Tamul version is now finally settled, (like the English,) the society might print the Bibles at home, and send out twenty thousand copies every year.*

"I have conversed with many Hindoos of the Brahmin and other casts, who appear to be true members of Christ's body. I have seen in the feeble-minded native of Hindostan, truth, generosity, a spirit without guile, ardent zeal for the faith, and a love for those who love the Lord Jesus Christ in sincerity. I am satisfied that our Saviour hath a church here, and that in process of time all casts will come into it.

"I remain, dear sir, very sincerely yours,

C. BUCHANAN."

On the 20th of September, Dr. Buchanan again writes to Mr. Brown, from Ramnad pooram, as follows:

"In the province of Madura the Romish churches are frequent. At Aour, or, properly, Aughoor, near Tritchinopoly, is a church where the priest reads the Syrian mass, instead of Latin, which he does not understand. Nor do his people understand the Syrian; for to them he preaches in Tamul. He

* Nothing effectual appears to have been done towards supplying this pressing demand for Bibles till the year 1810, when Mr. Brown preached a sermon at Calcutta upon the subject, and a subscription of one thousand pounds was in consequence raised towards the purchase of copies of the Tamul scriptures, and the encouragement of a new edition. See Christian Researches, p. 89.

gave me a Syrian letter to his brethren at Cranganore. At this church there is an union of Romish ceremonies and pagan superstitions. They have their Rutt Jattra. I examined the Rutt, which is built in the usual manner, with three cables to pull it. Only that, instead of the Hindoo devices, it has hell and the devils on the lower part, heaven and the blessed in the higher, and, above all, the pope and the cardinals. The priest, my friend Joachim, is so ignorant, that he did not seem conscious of any impropriety in having the Rutt. I asked him how many thousands of christians attended the festival: he said, generally about ten thousand; which number corresponds with the report of the collector of the district.

"The English here know little of these matters. Mr. C., a Judge of circuit, told me he would proceed immediately to Aughoor, to see this sight. I told him he might see it in many other places.

"I passed three days among the ruins and antiquities of Madura. This is a fine station for the gospel.

"I proceed from this place to the Juggernaut of the south, Ramisseram. There Mussulmans and Hindoos have consecrated the names of Adam and Abel."

An interval nearly of a month occurred between the date of the preceding letter, and that of Dr. Buchanan's next communication to the same friend and correspondent; during which he had visited the island of Ramisseram, and from thence had crossed to Ceylon. Of his visit to the latter island, both at this time and again about eighteen months afterwards, Dr. Buchanan gave some account to the public in his Christian Researches; but of Ramisseram, as well as Ceylon, it may not be uninteresting to add the following particulars:

"Borders of Travancore, 18th October, 1806.

"The Ranny of Ramnad gave me a letter to the Pandarum or chief priest of the Pagoda of Ramisseram, desiring that he would give me a catalogue of the Shanscrit books preserved in the temple from time immemorial. The Ranny is the patroness (by hereditary right) of the temple. When I delivered the letter, the Pandarum informed the priests of its contents. They observed, that no catalogue had ever been given before. The Pandarum said he would give me an answer next day. In the meantime I paid him a visit of ceremony, and presented a nuzzur. The next day he sent to acquaint me that the catalogue was preparing, and would be ready for delivery in the evening; when I was requested to proceed to the Pandarum's house. At five o'clock he came himself to accompany me, attended by his elephants and music, and the whole band of priests. In this procession I moved round the temple to the Pandarum's house, where all the books were exhibited in order. They are all written on ollas; and had generally the aspect of antiquity.

"The Pandarum then presented the catalogue written on four ollas. It contains ninety-six Shanscrit volumes, and seventy-two Tamul.

"It was Mr. E. who suggested to me the attempt to procure this catalogue.

"Ramisseram, or rather Ramacoil, or Ramacovel, that is, Rama's temple, is a noble building. The aisles, or porticoes, of majestic height, are about six hundred feet long. No abbey or cathedral in Europe is of such magnitude. Like the other temples in the Deccan, its revenues are wasting away. But Juggernaut will fall, I think, before Ramacoil. I saw no human bone in the island of Ramisseram. Christianity in its worst shape has civilized the Deccan. All descriptions of people are more humane and intelligent than the Hindoos of Bengal.

"The Pandarum presented to me a fine shawl, (the Ranny gave me two,) and then procured a donie to carry me to Jaffnapatam. The wind was fair, and I was only one day on the deep. I had letters to Mr. T., the civil magistrate of Jaffna. I slept the first night on the island of Leyden, at the house of Mr. T., the custom master. Next morning he showed me three Roman Catholic churches lately built, and assured me that every person on the island was a christian. I passed through a bazar, and spoke to some christian women selling turtle, which they cut in pieces to make curry. They were not so intelligent as Mr. Kolhoff's christians.

"I next day visited the chief Romish church in Jaffna town; built by Padre Leonardo, who now presides in the island. This church is the largest structure of slight building which I ever saw. Every Sunday about a thousand or twelve hundred people attend, and on feast days three thousand and upwards. Leonardo introduced me to four of his brethren, who all conversed very fluently in Latin. There are five priests in Jaffna, and ten in Ceylon. They are all of the same order, St. Philip Nerius; and no priest of any other order is ever admitted to the island.

"I passed half a day with Dr. S., mentioned by Thunberg. Dr. S. was at Japan, and brought from thence a valuable collection of Japanese books in print. They are chiefly on subjects of natural history, having drawings of animals. He has a very extensive museum of oriental curiosities. I went patiently through his library, and found some information I wanted.

"Among the Dutch ladies are some examples of serious religion. Mrs. M. is a pious woman. She could not speak English; but she produced a quarto Dutch Bible, well worn, and we conversed with each other in texts.

"The chief justice spoke respectfully of Mr. Palm, and so did the other gentlemen at Jaffna. They wished me to go to Columbo, and report to the Governor: he has himself already visited Jaffna, and Dr. S.'s collection.

"From Jaffnapatam I proceeded by land to Manaar, through the woods; a journey of three days. The elephants, bears, and buffaloes abound. Every night two men preceded my palanquin, carrying each a flaming log of gum-wood, to frighten the wild beasts. In the open spaces in the woods, I saw the Ryots guarding their cattle with gum-wood torches. The cheetah is very destructive here.

"Governor North built three caravanseras in these desolate woods.

"At Manaar I found Captain B., commandant of the Fort. He was a shipmate in the Busbridge. At his house I met Mr. M., son to the old lady at Jaffna. He happened to mention that he had Busching's Magazine in German, containing Moen's (the Dutch Governor at Cochin) account of the Jews at that place. This book is referred to by Forster, who writes notes to Bartolomeo, as the last and most authentic account.

"Mr. M. has promised to translate the whole into English, and send it to me in a fortnight.

"At Manaar I embarked in a donie, an open boat, about the size of a burr, for Ramisseram. A storm arose, and I went on shore at a fishing village, situated near the north-west extremity of the island Manaar. They were all Romish christians, and I slept in their church. The priest was absent; and his catechist had never heard that there was such a book as the Bible. The dandies of my own boat were also christians, but had never heard of the Bible. They had, however, a very good christian custom. Before they hoisted the sail, they all joined in prayer to God for protection. Every man at his post with the rope in his hands pronounced his prayer.

"Next morning I embarked again; and when we were nearly out of sight of land, the wind began to rise again. We could not gain any land before it was dark. At four o'clock in the morning we were alarmed by the noise of breakers; and in a few minutes we struck on Adam's bridge. I had expressed a wish to see Adam's bridge; and now I saw it in a perilous situation. The boatmen leaped out, and kept the boat's head to the sea till she floated, and then forced her through the waves like a Masoolah boat.

"At day-light I saw the towers of Ramisseram near at hand, when we landed at Pomben, next the continent. The boatmen offered up their christian thanksgiving for their deliverance from the peril of the sea. One of Mr. Swartz's catechists, who accompanies me everywhere, appeared to be a good deal edified by the scene.

"My friends at Ramnad sent bearers to me on my arrival at Pomben, and I was conducted once more to Colonel M.'s hospitable mansion.

"Tell H. that in the island of Ramisseram I saw Abel's tomb, which is about fifty feet long. It is guarded by a Mussulman, as I expected would be the case. In Ceylon the fable of Adam's flight from the island is very current. The truth seems to be this. The Hindoos called Ceylon a paradise, on account of its spices and pearls and precious stones. And the Mussulmans, believing it to be the Garden of Eden, introduced Adam and his family immediately.

"At Ramnad-pooran there is a good Protestant church and parsonage-house of stone, built by Colonel M. and the company about eight years ago. But they have no minister, and long much for a visit from some missionary.

"From Ramnad I proceeded to Tutycorin, where there is a rich Romish church, and a Dutch Protestant church.

"At this place there is a tribe of Hindoos called Parrawars, (not Pariahs,) whose chief is called Prince of the Parrawars. The whole of this tribe, without exception, are christians in the Romish communion. The wealth and dignity of the prince support the church, and exhibit more magnificence than is now generally to be found in the Romish churches.

"The Rutt is attached to this church, as at Aughoor. The priest told me he walked before it in procession. In the Hindoo temples it is usual to ring bells and strike gongs the moment the idol is unveiled. In analogy to this, bells are rung and drums beat at Tutycorin when the Virgin Mary is unveiled. There are three bells within the church of large size, which have a terrible effect on the auditory nerves. I requested the priest to undraw the curtain before the Virgin, that I might see the golden image: but I was not apprized of the thunder that was to accompany the exhibition.

"I visited the prince in form, and inquired into the moral state of his subjects. He was denominated by the Dutch the

Prince of the Seven Havens. The Dutch minister showed me his library, in which I was happy to find Fabricius's Lux Evangelii, in quarto. I went from Tutycorin to Tinavelly, in my palanquin, without taking my eyes off this book.

"Here is the pearl fishery. I saw the shells in heaps at the place where they are opened, and Mr. M., the Dutch merchant at whose house I lodged, made me a present of a large pearl, about the size of a pistol bullet, but of little value from its being clouded in various places.

"At Tinavelly I was hospitably received by the Judge, the Collector, and the Register. In Palamcotta Fort, which is close to Tinavelly, there is a Protestant church and parsonage-house. The christians in the district are numerous, and have suffered some persecution. Mr. Kolhoff wished me to represent the subject to the Judge and Collector, who have assured me that they will afford them every protection and encouragement in their power.

"Tell H. that I write this at the bottom of the lofty mountain, called Cape Comorin, whose rocky head seems to overhang its base. The birds which build the pendulous nests are here numerous. At night each of their little habitations is lighted up, as if to see company. The sagacious little bird fastens a bit of clay to the top of the nest, and then picks up a fire-fly, and sticks it on the clay to illuminate the dwelling, which consists of two rooms. Sometimes there are three or four fire-flies, and their blaze of light in the little cell dazzles the eyes of the bats, which often kill the young of these birds.

"I did not pass through Cape Comorin gate in entering Travancore, but through a gate some miles northward, called Arampalli gate. The mountain, called by sailors the Cape, is again to the north of this. Arampalli is thought to be the Arguropolis of the Greeks. Here there is a fortified pass, and lines of two miles in length, composed of stone walls and towers. The guard received me with frowning looks. I had unfortunately not yet received my passport from Colonel Macaulay. I did not know, therefore, how I should be received at the gate. But when I was approaching it, I sent some of the armed peons who accompanied me, to inform the commandant that I expected he would be ready to receive me at the gate, and to afford me an escort to the Rajah's presence. And thus I passed without opposition.

"Next day I arrived at Cottate, the Cottonia (hence the word cotton) of the ancients. It is still a flourishing place. The day after I came to Padmanburam, a fort and residence of the king, where his principal arsenal is established.

"From Padmanburam to Trivandram is a road, shaded by lofty trees, called the King's road, whereon Brahmins and Nayrs alone are suffered to walk. The lower casts do, however, walk on it; but if they meet a Brahmin, they immediately leave it, and seek a path in the woods. A person sometimes precedes the Brahmin to announce to passengers that he is near at hand."

The date of Dr. Buchanan's next letter is on the 27th of October, from the palace of the Rajah of Travancore, at Trivandram:

"I have received your letter of the 27th September, in which you answer mine of the first from Tanjore.

"I have not seen Geddes, but I am accustomed to read quotations from him. I shall endeavour to preserve some Syrian and Jewish relics for you.

"On my arrival here I found that Colonel Macaulay was a hundred miles off, at Cochin. But I received a letter from him, tendering his services in whatever way I wished to command them.

"I immediately informed his *excellency*, the minister, (a noble Nayr of able and liberal mind,) that I wished to pay my respects to his *highness*, the Rajah, for so are these illustrious persons designated by the Company.

"The Rajah sent his Vakeel to inform me that he would receive me in form next day. In the meantime he gave orders for my accommodation and table. The Rajah's servants accordingly came the next day to escort me to the gate of the fort in which he resides. The military were drawn out, and I was received on the steps of the palace by the minister and secretary, who conducted me to the Rajah's apartment. He was more gorgeously dressed than the Rajah of Tanjore. He was twenty-five years old on the day I entered Trivandram; and of five subjects of compliment which I had premeditated, this was one. He is an affable and sensible man. He conversed on political subjects for about two hours, and was extremely desirous to have my opinion of the chief persons, European and native, in Hindoston. His grand subject, however, was to learn the particular purpose of my various and extensive tour. Nobody had been able to satisfy him on this head. I was very candid with him, and declared my objects plainly. He appeared to be a little thoughtful, and I did not know what impression I had made on his mind. His whole court of Brahmins and Nayrs understood every word that was said. When I was about to take my leave, he expressed a hope that I meant to stay some days with him. I told him I should.

"On that same day I sent to him the Rajah of Tanjore's list of books, and also the Ramisseram catalogue. He read over both with great pleasure. I then requested that he would order his Brahmins to make out a similar list of their ancient books. He assented immediately, but the Brahmins resisted. The minister told me this. I asked whether the Brahmins governed the Rajah. At my next audience the Rajah told me the list was preparing.

"Understanding that I had the Rajah of Tanjore's picture, he requested to see it. He was so much pleased with the beauty of the painting, that he desired to keep it for a day or two to show it to his ladies. It was three days before I could get the Rajah of Tanjore out of the Zenana. I mean to tell the Rajah of Tanjore this.

"Mr. Swartz's catechist, who accompanies me, is called Pascal. He was heir to a person of property, who died some years ago at Trivandram. He proceeded from Tanjore, accordingly, to claim his inheritance about four years ago; but, being a poor man, and ill supported, he was told by this court that his claim was not just. Mr. Kolhoff requested I would take Pascal with me, and represent his case to the Rajah. I did so; but, having no hope of getting any thing for him, I gave him an allowance as my interpreter. On my second audience, I represented his case to the Rajah. The matter was investigated in public next day, and on the day following (to the great astonishment of poor Pascal, and all my servants) the Rajah put him in possession of a house and land in this place, and granted him the option of inhabiting it, or selling it immediately. He also delivered to Pascal bonds amounting to about six thousand rupees, and a great number of jewels. Pascal says he must build a church for all this."

Dr. Buchanan then mentions a second successful application to the Rajah in behalf of a small body of native christians at Moiladdy, a district of Travancore, who had hitherto been refused permission to build a church.

"I asked the Rajah," says Dr. Buchanan, "whether he had ever read of any people who were not allowed to worship their God? The minister was willing. At last the Rajah told me he would himself soon visit the district of Moiladdy, and would then point out a proper place for the church. The Brahmins, I hear, first opposed the measure, alleging that the English would soon have the country, if they were allowed to introduce their religion into it.

"At my last audience the Rajah was very gracious. He presented to me some shawls; and when I was taking leave, he put an emerald ring on my finger. He at the same time gave orders that two of his officers (Nayrs) should attend me throughout his dominions, wherever I was pleased to go. This last favour was of a very peculiar nature, and altogether unexpected."

Dr. Buchanan thus continues his correspondence:

"1st November, 1806.

"From Trivandram I went to Poontara on the sea-coast; and here I first saw a Syrian church in the Romish communion. I mean in Travancore; for I before mentioned to you that I had visited one near Tritchinopoly. From Poontara to Angengo I travelled by the sea-coast, and had the pleasure to see a church every four or five miles. From Cape Comorin to Cochin there are about a hundred churches on the sea-shore alone. Of these the chief part are the Syrian Latin, or, more properly, the Syrian Romish churches. The priest reads the Syriac Liturgy, not one word of which the people understand, and then he walks off; or he reads the Latin Liturgy, with which the poor christians are equally edified. Some of them (the private christians) have, however, the prayers translated into Malayalim, or, proper Malabar. The churches are snow white, and are generally built in a grove of shady trees. Before each, on the sand of the shore, is a lofty cross, which, like the church itself, is conspicuous at a great distance.

"There was an insurrection of the Nayrs in Travancore last year, against the Rajah; three battalions of his Nayr body guards revolted, and sought to kill the British Resident, and the Rajah, and the present minister. Colonel M. fled to Cochin. The Rajah called in the *christian* fishermen from the coast to defend him against the Nayrs. They assembled at Trivandram in immense numbers, each man armed with a short bludgeon. The bowmen from the hills appeared at the same time in the Rajah's behalf, and the Nayrs laid down their arms and fled. About fifty of the ringleaders were seized and hanged. The battalions were broken, and the Rajah accepted of a subsidiary force from the English. This was a dreadful blow to the Brahmins, whose influence in Travancore is identified with that of the Nayrs.

"At Angengo I found apartments prepared for me by the British Resident, Mr. H., who is appointed by the Bombay government. Angengo has been in possession of the English since 1628.

"At Quilon, Dr. M., nephew to the Colonel, entertained me. The subsidiary force is at present encamped here. At this place I saw Dr. H., the Hindostanee scholar. He told me, that though he had been many months here, he had not yet met with any one who could give an account of the schismatic Syrians, as their churches were all in the interior, where Europeans cannot go without permission from the Rajah."

The next letter, in which Dr. Buchanan announces his approaching departure to the interior of Travancore, will be read with lively interest by those who have followed him in his progress hitherto, and who are aware of the important result of his researches.

"CALYCOULON, 4th Nov. 1806.

"I am now about to proceed northward and eastward from this place, to visit the Syrian churches. There is one very near at Mavelicar. The others are remote, situated (according to Dr. L.'s account) in impenetrable forests, where jungle fevers and tigers abound.

"The weather is dry and clear, and I have received a very different account of the regions I wish to visit. I shall, however, proceed no farther than may be prudent. I have told my servants, that they may remain behind, if they please. But they choose to accompany me. The Rajah's men encourage them. The Lord, who hath graciously led me from Cambuslang to Calcutta, and from Calcutta to Cape Comorin, will lead me in safety, I trust, through the mountains of Travancore. In many instances, already, mountains have been made a plain before me; and I am ready to believe that some good will result from a journey, hitherto so remarkably favoured by Providence.

"I, however, think it right to 'put my house in order' at this place, and leave the event to Him who disposeth of the lives of his servants according to his eternal purpose and righteous will.

"At a village near Calycoulon lives Captain W., an old officer of a former Rajah. He is now blind, but his wife reads the Bible to him. Hearing of my approach, he had prepared some questions to ask me, which had long been on his mind, relating to the doctrine of salvation. After supper, he quoted several passages from the Epistles to the Romans, Ephesians, and first of St. Peter; and asked, how can these things be?

"After an hour's discourse, the old man said, 'It is even so, as I hoped.' And he began to weep aloud."

It was surely worth a journey from Calcutta to Travancore

Front View of the Church of Udiamper.

From an Original Drawing by Dr Buchanan.

to resolve the doubts and to shed light upon the path of this aged christian!

On the 5th of December Dr. Buchanan communicated to his excellent correspondent in Bengal a long and detailed account of his visit to the Syrian churches in Malayala. As it has been already observed in respect to Juggernaut and Ceylon, the narrative in this letter is substantially similar to that which has been long since published,* and excited such general attention and interest. It will not, however, be deemed unnecessary to give a sketch of Dr. Buchanan's introduction to the Syrian christians, and to add a few extracts, containing some circumstances which have not yet met the public eye.

"Cochin, 5th Dec. 1806.

"My last letter from Travancore informed you that I was about to leave the sea-coast, and to proceed into the interior of the country to visit the ancient Syrian churches. I have been enabled to accomplish my purpose. I have visited the remote churches situated amongst the hills at the bottom of the great Ghauts. The scenery of the country was everywhere delightful; the weather was cool and pleasant; and I have returned from an expedition, which was represented to be dangerous, in perfect health.

"Early in November I left the sea-coast, having first supplied myself with plenty of gold and silver. I directed my course towards Mavelicar, the first Syrian church.

"The *kasheeshas* (priests) received me on my arrival with much civility, perceiving that I was accompanied by the Rajah's servants. Their curiosity to know the object of my visit was very great; still greater when I took up their Syrian books and began to read; and when I showed them my printed Syriac books, which they could read. They produced the scriptures, and their liturgy; also lexicons and grammars, Syrian and Malayalim. The Malayalim, or proper Malabar, is a dialect distinct from the Tamul; but the character is nearly the same. It is considered by the learned Brahmins of this coast, as the eldest and legitimate daughter of the Shanscrit.

"In the evening the church was lighted up for prayers, at which a good many of the people attended. Nothing objectionable appeared at this service. The priests pronounced the prayers without book, and chaunted their hymns, having their faces turned towards the altar. They have no images, but on the walls were paintings from subjects of scripture history.

* See the Christian Observer, vol. vi. and Christian Researches, p. 112—150

"Next day being Sunday, I had an opportunity of seeing the whole service, morning and evening, as I sat in the chancel, with one of their books in my hand. The people were very decently habited, and filled the church.

"On Monday morning the four chief elders of the church came with the priests to visit me. I told them I knew their history, and came as their friend, and the friend of their religion; that I knew they had been an oppressed people during a long period. To all this they listened evidently with deep thought and perplexity. They then put a few questions to me. I told them I was about to visit their remotest congregations, intending to penetrate to Ranniel itself.

"Their countenances began now to assume great distrust, and, after a few civil sentences, they begged leave to withdraw. I certainly appeared in a most questionable shape among these simple people, who had so little commerce with the world. In the evening I invited them to another conference. I told them I should set off the next morning for the mountains; that I was much obliged to them for their hospitable entertainment, and begged they would accept something in return. I gave each of the priests some gold, and some to the elders of the church, for the poor; and desired their benediction, that I might go in peace. They then retired with apparent reluctance, looking at the money with dubious countenances.

"I afterwards learnt that they immediately called an assembly. An old man arose and said, 'What if this stranger should prove to be a true christian, and a real friend? What proof have we that he is our enemy? It is true no European ever visited us before; but what say you to this man's knowledge of our church at Antioch, to his Syrian books, his money? Besides, it is said that the Rajah put an emerald ring on his finger. If he do not intend our good, he may have power to hurt us.'

"They then conferred with Mr. Swartz's catechist, and my other servants of all casts, concerning my family, country, profession, my present journey, where I had been, and what I had been doing, and what I intended to do.

"After this ordeal, I was permitted to appear before their tribunal once more. The old priest said he was afraid they had judged me too hastily; but that there were some circumstances which he would now communicate as an apology for their suspicions."

Dr. Buchanan then relates the account which the venerable priest gave him of the various attempts of the Roman Catholics to force the Syrian churches to join their communion, as the ground of their suspicions respecting his present visit, and the manner in which he at length succeeded in removing their fears and gaining their confidence.

He next proposed to send a standard translation of the scriptures, in Malayalim, to each of their fifty-five churches, on condition that each church should multiply the copies, and circulate them among the people. To this they thankfully assented.

"One of the elders, named Thomas, or, Didymus, stepped forward and said, 'To convince you, sir, of our earnest desire to have the Bible in the Malayalim tongue, I need only mention that I have lately translated the gospel of St. Matthew, for the benefit of my own children. It is often borrowed by the other families. It is not in fine language, but the people love to read it.'

"'But how,' said the old priest, 'shall we know that your standard copy is a true translation of our Bible? We cannot depart from our own Bible. It is the true book of God, without corruption; that book which was first used by the christians at Antioch. What translations you have got in the west, we know not: but the true Bible of Antioch we have had in the mountains of Malabar for fourteen hundred years, or longer. Some of our copies are from ancient times; so old and decayed, that they can scarcely be preserved much longer.' I rejoiced when I heard this.

"'But how,' repeated the aged priest, 'shall we know that your western Bible is the same as ours?' 'I have here,' said I, 'a western Syrian Bible, which yourselves can read; and I have an English Bible, which will be interpreted to you. Let some portion of scripture, selected at a venture, be accurately examined. You can compare the whole, at your leisure, hereafter.' They turned over the leaves of my Bible with surprise, having never seen a printed Syriac Bible before. After some consultation, they proposed that the 3d chapter of St. Matthew's gospel should be critically compared, word for word, in the eastern Syrian, western Syrian, and English. St. Matthew was selected, I believe, at the suggestion of Thomas, who had got his Malayalim translation in his hand.

"It was an interesting scene to me to behold the ancient English Bible brought before the tribunal of these simple christians in the hills of Malabar. They sat down to the investigation with great solemnity, and the people around seemed to think that something important depended on the issue.

"I held a Greek Testament in my hand, and proposed that the sense of the Greek copy should be first explained, as the New Testament was first given to the world in Greek."

Here a discussion arose respecting the comparative merits of the Greek and Syriac scriptures, which Dr. Buchanan has given at length in his Researches.* After which he adds, "Not thinking it prudent to proceed further in this argument, I proposed that Jona (the aged priest) should first read his own Syriac, as the standard, with which the other versions should be compared. We accordingly began, and soon finished the collation of the chapter. Jona was satisfied that the English Bible was a faithful translation. As for the western Syrian, it agreed with the eastern nearly word for word. Thomas' Malayalim translation alone was faulty.

"We next considered the establishment of schools; the proposal of which seemed very acceptable to them.

"My business was now done. The priests observed, that it would be necessary that their Bishop and Metropolitan, Mar Dionysius, now residing at Candenad, near Cochin, should be made fully acquainted with all that had passed; as without his concurrence nothing could be done with energy in so extensive a diocese. I told them I had already ascertained that the good Bishop would willingly give his sanction to measures so beneficial to his people, and that he would signify it to them officially in due time.

"The people now informed me they had determined that one of the priests, and one of the elders, should accompany me to the other churches; and that letters should be sent before to announce our coming.

"Next day we took our departure from Mavelycar, and arrived in the evening at the church of Chinganoor. The priests and people came out, women and children in their holiday clothes, to meet us at a little distance from the town. The church is a spacious building, far superior to any that I had yet seen. Near the altar are two shrines of bishops who died here. I requested Jesua the priest to select four of the chief elders, as representatives of the people, to hear what had passed at Mavelycar. They received the proposal for diffusing the scriptures and establishing the schools with the utmost cordiality.

"I was here told, that no European, or even Romish priest, had ever penetrated farther into the country than this place. Bartolomeo was not here; for there is not a single Roman church in this district of Malabar.

---

* Christian Researches, pp. 114—115.

"Calicherry was our next church. It is built on the top of a hill. The chief priest is Matthew, aged eighty years. He gave me the history of ancient times; and also a very accurate account of the present state of the Syrian church. The people here manifested the same favourable disposition which had appeared at the former places.

Still journeying towards the East, we arrived at the church of Puttencow; from whence we had a view of the delectable mountains, the utmost bound of the Syrian churches. The church of Puttencow was built by the present bishop about fourteen years ago. At this place I met a greater number of aged persons than I had yet seen. They suggested many useful improvements in the plans to be adopted, and pointed out where they were most liable to fail. Andrew, the priest, appeared to be very zealous for scripture translation.

"We came the next day to Maraman, a small church, over which presides the aged Zechariah. I found him reading his Masmora (Psalms) in the porch of the church. This part of the country is interspersed with hills, round which the rivers from the Ghauts wind their course. The christians go from place to place in little canoes. Sometimes a woman may be seen with the oar in her hand; sometimes a little boy; some of the canoes being so small as to admit of two persons only.

"The church of Colancherry was next in our course. It is built in the bosom of the forest, but not far from a river. The people were poor, but very hospitable. An old lady wished me to make a promise that I would come back again in a year or two, or at least that I would write to them. She would take care that the Cassanars did their duty.

"Next day we arrived at Ranniel, the remotest church in these regions, and the limit of my proposed tour. This church is built on a steep hill, or rather rock, in which a few steps are cut to ascend. The people assembled from all quarters, and seemed delighted with the novelty of my appearance, and that of my attendants. The two priests were Lucas and Matthew; and the four elders, Abraham, Thoma, Georgius, and Philip.

"I found Abraham to be rich; and to be withal deeply interested in the success of our measures for the extension of religion. He had travelled a little. He said there was a great difference between the religion of the heart and the doctrines of the head; and it was to be lamented that many priests were ignorant of this. 'You were right,' said he, 'in taking a pledge of the four chief elders, rather than of the young Cassanars. For want of colleges* and places of religious instruction, the young priests are sent to teach us before they are taught themselves.' They are obliged indeed to lead moral lives, for otherwise they would not be endured. But no man should go forth to the ministry until he has studied the whole Bible, and can quote it fluently in his christian discourse. For three hundred years we have been quarrelling with the Romish Church about supremacy, rites, and ceremonies, but the Bible has been out of the question. The Bible, sir, is what we want, in the language of our own mountains. With the Bible in his hand, every man can become the priest of his own family.'

"While Abraham was thus discoursing, I thought of that other Abraham, who was called 'the friend of God' in a strange land. He gave me much useful information, and conveyed it too with some authority; for he seemed to consider me as a young man who professed a good purpose, but who was not likely to bring it to a happy issue, without being well directed and well supported. 'After you are gone,' said he, 'evil men will endeavour to frustrate your counsel.' Nothing will complete your success but the authority of the English government interposed in our behalf. Before any thing can be done in India on a great scale, kings, and men in power, must range themselves on God's side. When the christian religion is left to itself, as a thing indifferent, the solid dominion of the devil will soon overwhelm it; unless indeed it should please God to send forth in these days his divine power in a miraculous way, as in the first ages. But this we are not to expect, and therefore we ought to pray, as in our Syrian Liturgy, 'that kings and ministers would work with God.'

"I proposed to Abraham that he should correspond on these subjects with the most learned and pious persons of his church; and requested he would inform me from time to time what was proper to be done. At parting I put a ring on Abraham's finger, before the people. He said he should ever wear it, and it should be a memorial of what had passed. At the request of the priests I recorded my visit in the church books, in the Syrian language; being willing that there should be the appearance of as much solemnity as possible in my visit to this remote people; in order that the objects of it might not soon be forgotten.

---

* It may be gratifying to the reader to know, that Major Munro, the present British Resident in Travancore, has succeeded in procuring the establishment of a college for the better instruction of the Syrian priests.

"At all these churches I passed some time in examining their Syrian books. At most places there are ancient copies of the scriptures, or of some parts of them; for the whole scriptures are with them seldom bound up in one volume. They are most generally in four: the *Oreta*, or former part of the Old Testament; the *Evangelion*, the *Praxeis*, and the *Egurta*. The Prophets are rarest.

"In the vicinity of Ranniel, there is a high hill, from the top of which the people told me I might have an extensive view of the country. The hill was steep, and of laborious ascent, and I left my servants below. When I had gained the summit, I felt myself much fatigued, and sat down to contemplate the delightful prospect. The mountains of the Ghauts were at some distance, but from their great height they appeared to be close at hand.

"In a few minutes I saw a man coming up from a village below, with a cocoanut in his hand. I drank the cooling water, and was much refreshed. He said he was a christian; that seeing me ascend, he thought the cocoa-water would be acceptable. I said I was a christian too. He smiled doubtingly, looking at my English dress. He said he was never farther from home than the adjacent mountains, where he sometimes went to fell wood. He did not seem to understand that there were christians in any other part of the world than the mountains of Malayala. He pointed out to me by name the christian parishes which I had visited, but most of the churches were concealed by the trees. The christians are forbidden to have steeples, as they would appear too pre-eminent among the pagodas of the heathens.

"While I surveyed the christian districts all around, I reflected on the inscrutable counsels of God, in finding this asylum for the Bible during so many ages; and yet in confining it for so long a period to this region of the heathen world. I indulged the hope that the same Providence was about to unfold itself by dispensing the Bible throughout the East, by means of this people.

"I passed two hours on the top of this hill. I do not know its name. But I called it Pisgah; for I believed that I had a sight of kingdoms promised to the Messiah in the second psalm. 'I will give thee the heathen for thine inheritance, and the uttermost parts of the earth for thy possession.'

"On my return from Ranniel, I visited most of the churches a second time, and then proceeded to Nerenam, which was formerly the residence of the Syrian Bishops. The episcopal chair, covered with red velvet, and decorated with copper studs, is evidently the workmanship of a former age. In a corner lay the pastoral staff. The church itself is supposed to be nine hundred years old. The chief Kasheesha here was Thoma, aged 62 years. He has five colleagues and one shumshana (student.) The christians here are said to be wealthy; but they must conceal their wealth. Their chief elder is named Jacob Terragon: the latter word is an addition conferred by the Rajah on persons of condition. Jacob intimated to me, that he was ready to support the cause with money.

"Next day we arrived at Mavelycar, where I received a better welcome than on my first visit to that place.

"In all these churches which I visited, I found the same zeal and affection for the religion of their forefathers. In every church the elders stepped forth with patriarchal simplicity and zeal, as the natural guardians of the people. The women in general were affable and courteous in their manners, and appeared to be as much interested in the objects of my visit as the men. The children showed nothing of the Hindoo shyness and alarm at a stranger. They used to mount my palanquin, and sometimes get into it. The manners indeed of the Nayrs of both sexes have much of the same independent frankness. As to the Brahmins, their families live in entire seclusion, as in a Romish convent; unlike any thing that is known elsewhere in Hindostan.

"From Mavelycar I went to Aleppe on the sea-coast; and thence I returned into the interior of the country as far as Changanacherry, to visit the Romish churches in that quarter. At Pulingunne is a Syrian academy for the Cassanars of the Romish Church. It is under excellent management; and, if its objects were well directed, it would become a useful institution. The Romans were surprised at my condescension, as they termed it, in visiting them, having understood that I had visited the Syrian congregations, and favoured their religion. For it seems the rumour of my progress to the mountains had already gone far abroad. 'It is true,' said I, 'I am a schismatic. Colonel Macaulay and the Governor General, and all the English, are schismatics from the Romish Church.' The priests were very polite, and would not allow that the English were either heretics or schismatics. 'Indeed we are,' said I, 'as much schismatics as the Syrians in the mountains. It will be expedient for you, therefore, to change the name for the future, if you have any respect for the English.' This speech, as I afterwards heard, was carried before me to the

Front View of the Church of Candenad

From an Original Drawing by Dr. Buchanan.

Romish Bishop at Verapoli, near Cochin; for whose use, indeed, I chiefly intended it."

Dr. Buchanan next directed his course to Candenad, the residence of Mar Dionysius, the Metropolitan of the Syrian Church.

"On my arrival," he says, "I found that a great number of his clergy had assembled from different parts of the diocese in expectation of my coming. The old bishop is infirm, being now seventy-eight years of age, and received me in an upper chamber. He saluted me with 'a holy kiss,' after the apostolic manner. He said he had learnt all that had passed in my progress through his churches. His fears from the power of the Romish Church had now subsided; and he was satisfied that the English were the friends of his church. 'His joy was like that of the Jews, when Cyrus sent forth his mandate to rebuild the walls of Jerusalem.'

"Next morning I delivered to him a paper containing some subjects for the consideration of himself and his clergy."

This related to their disposition to an union with the English Church, to such extent as should seem practicable to both; to the translation of the scriptures into the Malayalim language, and to the establishment of christian schools in all the parishes of his diocese. Upon these subjects some very interesting discussions took place, the substance of which will be found in the Christian Researches, pp. 128—134.

"At the close of the conference the bishop added, 'I am in a declining state of health, and cannot expect to live to see these pleasing prospects realized, which now open to our view. But I am the father of fifty-five churches in a heathen land; and I must soon give up my account to the bishop of souls. I have been thus explicit in declaring to you my sentiments before my clergy, that they may act wisely, and remember them when I am gone.' He then introduced me to two of the priests, whom he authorized to communicate with me, as occasion might require, on the subjects of the present conference.

"The next morning I visited the church of Udiamper, which is only half a mile from Candenad. This is the church in which the celebrated synod was held in 1599, by Menezes, Archbishop of Goa. It is a spacious edifice."

From Udiamper Dr. Buchanan proceeded to Cochin.

"On my arrival," he continues, "I slept the first night at the house of Mr. V., the old Dutch governor. Next morning I went over to an island about two miles from Cochin, on which Colonel Macaulay has a house. He received me with great kindness, and has paid me much attention during my stay in

Malabar. Colonel M. is a man of letters; and had, previously to my coming, collected various information and many manuscripts, Syrian and Syrochaldaic, for my inspection. He had also procured a copy of certain chapters of the Jewish scriptures, which he understood I wished to see.

"In a few days after my arrival, he accompanied me to the Rajah of Cochin's palace, and thence to Udiamper and Candenad. The old bishop was much gratified with this second visit, and considered it as a proof of our affection for his church. Colonel M. intimated to him that he perfectly accorded with me in the measures that had been proposed, and invited the bishop to dine with us at Cochin. This invitation his bad health would not allow him to accept; but he sent over two of his principal clergy to consult with me further on the affairs of the church."

From this place Dr. Buchanan visited Cranganore, the spot on which the Apostle Thomas is said to have first landed in India; Paroor, the church of which place bears the name of St. Thomas, and is said to be the most ancient in Malabar; and Verapoli, the residence of a Romish bishop, and the pope's apostolic vicar.

"Before my arrival, the bishop had lent some books to Colonel M., one of which was 'La Croze's Christianisme des Indes,' a book marked in the bishop's library as 'liber hereticus; prohibitus.' This book he wished to get back, lest it should fall into my hands. Colonel M. refused to give it, knowing it was his intention to burn it. I visited the bishop at Verapoli, and explained to him that I had not come to notice *his* church, but to take care of a flock who seemed to have no church of its own. It seems that he and all the priests at Verapoli had taken it for granted that my purpose was to subjugate them to the Church of England. 'How,' said I, 'could I possibly think of effecting such a change?' I shall not soon forget the answer. 'If the English government should desire it, and threaten to withdraw its protection if we did not comply, what alternative would be left?' I answered that I was glad to find they were so compliant, but I had no proposition to make to them on that subject. Only I should be much obliged to them to give the scriptures to the people. If they were afraid of the inquisition at Goa, I could promise that not one of them should be burnt.

"The bishop has opened his library to me, and shown me many important records of his church. He is indeed very cordial in his assistance, if I may judge from his endeavours to afford me information.

Front View of the Church of Alangatta.

From an Original Drawing by Dr. Buchanan

"You will perhaps think that my mission to Malabar has terminated very satisfactorily without noticing *manuscripts*. These are certainly of but secondary consideration with me, though the learned will probably consider them to be of primary importance."

Dr. Buchanan then relates his success in obtaining both Syrian and Hebrew manuscripts, and describes the brass tablets, fac-similes of which he procured at Cochin, and on which are engraved the privileges granted several centuries since to the christians and Jews by the native princes of Malabar. But of all these circumstances a particular account is already before the public.*

In the course of his tour, Dr. Buchanan made drawings of several of the Syrian churches on the spot; of which, though extremely simple, and, with one exception, exhibiting only the principal front of each building, it has been thought desirable to obtain engravings, as an accompaniment to this part of his memoirs. They represent the old church of Paroor, those of Candenad and Udiamper, and that of Alangatta. The three former have been already particularly mentioned. Of the latter it will appear, that Dr. Buchanan merely states his intention of visiting it. It is said to be the largest of the Syrian temples, and a very handsome and noble building.† The church of Paroor, as Dr. Buchanan remarked generally of the most ancient Syrian structures, is not unlike some of the old parish churches in England. The other three are more ornamented, and evidently in the style of architecture prevalent in Asia Minor and Syria. The sketches of these venerable buildings can scarcely be contemplated without exciting some tribute of applause to the christian zeal and energy which prompted Dr. Buchanan to explore the recesses amidst which they had been for ages concealed, and to shed around them that scriptural light which poverty and neglect had well nigh extinguished.

The following miscellaneous extracts from his letter to Mr. Brown, dated Cochin, may next be added:

"Colonel Macaulay has been fortunate enough to incline the Travancore court to the belief that all the christian churches are, and necessarily must be, cognizable, in respect of interior management, and the appointment of bishops, by the christian king, who is now sovereign of India. The bishop of Cochin, lately appointed from Goa, arrived while I was here. But he could not enter on the duties of his office until he was re-

* Christian Researches, pp. 128. 143. 232. 234.

† Asiatic Researches, vol. vii.

cognized by the British Resident, who gave him his authority to be presented to the government of Travancore. The bishop of Cochin presides over most of the churches on the sea-coast, towards the south.

"As to the christians in the territories of the king of Cochin, the Dutch constantly assumed the entire management of the churches, and even the collection of the revenues due to the Rajah from the christians. This was done to preserve the people from oppression. It would be desirable that a similar right were exercised by the English government in relation to the christians in the territories of the king of Travancore.

"—— I was present the other night at the marriage of the daughter of Nathaniel, the richest Jew of the place. It was a very splendid solemnity. The women were covered with gold and silver Dacca and Surat muslins, that being the costume on such occasions from time immemorial.

"The weather on the coast is still dry and pleasant. I have had no cold as yet this year; an indisposition which I never escaped in Calcutta in the months of October and November. I expect to leave Malabar in about a fortnight, and shall probably be with you in Bengal about the end of February. Swartz's catechist is still with me. I forget whether I mentioned to you that one of Mr. Swartz's brass lamps is destined for you. It is called the Halle University lamp. It gives a bright and steady light, and a square moveable canopy shade preserves the eyes. It is worn thin by the midnight lucubrations of the old man; for he was a hard student to the last year of his life.

"I am now about to visit the interior of this country a third time, and shall first proceed to Angamalee, formerly an archbishopric of the Syrian christians. I have written to you thus particularly of my tour through Malabar, in order that, if I should be long delayed in my return, you may know what has been done. I have succeeded certainly in the general objects of my inquiry beyond my most sanguine expectations.

"Mr. H., at Angengo, has heard of an ancient history of Malabar in the Malayalim language, which his linguist has promised to procure. The Rajah's dewan tells me that it is referred to in public acts. Mr. H. says, there are in the episcopal library at Verapoli some volumes on Shanscrit literature from the Propaganda, which, if possible, I shall procure for Mr. Colebrooke's inspection. I wish Mr. C. himself were here. The Brahmins still aver that Malabar is the cradle of Shanscrit science; and Colonel Macaulay has adopted that opinion fully. It possibly existed here at as early a period as in the north, but not with the same advantages of improvement."

The date of Dr. Buchanan's next letter is December 14th, from Angamalee in Malabar. Though the name of this place occurs in the extracts published by himself from his Journal,* the following account of it will be found to be fuller and more interesting:

"Angamalee was formerly the seat of the archbishop of the Syrian churches in the mountains of Malabar. In the town of Angamalee there are three churches within a quarter of a mile from each other, in all of which service is still performed. The cathedral church is the largest, and contains the tombs of bishops and archbishops for many centuries. As I approached the town of Angamalee in the evening, I heard the 'sullen roar' of the great bell reverberating through the mountains. When the Romish archbishop Menezes visited this place in 1599, the christians strewed the way up the hill with flowers as he advanced. And yet he came to burn the ancient libraries and archives of Angamalee. As the flame ascended, the old priests wept; but they were obliged to hide their tears, dreading the inquisition at Goa. The archbishop presented himself next day to the multitude, arrayed in his pontificals, resplendent with gold and precious stones. To this day they have a lively tradition of the splendour of his robes blazing in the sun, and forming a striking contrast with the plain white garments of their own primitive church. When Tippoo waged war with the king of Travancore, in 1791, he sent detachments in every direction to destroy the christian churches, and particularly the ancient edifices at Angamalee. Two thousand men penetrated into the mountains, and were directed to the place by the sound of its bells. They sprung a mine under the altar walls of each church, and the inhabitants who had fled to the higher mountains witnessed the explosion. But the walls of the grand front being five feet and a half thick, (I measured them yesterday,) they did not attempt to demolish them for want of powder. In the mean time Tippoo, hearing that Lord Cornwallis had invaded Mysore, suddenly recalled his church-destroying detachments. Next year Tippoo was obliged to sign any terms that were offered him; but Lord Cornwallis forgot to desire him to rebuild the christian churches. The inhabitants, however, have rendered them fit for public worship; and have proceeded some way in restoring the cathedral to its former state. The archbishop's residence and all the other public

* Christian Researches, p. 138.

buildings are destroyed. The priests led me over the ruins, and showed me the vestiges of their ancient grandeur, asking me if I thought their Zion would ever be rebuilt. Angamalee is built on a hill. I told them that their second temple would perhaps have more glory than their first.

"Two of the churches here are Roman, the third Syrian. But the two former would gladly return to their mother church.

"Colonel Macaulay accompanied me half way in my present excursion. I find the Syrian churches to the north much more splendid than those to the south. The books also are more numerous. I am now going to visit Alangatta and Edapalli, where formerly there was a Syrian monastery."

The preceding account of Dr. Buchanan's first visit to the coast of Malabar can scarcely be better closed than by the following letter to Mr. Henry Thornton, which comprises a brief but animated sketch of the whole; and which, notwithstanding the repetition of a few particulars which will be familiar to some readers, will not, it is presumed, prove uninteresting to any:

"Cochin, 24th December, 1806.

"Dear Sir,—In August or September last I addressed a letter to you from the Pagoda of Seringham, near Tritchinopoli. Since that period I have visited Ceylon, and many places in Southern Coromandel and in the province of Malabar. I passed a week at the palace of the Rajah of Travancore, who aids me very liberally in all my pursuits. The Brahmins and present minister had taught the young man (he is only twenty-five) to oppress the christians. But he promises milder treatment in future. This favourable change is produced by the exertions of Colonel Macaulay, the Resident, who I am happy to say is much alive to the interests of religion.

"From the sea-coast I proceeded into the interior of the country, to visit the ancient Syrian christians who inhabit the hills at the bottom of the great mountains of Malayala. The weather was cool and pleasant. The country is picturesque and highly cultivated, diversified with hill and dale, and winding streams. These streams fall from the mountains, and preserve the vallies in perpetual verdure. The christians received me courteously, seeing I travelled in some state, escorted by the Rajah's servants. But when they found my object was to look into their books and religion, they surveyed me with doubtful countenance, not well understanding how an Englishman could have any interest in the christian religion. And the contrary was only proved to them by long and serious discussion, and by the evidence of facts which for the first time came to their knowledge. But when their doubts had been dispelled, they sent deputies with me, who introduced me to all the other churches. No European, or even Romish priest, had ever, as they told me, visited that remote region. There are no Romish churches in its vicinity, and the Rajah gives no permission to Europeans to travel into the interior of his country.

"The Syrian is still their sacred language, and some of the laymen understand it; but the Malayalim is the vulgar tongue. I proposed to send a Malayalim translation of the Bible to each of the churches; and they assured me that every man who could write would be glad to make a copy for his own family. They also agreed to establish schools in each parish for christian instruction, which are to be under the direction of the four chief elders of each parish, and in which the Bible in the vulgar tongue is to be a principal class-book.

"Their doctrines are not in essentials at variance with those of the Church of England. They desire an union, or at least such a connexion as may be practicable or desirable for the better advancement of the interests of christianity in India.

"As to manuscripts, I have succeeded far beyond my most sanguine expectations.

"It had been supposed that the Roman Catholics had destroyed in 1599 all the Syrian books. But it appears that they did not destroy one copy of the *Bible;* and I have now in my possession some MSS. of the scriptures of a high antiquity. The collation of these with our western copies is very interesting. There are some other MSS., which were not condemned by the Synod of Menezes. I have also found some old Hebrew MSS., biblical and historical.

"It is sufficiently established by the concurrence of oral tradition with written records, that the Jews were on this coast before the christian era.

"I propose to send home some Syrian youth to England for education and ordination, if practicable. And I take with me to Bengal a Malayalim, a Syrian, and a Jewish servant. They will, however, be but nominal servants. I should have engaged them as moonshees; but I see there is no college now in Bengal.

"The Roman Catholics here were at first very jealous of my attention to the Syrians. The Romish bishop, however, who is a *bon vivant,* perceiving that my chief object was to diffuse the scriptures among the people, began to think that it might be politic in him to circulate them among his people too, and to please the English rather than the inquisition. Colonel Macaulay thinks the bishop will adopt the measure the moment we seriously propose it. He lives in some state, and fires a salute of eleven guns on occasion.

"Cochin is rich in Hebrew literature, and I am purchasing what is to be sold.

"The Rajah of Cochin has followed the example of the Rajahs of Travancore, of Tanjore, and the Ranny of Ramnad, and Ramisseram, in giving me catalogues of the Shanscrit books in the temples. I hope the Coorga Rajah will do the same.

"This opening of the Pagodas is a new scene in India. Mr. Swartz was the remote instrument. He opened the Rajah of Tanjore's heart; and the Rajah of Tanjore opened the Pagodas, those chambers of imagery, the emblem of the heart.

"The Rajah of Tanjore wishes me to visit him again. If practicable, I shall open a correspondence with him.

"I propose to leave this coast in a fortnight, and proceed to Bombay, from whence I shall probably go across to Benares, and thence down to Calcutta by the Ganges.

"Having arrived at the extreme boundary of my tour, and accomplished its object, I thought it would be acceptable to you to have some short notices of it. Be pleased to tell Mr. Newton that I am well. I wrote him a long letter from Tanjore. It is with pleasure I see that, amidst the agitations of the world, he is tranquil, and at peace, and nearly arrived at the haven where he would be. Mar Dionysius, the bishop of the Syrians in the mountains, has somewhat of Mr. Newton's manner and appearance; only that the bishop has a venerable long beard, which reaches below his girdle, and through which you may see a large gold cross beaming at intervals. He is now seventy-eight years of age, amiable in his temper, and devout according to his knowledge.

"I read at this place, in Hayley's third volume, Cowper's correspondence with Mr. Newton, and was pleased to see the name of the good man honoured.

"I remain, dear sir, very sincerely yours,

C. Buchanan."

In his next letter to Mr. Brown, Dr. Buchanan announced his intention of shortly returning to Bengal, together with a farther plan which he was projecting respecting a visit to the christian churches in Chaldea and Syria.

"COCHIN, 23d Jan. 1807.

"I am happy to hear that the first gospel in Chinese and Shanscrit is ready.

"I should have left Cochin before now, but some splendid events have taken place. The Syrian church, finding I was their friend indeed, opened new sources of antiquity. I visited them once more; and the bishop presented to me an ancient copy of the Old and New Testament, in Syriac, on thick vellum, reputed to be as old as the Alexandrine. On the other hand, the Jews were softened by gold, and a singular discovery was made."

This referred to some valuable Hebrew manuscripts, of which Dr. Buchanan gave a full account in his Christian Researches, and which will be again noticed hereafter. The letter thus proceeds:

"I despatched, on the 3d instant, three chests of books and MSS. to my own address, and to your care. Be pleased to open them and air the contents. I shall carry round with me three chests more. My hands are so fully occupied here, that I cannot proceed farther up the coast at this time; besides, I see you are desirous that I should return. I therefore purpose to take my passage in a large Danish vessel, now here, and ready to sail. I have promised to visit the Syrians and the Jews once more before I leave the country, if practicable. The information I have received from the Syrian christians, strongly inclines me to visit their fellow churches in Chaldea and Syria. The ancient patriarchate of Antioch is just expiring, unless supported by the English church. As it will be more convenient for a sea-sick traveller to go by land, I had always proposed to myself that route. And this new inducement will probably lead me to adopt it about the conclusion of the present year, or whenever the monsoon will carry a ship rapidly into the Persian Gulf. These things I have thought of, not thinking that I can do much more in India; but I leave them to the issue which God, in his all-wise counsel, shall be pleased to give. I have certainly no pleasure in the thought of returning to England, or of staying in India. The world (as the world) is equally distasteful to me everywhere. If I knew where it was the will of God I should pass my days, I should there lie down contented, and endeavour to do some good in a quiet and humble way.

"In one of the chests you will find some shawls. Let J. and H. choose one each; and each of the boys may choose a Hebrew book."

Dr. Buchanan's last letter to his friend, previously to his

embarking for Calcutta, contained the important information of his having actually made arrangements for the translation of the scriptures into the native language of Malabar. His success, therefore, as to the great objects of his journey, had been complete.

"Cochin, 29th Jan. 1807.

"I recived your letter of the 31st ultimo, and am glad to hear that you have ended the year so well and so happily.

"I embark to-morrow in the Danish ship Danesberg, for Calcutta, and shall touch at Columbo. I hope to be with you early in March. I send a chest of books and MSS. to England by the Bombay ships, which touch here.

"I am now about to encounter sea-sickness for a while. If I call at Mr. T.'s, in Columbo, it will be some relief, for I have much to do there. It is understood, by all ranks here, that I shall call on them six months hence on my way to the Persian Gulf. I have expended a large sum here. Mr. F. told me he had orders from his government (Madras) to supply me with any money I might want. But I did not avail myself of this kindness.

"My servant, who came from Calcutta, is still with me. He was formerly a ship-cook, and will be useful now by sea, as he has long been by land. Mr. Swartz's catechist, and other attendants, wait here to see me on board, as do various Syrian, Romish, and Jewish priests. I am glad to get out of the throng.

"I hope I have come to this place for good, and not for evil. The goodness is God's, and the evil is my own. It is wonderful that I should have travelled so far in safety; and that, after the strange events that have occurred, I now leave the coast in peace. If I should never see you, my testimony is gone forth to the world, and others must carry on what is now begun.

"The Tamul copy of the scriptures (complete) is only arrived to-day from Carnatic; I proceed with it to-morrow to the Syrian bishop, who is now engaged with three learned Syrian and Malayalim scholars in the translation into the language of Malabar. The bishop longed to see the Tamul, he being a good Malayalim scholar himself.

"I leave the three translators at monthly wages, and Col. Macaulay superintends when I am gone.

"The Romish bishop has consented to the circulation of the scriptures throughout his diocese, so that there will be upwards of 200,000 persons who are ready to receive the Malayalim Bible."

Dr. Buchanan did not leave Cochin quite so soon as he had anticipated in the preceding letter; but on the 6th of February he embarked on board the Danesberg, after having despatched the following letter to his valuable friend and coadjutor, Col. Macaulay:

"My dear Sir,—I have directed Messrs. Harrington and Co., at Madras, to honour all drafts of yours for any sums you shall have the goodness to lay out on my account. I leave to you to settle the sum for the Verapoli Cassanar.

"Mr. Swartz's catechist stays a month at Candenad, to show them the best plan of proceeding in the translation. If any obstacle to their progress should occur from the Tamburan, or Mar Thoma's fear, I shall be obliged to you to transfer the translation establishment to Tanjore, whither the chief man has no objection to go. If a Verapoli Cassanar, of Syrian and Malayalim learning, could be prevailed on to go to Tanjore also, the establishment would be complete.

"I cannot leave you without expressing my sense of the peculiar obligations I am under for your uniform assistance in every subject which has engaged my attention on this coast. Without your direct countenance, I certainly could have done little or nothing. Something beneficial to the country will, I trust, result from what has been done, though the circumstance of your leaving it presents but a doubtful aspect.

"Believe me to be, my dear sir, very sincerely yours,

C. BUCHANAN."

CHAPTER VI.

DR. RUCHANAN arrived safely at Calcutta, after a voyage of five weeks, on the 15th of March. On his return he found that the college of Fort William, which had flourished nearly seven years, during which period it had been productive of the most important benefits both to the service of the East India Company, and to oriental learning and religion, had been reduced within very narrow limits on the first of January. The offices of Provost and Vice-Provost were abolished, and the Professorships restricted to three; viz:—the Hindostanee, Bengalee, and Perso-Arabic; it being intended that the students should only be attached to it, on an average, for a single year.

The public letter of the Court of Directors which conveyed this order was dated in May, and reached Calcutta in December, 1806. On its arrival, Mr. Brown, deeply impressed with the importance of the moral discipline which had hitherto been exercised in the college of Fort William, and which was now superseded, felt it to be his duty to submit his sentiments upon the subject to the Governor General, and acccompanied his representations with the offer of continuing to superintend the institution, and, if that were deemed necessary, to officiate without salary.

In making this communication to Sir George Barlow, Mr. Brown referred to his highly esteemed colleague, Dr. Buchanan, as follows:

"I particularly regret that there should be a necessity for any material change during the absence of the Vice-Provost, without his concurrence or knowledge, from consideration of his having, throughout, so eminently devoted his superior talents, with the utmost zeal, and by every exertion, for the benefit of the public service, in the success of the college. In his absence I take it upon me to communicate faithfully my thoughts, and to submit them, with respect and deference, to the consideration of the honourable the Governor General."*

Sir George Barlow, on receiving the representation and offer of Mr. Brown just referred to, expressed himself deeply struck and gratified by his philanthrophy and disinterestedness, and assured him that "he should consider of his proposal." No farther notice of it, however, appears to have been taken; but the new modification of the college immediately took place, and the offices of Provost and Vice-Provost were accordingly abolished.

The labours, the influence, and the income of Dr. Buchanan were, in consequence of this arrangement, materially diminished. The reduction of the former was not only grateful to his taste and inclination, but necessary to his health; while that of the latter affected him only as it tended to abridge his means and opportunities of usefulness. The subject occurs but once in his various correspondence with his friends, and is then stated merely as a matter of information, in which he did not seem to be particularly interested.

His grand object was the promotion of christianity in India. This he had kept steadily in view during the period of his

* Memorial Sketches of the Rev. D. Brown, p. 313.

Vice-Provostship; for this, as we have already seen,* he made some provision when anticipating its abolition; and it was in pursuance of the same important object that he undertook the extensive journey through which we have lately accompanied him.

During his voyage, or immediately after his return to Calcutta, Dr. Buchanan had drawn up a paper, under the title of "Literary Intelligence," containing a sketch of his proceedings on the coast of Malabar, which he was desirous of publishing, both at Madras and Calcutta, for the information of those who were interested in the promotion of christian knowledge in India. To the great surprise, however, of Dr. Buchanan, and of many of the most learned and respectable persons at both Presidencies, it was not thought expedient to permit such a publication to be inserted in the government gazette. It was, in consequence, printed and circulated in a different form; and, without producing any of the ill effects which some had anticipated, it conveyed intelligence which was as gratifying to the friends of learning and religion in India as the same information afterwards proved to persons of a similar character in England.† It is to this circumstance that Dr. Buchanan refers in his subsequent correspondence with Colonel Macaulay, which will afford a connected view of his proceedings after his return to Calcutta. The following is an extract from one of his first letters to that gentleman:

"CALCUTTA, 4th April, 1807.

"The alarm of this government, *quoad* ευαγγελιον, is subsiding. Your government also seems well again. At least so writes the Rev. Mr. Thompson, to whom Lord William declared, 'that the promotion of christianty is on his heart, and that he wishes for more missionaries.'

"This society anxiously anticipates the confirmation of the report, that Lord Wellesley has been appointed a secretary of state. I believe it would be as agreeable to them, as to hear that Bonaparte had *lost a leg*, which is also reported.

"Major Wilks' letter has been read here with much interest. I think you are doing more in the Deccan, than we in Hindostan.

"I send you a letter from the bishop of Llandaff, which has

---

* See page 206

† The "Literary Intelligence" appears, however, to have been admitted into the Bombay Gazette, by which means it reached Europe. It was afterwards published in England by the late Bishop Porteus. See Dr. Buchanan's Apology for Promoting Christianity in India, p. 87; and Owen's History of the British and Foreign Bible Society, vol. i. p. 320.

made some noise here. Had the Literary Intelligence not been suppressed, the bishop's letter would not have been published."

The letter thus referred to was afterwards inserted by Dr. Buchanan at the close of his Christian Researches. The extracts from it, which follow, while they are honourable to the christian zeal of the late learned and eloquent prelate whose name it bears, will not here be deemed irrelevant.

"Calgarth Park, Kendal, 14th May, 1806.

"Some weeks ago I received your memoir of the expediency of an ecclesiastical establishment for British India, for which obliging attention I now return you my best thanks. I hesitated for some time whether I ought to interrupt your speculations with my acknowledgments for so valuable a present; but, on being informed of the noble premium by which you purpose to exercise the talents of graduates in the University of Cambridge, I determined to express to you my admiration of your disinterestedness and zeal in the cause of christianity.

"Twenty years and more have now elapsed since, in a sermon before the House of Lords, I hinted to the then government the propriety of paying regard to the propagation of christianity in India; and I have since, as fit occasions offered, privately, but unsuccessfully, pressed the matter on the consideration of those in power. If my voice or opinion can, in future, be of any weight with the king's ministers, I shall be most ready to exert myself in forwarding any prudent measure for promoting a liberal ecclesiastical establishment in British India: it is not without consideration that I say a liberal establishment, because I heartily wish that every christian should be at liberty to worship God according to his conscience, and be assisted therein by a teacher, at the public expense, of his own persuasion.

"The subjects you have proposed for the work which shall obtain your prize, are all of them judiciously chosen, and, if properly treated, (as my love for my Alma Mater persuades me they will be,) may probably turn the thoughts of the legislature towards the measure you recommend.

"God, in his providence, hath so ordered things, that America, which three hundred years ago was peopled by none but pagans, has now many millions of christians in it; and will not, probably, three hundred years hence, have a single pagan in it, but be occupied by more christians, and more enlightened christians than now exist in Europe.

"Africa is not now worse fitted for the reception of christianity than America was, when it was first visited by Europeans; and Asia is much better fitted for it, inasmuch as Asia enjoys a considerable degree of civilization, and some degree of it is necessary to the successful introduction of christianity. The commerce and colonization of christian states have civilized America; and they will, in process of time, civilize and christianize the whole earth. Whether it be a christian duty to attempt, by lenient methods, to propagate the christian religion among pagans and Mahomedans, can be doubted, I think, by few; but whether any attempt will be attended with much success till christianity is purified from its corruptions, and the lives of christians are rendered correspondent to their christian profession, may be doubted by many: but there certainly never was a more promising opportunity of trying the experiment of subverting paganism in India, than that which has for some years been offered to the government of Great Britain.

"Your publication has given us in England a great insight into the state of christianity in India, as well as into the general state of learning amongst you, and it has excited in me the warmest wishes for the prosperity of the college of Fort William. It is an institution which would have done honour to the wisdom of Solon or Lycurgus. I have no knowledge, personally, of the Marquis Wellesley, but I shall think of him and of his coadjutors in this undertaking, with the highest respect and admiration, as long as I live.

"I cannot enter into any particulars relative to an ecclesiastical establishment in India; nor would it, perhaps, be proper to press the government to take the matter into their consideration, till this country is freed from the danger which threatens it: but I have that opinion of his majesty's ministers, that they will, not only from policy, but from a serious sense of religious duty, be disposed to treat the subject, whenever it comes before them, with great judgment and liberality. May God direct their counsels!"

A few days after the date of his former letter, Dr. Buchanan wrote to Colonel Macaulay as follows:

"CALCUTTA, 13th April, 1807.

"My dear Sir,—I have been favoured with both your letters, with their enclosures, and return you many thanks for your kind attention. Your first contained the Hebrew MSS. I am perfectly satisfied with Levi's explanation of the cause of its detention. But I am not equally satisfied with his candour *quoad* the opprobrious omission of the word כל in the last verse of the 27th of Deuteronomy. It is true, as you observe, that there is one כל in that verse, 'all the people;' but there ought to be another, viz: 'all the words;' which the modern Jewish copies have not. But it is in the Samaritan copies, and also in the Syriac copy I brought from Travancore. I one day read the verse to Levi in a Jew's house in Mattinceri, and pointed out the omission. He ought, therefore, to have been candid enough to have recollected that. But poor Levi's ideas are always in a whirl.

"Your second letter, which I had the pleasure of receiving yesterday, contained Major Wilks' very interesting letter, and that of your writer, not less important. But what relates to yourself ought first to have my attention. I am much concerned to hear that your health is declining, and that you must leave India so soon.

"In November next, I propose to sail for Cochin and Bombay, and thence to the Persian Gulf. My purpose is made known to government, and also the objects of a route overland.

"Since I shall be myself at Cochin in November or December, it will not be necessary for you to make any arrangement at this time for sending home the Syrian youths. I shall then be better able to judge of the prudence and importance of the measure.

"I could have wished to have a Syrian moonshee with me here for a few months before I go; but if it be not perfectly convenient to ship him off in time, you need not think farther of it.

"I am happy to hear that the Malayalim translation proceeds with such spirit. Mr. Kolhoff writes to me, that he is very ready to undertake the superintendence of that work, if untoward circumstances should impede its progress in Travancore.

"The reason why I did not communicate to you the 'Literary Intelligence,' was that you might be exonerated from the consequences of the publication of that paper, should there be any unpleasant result in a political way. The Madras government deemed it to be so dangerous, that they refused to publish it. The government here (*par nobile*) refused also. This suppression of what almost all sensible men accounted to be merely 'literary intelligence,' has given great offence to the men of letters in the settlement. The consequence has been, that it is printed in the form of a pamphlet, in large 4to, and in large type, with *Bulmer's blaze*, and there is added something yet more offensive, viz: the Oxford and Cambridge notifications of the five hundred pound prizes, (which were also suppressed here ;) and, what is more offensive than the last, a copy of the second Latin letter addressed to me by the University of Cambridge, on the subject of diffusing a knowledge of revealed religion amongst the nations of Asia. This pamphlet of twenty-eight pages will be exposed for sale next week.

"—— and I are on terms of high civility; but he is no friend to my evangelical purposes, and he does not like my (and your) steady adherance to the principles of Lord W.'s administration. But I wish to be at peace with all men, and I ever desire to conciliate my enemies. I mean enemies made by my evangelizing plans, for I have no other; and perhaps these are few in number.

"The christian tablets, Syrian Bible, and Hebrew roll, are here objects of great curiosity. Mr. Carey beheld them with veneration. The public mind is strongly attracted towards Malayala, and the wall between Hinduism and christianity seems to be tottering.. You have applied the battering-ram to that wall with good effect in Travancore; and I sincerely wish that you could stay to give it a few more shocks. But you will be useful at home. I go home also; but only perhaps for a season. At least in the pamphlet now printed it is mentioned that I am going home overland, 'for the purpose of visiting the ancient christian churches in Mesopotamia and Syria, and that I shall return to India in a short time.' Some were ready to *wish me a good journey*, but they did not expect this last clause of *returning*. It has, however, given great satisfaction, I understand, to almost all the settlement. For you must know that ——'s persecution (as it has been called) of a good work, has procured it much success and many friends. —— is faithful. —— dubious of what is right. Sir H. Russel, Sir J. Royds, and Sir W. Burroughs, are all friendly. So is Mr. Harrington. The Malayala battering-ram is said to have given C. a violent and unexpected shock, which is likly to crumble his wall of hostility into the ruins of indifference. For so our Persians speak.

"I have had a letter from the Bishop of London, dated 1st September last; in which he says, that 'it was too late last session to bring forward the proposition of an ecclesiastical establishment for British India; but that the Archbishop of Canterbury intends to move his majesty's ministers on the subject next session.'

"His lordship also says, that money will probably be sent out to support the great work of translating the scriptures into the oriental languages. Lord Barham writes to the same effect on both subjects.

"I have placed the young Malayalim moonshee, from Paroor, in the missionary school at Serampore, where he is very happy and in good health. I should be glad that your writer would communicate this to his mother. My Hebrew moonshee is well also.

"Lord Minto's arrival is anxiously looked for by this settlement. I shall write to you again shortly, and remain, with much esteem, yours sincerely, C. BUCHANAN."

The plan of a journey overland to Europe, mentioned in the preceding and in some subsequent letters, was proposed and long cherished by Dr. Buchanan, not merely as obviating his well-founded objection to a sea-voyage, but as calculated to promote his benevolent researches into the state of the ancient and declining christian churches in the east. It will, however, be seen that, after many inquiries, he was at length reluctantly compelled, by political and military obstacles, to abandon this interesting expedition.

It may seem extraordinary, that of the addresses to Dr. Buchanan from the senate of the University of Cambridge, no more distinct or complete information should be contained in these memoirs than the reference to the second of them in the foregoing letter. They probably expressed the sense which that learned body entertained of Dr. Buchanan's meritorious exertions in promoting the interests of learning and religion in the east, and of his munificent encouragement of those important objects by the series of prizes offered to the members of the University. No traces, however, of the letters in question have been discovered amongst his papers; nor is it known that any copy of the pamphlet in which the second was printed in India has reached this country. It is therefore only to be regretted that no farther account can be given of documents which were, doubtless, highly valued by Dr. Buchanan, and equally honourable to him and to the distinguished body from which they proceeded.*

Of the several objects of Dr. Buchanan's late tour, it was stated to be one, to discover fit instruments for the promotion of learning, and for the dissemination of the scriptures in India. It may now be observed, that it was in the course of his journey that he first thought of a plan which might effectually accomplish that object. The reader will probably recollect the meditation of Dr. Buchanan on the banks of the Chilka Lake,

* The Vice-Chancellor of the University, upon an application being made to him for copies of these letters, declined granting them.

where, on the morning of the Sabbath, while reflecting on the painful scene which he had just witnessed, with the lofty tower of Juggernaut still in distant view, he conceived the design of some christian institution, which might gradually counteract, and at length extinguish, the idolatry of the eastern world. The historian of the Decline and Fall of the Roman Empire, informs us that he first conceived the thought of his elaborate and eloquent work amidst the ruins of the capitol. It was an association of a more sublime and sacred nature which suggested to Dr. Buchanan the design of the institution, the general plan of which he then briefly described. Soon after his return to Calcutta he employed himself in digesting and arranging its form and constitution; and on the 28th of May he thus adverts to the subject at the close of the following letter to Colonel Macaulay:

"My dear Sir,—I had the pleasure to receive your letter of the 1st inst. two days ago, accompanying the Dutch translation.

"I am happy to hear that you have two Hebrew books for me. If any thing interesting in Hebrew or Syriac, printed or in manuscript, should offer while you remain on the coast, I shall be obliged to you to secure it for me.

"I presented the bishop's* demand on Baretto's house, and enclose the answer. My compliments to the bishop. I shall take care of his affairs, and send him *cauliflowers* when the season arrives.

"Dr. Leyden proceeds by sea to Madras to-morrow. He is in better health. He has been looking at a variety of my MSS. for some weeks past, but with little success. He can make nothing of the christian plates, but means to renew his attack on the Malayalim part of them when he arrives at Madras. He thinks the old Syriac Bible, on vellum, is as early as the fifth or sixth century. But that is certainly too high a period.

"The Indus sails as a packet for England in a few days. I have said in a letter, that you are meditating your return this season. By the Indus I send home a small work for publication; not in relation to Malabar, but to Juggernaut; nor to him directly, but to a literary institution, whose object shall be to promote christian knowledge in Asia by means of books; which institution shall be exclusively literary, and shall have no connexion with any mission society. The institution al-

* Of Verapoli.

ready exists, and is in extensive operation. I shall copy the heads of the sections on the opposite page. Nothing yet from England.

"I remain, my dear sir, very sincerely yours,

C. BUCHANAN."

Instead of inserting the short sketch to which Dr. Buchanan refers, it will be more satisfactory to give a fuller abstract of a work, which, though printed, it was afterwards deemed not expedient to publish. The title was as follows:—"The Christian Institution in the East, or the College for translating the Holy Scriptures into the Oriental Tongues."

The origin and objects of the institution were described nearly in the terms of the preceding letter. It was dedicated to all good men, to be an instrument in their hands of extending the knowledge of revealed religion by the translation of the holy scriptures, and was placed under the immediate patronage of the Archbishop of Canterbury, as President of the Society for the Propagation of the Gospel in Foreign Parts, and of the Society for Promoting Christian Knowledge. One of its subordinate objects was to print small tracts on certain branches of art and science, fitted for popular use and improvement.

The various instruments of the institution were next enumerated, comprising the venerable bishop of the Syrian church in Malayala; the British and Danish missionaries throughout India; Judah Misrahi, a learned Jew of Cochin, engaged by Dr. Buchanan as a translator of the New Testament into Hebrew; Professor Lassar for the Chinese language; and the late Rev. Henry Martyn, with two learned coadjutors, natives of the east, for the Persian, Arabic, and Hindostanee languages. With the exception of Mr. Martyn, who arrived at Calcutta during the absence of Dr. Buchanan, he stated that he had visited all the before-named persons at their respective residences, and had informed himself as to their abilities and principles.

It was not intended to form an expensive establishment; but that a professor should be stationed as a literary agent of the college in each of the principal provinces of the east, to study a particular language, to collect information, to correspond with the society at home, to compose and to print books, and to instruct the natives in printing. The literary agents were in general to be paid for *work done*; that is, for translations or for printing, previously agreed for, and faithfully executed. Care was also to be taken that, in cases where translations of the scriptures should be intrusted to the members of any particular sect, their exclusive tenets should not find admission into the work.

Dr. Buchanan proposed that the name of the institution should not be derived from any church or sect in Europe, but from the religion itself, the knowledge of which it was intended to diffuse; and that the instruments which it would recognize in promoting this great design, should be of all nations.

He next observed that, in order to secure its resources from failure, and that there might always be a copious supply of fit persons for the work, it was expedient that the institution should possess an organized body in England, and that its establishment should be sufficiently respectable to attach to it men of rank and learning. The college of the Propaganda at Rome owed its efficiency and perpetuity chiefly to its liberal establishment.

Dr. Buchanan grounded the necessity and importance of this christian institution upon a view of the present state of the Brahminical superstition at the chief temples of the Hindoos, and particularly at Juggernaut; and, in order to convey to his readers in England some idea of the spirit and effects of the religion of Brahma, he added some extracts from the journal of his visit to that place.

Provision was made for the transmission of copies of every work published by the institution in India to certain libraries in Great Britain; and it was stated that thirty-one volumes had accordingly been forwarded by the packet which conveyed the work in question. It was added that Dr. Buchanan would for the present continue to superintend the affairs of the institution.

Such is the outline of the college for oriental translation conceived by Dr. Buchanan. His intention, in short, was to establish a British Propaganda, which, in proportion to the extent of its objects, should be superior to that at Rome, the fame of which still survives in Asia. Objections would probably have occurred to different persons with respect to some of the provisions of this institution; and it was obviously never considered by its author as incapable of alteration and improvement. Its design and general plan were undoubtedly excellent, and would, probably, have been received with much approbation.

Upon its original formation,* Dr. Buchanan proposed to the Baptist missionaries at Serampore, as extensively engaged in

* See his Apology for promoting Christianity in India, p. 70.

translating the scriptures, that they should accordingly associate, merely in that character, with other fellow labourers in different parts of India; that the missionary pursuits, properly so called, and the individual establishments of each society, should remain peculiar and private, as before; but that the translators of the scriptures should act in concert, and maintain an amicable correspondence with each other, under the general direction of the superintendent, who would be responsible for the views and proceedings of the institution at large. The intention of this proposal was clearly not to supersede the meritorious labours of the Baptist missionaries; but to render them more effective, by incorporating them in one great and comprehensive plan for the same important object, and by rescuing their operations from the appearance of any thing private or sectarian, and investing the united labours of the learned translators throughout India with a more public and national character.

It may readily be imagined that the society at Serampore might feel some hesitation and even reluctance in acceding to this proposition, after the publicity which Dr. Buchanan had given to their extensive plan of oriental translation; and it was, perhaps, expecting too much, that they should voluntarily abandon the " vantage ground" which they were thus occupying. However this may be, the Baptist missionaries declined the proposal; and the name of " the christian institution" was in consequence but partially assumed. The other branches of which it was intended to be composed, including, besides those already named, one of the most distinguished oriental scholars of the present age, the late learned and lamented Dr. Leyden, who undertook the translation of the scriptures into the several dialects of the Malayan Archipelago, were generally associated, after Dr. Buchanan's departure from India, under the superintendence of the late Rev. Mr. Brown.

The " Christian Institution" was, however, carried but very imperfectly into execution. On the arrival of the manuscript in England, though it was printed in pursuance of Dr. Buchanan's instructions, some of his friends, to whom the work was communicated, conceived that its publication was inexpedient, and might even produce consequences injurious to the general cause of christianity in India. Under these impressions, they took upon themselves to suppress the publication of the work, more especially as Dr. Buchanan had announced his intention of returning to this country in the course of the following year. Their determination was, doubtless, guided by a sincere desire to promote the great object of his labours; and it will be seen that he acquiesced in their judgment.

With respect to the main design of the christian institution, as a college of acknowledged responsibility, embracing the associated learning and piety of the East for the grand purpose of sacred translation, and possessing commanding patronage, effective support, and enlarged superintendence and control, the failure of its establishment can scarcely be considered but as a subject of regret. The munificent donations of the British and Foreign Bible Society to its corresponding committee in Bengal, combined with the exertions of its eastern auxiliary branches, and those of other societies, have undoubtedly promoted, to a very splendid extent, the work of oriental translation. It is, however, well known that various circumstances, inseparable from private and unconnected labours, have hitherto impeded its more complete and successful execution; nor is it probable that these will ever be removed, but by recurring to the general plan so ably and comprehensively conceived and developed by Dr. Buchanan in his "Christian Institution."

Of the fate of this elaborate plan in England, its author was necessarily ignorant. He continued, therefore, to mention it, amongst other topics, in his succeeding letters to his friends, as if in the course of execution.

On the 9th of June, Dr. Buchanan thus wrote to Colonel Macaulay:

"My dear Sir,—I yesterday received your letter of the 10th of May, enclosing the regulation against spiritual encroachments. It is admirably done, and the bishop of Verapoli is saved. Your continuance in Travancore is important, if it referred to nothing else than the ecclesiastical concerns of the country.

"I am happy you stay a little longer on the coast. I shall hope to see you in November or December. All and every thing you have sent from the archives of Verapoli is interesting and important. Your account of the translation of the scriptures gives me and others here much pleasure. *That work will prosper.*

"The Turk impedes my plan of route. I now propose to go through Armenia. I have ever been very desirous to visit the Armenian churches. But I have not determined what I shall do; for we may expect many a revolution before January next.

"The Tinavelly impostor is one of many who are lifting up their voices in the desert. This is an age for, 'Lo here, and lo there.' There is a luxation in all the joints of the Brahminical superstition, and the Wahabian philosophy is eating out Mohammedanism, as doth a canker.

"The copper-plates are arrived at the custom-house here. I shall have them to-day.' I am greatly obliged to you for this rapid transmission of them.

"I thank Mr. Clephane for his friendly proposal as to the types. I shall confer with Mr. Kolhoff on that subject. A fount must be cut; that is certain. And from this fountain will flow a clear and living stream for the souls of men. I have despatched to the Archbishop of Canterbury, by the Indus, a copy of St. Matthew's gospel in Chinese, and two of the gospels in Shanscrit.

"I shall be obliged to your writer to inform Timapah Pullé (who is now employed in translation at Candenad) that I have received his letter; that I am pleased with his services; that if Colonel Macaulay deems it reasonable to add the Burdella Brahmin he speaks of to the list of translators, I shall approve of it; that I am happy he (T. Pullé) begins to consider the christian religion the true faith; and that I will stand his godfather, agreeably to his request, if he should prove worthy; that I shall be glad to hear from him again, and that he may write to me in Malayalim, as I have an interpreter in Calcutta; and that the young man, his relation, who lives with him at Candenad, may receive from Colonel Macaulay six rupees per month, and arrears from the time of his own appointment, if he can show that the lad is useful to him in his work.

"I remain, my dear sir, very sincerely yours,

C. BUCHANAN."

In the course of the ensuing month, Lord Minto, who had long been expected, arrived as Governor General in Bengal. In a letter to Colonel Macaulay, on the 17th of August, Dr. Buchanan notices his lordship's good example, and attendance on divine worship, and his attention to himself. "He wishes me," he adds, "to communicate fully with him on all the subjects which he knows have long engaged my attention." A subsequent paragraph in this letter thus mentions another very meritorious ecclesiastical servant of the company in India:

"I have not seen the publication of Dr. Kerr, to which you allude." This was probably the account of the St. Thomé christians, the Syro-Romish, and the Latin church in India, which was drawn up by that excellent man by order of the Madras government.*

---

* See the Christian Observer, vol. vi. p. 751, and Christian Researches, p. 146.

"But," continues Dr. Buchanan, "I received from him yesterday his 'Letter to Lord William Bentinck,' on the subject of chaplains, printed and sent home by the Indus. Dr. Kerr is an ardent and useful friend of the christian religion; and I think the court will make him one of his proposed vicars-general, or perhaps his suffragan bishop."

It appears, therefore, that the necessity of an enlarged ecclesiastical establishment in India had occurred simultaneously to Dr. Buchanan and to Dr. Kerr. The latter zealous and laborious chaplain, however, did not survive long enough to receive any additional authority, even supposing that it would have been conferred upon him.* His honour and his reward are in heaven.

Dr. Buchanan's next letter to Colonel Macaulay is dated September 15th, and contains some interesting notices respecting his intended journey overland to Europe, and the progress of the Malayalim translation of the scriptures. It refers, however, at the close, to a painful subject, which is afterwards more fully explained.

"My dear Sir,—I had the pleasure to receive the copies of your correspondence with government regarding the discipline of the churches. Every additional letter you write on that subject is an additional pin to the tabernacle.

"If I should go by Persia, I am prepared to spend twelve thousand rupees in presents. But I hope to be able to travel by the route of Bussorah, Mosul, and Aleppo. I proceed to Bombay in the Metcalfe, Captain Isaacke, who will sail from this place about the 10th or 15th of the next month, October. If practicable, he will set me down at Cochin. If not, I shall first arrange matters at Bombay, and then come down to Goa (which I wish much to visit) and to Cochin.

"I am greatly obliged to you for your letter of the 2d of August, containing Colonel Capper's sentiments on a journey through Persia and Armenia. His remarks are highly interesting, and may be useful to me hereafter. I am more afraid of the French than of the Persians.

I am happy at the arrival of the pontifical bull. A Protestant christian happy at the arrival of the pope's bull! Tell it not to the Church of England or to the Kirk of Scotland. Yea, I am happy, even though the object of it be a rosy bishop, who delights to quaff the essence of *sura;* for I hope through

* For an account of this truly pious man, see the Christian Observer, vol. xi. p. 80.

the medium of this bishop to diffuse the holy scriptures among thousands of my fellow creatures.

"Within the last few days arrived your eight packets of the holy Gospels, translated into the Malayalim language. They have been contemplated with mingled affection and admiration by the missionary corps. David Grant is now employed in reading them through, and prefixing the titles to the books, and numbering the chapters in English. People wonder here at this rapid fruit of my visit to Malayala. But yours is the praise, not mine.

"As we have no fount of Malayalim types ready cut in Bengal, I mean to take the MS. with me to Bombay, and to have it printed there under the superintendence of Sir James Mackintosh.

"The translators may take their rest now for a little while. Until we can ascertain the accuracy of the translation of the Gospels, we need not proceed to the Epistles. You may therefore settle accounts with the translators. I request you will thank them in my name for what has been done, and inform them, that I expect they will shortly resume their operations.

"I beg you will remember me to Dr. Macaulay, and to Mr. Hughes, the philosopher of the mountains. I fear he cannot tell me yet the mode in which a rock snake is killed by the hunters.

"I am on the eve, I fear, of a rupture with this government. The cause is the gospel. They are endeavouring to restrain the exertions of the missionaries in Bengal. I have not yet interfered. And I trust it will not be necessary; for I love peace, and not war; particularly at the moment of my leaving the country. But I shall do my duty, and leave the event to God.

"I am, my dear sir, yours sincerely, C. BUCHANAN."

On the 22d of September, Dr. Buchanan wrote to his two daughters. The following passage from his letter alludes to their lamented mother in a peculiarly affecting manner:

"I am now about to quit India, and to go home to see you. I propose to leave Calcutta in the course of next month. If I find it dangerous to go home overland, I shall proceed from Bombay by sea. I shall probably sail over those waters where your dear mother lies. Do you not know that at the resurrection of the dead she will come forth with a 'glorious body?' Though it be 'sown in dishonour, it is raised in glory.' Of this you may read in the Bible, and in the burial service. Your mother will come forth with a 'glorious body;' for she was a good woman, and remembered her Creator in the days of her youth. Perhaps I shall die too before I reach England. You ought therefore to pray that God would preserve my life, if it be his will, (for I desire to do his will in all things,) that I may see you, and show you the affection of a father, and receive the affection of daughters, and lead you onward with myself to that happy state, whither your mother is gone before you."

It is gratifying to reflect, that this affectionate and pious father was permitted to realize the delightful prospect which he thus anticipated. The following extract is from a letter to Colonel Macaulay, which occurs shortly afterwards:

"CALCUTTA, 12th Oct. 1807.

"Your letters of the 13th and 15th ult. arrived on this day. I have perused with pleasure and pain your public letter on the subject of expenditure at your residency; with pain, that your resources have been so scanty, and your fortune little; with pleasure, that you have upheld your character with such dignity, and have repelled the insinuations of ignorance with such temperance and effect. The highest compliment I can pay you, (and I seldom pay compliments,) is to say, 'that every word in your letter will be believed by the honourable court.'

"The attack I announced to you in my last has not been yet made. I wish you were at my side during the storm. I have friends, but they are not soldiers. I am the forlorn hope, and yet I have not twelve men. Nay, more, my friends tell me I shall certainly be killed.

"The assault however must be made, but whether by silent escalade at the midnight watch, or by heavy and hot battery at noon-day, I have not yet determined. I think the latter. You shall hear in a letter dated on or about the 1st of November, *me vivente, et Deo volente.*"

The rupture with the supreme government, to which Dr. Buchanan refers in the preceding letters, was of so serious and unpleasant a nature, and is so closely connected with the illustration of his character, that it demands some farther explanation.

Not long after his return from the coast of Malabar, Dr. Buchanan preached a series of discourses in the Presidency church, on the subject of the christian prophecies, which proved so acceptable to some of the congregation, that they expressed a wish that he would permit them to be printed; observing that, as he was about to return to Europe, they hoped he would bequeath these discourses, as a parting memorial, to his friends. To this request Dr. Buchanan acceded, and, accordingly, made preparations for their publication. These sermons related chiefly to the divine predictions concerning the future universal propagation of the gospel, and were intended to excite the public attention to that important subject, as well as to animate and encourage those who, from the purest motives, were labouring to promote the knowledge of christianity in India. Nothing could be more legitimate or laudable than such a design, conducted as it was by Dr. Buchanan, not in the spirit of violence and fanaticism, but of calm discussion, and reasonable and benevolent exertion. On transmitting, however, an advertisement to the government gazette, announcing the intended publication of his discourses, Dr. Buchanan was surprised to find that the insertion of it was refused, and that an order had been issued to the printers of the other newspapers, forbidding them to publish the obnoxious notice. Shortly afterwards he received a letter from the chief secretary to the Presidency, desiring that he would transmit the manuscript of his sermons on the prophecies for the inspection of government. To this unexpected demand Dr. Buchanan gave no immediate answer. It had long been the subject of painful observation to him, that on the departure of the Marquis Wellesley, during whose administration the spirit of promoting learning and religion in India had been general and ardent, a directly contrary disposition was manifested; as if it had been previously restrained by his presence. This first appeared under the administration of Sir George Barlow, and had been acquiring strength ever since. Lord Minto had now assumed the supreme government; and as several measures were adopted which appeared to Dr. Buchanan to operate very unfavourably for the interests both of learning and religion, he deemed it his duty, before he quitted Bengal, to address a memorial to his lordship, in which he particularly directed his attention to the character and tendency of those measures; and, in so doing, explained his reasons for declining to comply with the wishes of government respecting his sermons on the prophecies. The memorial was introduced to Lord Minto by the following letter:

"*To the Right Honourable Lord Minto, &c. &c. &c.*

My Lord,—I beg leave respectfully to submit to your lordship some particulars regarding the present state of the christian religion in Bengal, which I have thought it my duty to communicate for your lordship's information at this time.

"I trust you will do me the justice to believe, that it is with the utmost reluctance I trouble your lordship with a letter on such a subject so soon after your entrance on this government, when as yet few, if any, of the circumstances noticed in it can have come to your lordship's knowledge.

"I have no other view in soliciting your attention to them, but the advancement of learning and religion. Perhaps no one has addressed your lordship on the subject since your arrival; and there are certainly many particulars, regarding their present state, which it is of importance your lordship should know.

"Being about to leave India, I feared lest I should hereafter reproach myself, if I withheld any thing at this time which I conceived might be useful, particularly as I have been farther encouraged to address your lordship, by your known condescension in reeeiving any communications which are honestly intended.

"I have the honour to be, my lord, with much respect, your most obedient humble servant, C. Buchanan.

"Calcutta, 9th Nov. 1807."

The memorial which accompanied the preceding letter, and which was published some years afterwards* by Dr. Buchanan in his own vindication and defence, evinces, as it has been well observed, "the temperate firmness of a man, who, knowing that the gospel is the power of God unto salvation, is neither ashamed to profess, nor afraid to defend it." It is introduced by a statement of the circumstances which have been just mentioned, as having led to this address to the Governor General. Dr. Buchanan gave full credit to the officers of his lordship's government, of whose conduct respecting the christian religion he complained, that they were acting according to the best of their judgment; but adds, with much force and propriety of expression, "not to promote christianity may, in certain circumstances, be prudent; but to repress christianity will not, I think, in any case, be defended." In proof of such a spirit of hostility to the progress of the gospel in India, which is the main subject of his memorial, Dr. Buchanan specified the four following facts: "First, the withdrawing of the patronage of government from the translation of the holy scriptures into the oriental tongues." "Second, attempting to suppress the translation of the scriptures." "Third, suppressing the encomium of the honourable, the Court of Di-

* See his Apology for Promoting Christianity in India.

rectors on the venerable missionary, the Rev. Mr. Swartz:" and, "Fourth, restraining the Protestant missionaries in Bengal from the exercise of their functions, and establishing an imprimatur for theological works."

The truth of the two first of the preceding allegations has been already proved by the course of these memoirs, and needs, therefore, no additional confirmation. The third rests upon the simple fact, that the Bengal government, instead of following the example of those of Madras and Bombay, in giving publicity to the honourable testimony which had been recently borne by the Court of Directors to the merits of the venerable Swartz, in sending out to Fort St. George a marble monument to his memory, with a suitable inscription, which was ordered to be translated into the languages of the country, had chosen to pass over the whole transaction in silence; and had aggravated this neglect by permitting the insertion of an article in the Calcutta Gazette, "the obvious tendency of which was to bring the chracter and labours of the christian missionary into contempt."

On the fourth head of the complaint preferred by Dr. Buchanan in his memorial, it will be necessary to be somewhat more particular. The success of the Protestant mission in Bengal, Dr. Buchanan affirmed to have been long a source of uneasiness to those officers of government who did not think it right to attempt the conversion of the natives. And some of the native moonshees, attached to the public offices, knowing the sentiments of their superiors, were not backward in seizing any occasion to complain of the missionaries, which might be presented to them. Some clamour of this kind had been raised at two different times within a few years, but had passed away without offence to the christian religion. The complaint of the moonshees against the missionaries on the latter occasion was, that they had in a certain tract "applied abusive epithets to Mahomet." This tract, being an account of the life of Mahomet, composed by a native convert, had issued from the missionary press at Serampore, but without the knowledge of the missionaries themselves.

In commenting on this charge, Dr. Buchanan observed, "the missionaries certainly mistake the proper method of convincing the minds of men, if they use epithets of abuse; the successful method of preaching is by argument and affectionate address; and I presume this has been their general method during the fourteen years of their mission.

"At the same time, christian teachers are not to speak with reverence or courtesy of Juggernaut or Mahomet; they must speak as the scriptures speak; that is, of false gods as false gods, and of a lying prophet as a lying prophet. The Mahometans apply abusive epithets and vulgar curses to the idolatry of the Hindoos, and to the faith of christians; and these epithets are contained in books: the government might, on the same principle, have been assailed with the petitions of christians and Hindoos against the Mahometans."

The complaint, however, of the Mohammedans produced various restrictions on the proceedings of the missionaries, which were defended on the plea that the public faith had been pledged to leave the natives in the undisturbed exercise of their religions. If by not disturbing the natives in the exercise of their religion, it is meant that we are to use no means for diffusing christianity among them, then, observed Dr. Buchanan, "this pledge has been violated by every government in India, and has been systematically broken by the East India Company from the year 1698, to the present time. The charter of 1698 expressly stipulates that they shall use means to instruct the Gentoos, &c., in the christian religion. Nor in this is there any thing at variance with the pledge in question. It is a very different thing to apply arguments to the mind, and violence to the body; to civilize and humanize, to address the understandings and affections of subjects, and to interfere with their superstitions by compulsory acts."

After various illustrations of the countenance afforded by the Company itself to christian missionaries, and of their successful efforts in different parts of India, Dr. Buchanan adds the following observation:

"It has been the usual conduct of Asiatic governments to let christianity alone. In the annals of the British administration in India, has there been no instance of the suppression of a christian mission."

Having presented the preceding considerations to the notice of Lord Minto, Dr. Buchanan recurs to the subject of his discourses on the prophecies. He had, at the opening of his memorial, professed that he would willingly transmit them to the perusal of the Governor General, and that he should be happy to receive such observations on them as his lordship's learning and candour might suggest. "But," adds Dr. Buchanan, "I now beg leave to submit to your lordship's judgment whether, in the view of the temper of mind displayed above, it would be proper in me to submit my compositions to the opinion and revision of the officers of your lordship's government. I incline not to commit them to the hands of those officers from another consideration: it would be a bad precedent. I would not that it should be thought that anywhere in the British dominions there exists any thing like a civil inquisition into matters purely religious.

"It is nearly two months since I received the letter from government on this matter, and I have not yet communicated my intentions. I now beg leave to inform your lordship that I do not wish to give government any unnecessary offence. I shall not publish the prophecies.

"At the same time I beg leave most respectfully to assure your lordship that I am not in any way disappointed by the interference of government on this occasion. The supposed suppression of the christian prophecies has produced the consequence that might be expected. The public curiosity has been greatly excited to see these prophecies; and to draw the attention of men to the divine predictions could be the only object I had in view, in noticing them in the course of my public ministry. Another consequence will probably be, the Prophecies will be translated into the languages of the East, and thus pave the way, as has sometimes happened, for their own fulfilment."

Dr. Buchanan closed his memorial with entreating Lord Minto, in case any circumstance should afford a pretext for renewing the attempt to suppress the translation of the scriptures, that the Chinese translation, in which, as its original proposer and patron, he felt peculiarly interested, might at least be spared; and with offering any farther evidence or explanation of the facts asserted in his letter, which his lordship might require. This offer, however, Lord Minto did not condescend to accept. He did not even honour Dr. Buchanan with a single word of reply. Instead of considering the memorial as a communication intended to inform his lordship on subjects with which he was likely to be unacquainted, he viewed it as disrespectful to his government, and transmitted it by the very fleet which conveyed Dr. Buchanan himself to England, to the Court of Directors, accompanied by a commentary, of which Dr. Buchanan remained perfectly ignorant till some years afterwards; when, with many other documents relative to christianity in India, it was laid upon the table of the house of commons. It then attracted his notice, and called forth some remarks, which will be better considered when we arrive, in the course of this narrative, at the period of their publication. The Bengal government, however, not having thought proper to pay any attention to his memorial, Dr. Buchanan deemed it to be his duty to transmit a copy of it to the Court of Directors, which he did immediately before his departure from Calcutta, accompanied by a letter, in which he expressed his hope that some general principles on the comparative importance of religion in political relations in India, might be established at home, and transmitted to our eastern government for their guidance. Dr. Buchanan concluded his address to the honourable court, by recalling to their notice the solemn charge which he had received about eleven years since from their chairman, the late Sir Stephen Lushington, the tenor of which has been already stated. "In obedience to these instructions," observes Dr. Buchanan, "I have devoted myself much to the advancement of the christian religion, and of useful learning, since my arrival in India; using such means as I was possessed of, and directing the opportunities which have offered, to the accomplishment of that object. I am yet sensible that I have fulfilled very imperfectly the injunctions of your honourable court. It suffices, however, for my own satisfaction, if what I have done, has been well done; that is, with honesty of purpose, and with the sanction of truth. In my exhibition of the religious and moral state of British India, I might have palliated the fact, and presented a fair picture, where there was nothing but deformity. But, in so doing, I should not have done honour to the spirit of the admonitions of your venerable chairman, now deceased. And however grateful it may be for the present moment to suppress painful truths, yet as my labours had chiefly reference to the benefit of times to come, I should not, by such means, have conciliated the respect of your illustrious body twenty years hence."

Under these impressions, Dr. Buchanan requested that the court would be pleased to investigate fully his proceedings, with respect to the promotion of christianity in India, that the company at large might be enabled justly to appreciate them; and that he might be encouraged (if it should appear that encouragement were due) to prosecute an undertaking which seemed, he said, to have commanded the applause of all good men, and which had certainly commenced with omens of considerable success.

The preceding letter to the Court of Directors was not published with the memorial to the government at Bengal, nor does it seem to have been noticed by the court. Neither of those addresses, however, though unacknowledged at the time, was unproductive of effect. In Bengal, a more favourable disposition on the part of the government, towards the promotion of christianity, shortly afterwards appeared; and the reply of the Court of Directors to the representations of the Governor General in council, though not friendly to Dr. Buchanan, was, as we shall hereafter perceive, strongly marked by those enlightened and liberal views which he had been so anxious to see established for the guidance of our Indian governments. The favourable change which took place in the conduct of the Bengal government towards the mission at Serampore, is, however, chiefly to be ascribed to the memorial presented by the missionaries themselves to the Governor General in council; which, when published a few years afterwards in this country, excited general admiration.

The painful transaction which has now been detailed was nearly the last of a public nature in which Dr. Buchanan was engaged in Calcutta. The time was now approaching for his second and final departure from that city. Accordingly, in the month of November, he preached his farewell sermon to the congregation at the mission church from the words of St. Paul to the Philippians, chap. i. 27, "Only let your conversation be as it becometh the gospel of Christ: that whether I come and see you, or else be absent, I may hear of your affairs, that ye stand fast in one spirit, with one mind, striving together for the faith of the gospel." From this appropriate and interesting passage, Dr. Buchanan delivered a discourse remarkable for the importance of the practical truths which it enforced. After an introductory view of the origin and progress of the church at Philippi, Dr. Buchanan considered the two particulars, of which the parting request of the apostle to his favourite converts consists. The first respects the holy practice which they were exhorted to maintain.

"Without a highly moral conversation," observed Dr. Buchanan, "a congregation of christians cannot be said to have substance or being; for faith without works is dead. Unless the world see something particular in your works, they will give you no credit for your faith; or, rather, they will not care what your faith may be. In such circumstances, your faith will give them no trouble. But when 'wonderful works' appear, they will begin to ask what 'power hath produced them.' In this very epistle, the apostle calls the christians at Philippi, 'the sons of God,' and the 'lights of the world;' and he expresses his hope, that their conduct would be correspondent with these noble and distinguishing appellations."

"Now," continues Dr. Buchanan, "when this light shineth to the world, even the light of a holy life and conversation, it will be manifested by these two circumstances: First, it will not be agreeable to some. And, secondly, some will misrepresent your motives, or attach to your conduct an evil name; accusing you of hypocrisy, or of unnecessary strictness. And if no man allege any thing of this kind against you, if the worst of men make no derogatory remark on your conduct, then may you doubt whether you are walking in the steps of the faithful servants of Christ. They all were marked out by the world, as being in a greater or less degree singular and peculiar in their conduct, as persons swayed by other principles and subject to other laws. If these things be so, you will perceive how little concerned you ought to be about the praise of man, or the honour which cometh from the world."

Dr. Buchanan then proceeded to the second part of the apostle's exhortation; and, in urging the duty of "striving for the faith of the gospel," he observed, "this will appear strange to nominal christians, both preachers and hearers. But when once a man's heart comes under the influence of the grace of God, he will discover (perhaps in old age for the first time) that it is his duty, and it will be his pleasure, to promote the faith of the gospel, by every way; by his means, by his influence, by his exhortation, by his example. Every true disciple of Christ, however humble his situation, or peculiar his circumstances, will find opportunities of doing something for the faith of the gospel. And, indeed, the poor often enjoy means of usefulness, which, from many causes, are denied to their superiors."

Dr. Buchanan next directed the attention of his hearers to the apostle's rule for the successful pursuit of this great object, "that ye stand fast in one spirit, with one mind—that they should preserve unity; unity in the faith, and in the church." The following passage, relative to this important point, displays considerable acuteness of observation:

"You will generally observe, in the present day, that new opinions concerning forms and doctrine are chiefly introduced by men who have had little learning in their youth; so that, when in advanced life they begin to be serious and to acquire knowledge, the novelty flatters their understandings for a time, and leads them to adopt new systems, as they acquire new knowledge. This is very natural. Whereas those in whom serious piety and sound learning have united in early life, are seldom subject to such changes. But the unsettled man is designated by St. Paul under the appellation of a 'novice,' whatever his age may be; one who, being lifted up for a time in his own conceit, gradually loses his reputation, or perhaps has a fall in the face of the church. And, when his pride has been thus humbled, he generally returns to meekness of conduct and sobriety of speech."

Dr. Buchanan noticed, in the third place, the nature of that faith for which christians ought to strive.

"With respect to this," he observed, "it is not necessary for me now to declare it. It hath often been described to you from this place, even that 'faith which was once delivered unto the saints;' and which hath descended from age to age, like a pure stream of the water of life, gladdening the hearts of men, and nourishing their souls unto everlasting life. Amongst yourselves have there been some, who drank of it deeply, and have now passed away into glory; good and holy persons, who bequeathed to you an illustrious testimony, and pointed out to you the 'true way.' These all died in faith, and now inherit the promises. These are your 'cloud of witnesses;' that you should 'run with patience the race that is set before you.' These once, like some of you now, endured suffering for conscience' sake, some trouble of body, or some distress of mind. But all was sanctified to them, as it will be to you; they endured unto the end, and their names shall be had in everlasting remembrance."

The sermon was concluded by a faithful and solemn exhortation to the young and to the old, to those who doubted as to "the true way," to the sinner and the saint, to strive to obtain, and, having obtained, to adorn and recommend the faith of the gospel. "It only remains," added Dr. Buchanan, "that I implore the solemn benediction of God on this congregation.

"I pray, that the word of Christ may 'run and be glorified' amongst you; that from this place, as from a fountain, streams of truth may flow far and wide; that you may be ever blessed with wise and learned instructors, 'able ministers of the New Testament,' who shall take delight in dispensing the word of life, and in tending the flock committed to their care; and, finally, that the honour of your church may ever be preserved pure from any stain, that ye may uphold a conduct 'blameless and harmless,' as examples to men, as 'the lights of the world;' striving together, with one mind and in one spirit, for the faith of the gospel."

Such was the simple but impressive strain in which Dr. Buchanan took leave of the congregation which contained the greater proportion of religious persons in Calcutta. His farewell at the Presidency church was probably of a different nature, though characterized by the same pastoral fidelity and practical wisdom as that which we have just observed. There were, doubtless, some in each congregation from whom he would regret to be separated, and many who would lament his departure. Mr. Brown would particularly feel the loss of his able and affectionate coadjutor and friend, with whom he had taken "sweet counsel" in the house of God, and had shared the burthen and the heat of many a laborious day. Of the sentiments entertained by this excellent man respecting his learned and valuable colleague, the following brief extract from a confidential letter to his brother, written just as Dr. Buchanan was on the eve of his departure from Calcutta, will be a sufficient testimony.

"You ask me," says Mr. Brown, "if Dr. Buchanan is my friend? I answer, I know no man in the world who excels him in useful purpose, or deserves my friendship more. Perhaps there is no man in the world who loves him so much as I do; because no man knows him so well. Further, no man I believe in the world would do me service like him. We have lived together in the closest intimacy ten years, without a shade of difference in sentiment, political or religious. It is needless to add, without a jar in word or deed. He is the man to do good in the earth, and worthy of being Metropolitan of the East."

The private and unaffected nature of the letter from which the preceding passage is extracted, the well known simplicity and integrity of the writer's character, and the perfect competency of his testimony, render this warm and energetic tribute to the merit of his friend peculiarly valuable. To separate from such a colleague must have been a subject of sincere regret to him. But, with this and a few other exceptions, Dr. Buchanan's ties to India were neither strong nor numerous. The society of Calcutta is necessarily fluctuating. One of the most important branches of his employment no longer existed; he had laid the foundation of a great work for the promotion of christianity in India, which he could in future more advantageously forward and defend in his native country; and thither he felt attracted by the associations of early and maturer life, by filial duty, and paternal affection. For this return, therefore, after making a variety of arrangements to ensure the continuance of the works carrying on under what he considered to be the "Christian Institution," more particularly of the Chinese class at Serampore, he at length prepared.

On the 27th of November, Dr. Buchanan left Calcutta, and reached Fulta the next day; and from this place he wrote to Colonel Sandys as follows:

"Dear Sandys,—I am thus far on my way to Europe. I sail in the Baretto to Goa, to look into the inquisition there, and examine the libraries. Thence I proceed to Bombay.

"A few days ago I received your letter of the 28th of May, 1807, dated from Northwold, containing the signatures of the little girls. They write very well, and have made a flattering progress in their education. I am much obliged to you for your particular account of the two children, which is very correct, I believe, and very pleasing. Being long estranged from them, and hearing none converse about them, I seldom think of them now comparatively. But when we meet again, I suppose we shall fall in love.

"You observed in some of your late letters that you heard I was likely to be married again. It so happens that I have not once thought of it. It is possible that I may marry some time after my arrival in England. But yet I would avoid it, for some reasons. It is a subject I think not of.

"Instead of love and marriage, I am engaged in war and fightings. I have been obliged to address this government publicly on its hostility to religion and to its progress in India. All Calcutta wondered what step government would take. In the midst of this strange scene, I paid a farewell visit to them all, and left every creature, from the Governor General to the pilots, on good terms.

"I have now finished my labours, and pray that God may bless them.

"I have been down here for eight days, waiting the despatch of the ship. The Calcutta people have not been uninterested in my late contention with the government; and I hear some of them have called a ship by my name, since I came down here. The 'Christian Institution in the East' is unknown in Calcutta to this hour, though active in its operation.

"Yours affectionately, C. BUCHANAN."

The ship in which Dr. Buchanan sailed left Saugor on the 9th of December; but no memorial of his voyage occurs until the 23d of that month, when he wrote to Mr. Brown as follows, from Columbo, in the island of Ceylon:

"Ceylon again! In crossing the Gulf of Manaar, we encountered a gale, and put into Columbo. I had requested the captain to touch here when I left Calcutta; and now he was obliged of necessity. I have been well on board, and well treated. Many causes for thankfulness, as usual. The Adele was taken by the Russell the day before we came up to her, and we had parted convoy. In the Gulf of Manaar we were about to throw over our cargo, when the gale abated.

"On my arrival here, many of the chief persons waited on me. From my having touched last year at so many Dutch settlements, I found all the families knew me. I have only been here three days, having arrived on Monday last, and the ship proceeds on her voyage on Friday. I have some thoughts of letting her go, and following at my leisure; for I find there is something for me here to do. What a field for English, Dutch, and Cingalese preachers in this fertile and renowned land!

"I propose to proceed straight to Cochin from this place. Sir James Mackintosh is on the Malabar coast, I hear, with his family. Two Bombay civil servants now here wish me to travel by land from Cochin to Goa. They have been judges and collectors for fourteen years on that coast, and allege they know more about the christians than any other persons in India. They complain much of the undue influence of Goa, exercised sometimes cruelly on all christians who are not Catholics. Mr. B. carries me out to-day to his country house, to visit some of the Cingalese christian churches.

"My affectionate regards to all your family."

By the date of his next letter, Dr. Buchanan appears to have left the Baretto, in which he originally embarked from Calcutta, and to have exchanged that ship for the Canton, from which, on the 26th of December, he thus wrote off Cochin to Colonel Macaulay:

"I had flattered myself with the hope of being landed here, but the commander of the ship cannot wait, and I am disappointed. He has engaged to put me down at Goa, where I propose to remain some time, and from whence I shall write to you particularly. I left Calcutta on the 8th inst. and touched at Columbo, where I staid some days, and found flattering assurances of support in our evangelizing plans for that island. There is less prejudice there than in the Company's settlements. This is the third time that I have visited Ceylon; so that the people begin to think I have some serious design against them.

In my last I believe I informed you that I was *standing in the breach*. I have now the pleasure to announce that the battle has been fought. Long consultations were held how to proceed. It was at last decreed that I should be permitted to depart in peace.

"I have the copy of the Malayalim scriptures with me, and mean to print when at Bombay: five thousand copies will suffice for a beginning, I suppose.

"I left Misrahi, my Jew, in Calcutta, with his own consent. I have advanced him in the whole a thousand rupees; so I suppose he will trade there.

"I hope to see you before I leave India; but I do not know at this moment where or how. May all our resolves and purposes be acceptable to the divine will!

"Mr. Johnston, Judge at Columbo, will furnish me with some important official documents relating to the state of christianity in that island. The Governor was absent; but Major Maitland (Lord Lauderdale's son) came to inform me that he would return in two days, if I would stay to see him. I could not stay; but I communicated to him that, if he would give to the Cingalese translation of the scriptures his *countenance*, I would give *money;* and Judge Johnston would find instruments. Mr. J. is an excellent Cingalese scholar himself."

Notwithstanding the disappointment of which Dr. Buchanan expressed his expectation at the commencement of the preceding letter, we find him two days afterwards safely landed at Cochin, and under the roof of his friend, Colonel Macaulay. He thus writes to Mr. Brown:

"COCHIN, 28th Dec. 1807.

"On the 24th, Christmas-eve, we left Columbo, crossed the Gulf of Manaar on Christmas-day, and arrived here on the 27th, yesterday. I found all my Jews and Christians in fine health and spirits, and highly gratified at my unexpected arrival. I reside with Colonel Macaulay. After passing some time in these regions, he accompanies me up the coast, by land, through all the christian territories, as far as Cananore, perhaps Mangalore, whence I proceeded by sea to Goa.

"The Jews have lately had a meeting about the prophecies. And I am about to call another Sanhedrim on the subject before I go. It is a strange event.

"I am happy I have visited this place a second time. May God direct all these things to his own glory, and to the good of men! I have need of watchfulness and prayer. Much lies before me, ere I leave India, yet; if ever I leave it.

"Tell H. that the poor Jews, blind, lame, and halt, are come this morning, exclaiming, as usual, 'Jehuda Ani.' I wish I could impart a better gift than silver or gold. The Rajah of Travancore has desired I will visit him. I do not know what to do. The Rajah of Cochin has offered to come over to see me. Ambassadors from the Syrian christians are expected to-morrow."

On the 2d of January, 1808, Dr. Buchanan left Cochin, accompanied by Colonel Macaulay, on a second tour upon the coast of Malabar. The following letter to Mr. Brown will afford an interesting account of their progress:

"TELLICHERRY, 14th Jan. 1808.

"I write this from the fort which the English first built in India; and where, as Tippoo observed in his official manifesto, the English pedlars 'first exhibited their scissors and knives.' Tellicherry lines enclose nine miles in circumference; and the natives have enjoyed the protection of the English for about one hundred and sixty years. The enemy was never suffered to destroy them. *But no English church, or house of prayer, has yet been built.* From this spot we extended our power to the utmost limits of India.

"Colonel Macaulay has accompanied me thus far. We first proceeded from Cochin to the famous Shanscrit college at Trichiur, and thence to a district of the Syrian christians which I had not before visited. It was named, by Hyder, Nazarani Ghur, or the city of the Nazarenes. It is a beautiful place, fertile and populous. The town is four square, having four gates, built on the side of a hill, with steps cut in the rock from street to street, surrounded by lofty groves of palm and other trees. A verdant meadow winds about the foot of the hill, and the whole country is a scene of hill and dale. The priests and people knew me, and received us with great affection. Colonel Macaulay accompanied me to the principal church. Having signified my intention of presenting a large gold medal to this church, in the name of all the Syrian churches in Malayalim, a vast concourse of people assembled. There is no person in the town but Nazarenes. The medal which I presented to them was that which Mrs. J. gave me before I left Calcutta. It is about three times as large as a college gold medal, and exhibits the baptism of Jesus in Jordan, eleganty executed; and, on the reverse, a child brought to be baptized. I placed it on the altar, in the presence of the people, with due solemnity, and, beside it, a gift to the poor. This town is in the territories of the Rajah of Cochin, whom I visited a fortnight ago. Tippoo invaded this Syrian colony in 1789. The people pointed out to me the grove of trees on which the christians were hanged. They are now so respectable for number and opulence, that the Rajah of Cochin is obliged to treat them with indulgence; and the more so, as they are within four miles of the English territories in Malabar. Nazarani Bazar (as it is sometimes called) is due east from Paniani, and is near Palghutcheri. This second visit to the Syrian churches has been useful.

The Jews at Cochin are very unsettled in relation to the prophecies. They wonder at the attention paid by the English to these subjects, for the first time. You will read in the Bombay Courier an account of a ceremony in the synagogue at Cochin, which took place at Christmas last, a few days before I arrived. Some of the Jews interpret the prophechies aright, and some in another way; but all agree that a great era is at hand.

"I visited Mahé, a beautiful place, formerly a French fort, but now in ruins, and Calicut. At this last place Vasco de Gama landed in 1497, at a fine bay a little above the town. I saw the ruins of the Samorin's palace, in which he was first received. The Mahometan towns on the sea-coast are large and populous. The Romish christians are numerous. The English christians complain that there is no Protestant church or minister on this coast, except a chaplain to the garrison at Cananore.

"The march of Menou prevents my going home by land.

"I propose to proceed to Goa in a day or two, and thence to Bombay, if time permit. I reside here at the house of Mr. C., the Judge of the province.

"I enjoy good health in this favoured land. Amidst all my researches, the importance of the gospel appears everywhere conspicuous. Every evil I witness, and every defect, might be remedied by the gospel, whether among the natives or the Europeans."

Dr. Buchanan's next letter to Mr. Brown is dated "Goa, 25th January, from the great hall of the Inquisition." It contains an account of his bold and interesting visit to that metropolis of the Roman Catholic religion in the east, and is similar to that with which the public in general is already well acquainted.* Instead, therefore, of repeating that admirable narrative, in which the ardour of christian research, and of christian courage and benevolence, are strikingly displayed, a sketch of this enterprising expedition only shall be given, which occurs in a letter to Colonel Macaulay.

"On my arrival at Goa I was hospitably entertained by Captain Schuyler. He and Colonel Adams introduced me next day to the Viceroy, who affects great pomp, rails at the French, and is a true Frenchman at heart. Next day Major Pareira went up with me to old Goa. The archbishop received me cordially. I professed a purpose of remaining some days there. This, it seems, was unusual, and it occasioned

* Christian Researches, pp. 155—178.

some discussion and difficulty. At last I was received by one of the *Inquisitors;* not *your* friend, (who lives at a distance from the place,) but by the second Inquisitor, Josephus à Doloribus, the chief agent of the Inquisition, and the most learned man of the place. By this *malleus hereticorum* was I received in his convent of the Augustinians, in a suit of chambers next his own. He was extremely communicative. All the libraries were opened, and were extensive and valuable beyond my conception. That of the Augustinians, alone, appeared to be larger than the library of the college of Fort William.

"My object all this time was the Inquisition, and I gleaned much information imperceptibly. I disguised my purpose for the first three days, and the Inquisitor referred me to various books and documents elucidating the very subject I wanted to investigate; so that, on the fourth day, I attacked him directly on the present state of the Inquisition.

"I had already discovered that it was abolished in 1775, by the court of Portugal, on account of its inhuman rigour; that in 1779 it was restored on the accession of the present queen; and that it has been in operation ever since. On its restoration its rigour was qualified in some points. It was not to have a public Auto da Fe; but it was permitted to have a private one annually. The dungeons and torture remain the same. It has power to incarcerate for life; and there are now victims in its cells. The tribunal is supported in its ancient pomp, and its establishment is full. In fact, it is the only department which is *alive* in ancient Goa.

Josephus à Doloribus was alarmed when he discovered the real drift of my inquiries. I told him that he had now said so much, he might as well tell me all; and that I should not leave Goa till I had seen the Inquisition. He at last consented to show me the great hall. I accompanied him, clothed in the solemn robes of his office. When I had surveyed the place awhile in silence, I desired that he would now let me go below and visit the dungeons. He refused; and here our first contest began. I told him that if he did not open the dungeons, and let me count the captives, and inquire into the periods of their imprisonment, and learn the number of deaths within the last year, I should naturally believe that he had a good reason for the concealment, and that the ancient horrors of the Inquisition still subsisted. Whereas, if he would now unbar his locks, I could only declare to the public the truth as it was, and nothing would be left to imagination. He felt the force of this; but answered, that he could not oblige me, consistently with his oath or duty as an Inquisitor. I observed that he had broken that oath frequently during the last four days, and that he had himself noticed in his own justification, that the ancient regulations of the church were in many instances obsolete. I then put the following question solemnly, 'Declare to me the number of captives which are at this moment in the dungeons below.' 'That, sir, is a question,' said he, 'which I must not answer.'

"I was now in the hall where the captives were wont to be marshalled when they proceeded to the flames. I contemplated the scene awhile with mournful reflection, and then retired. The alcaides and familiars of the holy Inquisition stood around me, wondering at my introduction into the hall, and my conversation with the Inquisitor. I went into a neighbouring church and ruminated on what I had seen and heard. I resolved to go again to the Inquisition. The familiars, thinking I had business with the Inquisitor, admitted me. I immediately saw a poor woman sitting on a bench in the great hall. She appeared very disconsolate, and was waiting to be called before the tribunal in the next room. I went towards the tribunal, and was met at the door by Josephus à Doloribus, who seemed to have lost his temper at this intrusion, and exclaimed, '*Quid vis tu, Domine?*' All our discourse was in Latin. I told him I wanted to speak with the chief Inquisitor, who was then on the bench. I then looked at the poor woman very significantly, and then at him—And what has this poor woman done? He was silent and impatient to lead me out. When we came to the head of the stairs, I took my last leave of Josephus à Doloribus, and repeated once more in his ears, what I had pleasantly pronounced before in our amicable discussions about the Inquisition, '*Delenda est Carthago.*'

"Before I left Goa, I communicated to him my intention (I first declared it to him in his own cell) of addressing the archbishop in a Latin letter, which would probably be published, on the four following subjects:

"1. The Inquisition.

"2. The want of Bibles for the priests.

"3. The disuse of public preaching and instruction in his diocese.

"4. The state of the public libraries.

"This letter I began and dated from the convent of the Augustinians, 25th January, 1808. I shall probably print it before I leave Point de Galle.

"My visit at Goa has excited a very general alarm among the priests. The Viceroy wishes success to my endeavours.

The English at Goa seemed to know little or nothing about the subject. The whole Catholic body there are awed by it; and it was said that some would suffer in consequence of my visit; for Major B., and others of the Viceroy's household, were known to furnish me with every information in their power. But at last I perceived that even B. himself, the philosophic, liberal, learned B., was cowed, and endeavoured to draw off."

On quitting his friend, Josephus à Doloribus, whose favour and forbearance had perhaps been conciliated by the present of a small purse of moidores, previously to his admission into the *santa casa*, Dr. Buchanan confesses, in his letter to Mr. Brown, that his own mind was much agitated.

"I began to perceive," he says, "a cowardly fear of remaining longer in the power of the Inquisitors. My servants had repeatedly urged me to go, and I set off about twelve o'clock, not less indignant at the Inquisition of Goa, than I had been with the temple of Juggernaut."

Dr. Buchanan's great object in this, as in all his researches, was not so much the gratification of personal curiosity, as the discovery of useful and important information, with a view to the detection and the removal of spiritual and moral evils. The suggestion in the published extracts from his journal, as to the propriety of an interference on the part of the British government with that of Portugal, for the abolition of the dreadful tribunal of the Inquisition, had been happily anticipated, but did not render his animated appeal upon that subject superfluous; while his inquiries relative to the moral and religious state of the Romish and Syro-Romish churches, on the coast of Malabar, led to efforts to disseminate the holy scriptures, for the instruction and illumination of that numerous and long-neglected body of christians.

"In two hours," continues Dr. Buchanan in his letter to Mr. Brown, "I reached New Goa. The alarm of my investigations had gone before me. The English came to inquire what I had seen and heard, and I told them all. I staid a day or two with them, and embarked in a pattamar (an open boat) for Bombay. The wind was contrary, and I was ten days on the voyage. I touched at three different places on the Pirate coast; Gheria, the celebrated fort of Severndroog, &c. One day we were driven out to sea, and in considerable danger. At length, however, on the 6th of February, I reached Bombay."

On his arrival at this Presidency, Dr. Buchanan was kindly received by Governor Duncan, and took up his abode at the house of Mr. Forbes. He experienced the utmost civility from the principal persons of the settlement, and was particularly gratified by the attentions of Sir James Mackintosh. "I passed five hours," he observes in a letter to Colonel Macaulay, "with Sir James in his library. It is uncommonly numerous and valuable. He is a friend to religion, and professes a desire to support me in all useful plans for India."

Dr. Buchanan had taken with him to Bombay the manuscript translation of the four Gospels into the Malayalim language, which had been completed by the Syrian bishop and his clergy, and transmitted to Colonel Macaulay, intending to print it at his own expense, an excellent fount of types having been recently cut at that place. When Mr. Duncan, however, heard of this intention, he intimated his wish that Dr. Buchanan would address a letter to the government upon the subject, promising to give it his countenance and support. He accordingly availed himself of this hint, and, in an address to the governor in council, briefly detailed the circumstances of his visit to Travancore, and its result relative to the version of the scriptures into the Malabar language. He also stated that, on his arrival at Bombay, he had submitted the translation of the four Gospels to the judgment of Mr. Drummond, of that Presidency, author of the Malabar Grammar, who had reported that he considered it to be a faithful version of the sacred original, and easily intelligible by the common people. Dr. Buchanan took the same opportunity of representing to the governor in council the importance of a cheap edition of the English Bible for the use of the army, and of the English inhabitants, generally, of that country. In reply to this communication, the secretary to government informed him that the governor in council readily extended his countenance to the good work which he was so laudably meditating, and would, for that purpose, be disposed to accede to such ulterior measures as might tend to promote it; but that the communities of Malabar christians to whom he had adverted, being chiefly within the jurisdiction of the Presidency of Fort St. George, the governor in council felt it to be his duty to transmit thither his representations upon that subject. With respect to the supply of the English scriptures, the governor in council expressed his intention of shortly recommending that part of Dr. Buchanan's suggestions to the consideration of the Court of Directors, who, he doubted not, would be desirous of ensuring to the Europeans at Bombay the edification to which the dissemination of the holy scriptures must materially contribute.

In consequence of this favourable disposition of the government, Dr. Buchanan drew up an advertisement for a subscription towards defraying the expenses of the printing of the Gospels in the Malayalim language; the governor himself professing his intention to subscribe, and to lead the way in this laudable design.

"I took no steps, however," says Dr. Buchanan in a letter to Colonel Macaulay, dated off Calicut, February 27th, "till the last day of my stay at Bombay, when I told Mr. Money that I had a delicacy in pressing the subscription when I was on the spot, but that I should leave it in his and Mr. Forbes' hands, and trust to them for its success.

"I left a note of instructions with Messrs. Forbes regarding the appropriation of the funds; and they are authorized to pay all bills relative to the expense of translating the scriptures into the Malayalim language, and of sending learned persons to Bombay to superintend the printing, which shall have received your signature.

"The types are ready, but they have not one Malayalim learned native in Bombay. The first thing that I request of you is to send round two persons qualified to superintend the printing. Mr. Drummond will superintend *them*. It will be expedient that one of the moonshees be a Romish or Syro-Romish priest, for the reasons mentioned in the advertisement.

"The prefaces peculiar to the Syriac may be omitted, and it may have a general conformity to the Vulgate.

"Some of the Romish priests will, perhaps, oppose the design; but I have warned the gentlemen at Bombay of that circumstance. A Padre L. is Italian instructor in Sir James Mackintosh's family, and assumes consequence. Mr. Duncan told me that this priest (who occasionally visits him) had come to him in evident alarm, and announced that I was about to destroy the Inquisition, and to declare to the world that the old horrors still exist, which, said he, is not true. I took this opportunity of giving Mr. Duncan some account of my inquiries; when he expressed his approbation fully of my intention, and urged me to weaken the Romish interest as much as possible in India. It seems the priests have given government some trouble lately; and he has proposed something to the Madras Presidency on the subject.

"It would take a fortnight to detail what passed during my fortnight at Bombay, and therefore I must conclude.

"I have taken my passage in the Charlton, and have secured the first officer's cabin, which is large and commodious, for myself and Master Drummond. We have ten ladies on board, and Dr. Pouget of Surat, a man of information.

"If you write a note to Point de Galle I shall probably receive it.

"I have often recommended your going home, and now I wish you to stay two or three years. If your health will allow this, your stay will accomplish a great object for the church of Christ.

"Your friend, Ribeymar, the chief Inquisitor, received me very kindly, and made a feast on the last day but one of my stay, at which were present the whole staff of the Santa Casa. He said he would answer your letter. The 'thieveless errand' I had to visit the Inquisition a second time, was to inquire whether the chief Inquisitor had written his letter.

"I did not touch at Cananore or Mangalore. I was afraid of losing the Inquisition and my passage.

"On my arrival in England, I shall not fail to give you some account of affairs, if I mix with men, which I much doubt; for I am tired of fighting, and sigh for quiet and retirement.

"I remain, my dear sir, very sincerely yours,

C. BUCHANAN."

It may be satisfactory to add that the letter from the chief Inquisitor to Colonel Macaulay, above referred to, strongly expressed his respect for that gentleman, and the pleasure which he had received from Dr. Buchanan's visit, notwithstanding the freedom of his inquiries and observations.

In another short communication to Colonel Macaulay about the same time, Dr. Buchanan mentions a pleasing mark of kindness which had been shown him by one of his friends at Calcutta, and informs him of a proposal which he had made relative to one of the most stupendous and interesting objects of curiosity in India.

"Mr. Speke has sent a beautiful large quarto Bible after me, as a keepsake. He had heard that I complained of my sight in reading small print at night. And this is my last communication with the learned of Calcutta. *Hoc Deus fecit.*

"I have put them on restoring Elephanta at Bombay. I found the cavern and figures in a state of progressive annual dilapidation. Mr. Money has taken up the subject warmly. If government does not execute it, I have proposed a subscription, with a promise of five hundred rupees as soon as the work shall commence under a scientific superintendent. I have left a memorandum of the subjects of improvement, and re-edification, according to my idea. I have a reason for wishing that the Trinity in Unity at Elephanta may remain while this lower world exists."

Dr. Buchanan thus adverts to the same extraordinary remains of antiquity, in writing to Mr. Brown:

"I have visited Elephanta; a more wonderful work than the Pyramids of Egypt. But the works of Providence are yet more wonderful; at least so I should esteem them; for in every region, and in every clime, the loving-kindness of God is magnified in my experience. May his grace also be magnified in me! My love to all your family."

On the 13th of March the Charlton arrived off Point de Galle, from which place Dr. Buchanan again wrote a few lines to Mr. Brown.

"I had intended," he says, "to have published my letter to the Archbishop of Goa at this place. But if we do not go on shore, I shall have no opportunity. I shall therefore publish it at home.*

"I have just been on board the Piedmontaise frigate, which has been captured by the St. Fiorenzo. The Piedmontaise lost one hundred and sixty-five men, killed and wounded, and exhibited a scene of vast carnage. Captain Hardinge of the St. Fiorenzo is killed.

"I have extensive commissions for sending good books and Bibles to Bombay, Malabar, and Ceylon. For, if they have no preachers, they must read.

"All is well on board this ship, and I hope some good will be done.

"With unfeigned prayers for the best of spiritual blessings on you and your family,

"I remain, my dear sir, very affectionately yours,

C. Buchanan."

To Colonel Macaulay Dr. Buchanan wrote the next day, as follows:

"My dear Sir,—We have just arrived at this place, and see the Bengal fleet ready to sail; so that I have only time to bid you farewell. We staid three days at Colúmbo; one of which I passed with General Maitland at Mount Lavinia. After long and interesting conversations, he was pleased to promise that he would recommend to his majesty's government 'an ecclesiastical establishment for the island of Ceylon.' By the next

* On his arrival in England, Dr. Buchanan found it unnecessary to publish this letter, the Inquisition at Goa having been abolished.

despatch he will send me, under cover to the Bishop of London, copies of all the papers I wanted relating to the ecclesiastical state of the island for the last two centuries. He has agreed to support the translation of the scriptures into the Cingalese language. I resided with the honourable Mr. Twisleton, whom I found well disposed to second all my views. Mr. Heywood did more. I think he is disposed to be zealous as a pastor to his people. I shall correspond, I hope, with both. They are surprised at the Governor's full acquiescence in the above important measures. I hope he will not retract.

"I received your letters for your brother, which I hope to deliver into his hands. I am much obliged to you for your introduction to him.

"The fleet is now under weigh for St. Helena. Farewell.

C. BUCHANAN.

"H. C. Charlton, Point de Galle,
"14 March, 1808."

Here we also must for the present take our leave of Dr. Buchanan; and, while he is pursuing his homeward voyage, resume our account of various events and circumstances connected with his history, which occurred during the interval between the publication of his ecclesiastical memoir, and his return to this country.

Memoirs of the Rev. Dr. Buchanan.

PART III.

CHAPTER I.

OF the events referred to at the close of the preceding division of this narrative, the first in order of time relates to the determination of the munificent prizes proposed by Dr. Buchanan to the universities of Oxford and Cambridge, in the year 1805. It has been already stated, that the time assigned for this purpose was the 4th of June, 1807; on which day, the prize was adjudged at Oxford to the author of these memoirs. At Cambridge some circumstances occurred which prevented any decision upon the subject; and which the following letter, from the Vice-Chancellor of that university to Dr. Buchanan, will sufficiently explain.

"Reverend Sir,—The sum of five hundred pounds proposed by you for the best essay on 'The probable Design of divine Providence in subjecting so large a portion of India to the British Empire,' &c. was accepted by the university; and Dr. Milner, Dr. Jowett, and Dr. Outram, appointed to read the compositions, and decide upon their respective merits.

"Of all that were sent in within the appointed time, not one was deemed worthy of so magnificent a prize. Another came a few days after the time, which was unanimously preferred to all the rest; and to which the examiners would without the least hesitation have adjudged the prize, but did not think themselves authorized to do so, without your special permission, as one of the conditions, the presenting the composition within such a time, had not been complied with.

"The author has since avowed himself to be the Rev. J. W. Cunningham, M. A. of St. John's college.

"Dr. Pearce, Vice-Chancellor at the time when the examiners made their report, having heard that you were on your passage to England, deferred writing, as he daily expected to have a personal interview with you: and thus has devolved to me the office of communicating to you the thanks of the whole university for your very liberal offer, and their regret that your design has not been completely carried into execution.

"Though I have not the honour of being known to you, yet in admiration of your character as the munificent patron and promoter of literature,

"I subscribe myself, with the greatest respect, your very humble servant, FRANCIS BARNES.

"St. Peter's College, Cambridge,
Jan. 19th, 1808."

It appears that Dr. Buchanan did not feel himself at liberty to make any decision upon the point stated in the preceding letter, and that the university was unwilling to resume the official consideration of the subject. Dr. Buchanan, however, offered to bear the expense of printing Mr. Cunningham's work.

On the 10th of May and the 28th of June, 1807, two sermons were preached before the university of Cambridge, by the Rev. Francis Wrangham, of Trinity College, and the Rev. John Dudley, of Clare Hall, pursuant to the proposal of Dr. Buchanan in the preceding year, on the translation of the scriptures into the oriental languages. Two discourses on the same important subject were preached before the University of Oxford, on the 8th and 29th of November following, by the Rev. Dr. Barrow, of Queen's College, and the Rev. Edward Nares, of Merton College. The two former of these sermons were published in the course of the year 1807, and the two latter early in 1808. All of them, with different degrees of ability and eloquence, and by various considerations and arguments, supported the duty and expediency of translating the sacred records into the principal languages of the East; and all strenuously maintained the general obligation of this country to attempt, by every wise and rational method, to promote the knowledge of christianity in India. But the authors of these excellent discourses, like those of the first series of prize compositions, though a most able and efficient corps, formed the advanced guard only, if the expression may be allowed, of the main body which was now hastening to its support, and whose united exertions were eventually crowned with the most gratifying and decisive success.

Dr. Buchanan's memoir on the expediency of an ecclesiastical establishment for British India, produced, as might be expected, a considerable sensation on the public mind. The subject was not only highly important, but it was new. The world had, indeed, heard much of East Indian commerce, policy, and conquests; but of East Indian religion, little or nothing. Now and then the name of a chaplain to the company had been mentioned, and, still more rarely, that of a missionary to the Hindoos. But, generally speaking, the whole subject of the religion of India was little known, and still less regarded. Its European population was presumed, without thought or inquiry, to be sufficiently provided with the means of christian instruction; and as to the natives, they were considered as a race so completely separated from ourselves, and at the same time so religious and even moral in their own way, that, with the exception of those who had heard something of the Danish mission on the coast of Coromandel, the idea of converting any considerable number of the Hindoos was either treated as altogether unnecessary, and even unjust, or deemed in the highest degree visionary and impracticable. The admirable writings of Sir William Jones had illustrated the history, the antiquities, and the laws of India, and had excited some degree of literary and even political interest in favour of its native inhabitants; but the peculiarly christian consideration of them and of their country was a topic which had hitherto been but incidentally noticed. In this state of things, a work like the memoir of Dr. Buchanan, exclusively devoted to this momentous and unusual subject, and characterized by great boldness, decision, and ability, might naturally be expected to produce a powerful and various impression upon the public. The more religious part of it hailed this production as presenting facts and arguments of a most important nature, and as opening a boundless sphere of exertion to the newly-awakened and expanding energies of christian benevolence and zeal; while others, and those a numerous and respectable class, considered it as at best a rash and unauthorized publication, and even deprecated it as tending to excite dissatisfaction at home and disturbance abroad. The growing extent and influence of the British and Foreign Bible Society, and the anxiety which it had evinced to promote the translation of the scriptures into the oriental languages, added materially to the displeasure and alarm of the persons last alluded to.

It was not long before sentiments and feelings of a hostile nature were publicly avowed; and it forms a very remarkable coincidence of events in either hemisphere, that while attempts were, as we have already seen, making at Calcutta to arrest, or at least to impede, the progress of scriptural translation, and to restrain the efforts of christian missionaries, a formidable attack was carrying on in this country, with a view to check the ardour which had been kindled in the minds of multitudes in favour of both those great and interesting objects, and to provoke authoritative interference of government to extinguish at once their hopes of effectually promoting them. The attack in question originated in a pamphlet published in the month of October, 1807, under the title of "A Letter to the Chairman of the East India Company, on the danger of interfering in the religious opinions of the natives of India, and on the views of the British and Foreign Bible Society, as directed to India." This pamphlet, though at first anonymous, was shortly after avowed by Thomas Twining, Esq., a senior merchant on the Bengal establishment; who announced it as only the precursor of a motion, which he intended to bring before the Court of East India Proprietors, for expelling from Hindostan all the christian missionaries who were then labouring in that extensive but neglected field; and for preventing the holy scriptures from being circulated in the languages of the East. The alarm of this gentleman, which could excite so formidable an intention, was no doubt genuine and extreme; though, as it has been well observed, the changes which have taken place since the date of his publication, both in the religious state of India, and in the opinion of the public at large, respecting the propagation of christianity in the East, give to his distorted representations the air of irony and satire, rather than of grave complaint and serious expostulation. Mr. Twining's pamphlet was chiefly composed of partial extracts from the reports of the British and Foreign Bible Society, and from Dr. Buchanan's memoir, which undoubtedly indicated the wish and the design to promote the knowledge of the gospel throughout the world, and, amongst other quarters, in which that knowledge was particularly needed, throughout the British dominions in India. This laudable intention Mr. Twining interpreted as evidence of a strong disposition to interfere, in some violent and unwarrantable method, with the religious opinions of the native inhabitants, and as exposing our eastern possessions to the most imminent and unprecedented danger.

With respect to the share of the British and Foreign Bible Society in this extraordinary charge, it is only necessary to refer to the able reply published by the Rev. Mr. Owen, in the month of December following, and to that part of his history of the society which relates to this controversy.

The attack of Mr. Twining upon Dr. Buchanan was founded partly upon some passages in his memoir, in which he discusses, in the most calm and benevolent manner, the duty, the practicability, and the advantages of endeavouring to promote christianity in India; and partly upon the misconstruction of one sentence, in which the acute sensibility of the former gentleman led him to imagine that Dr. Buchanan, in expressing his opinion as to the expediency of *coercing* the contemptuous spirit of the *Mohammedans*, was desirous of exercising some species of *compulsion* with respect to the religious sentiments of our native subjects in general. The term thus used by Dr. Buchanan may perhaps be considered as unfortunate, and he himself, on being informed of the perversion which it had suffered, omitted it in a subsequent edition of his memoir; but even as it originally stood, no one, who had read that publication with common attention and candour, could so far mistake the whole object of the writer as to suppose him guilty of the absurdity of recommending that the natives of India should be converted to the christian faith by *force*.

Notwithstanding the vague and unsatisfactory nature of this attempt to arrest the progress of christianity in India, there were not a few who, from the respectability of the quarter from which it issued, from ignorance or misconception of the subject, from mistaken views of worldly policy, from the want of any lively sense of the infinite value of the gospel, and from a morbid dread of every thing which was pronounced by persons affecting local knowledge, as likely to endanger the security of our eastern empire, were disposed to favour and support it.

The prejudice and alarm which began to be excited by Mr. Twining's pamphlet were increased by the publication of one, and subsequently of a second, by Major Scott Waring, who inveighed with even greater warmth and violence against the Bible Society, the missionaries in Bengal, and the memoir of Dr. Buchanan; and, in addition to the misrepresentation of his sentiments, which has been just referred to, discovered in his benevolent recommendation of adopting destitute Hindoo children, with a view to their education in christian principles, another proof of his wish to introduce a system of compulsion in India!

But the exertions of the friends of religion were successful in checking the rising spirit of jealousy and opposition occasioned by these publications; so that on the 23d of December, when the Court of Proprietors met at the India House, Mr. Twining found so little encouragement to propose his threatened motion, that he withdrew it, and the Court, in consequence, adjourned.

The important controversy, however, which had been thus begun, did not terminate here. Early in the year 1808, it was renewed by the publication of a pamphlet entitled, a "Vindication of the Hindoos from the aspersions of the Rev. C. Buchanan, M. A., with a refutation of his arguments for an Ecclesiastical Establishment in British India. By a Bengal Officer." This extraordinary publication was distinguished by the bold avowal that the Hindoo system little needs the ameliorating hand of the christian dispensation to render its votaries a sufficiently correct and moral people, for all the useful purposes of civilized society. Its military author, therefore, endeavoured strongly to maintain the excellence of the moral and religious doctrines of the Hindoos, and of the moral character of the Hindoos themselves. With much pretension, however, to local knowledge, he, in fact, betrayed much local ignorance, and with some partial information as to the speculative system of the Brahminical religion and morals, great disregard to its practical influence, and total deficiency in all large and general reasonings.

The "Bengal Officer," like his predecessors in this warfare, dealt much in general abuse of Dr. Buchanan's statements in his memoir, but adduced no one definite proof of their incorrectness. And here it may be right to observe that, while a few expressions in that work relative to the apparent absence of religious views and feelings in the Europeans, generally, resident in India, might be considered as somewhat too strongly and indiscriminately hazarded, no well-grounded objection to his representations upon any point connected with his main argument, was ever substantiated. So convinced was Dr. Buchanan himself of his correctness and integrity as to the statements contained in his memoir, that in a note to his letter to the Court of Directors from Calcutta, in December, 1807, which has been already mentioned, he ventured to make the following appeal upon this subject:

"The Memoir of the expediency of an Ecclesiastical Establishment for British India has now been in the hands of our Indian governments for a year and a half, and I have not heard that any one fact or deduction contained in that volume has been disputed or disproved; which, in this country, where the merits of such a work can be best understood, and where only just information of the local circumstances therein detailed can be obtained, and where, moreover, there are *fourteen* weekly publications to animadvert on that information, may be considered as some testimony to its general accuracy, as well as some acknowledgment of the necessity of the great measure therein proposed."

The labours of the friends and advocates of diffusing christian knowledge in India, more than kept pace with those of its adversaries. Amongst others, the venerable Bishop Porteus,* wrote some remarks on Mr. Twining's pamphlet, which were published anonymously, and which, in a strain of animated and well-directed irony, defended the measures of the British and Foreign Bible Society, and what his lordship termed "Dr. Buchanan's invaluable memoir."

Early in the spring appeared Mr. Cunningham's "Essay on the duty, means, and consequences of introducing the christian religion among the native inhabitants of the British dominions in the East;" forming a part of the work which he had submitted to the University of Cambridge, as a candidate for Dr. Buchanan's prize. The main argument of this able and elaborate publication was founded upon the malignant and pernicious nature of the Hindoo superstition; which was here so completely developed, as not only to form a decisive answer to the statements of such writers as the Bengal Officer, but to prove the obligation of Great Britain to communicate that divine system of faith and morals, by which alone the civil and religious character of the natives of India can be effectually improved.

Mr. Cunningham's essay was followed by the prize dissertation of the author of these memoirs; of which he will only observe, that he will ever esteem it one of the chief privileges and blessings of his life to have contributed, in whatever degree, to the accomplishment of the great end which the admirable proposer of the subject had in view; the infinite importance of which is confirmed by every year's experience, and cannot fail ere long to be universally acknowledged.

One other work remains to be mentioned of singular excellence and authority; and of which it has been justly remarked, that had it appeared in an earlier stage of the controversy, it would have superseded every other. This was the production of Lord Teignmouth; who, together with the principles of christian piety and benevolence, brought to the consideration of the weighty subject in question the correct and extensive local knowledge and the practical wisdom and experience which were the result of the high stations he had occupied in India. The temperate and dignified manner in which his lordship discussed the various topics connected with the controversy before us, deserve the highest admiration; nor is it too much to assert, that his "considerations on the practicability, policy, and obligation of communicating to the natives

* See Owen's History of the British and Foreign Bible Society, vol. i. p. 350.

of India the knowledge of christianity," were not only conclusive of the temporary contest in which they appeared, but will remain a standing testimony to the duty of a christian nation towards its ignorant and unconverted subjects.

It would be unjust to close this brief enumeration of the principal writers in this controversy, without mentioning the eminent services of one periodical publication, distinguished by the zeal and ability with which it originally embraced and steadily supported the great cause of christianity in India. It is scarcely necessary to add the name of "the Christian Observer;" which, whether in the examination of the productions on either side of the question, or in original communications, may justly claim a very considerable share of the praise which belongs to its successful termination.

Thus, as in the instance of the rising opposition at Calcutta, the storm which threatened to overwhelm the efforts of christian benevolence in this country to diffuse the knowledge of the gospel in the East, was quickly dispersed; and the advocates of this important and salutary measure were for the present permitted to pursue their peaceful and charitable course without farther interruption or disturbance.*

---

* The following interesting statements in relation to the subject of this chapter, are from a sketch of the life of Lord Teignmouth, in the Christian Observer for May, 1834.

"Many years before the general discussion of the question of unbarring India to christian light at the renewal of the Company's Charter, his lordship and his friends were zealously endeavouring to prepare the way, in private and official intercourse, for that great consummation; but it was not till the year 1808 that he was known to have come forward as an author upon the subject; and, even then, his publication was anonymous, under the title of 'Considerations on the Practicability, Policy, and Obligation of communicating to the Natives of India the Knowledge of Christianity, with Observations on the Prefatory Remarks of Major Scott Waring; by a late Resident in Bengal.' We have it in our power, however, to show, that even two years before the publication of this pamphlet, his mind was actively at work upon the question, by informing our readers of one of our literary secrets,—that it was his lordship who wrote the Review in the Christian Observer, in 1806, of Dr. Buchanan's 'Expediency of an Ecclesiastical Establishment for British India, both as a Means of perpetuating the Christian Religion among our own Countrymen, and as a Foundation for the ultimate Civilization of the Natives.' His lordship thought, indeed, that Dr. Buchanan had advanced somewhat beyond the bounds of prudence and practicability; and few persons were there at that time—not, we believe, even Mr. Wilberforce or Mr. Grant—who did not feel some hesitation respecting the large plans of Dr. Buchanan; and, even Dr. Buchanan himself, the Luther of India, whose zealous writings and unwearied personal exertions, added to his munificent premiums for publications upon this momentous question, did more to enlighten and stimulate the public mind than the labours of any other individual, did not venture to adopt on his title-page a stronger word than 'civilization,' as applied to the natives of India. The idea of 'conversion' would have been accounted insanity. Looking back, therefore, at the circumstances of the times, and considering Lord Teignmouth's

CHAPTER II.

WHILE the controversy, of which a brief view has been given, was thus carrying on, the person, whose zeal and activity had principally given occasion to it, was quietly pursuing his voyage from India to his native country. Of the incidents which occurred during the five months which intervened between Dr. Buchanan's departure from Point de Galle in Ceylon to his arrival in England about the middle of August, no memorial appears to have been preserved. The following extracts from letters to several of his friends, though they fail in expressing his emotions on revisiting his native shores, after an absence of twelve years, during which he had been employed in so important and honourable a manner, and had experienced such vicissitudes of joy and sorrow, of repose and toil, of gratification and trial, will yet afford some notices of his proceedings. They will serve also to show his filial affection, his wish for retirement, yet his desire of usefulness as a minister of the gospel, and his lively interest in the progress of true religion in this country.

official habits, his characteristic caution, his serious responsiblity, and his practical knowledge of the obstacles to be surmounted, we are far from being surprised that he thought some of Dr. Buchanan's statements over-sanguine: on the contrary, we are rather inclined to express our admiration and gratitude that his lordship was so far in advance of most of his oriental contemporaries, even including men of undoubted piety and zeal, as to have penned the sentiments contained in that review. At that period not only was India almost hermetically sealed against christian missionaries, but even the circulation of the holy scriptures, without note or comment, was opposed by the Indian government, both at home and abroad, as a proceeding which involved great danger; and as to sending out a bishop to Calcutta, such a step, it was urged, would cause a general revolt of the natives, and end in a deluge of blood, and in our certain expulsion from the country. We may look back upon these astounding predictions, after more than a quarter of a century, without dismay; but, at the time they were uttered, they created strong impressions of alarm. Yet, triumphing over the general prejudice which then prevailed, especially among gentlemen who had passed much of their lives in the East, we find our respected correspondent and co-adjutor expressing his extreme anxiety for a 'sufficient' ecclesiastical establishment in India; hoping that it would be 'speedily and effectually supplied;' contending for the wisdom, duty, and safety of that great experiment, combating the vague apprehensions which were afloat, and fully concurring with Dr. Buchanan, not only in that part of his proposition which related to the European population, but also as to 'the practicability of civilizing the Hindoos, by instructing them in the truths of christianity, *and the undeniable policy of the attempt.*' His lordship, in that review, expressed strongly his opinion, that nothing will ever 'improve the morals' of the people of India but 'the principles of the christian religion.' "

His first visit, on his arrival in London, was to the house of Mr. Newton; "but judge," said he, to one of his correspondents, "what were my feelings, when I was informed that my venerable friend had entered into rest some months before. I next proceeded to Cadell's, expecting to have had the 'Christian Institution' put into my hands; but here also I was disappointed."

Thus deprived of two of the principal objects of his immediate attention, Dr. Buchanan turned to others of a more private and domestic nature.

"LONDON, 20th August, 1808.

"I arrived here two days ago, and was happy to hear that you and your family were well. I go down to Northwold in a day or two, whence I shall proceed to Scotland to see my aged mother; and on my return I hope to pay you a visit in Cornwall.

"I have enjoyed good health on board ship. I have no thoughts of ever returning to India again. My wish is, to take a cure of souls, and to grow old preaching the gospel; and I look out for retirement. The chairman and his deputy were desirous that I should conciliate the directors, by waiting on them individually in the usual manner. I have accordingly paid my respects to them all. It seems, that on Wednesday next there is to be a grand discussion on Indian missions. Lord Minto has sent home my letter to him, to the court, and this is the subject which calls for its attention on Wednesday.

"In the mean time I dismiss it from my mind altogether, being careless of the result, as it affects myself. I read no pamphlets, and scarcely know what has been doing. Nor do I wish to know any thing, till I have seen my family in England and Scotland, and have enjoyed for a time their tranquil society."

"NORTHWOLD, NORFOLK, 30th Aug. 1808.

"I received your letter as I was leaving London. Your affectionate expressions well accord with your long proved kindness to me and my family. It would indeed give me a sincere delight to visit you at this time with my two little girls; but I have not lived with my mother these twenty years, a fortnight excepted. I have a long arrear of filial affection and personal attention to bring up, and must first fulfil this duty.

"I shall probably stay over the winter in Scotland. There is an Episcopal church in the vicinity of my mother's house, where I may exercise my ministry, and where I may possibly remain, if I should find my labours useful.

"Charlotte and Augusta are so much grown, that I should scarcely have known them. The natural feelings of children to a father, and of a father to his children, have been displayed in a remarkable manner in many instances, and with such powerful sympathy, as has been delightful even to the beholders."

"STAMFORD, 12th Sept. 1808.

"Much more good has been done by the proposition of the literary prizes than I ever expected.

"Wherever I go, some commotion prevails; a conflict between light and darkness, which was not known when I left England twelve years ago."

"GLASGOW, 28th Sept. 1808.

"We arrived here on the 20th instant, and found my mother and family in fine health, both in body and spirit. We stopped on Sunday at Stamford, on Wednesday at York, and on Sunday at Carlisle. The Dean of Carlisle, with whom we dined, lifted up his voice against the races for the first time. He had long been oppressed in spirit on the subject; and he devoted his last day of preaching this season to the consideration of it. The cathedral was crowded, and he preached the word with great energy and eloquence.

"Mr. S—— has written to me, hoping I am not offended at his interfering with the publication of the book. I have answered, that on the contrary I consider his and Mr. G——'s interference as the act of christian friends; that I doubt not they acted for the best, according to their judgment; but that I can form no opinion on the subject myself, as I have not yet read the publications of the controversy."

When the attachment of Dr. Buchanan to the plan developed in the work just alluded to is considered, his acquiescence in the judgment of his friends affords a striking proof of his diffidence and humility.

"On Sunday last," Dr. Buchanan again writes from Glasgow, "I preached in the English church here to a crowded auditory. The Presbyterians come to hear, notwithstanding *the organ*. Both in England and Scotland a more tolerant spirit seems to pervade the different sects than formerly.

"In a few days I propose to leave Scotland, and to proceed with my little girls to Bristol. If I stay any longer at Glasgow, I fear I shall never get away."

Dr. Buchanan arrived at Bristol on the 21st of November, and on the 25th gave the following account of his journey from the North.

"I returned from Scotland by the way of Newcastle and Durham, after passing a week at Edinburgh. I was frequently with Professor ——, with whom I discussed the Edinburgh Review, which I told him was denominated in the middle counties of England, 'The Northern Blast.' He assured me that he had now nothing to do with that work, directly or indirectly; and seemed to lament that it was conducted with so little judgment. I asked him whether it was too late to retrieve its character; I was anxious for the fame of my countrymen; the bishop of Durham had already renounced it, and his example would soon be followed by others. The reviewers observed in defence, that most of the obnoxious articles have come from England. —— told me that it was with the greatest reluctance the editor admitted the Review on Indian missions, and that he wrote a long note in qualification of the text.

"I passed two days at Bishop's Auckland. The bishop entered into various subjects of religion and literature with great spirit. He told me it was true he had forbidden the Edinburgh Review to lie on his table. He did not think it right to sanction a work which had so grossly insulted religion. Some other gentlemen had expelled it on the same ground.

"I took an opportunity of mentioning to his lordship, when he was asking what appeared strange to me after a twelve years absence, that I thought the bishops seemed to have too little correspondence with each other on the interests of religion; that they were like twenty-four insulated kings or barons in their castles, while the enemy were scouring the plains, and did not sufficiently encourage men of learning and piety to come near them, and offer their counsel on subjects connected with the church at home and abroad.

—— "I visited Mr. Cecil yesterday, who is close by me here. He is much better, and is very anxious that I should write the life of Swartz. I was happy to hear him talk with such spirit."

For the various excellencies of the eminent minister of Christ, whose name occurs in the preceding sentence, and who was then near the close of his earthly career, the author of these memoirs gladly seizes the opportunity of testifying his affectionate veneration. In a subsequent letter Dr. Buchanan adds another brief notice of this admirable man:

"Notwithstanding his weakness, he seems to feel a singular pleasure in hearing me talk on oriental subjects, and the diffusion of the gospel generally. It seems he once preached a sermon* which led him to some inquiry on these subjects; for most people, I perceive, know little about them.

"You notice the spirit so hostile to you among your relations. If it be merely on account of the gospel, there is nothing more to be said or thought of it than this, 'That the reproach of Christ is great riches; and that to you it is given not only to believe, but to suffer for his sake.'

"I have been called to preach a charity sermon for the Bristol Infirmary. And they now wish me to preach the annual sermon at Mr. Biddulph's church, for 'Missions to Africa and the East.' They think more highly of me than they ought to think; but, being now somewhat of a public character, my testimony is acceptable. But my chief employment is at St. Mary Redcliffe.

"I have no thoughts of going to India. There is no peculiar sphere of usefulness for me there; nor is it probable that any will offer. As for my place of residence for the remaining years of my life, I have no partiality. I care not where I live or go. It sufficeth that I am employed for the present."

In the course of the autumn in this year, Dr. Buchanan received two letters from his friend, Mr. Brown, dated about two months after his own departure from India; the following extracts from which are strongly expressive of that excellent man's esteem for his late valuable colleague:

"I begin," he says, "with acknowledging the receipt of all your letters from Columbo, Cochin, Tellicherry, Goa, Bombay, and, lastly, from Point de Galle. The news all good. Your journey prosperous, and promising the best fruits.

"Well! you have fought your fight, and finished with the Archbishop of Goa, and are gone. May peace and safety attend all your paths; and may the providence of God preserve you to embrace your children, and to do good in the world!

"I have the best accounts of Martyn, Sabat, and Mirza. The Persian and Hindostanee are both ready. You will see we want a press for Martyn.

"I send you a copy of the archbishop's letter. No name was upon it. The inscription on the cover was 'The Vice-Provost,' and it was brought to me.

* This was Mr. Cecil's able and impressive sermon before the Church Missionary Society, in the year 1803.

"Since you left me, war has been in all my gates. But I have nothing to lose; neither fame nor money. Let them burn me, if they please. I shall make as good a fire as Brahmin women; two of whom were burnt last week near us; one before my eyes. I get disgusted and indignant on these occasions, and am always weighed down for some days after witnessing such horrible sacrifices to Moloch. Surely the 'Christian Institution' will demolish this most diabolical religion.

"I now send you two copies of Lord Minto's college speech. Mr. Harrington, to whom I had sent the report of the Chinese examination, took it to his lordship. He doubted at first whether all this was real. To be certain, he sent Dr. Leyden to me, to whom the whole was rehearsed, and who gave 'confirmation strong' to the report. Lord M. made several inquiries of me, and seemed pleased with what had been done.

"While I am writing I have received a long account of the particulars of ——'s death, from his son. His end was most blessed. The victory was complete. He was surprised to be told he was dying, but it did not discompose him for a moment. His language was, 'Whom have I in heaven but thee?' He broke out in Dr. Watts' translation of these words, which were his last. I shall find, a week or two hence, some interesting things to say in a funeral sermon, which I am requested to preach, and should have preached, if not requested; for these are our best occasions for working on the dead mass, and you were always diligent to improve them.

"I used to think you would make some improvement of my death. It must now be left to Limrick. Let him say, Alas! my brother, and I shall be satisfied. I have been a brother to him, and am yet, and shall be when I die, if I die before him. I shall have something to add, perhaps, but I say here, yours, affectionately, D. BROWN."

The letter to which Mr. Brown refers in the preceding extract was from the Archbishop of Canterbury; and it is here added, as a proof of his grace's approbation of the important measure which it was the great object of Dr. Buchanan's Ecclesiastical Memoir to recommend, and of his anxiety to promote its accomplishment.

"LAMBETH PALACE, Oct. 3d, 1807.

"Reverend Sir,—When I look back on the date which the manuscript transmitted through your means, from the college of Fort William, to the archiepiscopal library at Lambeth, bears upon its earliest pages, I am fearful lest I should appear to yourself, and to those with whom you are connected, insensible to the value of this splendid gift, or strangely negligent of common courtesy. At the time it arrived, I was anxiously employed in communicating with those, as well in office as out of office, who were best acquainted with the wants of the Protestant Church in British India, and best able to supply them. If, in my answer to your letter, written in the first pages of the Koran, I could have reported some progress in the great work of regulating the church in India, I should have felt that in fulfilling my duty I had made the best return in my power for the munificence I had experienced from you. Under this expectation, I have been led imperceptibly to a longer silence than ought to have been permitted; and I am now obliged to break it, without making that report, which would have been its best apology. Nevertheless, sir, I will not despair of ultimate success. The object we have in view is a reasonable object, and must not be lightly abandoned. It is not the spirit of making proselytes by which we are actuated, but the sober wish to maintain, in its purity and strength, christianity among christians. If it shall please God, through these means, the best, I had almost said the only means, in the hands of man, to spread the blessings of christianity, it is a result devoutly to be wished, but not impatiently pursued. Experience may have taught us that they are blessings that will not bear to be crudely and prematurely obtruded; they must be left to grow at their ease, and to ripen out of the character, and discipline, and doctrine of that church which is planted in India, and which is necessarily the object of daily and curious observation.

"I have the honour to be, reverend sir, your faithful, humble servant, C. CANTUAR."

The speech of Lord Minto, copies of which Mr. Brown mentions that he had transmitted to Dr. Buchanan, was that which his lordship delivered on the 21st of February, 1808, after the annual disputations in the college of Fort William; and in which, amidst his testimony to the progress of oriental literature in that institution, he took occasion to advert in terms of high praise to the proficiency in the Chinese language of the missionaries at Serampore, which must have been peculiarly gratifying to Dr. Buchanan, as the early friend of that most important pursuit.

"I must not," said his lordship, "omit to commend the zealous and persevering labours of Mr. Lassar, and of those learned and pious persons associated with him, who have accomplished for the future benefit, we may hope, of that immense and populous region, Chinese versions, in the Chinese character, of the Gospels of Matthew, Mark, and Luke; throwing open that precious mine, with all its religious and moral treasures, to the largest associated population in the world."

To this liberal and enlightened tribute of applause to the importance of the Chinese translation of the scriptures, Mr. Brown, in the second of his letters to Dr. Buchanan, added the gratifying and unexpected intelligence, that Lord Minto supported the translations, generally, and had subscribed to some of the works then carrying on at the Serampore press.

The following extract from one of Dr. Buchanan's letters to a friend, in January, 1809, on the dangerous illness of a near relative, as well as the tenor of the concluding remarks, shows the prevailing piety of his mind:

"I sincerely sympathize with you on this affliction; but the excellent accounts you give of her spiritual state must be your chief consolation. Happy for her that her affliction hath been sanctified! Whatever be the event, there is great room for praise and thanksgiving. I feel this the more from having just heard that a beautiful young lady, of good family and great fortune, has finished her course at the Wells here, and died without a ray of hope. Blessed, then, is your family, which hath 'this hope,' in the midst of a perverse generation. May it be your hope unto the end!

"All is well in India: only Bonaparte is expected. And, if the news of this day be true, he *may* be expected. But 'the Lord reigneth, be the earth never so unquiet.' I behold the tumult of the present scene with much tranquillity. But we must be in the circumstances in which Miss —— now is, to be able to view it aright, and to see the utter insignificance of things temporal, when weighed in the scale with things eternal."

In a letter to Mr. Brown, about the same time, the following passages occur:

"People imagine that I am meditating war. Nothing is farther from my thoughts. I am, at present, reading the Bible, and studying some subjects for sermons to poor people.

"I stand remote from the world. I do not even know whether the Court of Directors pays my furlough allowance. But on this, and other subjects, I shall be able to say more after I have been a year in the country.

"The Chinese printing" (which had been sent to him by

Mr. Brown) "is very admirable. You are cheaper, too, than I was, when I gave four annas for every character.

"The arrival of Mr. Thompson will brighten your prospects. I told Mrs. M. her prayers would bring good men.

"Mr. B., here, is a most useful evangelist. I shall enclose to you an account of the death of his daughter, aged fourteen. He lost four children in a year, and preached nobly to the hearts of his large congregation during the whole period. So you see good men have their trials on the banks of the Severn, as well as on the Ganges.

"You will regret to hear that Henry Kirk White was first proposed to Mr. Thornton," (meaning for his own benefaction to some student at the University,) "and," for reasons which do not appear, "was rejected."

On the 26th of February Dr. Buchanan preached his sermon entitled "The Star in the East," at the parish church of St. James, Bristol, for the benefit of the Church Missionary Society. This was the first of that series of able and well-directed efforts by which its excellent author, in pursuance of the resolution he had formed in India, endeavoured to cherish and extend the interest he had already excited for the promotion of christianity in the east. The object of this sermon was to detail some of the more prominent proofs that "the day" had at length begun to "dawn," and "the day-star to arise," on the benighted inhabitants of Asia; and its peculiar excellence consisted in the strength and simplicity with which these evidences were exhibited.

After stating the labours and the success of the Church of Rome, and of the Protestant missionaries, more particularly of the venerable Swartz, Dr. Buchanan introduced the highly interesting account of the martyrdom of Abdallah, and the conversion of Sabat; which can never be read without the deepest emotions of admiration and pity.

The subsequent apostacy of Sabat from the faith which he once appeared to have so cordially embraced, while it affords a lamentable proof of the depravity of the human heart, does not, in the slightest degree, affect either the truth of the narrative, or the object to which it was applied, of illustrating the divine efficacy of the gospel. That will still remain the same, whether the unhappy apostate should, as there seems to be some faint reason to hope,* once more be "renewed to repent-

* In a letter published in the Asiatic Journal for January last, from a Prince of Wales' Island Gazette, this wretched man refers to Dr. Buchanan's account of him in the "Star in the East," and affirms that he has never ceased to believe the truth of the christian religion.

ance," or become the final victim of impenitence and unbelief. Nor ought the deplorable defection of this once promising convert to be adduced as any proof of the want of judgment or penetration in Dr. Buchanan, and others,* who, in common with him, trusted to the fair appearance and the striking evidences of sincerity which this learned, but deluded, Arabian manifested during several years; though it may, and undoubtedly ought to, teach a lesson, both of caution to the christian minister, and of humility and self-distrust to the professed convert, not only in the East, but in every quarter of the world.†

---

* Particularly the late Rev. Henry Martyn.

† Whether the faint hope above expressed, respecting *Sabat*, has ever been realized can only be known by the revelations of a future day, when the secrets of all hearts shall be disclosed. The following particulars of his subsequent career have been related by Colonel MacInnes, a British officer, and appear in an appendix to a French translation of Martyn's life, published at Geneva:

"'I became personally acquainted with Sabat at Penang, a little after his public abjuration of christianity at Bengal. This deplorable act was followed by an unsuccessful trading voyage to Rangoon, after which he re-appeared at Penang, with the wreck of his fortune, in hope of better success.

"'During his stay in this island, I had the opportunity of knowing him thoroughly. I saw in him a disappointed man, uneasy and agitated in his mind. He attributed all the distress of his soul to the grief he felt for having abandoned christianity. He desired to receive again this holy religion, as the only means of reconciling himself with God. He declared that he had not had a moment's peace since (at the instigation of Satan) he had published his attack upon Revelation, an attack which he called his '*bad work*.' He told me, also, that what had led him to this fatal step, was the desire of revenging himself upon an individual to whom he thought an attack upon christianity would be more painful than any personal injury: but he had no sooner executed this detestable project (he added) than he felt a horror of the action, and now he only valued his life that he might be able to undo the pernicious tendency of his book, which he thought would be great in Mahometan countries. He never spoke of Mr. Martyn without the most profound respect, and shed tears of grief whenever he recalled how severely he had tried the patience of this faithful servant of God. He mentioned several anecdotes to show with what extraordinary sweetness Martyn had borne his numerous provocations. 'He was less a man (he said) than an angel from heaven.' His apostacy had excited much observation in the East.'"

"'During his stay at Penang, this island was visited by a Malay prince, Jouhuroolalim, king of the neighbouring state of Acheen, (in the island of Sumatra,) from whence a revolt of his subjects had obliged him suddenly to flee." "Sabat offered his services to Jouhuroolalim, with no other end, as he assured me, than to discover and profit by any favourable opportunity that should offer of introducing christianity amongst the Acheenois, a nation which is particularly intractable and ferocious, and many of whom were cannibals. The imposing and even engaging manners which he could assume, his reputation as a man of talents, and the high esteem which the Indian nations have for Arabian auxiliaries, on account of their courage and intrepidity, procured him a favourable reception from Jouhuroolalim, in a moment when adversity had estranged from him all his European favourites. Sabat accompanied this prince to Acheen, where he soon gained such an ascendency as to manage all public

The conclusion, however, which was drawn by Dr. Buchanan from the various facts he had enumerated, and which he afterwards strengthend by some other encouraging considerations, was sufficiently established, that the time for diffusing christianity in the East was come. The remainder, therefore, of this interesting discourse was occupied with an earnest and persuasive appeal to his hearers on the duty of cordially supporting this important measure; which is so appropriate to every period, and contains so valuable a testimony to the nature and necessity of spiritual religion, that it can scarcely be deemed irrelevant to introduce a part of it in this place:

"Behold, then, my brethren, the great undertaking for the promotion of which you are now assembled. If it were in the power of this assembly to diffuse the blessings of religion over the whole world, would it not be done? Would not all nations be blessed? You perceive that some take a lively interest in this subject, while others are less concerned. What is the reason of this difference? It is this: every man who hath felt the influence of religion on his own heart will desire to extend the blessing to the rest of mankind: whereas he who hath lived without concern about the gospel of Christ will not be solicitous to communicate to others a gift which he values not himself. At the same time, perhaps, he is not willing to be thought hostile to the work. But there is no *neutrality* here. 'He that is not with Christ,' in maintaining his kingdom on earth, 'is against him.' Every one of us is now acting a part in regard to this matter, for which he must give an account hereafter. There is no one, however peculiar he may reckon his situation or circumstances, who is exempted from this responsibility.

"Begin then at this time the solemn inquiry, not merely into the general truth of Christ's religion, but into its divine and converting power. You observe that in this discourse I have distinguished between the *name* of christianity and the *thing*. For it seems there are some persons in this country, who, having departed from the principles of our reformation, admit the *existence* of of the Spirit of God, yet deny his *in-*

---

affairs, and was regarded by his adversaries as the greatest obstacle to their final triumph. But, as months rolled away without producing any decisive event, and the issue of the struggle appeared still doubtful and distant, Sabat resolved to retire. Whilst occupied in effecting his retreat, he fell into the hands of his rival, Syfoolalim, who gave orders that he should be strictly imprisoned on board a vessel, and, after having made him suffer severely, he was tied up in a sack and thrown into the sea.'"

fluence; and who agree not with the apostle Paul, that the 'gospel cometh not in *word* only,' but 'in *power*, and in the Holy Ghost, and in much assurance.'

"The great author of our religion hath himself delivered the doctrine in the most solemn manner to the world. 'Verily, verily, I say unto you, except a man be born again, he cannot see the kingdom of God.' *Verily, verily;* it is an undoubted truth, an unchangeable principle of the heavenly dispensation, that, except a man be renewed in his mind by the Spirit of God, he shall not have power even to *see* or behold the kingdom of God. If our Saviour hath delivered any one doctrine of the gospel more clearly than another, it is this of a spiritual conversion; and the demonstration of its truth is found in all lands where the true gospel is known. Christians, differing in almost every thing else, yet agree in the doctrine of a change of heart, through faith in Christ. This is, in fact, that which distinguishes the religion of God in Asia from the religions of *men.* In every part of the earth, where I myself have been, this doctrine has been proclaimed as the hope of the sinner, and the glory of the Saviour."

The sermon from which the preceding extract has been taken was immediately published, and was not only universally circulated, but generally productive of a corresponding feeling in the minds of its numerous readers.

The services of Dr. Buchanan not being permanently required at Bristol, he was desirous of obtaining some settled employment; and, with the humility and anxiety to be actively engaged in his Master's service which had ever distinguished him, would gladly have retired to some country curacy. "I wish, too," he observed to a friend, "to be fixed for a time, if it were but to organize a library;" having brought scarcely any books with him from India, except the Bible.

In the meantime he projected a journey to the University of Oxford, where he arrived at the beginning of April, and remained about ten days. His object in this visit was to look into the libraries, and to compare and collate certain oriental manuscripts. He appears to have been received with much civility by the heads of houses, and to have been gratified by the society of several members of the university. During his stay, he preached at the parish churches of St. Martin and St. Giles.

It might perhaps have been expected that the university would have conferred some mark of its respect on Dr. Buchanan, as the munificent patron and promoter of oriental literature and religion. The University of Cambridge had not, indeed, as yet set the example of such a step, though it took the first appropriate opportunity of so doing. It may, however, be regretted that no proposal of any similar honour should have been subsequently made at this place; though Dr. Buchanan himself was so far from any feeling of this nature, that, in a letter to one of his friends shortly after his visit to both universities, he observed that they had been very kind to him, and had done every thing that he wished.

A few extracts from several letters written from Oxford, and its neighbourhood, will not be unacceptable. The first, it will be seen, is to one of the sisters of the late Mrs. Buchanan:

"OXFORD, April 3, 1809.

"This is the day on which I was united in marriage to your sister Mary. I rejoice when I think that you and M. are following her steps. She is now in the enjoyment of scenes of bliss, while we are afflicted by contests below. But she had her day of affliction also, and when she was sufficiently purified by the refiner, she ascended on high.

"I hope you and I shall be carried through in like manner, and leave some testimony that we were not of this world. How great is the change made by grace on a young person! May you be more and more conformed to his image, and learn to know (what St. Paul saith passeth knowledge) the length, and breadth, and height, and depth of the love of Christ to usward.

"My love to your husband; and believe me to be, very affectionately yours, C. BUCHANAN."

"WOODSTOCK, 4th April, 1809.

"I spent yesterday in the Bodleian Library, and I am to-day looking over the Duke of Marlborough's at Blenheim. He has a noble collection of oriental Bibles. I want to compare some Biblical MSS. from the East, with the Bodleian this week, with the aid of Drs. White and Ford. Dr. Ford is a well-informed, vigorous scholar; but Dr. White seems nearly worn out. There is nothing that wears well in old age but heavenly learning: a proof this, that there *is* a 'wisdom which cometh from *above*.' It is only the christian who can say,

"'The soul's dark cottage, batter'd and decay'd,
Lets in new light through chinks that time has made."'

"OXFORD, 13th April, 1809.

"In my last I asked you to aid me in doing a service to the *English* church in India.* Will you now grant a boon to the *Arabian* and *Persian* church? I want to send out immediately to Calcutta a fount of Arabic and Persian types for printing the scriptures and other works in these languages. The Persian is most urgent. I shall want to see a specimen of the type before the agreement be concluded.

"I have been at Blenheim two days, looking into the Duke of Marlborough's library, where I found my old fellow collegian, ———, author of ——, domestic chaplain. I had not known it was my own friend who was the author of that work. 'What,' said I, 'have you spent the last twelve years in writing *verses*, and to be mangled by the Edinburgh Review after all?' I urged him to run off immediately. He possesses noble talents; and looks forward, though not with much ardour, to the opportunity of making a better use of them than he has hitherto done."

From Oxford Dr. Buchanan proceeded to London from whence he wrote to Colonel Sandys as follows:

"LONDON, 28th April, 1809.

"I received your last while I was at Oxford. I stayed there about ten days; and left a manuscript of the Gospel of St. John in the Ethiopic language, which I found in the East, with the Oriental Professor, Dr. Ford, who is going to collate it. Other MSS. of the Hebrew and Chaldaic scriptures I propose to deposit in the public library of the University of Cambridge.† I proceed thither to-morrow, to preach on Sunday in Mr. Simeon's church.

"My friends here wish me to take Welbeck chapel, while Mr. White, the present preacher, goes to his living in the country. If I find that my endeavours are blessed, I shall probably remain in it. But it is rather my wish to retire to a parish in the country.

"The 'Star in the East,' I find, has excited a general interest. I breakfasted yesterday with the Bishop of London, who said he was sure it would do a great deal of good."

A few extracts from various letters to his friends will serve as a brief journal of Dr. Buchanan's proceedings at this period.

---

* This was respecting an organ, which Dr. Buchanan had been requested to procure for the mission church at Calcutta.

† For a particular notice of these MSS. see page 228.

"TERRACE, High street, 12th May, 1809.

"I returned yesterday from Hertford College, with which I was much pleased. Of course it owes its present efficiency chiefly to a wise selection of professors. Dealtry alone would do honour to any institution.

"My friends have found me out here, and my engagements multiply; but after a short time I hope to be at large. I find a great body of Indian families in these streets, who appear to have really less religion here than they had in the East. In the great multitude with whom they are now mixed, their conduct is not so easily recognized as in India; and, being less conspicuous, they think themselves less responsible. It is difficult to know what or how to preach to such. I must pray for divine direction.

"The Ethiopic Gospel is now at Cambridge; and one of the professors is about to examine and collate it, as soon as he has improved himself a little more in the language. Other persons will be appointed to examine the other MSS.

"A few Sundays ago I preached the annual charity sermon at the Lock Hospital, where I found a great body of the religious world of London of the higher cast. Instead of entertaining them with news from India, which, perhaps, some expected, I gave them an account of the spiritual resurrection."

In the letter which next follows, Dr. Buchanan notices the distinguished honour which had been just conferred upon him by the University of Cambridge, and adds some interesting particulars respecting his ministry at Welbeck chapel:

"Cambridge has conferred on me the highest honour in her gift. She petitioned his majesty to grant me the degree of Doctor in Divinity. The mandate was issued, and I received the degree on the commencement day last week. Dr. Ramsden, as Regius Professor of Divinity, delivered a speech on the occasion, in the name of the university, in which he referred to the evangelization of the East, and to my endeavours. The Duke of Gloucester and many of the nobility were present. I waited on the Bishop of Bristol after my degree, and received from his lordship an assurance that he would ever support the cause in which I had been so long engaged. He subscribed at the same time to the Bible Society. All the heads of houses whom I saw professed their gratification at the public notice the university had taken of the subject. I shall be shortly called to preach before the university.

"I live very retired at present; preaching regularly to my congregation, and attending little to public affairs. The nobility have mostly left town; but their seats at my chapel are filled generally by the poorer sort. The Duke of Gordon, Lord R. Seymour, and others, yet remain. I pray to be enabled to persevere to the end of my time with them, next November; and, after that, to the end of my race, wherever I shall be called to run.

"The christians in Travancore are suffering persecution, which may do them good. I foresee another conflict on missions: may we all be found faithful and prudent, wise and harmless!

"Before the nobility left town, I delivered to some of them at Welbeck chapel my views of the pious and useful life of the late Bishop of London. I noticed his exertions to preserve the purity of public morals; and gave them an account of my last interview with the bishop, a few days before his death, and of his testimony to serious piety. Speaking of a public trial then pending, in which some allusion had been made to the religious character of one of his friends, he observed that the character of public men professing religion was severely tried, and often greatly misrepresented in the present age. And, addressing himself to the master of a college in one of our universities, then in company, he added these words: 'The man who shall at this day conduct himself in a strictly religious manner, and make a profession of serious piety, must be content to be misunderstood by some, and called by a name of reproach.'"

The following is a somewhat fuller account of the effect of Dr. Buchanan's ministry at Welbeck chapel, from a letter to a friend soon after he had left it:

"The power of religion which I witnessed in Marybone was more among the lower than the higher classes; though even among them I have reason to believe that good has been done. A general spirit of conciliation was manifest. Lady —— retains an abiding impression, and does the works of righteousness. I visited her frequently. Lady —— also has evinced a just sense of true religion, and others of rank. But the glory of the gospel was chiefly manifested in Mrs. B., who died last month. She was but in humble life; but many of the nobility visited her, and benefitted by her example."

In the month of August Dr. Buchanan left London on a journey into Yorkshire; the object of which will be perceived by the following extract from a letter to Colonel Sandys:

"LONDON, 31st Aug. 1809.

"I have been absent from London the last ten days. My friends wished to know if I should like to fix at Scarborough, if the advowson of the living were purchased; and I went down to see the place and the people. There is but one church, and seven thousand inhabitants, besides the visiters. I found the Rev. Mr. Robinson of Leicester there; and we both preached last Sunday, he in the morning, and I in the evening. It was calculated that three thousand persons were in church. I do not think that I shall settle there; but I leave the event to Him whose providence governs all things.

"While at Scarborough, I was hospitably entertained by a family I have long heard of, and wished much to see, Mr. Thompson's of Kirby Hall.

"I am glad you are reading Milner's Church History. He has combined more real piety and sound sense in these volumes than are to be found in half the books of the day.

"I am engaged by Mr. Burn to preach two sermons at Birmingham on the 8th of October next, on some annual occasion. My journey has refreshed me, I think, after some months residence in London, though it was rapid, and chiefly in the mail. I am glad that William has such an awful sense of the importance of the ministry. That is more likely *in time* to lead him to it, than to drive him from it."

About the first week in October Dr. Buchanan took a second journey into Yorkshire, and returned at the end of a fortnight, for the purpose of preaching a series of sermons on the interesting occasion afforded by the fiftieth anniversary of the reign of our venerable sovereign; and with the last of these discourses he closed his engagement at Welbeck chapel.

CHAPTER III.

Early in the ensuing month Dr. Buchanan communicated to the friend to whom the preceding letter was addressed his intention of again entering into the marriage state. The lady with whom he formed this second engagement, was the daughter of Henry Thompson, Esq., of Kirby Hall, near Boroughbridge, in Yorkshire. Dr. Buchanan, as we have already seen, became acquainted with this respectable family during his first visit to Scarborough, and was attracted towards Miss Thompson by her piety, her active benevolence, and her filial duty and affection. This connexion was particularly agreeable to Mr. and Mrs. Thompson, and was universally approved by the friends of Dr. Buchanan. The marriage accordingly took place in the month of February following; from which period he fixed his residence in Yorkshire.

A few extracts from his letters will describe the plan of life upon which he now entered, and show with how much promptitude and diligence he engaged in the duties of the ministry.

"KIRBY HALL, March, 1810.

"We live at Moat Hall, or Parsonage, within a quarter of a mile of the mansion. I have undertaken the whole charge of the parish of Ouseburn. On the Thursday and Sunday evenings I have a meeting of my parishioners in my own house. I read a portion of scripture to them, and expound it; and generally incorporate the subject of the lecture in a prayer. I ought to be thankful for the attentive ear of the people.

"Mrs. Buchanan enters into these plans with much ardour and affection.

"After staying here some months, I shall probably return to London; at least my friends urge me to resume Welbeck. I published three Jubilee Sermons, as a record that I was once there. They are passing through a second edition, to which is to be annexed 'the Star in the East.'"

The friend who originally introduced Dr. Buchanan to Welbeck chapel was anxious that he should be permanently fixed in that or in some similar station, which he had shown that he was so well qualified to fill. He therefore proposed the building of a chapel in one of the western parishes of London, and wrote to Dr. Buchanan for his approbation of the plan. To this he replied as follows:

"Accept my sincere thanks for your kind congratulations. I was about to write to you, that our correspondence might not cease on account of distance.

"I have next to thank you, in the name of the church in India, for your zeal in relation to the organ.

"I much approve your proposal for building a chapel; and I trust it will please Providence to bring the work to a conclusion. I take it for granted that you mean a building which will contain two thousand people, with all the latest improvements in church accommodation, and propriety of decoration.

"I know not how it may please God to dispose of my life and services in the revolution of years, but I consider the situation you propose as highly important; and I beg you will proceed with your plan of building the chapel, under the presumption that I shall be its minister.

"Great simplicity, I think, ought to be observed in the construction and finishing; approaching nearer to the Gothic than the Grecian taste, but not to be wholly in either style; for there is no such thing, I allege, as *truth* in architecture. An oval or oblong octagon is by far the best general plan of an edifice, having the pulpit in the phonic centre. But I shall submit to your judgment in all things."

Notwithstanding the apparently promising nature of this, and of a similar plan, which was supported by many opulent inhabitants of Marybone, various difficulties, well known to those who embark in such engagements, prevented the accomplishment of either; and circumstances in the life of Dr. Buchanan not long afterwards occurred, which proved that the expectations of his friends upon this point would, as far as *his* ministry was concerned, have been but too soon disappointed. In the meantime the idea was mutually cherished.

The Jubilee Sermons, to which reference has more than once been made, were published early in the year 1810, and were very generally read and admired. The threefold view Dr. Buchanan took of a subject, which the well-known circumstances of the occasion rendered peculiarly interesting, gave him an opportunity of embracing a variety of topics, which a more limited plan would scarcely have allowed. The first of these sermons exhibits a view of the Mosaic jubilee, as a religious, moral, and political institution; together with its analogy to "the acceptable year of the Lord," proclaimed by the Saviour of the world. The second was devoted to the British jubilee, and contained an animated review of the political and religious blessings which had been bestowed upon this favoured country during the lengthened reign of his present majesty; amongst the latter of which he particularly dwells on the preservation of our national church in her faith and polity, the increase of true religion throughout the empire, the general instruction of the poor, and the universal diffusion of the Holy Scriptures. The last of these excellent discourses, which is perhaps the most generally useful and important of the three, leads us forward to the closing scene of all, the heavenly jubilee. The employment and felicity of heaven, and the character of those who shall be admitted to the celestial jubilee, are here considered; and the whole is concluded by a copious application of the subject, which includes the most important practical topics adapted to the circumstances of the higher classes of society. Amongst these Dr. Buchanan introduced a powerful appeal as to the duty of propagating the gospel in heathen nations. Though the subject of these sermons partook of an occasional character, the general views they display will doubtless preserve them from oblivion, and render them more than temporary proofs of the various knowledge, the fervent yet rational piety, and the warm yet enlightened benevolence, which distinguish the writings of their author.

Of the second edition of his Jubilee Sermons, Dr. Buchanan sent a copy to his eldest daughter, accompanied by the following note:

"My dear Charlotte,—I have the pleasure to send you a book, which I hope you will receive as a mark of my affection. My chief desire in regard to you and Augusta is, that you may be prepared on earth for the *heavenly jubilee;* and in regard to myself, that I may meet you there.

"I hear from some, that you are not inattentive to religious subjects. This gives me real pleasure. It is a noble thing to see the young daughter follow the steps of her departed mother. That mother now rejoices in the heavenly jubilee, and looks for the time when her two children shall join her in singing the song of the Lamb."

In the spring of this year, Dr. Buchanan received letters from Mr. Brown, which announced to him the tranquil and even prosperous state of things in India, as to the promotion of christian knowledge, and the active labours of many learned and excellent persons in forwarding the designs of his christian institution, under the fostering care of the Corresponding Committee of the British and Foreign Bible Society. Mr. Brown dwelt with peculiar energy and delight on the exertions of Mr. Martyn and his associates, and pleaded strongly in behalf of the new Arabic translation of the scriptures, then recently undertaken by Sabat.

Another Indian letter which Dr. Buchanan received at this time was from the Rev. Mr. Kolhoff, the pious and excellent missionary in Tanjore. It is dated October 21, 1809, and is as follows:

"Rev. and very worthy Sir,—Your very kind letter of the 4th of January, directed to the Rev. Mr. Horst and myself, we had the pleasure to receive, on the 8th of July last, and beg you to accept of our hearty and sincere thanks for your kind remembrance of us, and for the affectionate regard and attention you have shown towards the mission committed to our care.

"Upon the receipt of your favours, Mr. Horst has, agreeably to your request, without delay, set about collecting materials for publishing the life of our much respected and beloved predecessor, the late Rev. Mr. Swartz, and has now ready about ten sheets, closely written, which will give nearly the same number in print, and which he would have despatched ere this, if he had not found out that he had unfortunately omitted several material points in the very beginning of Mr. Swartz's life.

"It gives us great pleasure to acquaint you that the Honourable the Court of Directors have taken into their benevolent consideration our humble petition addressed by us to the government of Madras, at the end of the year 1806, and have been kindly pleased to grant an addition of seven hundred to their former donation of five hundred pagodas on account of the Protestant schools of this mission.

"The resolution of government came to our hands on the 13th of this month, at a time when we were ready to despond and sink under the burden which oppressed us, and has given us a fresh motive for thankfulness to God for his fatherly care towards us. To you also, my dear sir, our warmest acknowledgments are due for having suggested that measure to us, and we beg you to accept the assurance of our most lively gratitude for your friendly advice, which has had such a beneficial effect on the cause of the mission, and of the gospel of Jesus Christ."

The life of that eminent missionary, the venerable Swartz, which is thus alluded to in his worthy successor's letter, was a favourite subject with Dr. Buchanan. He had proceeded so far with it as to be intending to publish it a year or two before his own death, but was prevented from executing his plan by the information he received of the same work having been undertaken by another person. The papers which he had collected for this purpose are now in the hands of his family.

The following extracts from Dr. Buchanan's correspondence, in the spring of this year, will illustrate his piety and christian sympathy, as well as the habitual activity and ardour of his mind with reference to the great object of his life:

"KIRBY HALL, 1st May, 1810.

"My dear Sister,—Your letter gave me great pleasure. You have a hope of being restored to your family and to active service a little while longer. I say a little while, for you must not look to long life, unless it should please God to restore you soon to strong and confirmed health. But let us not talk of life, but of how we are to live. I admire your expression, and the spirit which animates it, 'I trust I have an increasing desire to devote myself to the Lord.' May this desire, my dear sister, live in your heart till you die. It will be like 'a well of water springing up into everlasting life;' for this desire of which you speak has been imparted to you by the Holy Spirit, which our Lord compares to the water of life. 'If any man thirst, let him come to me and drink;' and then it is added, 'This spake he of the Spirit, which they that believe on him should receive.' John vii. 37. Blessed are they in whose heart this desire has been awakened! It is more to be valued than crowns and diadems. How beautiful is this desire in a female, and in a young person, and in the mother of children! For who led your steps to 'the waters' when you first heard the invitation, 'Ho, every one that thirsteth?' Behold the world around you, how few thirst for the waters!

"I now behold in you, your dear sister Mary thirsting after righteousness. The promise will be fulfilled to you, as it was to her. 'They shall be filled.' I have no admonition to give you. You are under heavenly guidance. One thing I will notice; this is your season of prayer. Let your prayers be offered up incessantly, at this time, for your husband and children; first, that he also may be a well of water, nourishing the souls of others unto eternal life; that he may 'increase,' if you are to decrease; and that new strength may be given him as he approaches the vigour of life and understanding. You know that, by the divine command, the persons appointed to the 'service of the tabernacle' were confined to the period between thirty and fifty; and that is certainly the period of the most effective service. And it will cost him and me many a sigh, if, when that period has elapsed, any thing should have interrupted our zeal and labour in the heavenly ministration. Secondly, that your dear children may grow up in the nurture and admonition of the Lord. For now is the time to lay up a treasury of prayers for them, which may be answering when your spirit is on high, and your body is in the dust. And pray for me also, that I may be found faithful. If I should survive you in life, it will be a great satisfaction to me to reflect that I once had your prayers. And pray for your brother in the ministry, and for your father and mother, and all your family. For when 'the spirit of grace and supplication is poured out,' (Zech. xii. 10,) its objects are indefinite. When we 'look upon him whom we have pierced,' we shall be anxious to bring all we love to behold the same glorious Redeemer. Then do we understand, for the first time, what is meant by 'charity;' that charity whose boundless praises are set forth in the 13th of the 1st of Corinthians, and which the world understands not.

"My love to your brother and to my little girls. Adieu.

C. Buchanan."

"KIRBY HALL, 16th April, 1810.

"I rejoice to hear that C. is alive and well, and that the Malayalim version of St. Matthew's Gospel has been *printed*. There are upwards of two hundred thousand christians, Catholic and Syrian, who can read it.

"I should gladly aid the ———, if I could; but the truth is, I have no papers by me, not even of a year's standing. When in India, I emptied my bureau every year, regularly, and committed papers and letters to the flames. But I shall think of something for you now and then.

"I am looking out with some solicitude to see what may be done, both in regard to England and India; and I think Providence will soon open a way. In the meantime, the gospel is preached both at home and abroad, and 'the kingdom' advances. It is ours to work 'to-day.' Το σημερον μελει μοι. Christ will see to his own church 'to-morrow.' I pray that I may do in the right spirit the portion of work assigned me, whatever it be; if indeed I belong to the family of Christ, and have found mercy to be faithful.

"I am not qualified to meet the public eye often. I am neither copious nor ready; and I can truly say, I never write what pleases myself. But I will give you bones now and then, if you will give them flesh. And I pray that you and I may increase in *zeal* in the great work. There is no zeal without *intemperance*, as the world defines it. For what is temperance? Ask first at the equinoctial line, and then at Nova Zembla. For so extensive are the latitudes of thinking among the servants of the gospel; even amongst those who are promoting most successfully the interests of Christ's kingdom."

"KIRBY HALL, 23d April.

"The ship Charlton, in which I returned from India, has been carried into the Mauritius by two French frigates. Poor Limrick went down in the Calcutta, together with L—— and his heaps of paper.

"The organ for the mission church has been shipped. It is a noble one.

" * * * * * Hebetude and illiberality are apt to creep on our minds after a long retirement in a nook of the vineyard. We need to be 'withstood to the face,' like St. Peter, and to receive the bastinado on the soles of our feet once a month, at least, to keep us active and operative, according to 'the gift that is in us.' Men who walk in and about a house for a whole life are at last afraid of people who walk abroad, and begin to criticise and to despise them; for they really do not understand what they are doing. And we must bear with such. For we should have been just the same had we vegitated in a corner."

It has been already observed that, on his first visit to the University of Cambridge, after his return to this country, Dr. Buchanan presented to the public library several valuable oriental manuscripts, which he had procured during his journey to the coast of Malabar.* They were twenty-five in number, chiefly Biblical, and written in the Hebrew, Syriac, and Ethiopic languages. The most curious and important of these manuscripts are a copy of the Hebrew Pentateuch, written on goat-skins, and found in one of the Black Jews' synagogues at Cochin; a copy of the Bible, cantaining the books of the Old and New Testament, with the Apocrypha, written on large folio vellum, and in the ancient or Estrangelo character, which was a present to Dr. Buchanan from the venerable Bishop of the Syrian churches; and a version of the New Testament into Hebrew, executed by a learned Rabbi in Travancore, about one hundred and fifty years since. This version was transcribed by Mr. Yeates, at Cambridge, by the appointment and at the expense of Dr. Buchanan, chiefly with a view to promote the production of a translation of the New Testament in the pure style of the Hebrew of the Old, for the benefit of the Jews, and in aid of the laudable design, for this purpose, of the London Society for the conversion of that ancient people. The same laborious scholar, in the year 1813, published a collection of the Indian copy of the Pentateuch, which had been also made at the expense of the munificent donor, and was printed by the Syndics of the University press for the benefit of Mr. Yeates.

On the 12th of June, Dr. Buchanan preached the annual sermon before the Church Missionary Society, at St. Anne's, Blackfriars. It was a grand occasion, and a collection of nearly four hundred pounds proved the interest excited by the preacher on behalf of the great objects of that important society. From the text, "Ye are the light of the world," Dr. Buchanan made a forcible appeal to his christian audience on the solemn duty attached to their profession of giving light to a benighted world. After some excellent observations on the sermon upon the mount, for the purpose of pointing out the moral character of the "children of the light," the preacher observed that, if christians wished to be "the light of the world," they would draw their light from Christ, and send forth preachers bearing the

* See letter descriptive of these manuscripts at p. 323.

character which he hath delineated; and that, if they were instruments of the "true light," they would be zealous in adopting the most effectual means of diffusing it. In discussing these two propositions, Dr. Buchanan recurred to a subject he was so well qualified to describe, the moral darkness of the pagan world; gave much interesting information, and suggested many valuable hints relative to missions to the heathen.

The following observations on the society before which this discourse was delivered, and on the British and Foreign Bible Society, are added for the purpose of recording some express testimony to his warm approbation and support of both those admirable institutions.

"Your object and that of the Bible Society is the same. It is—to give the Bible to the world. But, as that sacred volume cannot be given to men of different nations until it be translated into their respective languages, it is the province of your institution to send forth proper instruments for this purpose. Your society is confined to members of the established church. You do not interfere with the 'Society for the Propagation of the Gospel in Foreign Parts,' nor with that 'for Promoting Christian Knowledge;' for neither of these professes the precise objects to which you would confine yourselves. It does not seem to be possible to frame an objection to your establishment. When the design and the proceedings of your institution shall have been fully made known, you may expect the support of the Episcopal body, of the two universities, and of every zealous member of the Church of England.

"It has been objected to that noble institution to which we have alluded, the British and Foreign Bible Society, that it is in its character *universal;* that it embraces *all*, and acknowledges no *cast* in the christian religion: and it has been insinuated that we ought not to be zealous for Christ's kingdom, if we must associate, in any degree, with men of all denominations. But, surely, there is an error in this judgment. We seek the aid of all descriptions of men in defending our country against the enemy. We love to see men of all descriptions showing their allegiance to the king. Was it ever said to a poor man, You are not qualified to show your allegiance to the king? You must not cast your mite into the treasury of your king? My brethren, let every man who opposes these institutions examine his own heart, whether he be true in his allegiance to the King of kings.

"For myself, I hail the present unanimity of hitherto discordant bands, as a great event in the church; and as marking a grand character of Christ's promised kingdom; when 'the leopard shall lie down with the kid; and the calf, and the young lion, and the fatling together, and a little child shall lead them.' Isaiah xi. 6. I consider the extension and unity of the Bible Society as the best pledge of the continuance of the divine mercy to this land: and, I doubt not, the time will come when the nation will reckon that society a greater honour to her, as a christian people, than any other institution of which she can boast."

One scene of exertion in the life of Dr. Buchanan was followed by another. On the 23d of June he thus wrote to a friend:

"I am appointed by the University of Cambridge to preach before them two sermons, on Commencement Sunday, the 1st of July next. I am rather weak in spirit at present, and not strong in bodily health; but I pray for strength, and I trust the Lord will sustain me. My sermons will be published."

Of Dr. Buchanan's Commencement Sermons we shall have occasion to speak more fully when we notice their publication. In the meantime, the following brief account of them, by himself, to one of his friends, soon after they were delivered, may not be unacceptable to the reader.

"London, July 11th, 1810.

"Your letter of the 30th ult. followed me to London; for I only stayed at Cambridge two days after I preached.

"I addressed the students on the importance of the sacred office, in conclusion; and intimated that the time was now come when every man, who stood on the side of religion, must be content to bear a name of reproach; for it was a necessary evidence of his character.

"I preached for three-quarters of an hour in the morning, and above an hour in the afternoon. There was the most solemn stillness. The church was crowded.

"On the Tuesday following, the Bishop of Bristol came up to me in the Senate House, and thanked me for the discourses, and expressed a hope that they would be published. Others did the same. Dean Milner, who is Vice-Chancellor, informed me, soon afterwards, that he thought himself authorized to grant the imprimatur of the University for their publication; and I am preparing them for the press accordingly. I mean to publish important matter as an appendix. Adieu. C. B."

"*To Colonel Sandys.*

"Scarborough, 24th Aug. 1810.

"I thank you for your excellent letter of the 27th July. A

letter from you is always worth something. Continue to pray for me, and to exhort me.

"Since my arrival here, I have been engaged in preaching regularly, on Sundays and Wednesdays, at the great church, to the strangers and residents at the Spa.

"I should have published my University sermons, and many other things, by this time; but the truth is, that the congregations at Scarborough, and the hope of some utility, have put Cambridge, and its scenes, almost out of my head. I preach here a fortnight longer, and then return to Kirby Hall. After my return, I shall sit down to the Cambridge lucubrations."

In the autumn of this year Colonel Macaulay, one of the most valued friends of Dr. Buchanan, returned to this country. It is to this circumstance, and to the intimate association between the name of that gentleman and the Malayalim version of the New Testament, that the following extracts from letters to him, and to his brother, Z. Macaulay, Esq., refer:

"Kirby Hall, 28th Sept. 1810.

"I rejoice to hear that your brother is soon expected, and that he comes by land. That will be a proper *finale* to his pilgrim life. I am happy to hear that two Gospels are finished in Malayalim. I had been informed that St. Matthew only had been printed, and that it had been distributed; and I said so in my sermon. But it is better now that the four Gospels should be distributed, bound up together. I shall write to Mr. Woodhouse on the subject. How many copies has he sent you? If he has sent many, I shall forward them to Calcutta, the fountain-head of distribution, with instructions to Mr. Brown.

"Will you have the goodness to send a copy, neatly bound, to the Rev. Mr. Kerrich, librarian of the University of Cambridge, for the public library?

"You may also send bound copies to the Bible Society, Bartlett's Buildings Society, and to the University of Oxford; also to the Universities of Edinburgh, Glasgow, St. Andrew's, and Aberdeen. To save you trouble, if you will put them into the hands of your bookseller, he will transmit them; and I will pay his bill, with thanks to you."

"9th October.

"This is great news. And so C. is thus far through the wilderness; once more in his native land! May he pass through the Jordan flood, at last, with the voice of triumph and thanksgiving!

"Will you have the goodness to forward the trunk to me as soon as it can be rescued from the India House? It contains some papers, I believe, which I wish to see before what I am now preparing goes to press.

"There is no person in this country who can improve the Malayalim translation, because it is performed by men to whom the language is vernacular. It is not like the versions executed by Europeans.

"The Bible Society may assume great credit to itself by patronising this version, for the demand for copies will be perpetual and inexhaustible; even until 'the mountains shall be cast into the sea.'"

"*To Colonel Macaulay.*

"7th November.

"I am concerned to find that Cheltenham is necessary for you. But I think you will not remain there long. A little of the waters is enough. Pray, retreat as soon as the cold weather warns you. The warm town is the place for you. I have been at Bath, Clifton, Cheltenham, Scarborough, since my return. But there is no place like warm and busy London in the winter; unless, like me, you had a fireside of your own, and a wife and hissing urn, and a sofa to wheel round, to read the book of four pages. Another argument for an early *hejira* from Cheltenham, is its unprofitable society. I have looked through all these places, and would rather pass a month at Chetwe or Trivandupuram with you, than be condemned to mix daily with the visiters at a watering-place in our own country.

"I find the difference of *cast* greater here than in India. I am thankful that I can aspire more, day by day, to be of the high cast. I wish to be a pure Namboory among christians. And, if the Sooders will not go off the road for me, I must go off the road for them. ——— is, in this sense, a Brahmin of high cast. He is, indeed, 'a gift of God' to his country; follow him, even as he follows Christ.

"I give you twelve months complete before you settle; and, if you settle then, I shall be thankful; though Providence perhaps has ordained that you should ever continue, like Abraham, 'a pilgrim and a sojourner in the land in which you have no inheritance,' but look forward to another country, 'to a city which hath foundations, whose builder and maker is God.' Blessed is the man who wishes not to build a city in this world. This is often a ruling passion with Indians; they come home to build a city and a tower. ——— is building a mansion, with seven turrets, on his estate.

"Adieu, my dear sir, C. BUCHANAN."

The following passage in a letter to another friend contains the first intimation of a tendency to serious indisposition which Dr. Buchanan appears to have felt since his return from India:

"KIRBY HALL, 7th Nov. 1810.

"We returned lately from Scarborough, where I passed two months, ministering twice a week in the large church there. Since my return, I have been visited with an indisposition which the faculty do not seem to understand very well. It is merely a great quickness of breathing, and great lassitude from slight exercise, without any other complaint whatever. I desisted from peaching for a fortnight; but mean to resume it. It is probably some illness induced by a hot climate; and it becomes me to 'work while it is called to-day.'

"My letters from India state that the gospel flourishes in almost every quarter. The seed sown is producing fruit where there has been very little cultivation; and now our attention is directed to the Malay isles; for the whole Dutch empire in the Eastern Ocean will probably soon be ours. The word of truth, I am happy to inform you, runs and is glorified in these parts" (in Yorkshire) "also; but the chief evil is, that it is rather *fashionable* among the lower classes. I find the most useful preaching is to draw aside the cloak of profession, and see what is under it."

Dr. Buchanan was now employed in preparing his Cambridge Sermons for the press. To these he was intending to add, as an appendix, a variety of new and interesting matter, connected with the great subject of his discourses, and illustrating the progress of the gospel in the East. Distrusting, however, his own judgment upon a few points, amongst which was the name which this appendage should assume, or willing, at least, to submit it to that of others, he referred the whole to the revision and ultimate determination of two or three able and judicious friends. It was to them that the following letters were addressed; and they will serve at once to evince the christian simplicity and humility which adorned the writer's character:

"KIRBY HALL, 22d October, 1810.

"Tell K. that the half of my Appendix is gone up. I requested —— and —— to expunge any thing they thought wrong: and intimated to them that I wished not to give any unnecessary offence in word or manner; but that it was my purpose to pronounce a faithful and unequivocal testimony to the truth of the gospel. I pray that God will overrule the evil of my work for good to the souls of men. For it hath enough of evil, although I trust the purpose is good.

"I do not want fame, (I mean as a carnal object,) but I wish to glorify Christ on earth, as I can, the few days that remain to me. I think with you that W. had enthusiasm and many infirmities. So had Luther. *Nihilominus sit mea anima cum illo!*"

The following passages were addressed to Colonel Macaulay; whose long residence in the south of India, and intimate acquaintance with the principal scenes of Dr. Buchanan's researches, peculiarly qualified him for the friendly office which he was requested to undertake.

"KIRBY HALL, 20th December.

"I shall be very thankful for your revision, particularly of the 'Syrian Christians;' for I quote much from memory and imperfect notes. Only finish it in your own words; for I am not very strong for study at present, and my church occupies my attention. What I say to you, I say to your brother: for you are both friends of the truth in an evil day.

"I expect no particular effect from the Christian Researches, farther than affording some gratification to the advocates for christianity, and some vigour, perhaps, to their hopes.

"If your alterations are important, you may just mention what they are, but it will not be necessary to return the manuscript; for I can rely on your just judgment. I have rather a rugged style. Be pleased to add a word, and qualify my abruptness when it offends you."

"31st December.

"I concur with you in every sentiment contained in your letter. My friends in India have long urged me to notice the exertions of the Church of England there, under the name of 'The Christian Institution in the East;' and I was preparing to publish a list of its members at the conclusion of the work. But the promotion of christianity is the grand object; and the expression of your fears is sufficient argument for me to suppress the name of the 'Christian Institution' for the present.

"Be pleased, therefore, to obliterate the name, and substitute that of 'Christian Researches in Asia;' and retain as much of the introductory pages as may comport with your view of utility. I have no copy by me; and I am in poor health, and have other avocations. I desire nothing but to promote the glory of the christian dispensation. I could wish to make my work as catholic as possible, so that *all* may love its object. If you will make it such, you will make me happy. I want the work to be printed by the 10th of February, for transmission to India. India is more in my view than England, in regard to its utility. If you find any *sarcasm*, pray expunge it: but do not sacrifice a word of truth.

"I should write to you more particularly, but Mrs. Buchanan's confinement has been attended with circumstances which endangered her life; and I think of little at present but what is momentous and eternal. She is now better."

The conclusion of the preceding extract referred to a season of great trial which had taken place a few days before, and which after much suffering had terminated safely. Mrs. Buchanan recovered, but the child, who was named Claudius, survived only three days. "On the morning of the first day of the new year," observed his pious father, "I committed the little stranger to his parent earth. Mrs. B. has more of joy than sorrow from these events."

Amidst the anxiety occasioned by the illness of Mrs. Buchanan, and the interruption of personal indisposition, Dr. Buchanan prepared for the press his University Sermons, and the "Christian Researches in Asia." The subject of these sermons was similar to that of his discourse before the Church Mission Society,—the diffusion of christian knowledge throughout the world. From the words of the divine *fiat*, "Let there be light," as applied to the course of the great "Sun of Righteousness," Dr. Buchanan noticed three distinct eras of this heavenly illumination; that of the first promulgation of the gospel, the reformation from popery, and the present period. After an able and interesting historic view of these three eras of light, he urged a series of arguments, to which a reference only can here be made, to convince the Church of England of her obligations to exert herself in the great work of evangelizing the world. Having led the way by patronising about a century since the Protestant mission to India, it became her, he said, to resume her former station, and, "standing as she does like a Pharos among the nations, to be herself the great instrument of giving light to the world." It is, however, only doing justice to the subject of these memoirs, to extract a few passages from the sermons in question, which convey his sentiments on the fundamental truths of christianity.

"That which constitutes a Christian is 'faith, hope, and charity; these three.' Much human learning is not essentially necessary to constitute a christian. Indeed, a man may be a profound theologian and not be a Christian at all. He may be learned in the doctrines and history of christianity, and yet be a stranger to the fruits of christianity. He may be destitute of faith, of hope, and of charity.

"Let us not then confound the fruits of religion, namely, its influence on our moral conduct, its peace of mind, and hope of heaven, with the circumstances of religion. True religion is that which its great Author himself hath declared. It is a practical knowledge of the love of God the Father, 'who sent not his Son into the wôrld to condemn the world, but that the world through him might be saved;' of the atonement of God the Son, by faith in whom we receive the remission of our sins, and are justified in the sight of the Father, and of the sanctification of God the Holy Ghost, by which we are made meet 'to become partakers of the inheritance of the saints in light.' The preacher who can communicate this knowledge to his hearers, (and it is true that, if he possess a critical knowledge of the Bible, and of the history of christianity, he will be likely to do it with the most success,) the same is a 'workman that needeth not to be ashamed, and a good minister of Jesus Christ.' 1 Tim. iv. 6.

"Let every student in theology inquire whether the religion he professes bears the true character. Instead of shunning the reproach of Christ, his anxiety ought to be how he may prepare himself for that high and sacred office which he is about to enter. Let him examine himself, whether his views correspond, in any degree, with the character of the ministers of Christ, as recorded in the New Testament. 'Wo is unto me if I preach not the gospel.' 1 Cor. ix. 16."

Dr. Buchanan thought it to be his duty to conclude his discourses to the University with again delivering his testimony to that divine change which constitutes the essence of real christianity.

"This change of heart," he observes, "ever carries with it its own witness; and it alone exhibits the same character among men of every clime. It bears the fruit of righteousness; it affords the highest enjoyment of life which was intended by God, or is attainable by man; it inspires the soul with a sense of pardon and of acceptance through the Redeemer; it gives peace in death, and a 'sure and certain hope of the resurrection unto eternal life.'"*

The substantial truth and honest freedom of these remarks

* Dr. Buchanan's Eight Sermons, pp. 255, 289, 291.

were no less honourable to the preacher, than was "the candid attention" with which he gratefully acknowledged they were heard, to the learned body to whom they were addressed. It is scarcely necessary to add that the repetition of such sentiments is far from being unseasonable. May they be universally prevalent.

It has already sufficiently appeared, in the course of these memoirs, that Dr. Buchanan was far from being a mere declaimer, either as to the evils which he lamented, or the remedy which he proposed. With respect to the former, he did not content himself with the representations of others, but exhibited the result of his own personal observations, and revealed the gloomy recesses of Asiatic superstition, the "thick darkness" which "covers the people" of that widely-extended region. Splendid too, and unlimited, as were the prospects which he unfolded of their illumination and relief, and sanguine as were the hopes which he indulged of their accomplishment, both were founded upon the vigorous and persevering adoption of the ordinary means within our power, and particularly of the universal circulation of the Holy Scriptures.

It was to the devlopment of both parts of this picture, of the light as well as of the shade, that Dr. Buchanan devoted his Christian Researches. He accordingly introduced them by an account of his own endeavours and those of Mr. Brown to promote the translation of the scriptures, and of his two journeys to the coast of Malabar, which have been before detailed. He then proceeded to notice, in a series of distinct articles, the Chinese, the Hindoos, with a particular reference to the relative influence of paganism and christianity, the Ceylonese and the Malays. The Syrian and Romish christians, and the inquisition at Goa, form the next objects of attention in this interesting work; which are followed by notices of the Persians, Arabians, and Jews, and of the versions of the scriptures which were then preparing, or the preparation of which was suggested, for the use of those various nations. The Bibliotheca Biblica, or repository for Bibles, in the oriental languages, comprising a library for the use of translators of the scriptures, founded by the late Rev. D. Brown, is next adverted to; and, finally, the Armenian christians. Before Dr. Buchanan concluded his Researches, he recurred to the subject of his first memoir, and advanced some new and forcible arguments in support of an Ecclesiastical Establishment for British India.

Though it has been thought necessary to give the preceding brief analysis of this important and valuable work, it will be obvious that more was not required; not only on account of its great notoriety and extensive circulation, but because many of the topics which it embraced have been already noticed in this narrative. The conclusion, however, of the Christian Researches demands more particular attention, because it comprises what may be called the practical application of the whole. Dr. Buchanan, like Lord Bacon himself, aimed not so much at inculcating new principles, as at exciting a new spirit; and, though he did, indeed, make some important discoveries, as to the moral necessities of an immense portion of the human race, it was one of his main objects to teach others to follow him in his course, and to point out the way to its successful pursuit. In this view the concluding observations of his work deserve the most serious consideration.

"In the progress of these researches, the author has found his mind frequently drawn to consider the extraordinary difference of opinion which exists, among men of learning, in regard to the importance and obligation of communicating religious knowledge to our fellow creatures. And he has often heard the question asked by others, What can be the cause of this discrepancy of opinion? For that such a difference does exist is most evident; and is exemplified at this moment in some of the most illustrious characters for rank and learning in the nation. This is a problem of a very interesting character at this day, and worthy of a distinct and ample discussion, particularly at the seats of learning. The problem may be thus expressed: 'What power is that which produces in the minds of some persons a real interest and concern in the welfare of their fellow creatures; extending not only to the comfort of their existence in this world, but to their felicity hereafter; while other men, who are apparently in similar circumstances as to learning and information, do not feel inclined to move one step for the promotion of such objects?' The latter, it may be, can speculate on the philosophy of the human mind, on its great powers and high dignity, on the sublime virtue of universal benevolence, on the tyranny of superstition, and the slavery of ignorance; and will sometimes quote the verse of the poet,

"'Homo sum: humani nil a me alienum puto:'

but they leave it to others, and generally to the christian in humble life, to exercise the spirit of that noble verse. This is a very difficult problem; and it has been alleged, by some, that it cannot be solved on any known principles of philosophy. The following relation will probably lead to principles by which we may arrive at a solution."

The solution of the problem thus proposed is derived by the author from the penitent humiliation of the great Babylonian conqueror, who, when "brought to himself," expressed the sincerity of his conversion to the knowledge of the true God, by proclaiming his greatness, asserting his glory, and inviting all nations to magnify him, and bow to his dominion.*

"Such a proclamation," says Dr. Buchanan, "to the nations of the earth, was a noble act of a king, and ought to be had in perpetual remembrance. It reminds us of the last charge of Him 'who ascended up on high:' 'Go, teach all nations.' It discovers to us the new and extended benevolence, greatness of mind, and pure and heavenly charity, which distinguish that man whose heart has been impressed by the grace of God. How solemn his sense of duty! How ardent to declare the glory of his Saviour! His views for the good of men, how disinterested and enlarged! It is but too evident that all our speculations concerning a divine revelation, and the obligation imposed on us to study it ourselves, or to communicate it to others, are cold and uninteresting, and excite not to action, 'until, through the tender compassion of God, the day-spring from on high visit us, to give light to them that sit in darkness;' to humble our hearts at the remembrance of our sins against God, and to affect them with a just admiration of his pardoning mercy.

"Let Great Britain imitate the example of the Chaldean king, and send forth to all the world her 'testimony' concerning the true God. She also reigns over many nations which 'worship idols of wood and stone;' and she ought, in like manner, to declare to them 'the signs and wonders of the Almighty.' And in this design every individual will concur, of every church, family, and name, whose heart has been penetrated with just apprehensions of the Most High God, who has known his judgments, and experienced his mercy."

The circulation of the Christian Researches was immense. The first edition of seventeen hundred copies was soon exhausted; and, before the end of the year, three others had been printed. The labour, however, which their excellent author had undergone in preparing this interesting volume for the press, probably led to a painful, though apparently unimportant seizure, which was evidently the prelude to one of a more serious nature. It is to this illness that he refers in writing thus to a friend:

* Daniel, chap. iv.

"KIRBY HALL, 19th Feb. 1811.

"I have had an illness of a peculiar kind; a slight debilitating stroke, affecting the voice and right hand, of the paralytic kind. My hand is not itself yet, as you may see; nor is my voice perfectly restored. The faculty ascribe the immediate cause to study, a sedentary habit, and anxiety of mind on Mrs. B.'s illness. But, whatever the cause may be, it is a *memento* from the Lord that this is not my rest. Nor do I wish it to be so.

* * * * "The town of Leeds have sent me an invitation to succeed the late Mr. Atkinson, their worthy minister, who died last week. I have not yet answered them; but my late repeated attacks of illness will determine me to decline it. My constitution is evidently not settled sufficiently for laborious study. But the Lord is my shepherd. He will lead me in green pastures, and make darkness light before me. The people of Leeds deserve a better pastor than I am, and the Lord will be their shepherd also."

"26th March.

"I am now well enough to be able to write a few lines. I have been gaining strength with the returning spring; for I love the sun, and to look at it in this cold climate. It is a fine object in this evil world. But I like the sun chiefly as it is an emblem of 'the Sun of Righteousness.' It gives light and heat. I love your letters for they have light and heat, reflected from the same glorious Luminary.

"You will be happy to hear that Mrs. L. has become a most serious and intelligent christian. Her only desire is to live to the glory of her Saviour. She weeps at the recollection of her obdurate heart in India, loves Mr. Brown, and thinks him 'a man to be wondered at.' I mean to send two of her letters to Calcutta, and to ask whether they can show such things in India! Perhaps they will answer, 'Yes, we can; behold S——.'

"My love to Mrs. S. and the sufferer. Surely she must be all pure gold by this time. The dross and tin, a miner would say, must now be at the bottom of the furnace.

"I have received letters from India so late as October. Mr. Martyn was expected in Calcutta, in fine health and spirits, with his Hindostanee and Arabic translations."

As the spring advanced, Dr. Buchanan's physicians having agreed that his complaint was chiefly a nervous debility, for the removal of which cessation from study was desirable, he formed a plan with a view to an object which he had long cherished, and which might, he hoped, prove beneficial to his health. This was no less an undertaking than a voyage to Palestine, with the view of investigating subjects connected with the translation of the scriptures, and the extension of christianity. We have already noticed his proposal of returning from India overland, for the purpose of visiting the churches in Mesopotamia and Syria, the names of upwards of one hundred of which he had received from the Syrian christians, and also of inquiring into the present circumstances of the Jews in those regions and in Palestine. This was the design to which he was now anxious to render an intermission from sedentary occupation subservient. Another object of Dr. Buchanan's inquiry, in his proposed visit to the Holy Land, was to be the state of the Syriac printing press of Mount Lebanon, from which various works have issued; and to ascertain whether it might be practicable to establish presses in Jerusalem or Aleppo, for the Hebrew, Arabic, and Syriac languages; and to open a correspondence with England for their encouragement and support. He wished also to learn what language (with a view to the translation of the scripture) is most generally used at this time in the Holy Land.

It was Dr. Buchanan's intention to touch at Alexandria, in his voyage to Palestine, and to return from his tour by Lesser Asia, through the region of the seven primitive churches. He proposed to pass over from thence to Athens and Corinth, to visit the principal christian churches in Greece, and afterwards those of the larger islands in the Archipelago. A chief object here was to ascertain whether a translation of the scriptures in one dialect of modern Greek would suffice for the continent of Achaia and the Archipelago, (which he did not think to be likely,) or whether some principal dialects had not been already cultivated.

In order to give publicity to his proposed voyage, Dr. Buchanan transmitted a notice of the preceding particulars to the Christian Observer,* adding a request that the queries of the learned concerning the present state of the countries he intended to visit, in connexion with the promotion of christianity, might be communicated to him, and intimating that he would take charge of Bibles for distribution in his way in Portugal, Spain, and Malta, and would endeavour to establish a channel of correspondence in those countries with England, for the supply of the authorized version of each country respectively, as

---

* For May, 1811, p. 321.

far as the existing governments might be pleased to countenance the design.

Such was the intention of Dr. Buchanan with respect to this distant and laborious undertaking. Greatly, however, as we must admire the ardour of his piety, which could prompt him to form such a plan, it was, perhaps, originally of too extensive and difficult a nature for the already debilitated state of his constitution. He seems, in some measure, to have felt this in announcing it to a friend, to whom he sent a notice of his design, adding, "I cannot tell the purposes of Providence. Perhaps I may lay my bones in the Holy Land."

Towards the end of May Dr. Buchanan paid a short visit to Buxton, where, intent as usual on doing good, he embraced the opportunity of preaching a sermon, the occasion of which may be explained in his own words:

"BUXTON, 3d June, 1811.

"Having had some revival of spirits these three last days, I was not willing to allow the day of Pentecost to pass without notice, particularly as the company here were desirous that I should preach. Viewing them from my window all day drinking at the medicinal waters, I composed a discourse from John v. 2, 3, 4,* which I delivered yesterday (Whitsunday) in the great dining-room here; Captain Payne, aid-de-camp to Lord Wellington, who returned wounded from Busaco, acting as my clerk. This sermon I mean to publish immediately, for the benefit of the company during the gay season. I shall not, however, send it to the press till my return to Kirby Hall, (whither we go on the 5th or 6th inst.,) for I have no Concordance here, nor indeed any other book than the Bible."

The sermon thus hastily, but benevolently composed, was published in the course of the summer, under the title of "The Healing Waters of Bethesda." It was, as might be expected, altogether of a practical nature. But, though devoid of that peculiar attraction which his preceding publications derived from their connexion with oriental objects, it abounded with sound scriptural instruction, and was well calculated to awaken, in the minds of those to whom it was originally addressed, a

---

* "Now there is at Jerusalem by the sheep-market a pool, which is called in the Hebrew tongue Bethesda, having five porches. In these lay a great multitude of impotent folk, of blind, halt, withered, waiting for the moving of the water. For an angel went down at a certain season into the pool, and troubled the water: whosoever then first after the troubling of the water stepped in, was made whole of whatever disease he had."

salutary train of feeling and reflection, and to lead them to associate with the spring, to which they were resorting for bodily health, the thought of that heavenly fountain which can alone purify and refresh the soul, and strengthen it unto life everlasting.

In the month of June Dr. Buchanan wrote to Colonel Sandys as follows:

"KIRBY HALL, 24th June, 1811.

"I have lately returned from Buxton, whither I was sent to drink the medical waters. I have not found much benefit from them; but we now proceed to Scarborough, and I doubt not I shall be refreshed by the sea air.

"I shall probably leave England in autumn, and be absent about a year. Had any important spiritual charge been assigned to me, I should not have thought of leaving England again; but circumstances at present are very favourable to a temporary absence. I mean to go down to Scotland in a few weeks hence, to take leave of my mother, who is in a declining state, and does not expect (or perhaps hope) to pass through this next winter.

"I have a good appetite, generally, and sleep well; but, when I speak, my spirits are easily hurried, and the slightest exercise fatigues me.

"I hope that you and your family continue well, and more particularly that 'your soul prospereth.' I make a little progress, perhaps, but it is scarcely sensible. *When I stand on Calvary, (if it be given me to see it,)* I hope my spirits will be refreshed, and my affections enlivened to love and serve *the Lord who suffered there.*—May I have a single eye to his glory."

"SCARBOROUGH, 20th July.

"The Bethesda Sermon arrived yesterday. One hundred copies have been sent here, and sell rapidly. I seldom see any review; for I wish to be hid from the strife of tongues.

"I am willing to go 'through evil report' unto the end. That is not my cross.

"We set off to-morrow for Scotland. I have acquired but little strength at Scarborough. The change of air in the north may possibly be more beneficial to me."

"GREENOCK, 5th August.

"I have found my mother in tolerable health of body and in high spiritual health at seventy-five. She astonishes Mrs.

Buchanan by her eloquence on the prophecies, which she utters in hard words, without affecting at all the English language. She can read the Bethesda without spectacles, and likes it better than the Star in the East.

"We have seen and entertained almost all the Greenock clergy, and have visited some of the best religious families. In a few days we return to Glasgow. Your future communications must be addressed to Kirby Hall, for I know not where we shall be in ten days hence.

"I find the sea air more refreshing here than at Scarborough. Somewhere in Bute is now reckoned the Montpelier of Scotland. It boasts, it seems, many recoveries from consumptions. I consulted the Edingburgh faculty in passing. Dr. Gregory delivered to me five quarto pages composed oracularly on the subject of my complaint, which he seems to understand well. The length of this letter will intimate I am rather stronger than before."

"Glasgow, 18th September.

"I have been favoured with your letter of the 10th inst. enclosing Mr. H.'s dedication. He seems animated by a noble spirit. I have had a letter from himself, and have recommended him to enlist under the banners of the Society for Promoting Christian Knowledge, and to think nothing of the Syrians, till he have passed a tranquil year in the bosom of his family in Coromandel. Thence he may proceed where he likes. He asked me what would be his principal difficulty. I told him it would be learning Malayalim (which is more useful than the Syriac) in his old age!

"The companion of my tour to Syria is already engaged; a fellow of a college in Oxford, whom I met at Scarborough, the son of a family intimate with that at Kirby Hall; a young man of strong health, good learning, good sense, and good fortune; of sound theology, and one who is likely to become an author.

"As to Rothley Temple, if it be practicable, we shall visit it; but the season advances, and we have not got through Ireland yet.

"We proceed on Monday next to Lainshaw, the abode of Mr. Cunninghame, late of India, and thence, by Ayr, to port Patrick. Letters addressed to me, at the post office, Dublin, will find me till the 20th of October."

Early in November Dr. Buchanan returned from his tour to Kirby Hall, from whence he gave his friends a sketch of that part of it which has not been yet mentioned.

"KIRBY HALL, November 20th.

"We arrived at this place about ten days since, and found all our family well. We spent a month in Ireland, and about a fortnight in Wales. Mrs. B. liked the tour very well, for we found friends everywhere. I am glad that I have had an opportunity of surveying the state of religion in Ireland. I had much intercourse with the members of Dublin College, and hope to engage them in the support of evangelizing plans. They seem in general animated by a good spirit.

"I visited Maynooth College, and investigated the Catholic question. I could consult the best authorities on both sides. My opinion is that Maynooth College may be extended with safety. It has already added to the number of Protestants; and the Roman Catholic bishops begin to be alarmed at the light and knowledge which proceed from it. I saw Messrs. C. and C., the priests who have recanted. They preach in Dublin; but when I arrived they had not received any cure or support from church or state. I expressed my astonishment at the delay and marked indifference which seemed to pervade the Protestant church on the subject. Government has now espoused the cause of the young men, and ordained them immediate provision and a cure in the church. They both appear to me to be converts on conviction.

"I passed a day with the Bishop of Bangor in my way through Wales. We had much conference on the state of religion. He is candid and earnest to do good in the church.

"The Scotch Kirk have almost wholly ceased to read the scriptures as a part of divine service. I have noticed the subject in the fourth edition of the Christian Researches now printing.

"I have proposed to the University of Cambridge to print an edition of the Syriac Scriptures; and have offered a considerable sum to commence; but I have not yet had their answer. I promised to send the scriptures to the Syrian christians, and am ashamed of the delay.

"I have gained a little strength by the journey, but I am easily exhausted."

In the autumn of this year arrived Mr. Martyn's eloquent and successful appeal, in a sermon at Calcutta, on the 1st of January, in behalf of nine hundred thousand Christians in India, who were in want of the Bible; together with the gratifying intelligence of the formation of an Auxiliary Bible Society at that Presidency, at the head of which appeared some of the chief members of the supreme government.* The letters which announced this auspicious event brought information also of the revival of the college of Fort William as a

---

* The Society whose formation is here noticed has been remarkable for its energy and zeal in promoting translations of the scriptures, and circulating them in the countries of the East. Previous to the year 1835 it had distributed 17,113 copies of the scriptures. The following remarks in relation to its establishment, and the benefits arising from the circulation of the scriptures in India, are from the address of Archdeacon (now bishop) CORRIE, at the meeting of the British and Foreign Bible Society, in 1835.—AM. ED.

"At the period of the formation of this Society," [1804,] "when I went to that sphere of labour to which Divine Providence, about that time, called me, namely, to the Chief Presidency of India, the scriptures, even in the English language, were extremely scarce there, and only to be had at a very enormous price. Pocket Bibles of the most common kind, and in the plainest and meanest binding, were not to be bought in the bazaars of Calcutta under a pound sterling each. You will conclude, therefore, that Bibles were not plentiful among the military, to whom my labours were, at first, in a great measure confined. But no sooner did we hear of the formation of this Society in England, than a small band set about endeavouring to procure assistance from it: and we did procure the scriptures in the English language. With what thankfulness and joy did we receive the first supply sent out from this country! There was still, however, a great want of the scriptures in South India; and a lamentable deficiency began to appear among those who professed the Christian name. This formed a sufficient plea—a plea which the most jealous in that country could not withstand—for the formation of an Auxiliary Society in Calcutta; and the call was responded to far beyond the expectations of the most sanguine. Ladies contributed their ornaments and the superfluous portion of their dress; and, in a few days, not less than 1000*l.* sterling was sent to the treasurer. An opportunity was now afforded for encouraging the translation of the scriptures into the languages of the East; and the work was set about accordingly.

"But at that time there was no disposition, generally speaking, in the minds of the natives of the East to receive the scriptures. I well remember that the first offer which I made of the scriptures to a native, was heard with surprise; suspicion began to take possession of his mind: he retreated gradually; and at length turned about, and flew away, as from a plague. But, by the persevering labour of faithful men, and by selecting the principal narrative portions of the scriptures to be read in the schools which were commenced in that country, light began to diffuse itself; by degrees, the scriptures were introduced into the languages of various provinces: and now I am happy to state that they not only are not refused, but are generally sought after by the heathen and Mahometan population of Northern India. And not only are they sought after, but we have assurance that they are read: it is a remarkable fact that, within the last two years, a few have begun to oppose christianity, as infidels have done in England, by arguments drawn from the Bible itself—which is a sure proof that the scriptures are read. The domestic chaplain (as I may call him) of the King of Oude drew up a pamphlet, extracted from the Prophecies and Gospels, in favour of Mahometanism, which he called "Glad Tidings:" and though, as it may be conceived, his arguments were very futile, yet it is another fact to prove that the circulation of the scriptures in their own language has not been in vain.

"Moreover we have instances of the good effect which these scriptures, by the blessing of God, produce. We offer the scriptures on the faith of that promise, that his word shall not return to him void. We give them as the word of the living God, and leave the consequence to him. In our schools, I recollect a youth, in appearance about sixteen, who was reading a chapter in St. Matthew's Gospel; when, all at once, he rose up, and said to the missionary,

fountain of scriptural translation, and a communication from Mr. Brown to Dr. Buchanan; the following extract from which, considering the circumstances of his departure from Calcutta, could not but afford him the liveliest satisfaction:

"PAGODA, SERAMPORE, 5th March, 1811.

"You are truly the root of our Bible Society. I have had long and full discussions with Lord Minto on all subjects of religion, missions, scriptures, &c.; and he is very desirous to tread back his steps and to atone for the mistake which he made at the beginning of his government.

"Your letter prepared the way for this reflux of sentiment. Neither that, nor the Chinese, nor any part of your labours, has fallen to the ground. Therefore go forward; and obtain the crown of righteousness which is before you."

On the 6th of December, Dr. Buchanan wrote to his friend, Mr. Macaulay, respecting new editions of his publications; desiring it to be observed in the dedication of his Memoir to the present Archbishop, that, although he had "deemed it right to make a few verbal alterations, he had seen no cause to change any one material sentiment of the work." In the same letter he intimated his intention of proceeding on his proposed voyage early in the month of February following. A few days, however, only had elapsed before a second and more alarming attack suspended, and ultimately dissipated, all thoughts of accomplishing that extensive and interesting undertaking. His letter upon this trying occasion exhibits his characteristic piety and submission, and is as follows:

KIRBY HALL, 17th December, 1811.

"My dear Sir,—I must use the hand of another to inform you that I was visited last week by an illness of the same nature with that in the beginning of the year. I have had a second paralytic stroke, affecting the half of my head and body, and forming a complete hemiplegia. My voice is not much affected, and the numbness is slight. But yet I consider that this may be a precursor of a third and last call to quit my earthly mansion. I view it, therefore, as a most merciful dispensation, and hope I shall ever retain my present thankful sense of the

'Sir, I wish to be baptized.' The missionary said, 'Why?' He said, laying his hand upon his heart, 'I am sure this is the word of God.' Many similar instances might be mentioned of the good effect produced by a simple reading of the scriptures. It is also a gratifying circumstance, that our most efficient teachers were formerly heathen schoolmasters, who now instruct the children out of the word of God, having themselves received the truth in the love of it."

Lord's gracious mode of bidding me prepare for my journey, and of calling me gradually to himself. Whether this event will hasten me to a warmer climate, or whether I shall wait the Lord's will at home, I have not yet determined.

"I had just finished the revision of my sermons when I was attacked; and I suppose they are now in the hands of the printers. If you should recollect any thing faulty in them, I hope you will send for the proof sheets.

"I remain, my dear sir, very sincerely yours,

"C. BUCHANAN."

On the 2d of January, 1812, Dr. Buchanan had recovered sufficiently from his late attack to resume with a faint and trembling hand his correspondence with his friends.

"My hand is recovering from the paralysis, and I can just hold the pen to inform you that scarcely any thing remains of my indisposition but extreme weakness. The faculty think they have at last discovered the source of my complaints, and have taken away about five pounds of blood. This has afforded a most sensible relief to my breathing, and has given rest during sleep, which before I had not. In addition, they have lowered and attenuated the body during the last month; so that all things are new. If, when the body is thus regenerated, the soul could also be renewed, it would be a salutary illness. I can indeed say, and with great thankfulness, that my soul has had more spiritual communion with God than formerly. It would be a blessed thing were it always to remain as it has been.

"I wondered at the peace I felt in the prospect of departing this life. It was perhaps greater than it will be when the time comes. 'Whoso endureth unto the end shall be saved.'

"Yesterday Cadell published the second edition of my memoir in octavo. Two editions of it were published in America this last year. On the 1st of February I hope all my sermons revised will be published in one volume.

"The University of Cambridge has done valorously, as you have seen. What fine youths these will be to preach to the people when you and I have winged our flight!"

Notwithstanding the severe shock which the constitution of Dr. Buchanan had received by his late paralytic seizure, the powers of his mind were evidently unimpaired, and, amidst great debility and languor, he retained all his ardour in promoting the cause of christianity in the world. This was very shortly evinced by the following communication to a friend, who had apprised him of an incorrect and injurious statement which, on the authority of the Danish missionaries in India, had been inserted in the Report of the Society for Promoting Christian Knowledge for the year 1811, respecting the Syrian Christians in Travancore. The substance of this communication was afterwards introduced into an able article in the Christian Observer,* forming a most satisfactory vindication of that interesting body of christians. The original observations, however, of Dr. Buchanan may still be acceptable to those who may retain any doubts upon the subject to which they relate.

"Kirby Hall, 18th Jan. 1812.

"All my books and MSS., concerning the Syrian christians, I deposited in the University Library, Cambridge; but I shall desire Mr. Yeates to look over the liturgy of the Syrians, and, if he can find the passage in which they abjure the errors of the Nestorians, to send it to you. When I passed through the Danish missionaries on the coast of Coromandel, on my way to Malabar, they told me the same things concerning the Syrians, which they have now stated to the society; but when I arrived in Malayala, I found they knew no more of the Syrian christians in that region, than people in England know of the Syrian christians in *Cyprus*. I suppose the missionaries have written thus by way of offering some apology for not advising the society to assist the Syrian christians.

"In regard to an *official* union, it is scarcely practicable, in present circumstances, and need not be thought of; but there is nothing to prevent a friendly connexion, or, as the bishop expressed it, 'such a connexion as should appear to both churches practicable and expedient.' The Romish church long solicited such an union, but could not attain it; nor did they regard their formerly having had (if, indeed, they ever had) Nestorian bishops, provided they would now qualify their system a little. They might even say mass in another tongue than Latin. But the missionaries cannot yield so much as this!

"The truth concerning the Syrians will be found, I allege, in my more full account of them, published by the Bishop of London.† 'Their liturgy is derived from that of the early church of Antioch, called *Liturgia Jacobi Apostoli*. They are usually denominated *Jacobitæ;* but they differ in ceremonial from the church of that name in Syria, and, indeed, from any existing church in the world.'

"That they worship the Virgin Mary is a flagrant error of

* Vol. xi. p. 105.

† In 1807. See the Christian Observer for that year.

speech. The practice might as well be charged on the Church of England.*

"In regard to their morals, learning, and civil state, I have merely recounted the conversations I had with their most learned members and noticed that 'I perceived all around symptoms of poverty and political depression:' that they were in a degenerate state, yet 'like a people who had known better days.' I also notice that 'they have some ceremonies nearly allied to those of the Greek church;' and I intimated to the bishop 'that there were some rites and practices in the Syrian church, which our church might consider objectionable or nugatory.' If I have not filled my page with these particulars, it was because I had no pleasure in describing them. Finding a church in their peculiar situation, possessing the Bible, and abjuring the Romish corruptions, what more was required to make them an useful people in evangelizing that dark region? And it is not decorous in the Church of England to seem to take pleasure in holding up to a kind of opprobrium an ancient people, found in such interesting circumstances; possessing, too, an ordination with which ours is scarcely to be compared. A former president of the Bartlett's Buildings Society (Archbishop Wake) negotiated for an union with Rome herself!

"As to the moral and civil state of the Syrians, Dr. Kerr has given them a higher character than I have, in his official document to the Madras government, which, on this subject, may now be quoted as a proper authority. All that he has said also concerning the facility and expediency of an union, may now be pressed with much advantage; for Dr. K. was

* A very different statement respecting the Syrian christians has been lately published in a letter from the Abbé Dubois, a Romish missionary in Mysore, inserted in the second report of the Bombay Auxiliary Bible Society. The respectability of the quarter from which this document has proceeded, may naturally seem to claim for it a considerable degree of credit. But whatever may be its value, as to points within the writer's own knowledge, it is undoubtedly erroneous as to the Syrian christians. Nor can this be a matter of surprise when it is considered that all his information concerning them is confessedly derived from other persons, who may, very probably, like himself, have never visited them, and be members of a church whose tyranny and oppression the Syrian christians in Travancore have for ages nobly resisted. "This sect," observes the Abbé, "still obstinately adheres to the religious tenets held by the heresiarch Nestorius." It is, however, somewhat extraordinary that the late venerable metropolitan of the Syrian church, in an official communication to General Macaulay, then resident at the court of Travancore, distinctly disclaimed the errors of Nestorius, as well as those of other heretics; and that Dr Buchanan and Dr. Kerr agree in representing their creed as not materially differing from that of our own church. It may be added, that their account of them is substantially the same as that of La Croze, Assemannus, and Mosheim. For further information upon this subject, the reader is referred to Dr. Buchanan's Christian Researches, and to the Christian Observer for December, 1816.

sent from the very place where the Danish missionaries dwell, to obtain information for government.

"But, on this subject, Colonel Macaulay is the highest authority in the world. If he will address the society in a respectful, conciliating manner, and urge the incontrovertible facts founded on his own knowledge and Dr. Kerr's official report, it will have immense effect.

"He may observe that an union is not to be thought of at present, on account of political considerations; but that such an interesting people deserve our countenance and every aid for mental improvement, by assisting them in the translation of the scriptures, and encouraging them to hold out against the Romish church. They are also proper subjects of occasional pecuniary assistance: for the oppression of the Hindoo government has of late been very great: but for the future they will, perhaps, be able to retain what they acquire.

"It would be proper that Colonel Macaulay should mention his own political transactions with the Travancore and the English governments on their behalf, and on behalf of the Romish Syrians. For *they* also want the Bible.

"My hand, you see, is a little better; but I am by no means strong. I can only sit up half an hour at a time."

It is surely to be lamented that no application was made on the part of the society to the two persons best qualified to afford information upon this subject, Dr. Buchanan and General Macaulay; and that no steps appear to have been taken to communicate that encouragement and support which the Church of England is plainly bound to extend to a community of christians thus brought into such immediate contact with the British government.

In the meantime, Dr. Buchanan continued his own exertions with a view to supply the Syrian christians with a translation of the scriptures. Thus he wrote in February and March to Mr. Macaulay:

"I enclose a letter, which I wish to go by this fleet. It is to give money to Timapah Pullé, who superintends the Malayalim version at Bombay.

"I have received a copy of the second edition of the memoir, and immediately discovered improvements. Many thanks to you for this service. And yet I have little satisfaction in looking at the book. I wish now to flee away to regions of peace with the wings of a dove—and be at rest."

"KIRBY HALL, 7th March.

"The day after I wrote to you last, I was obliged to leave

the writing table entirely, and have not resumed it since. The sensation of paralysis is but slight, but it appears to be now permanent; at least during the cold season.

"26th March.

"La Croze and Geddes are the principal authors for ——'s purpose, and I have neither.

"Gouvea, and Bartolomeo's India Christiana, and other curious works, I deposited, together with the MSS., at Cambridge.

"If you could call on Mr. Yeates, he could possibly furnish you with La Croze, or Simon, or Assemannus. It is a fine subject for ——'s contemplation, and one which would greatly interest the public mind. A few pages only, however, will suffice for the society. But, after he has done that, he may possibly meditate a larger work. These are times when *every thing a man has*, which may be in any way for the advantage of christianity, ought to be given to the world. For we shall soon die, and then shall 'all our thoughts perish.'

"Mr. Yeates writes thus in a late letter. 'Simon, in his Critical History of the Religion and Customs of the Eastern Nations, has ably vindicated the Syrian christians against the Catholics, and exposed their rage and persecution as the result of papal tyranny. I have read so much in Assemannus and other authors, as to know that the Syrian christians are the Protestants of the East. The Church of England, as a National Church, cannot extend her assistance to greater advantage, than in restoring and building up the ruins of the Syrian communion in Antioch, Mesopotamia, and India, by the immediate dispersion of copies of the scriptures. And when this is done, they will supply missionaries for the extension of the christian faith among the Mahometans and pagans.'

"I rejoice to hear that 'Ethiopia does not stretch out her hands' in vain. This will be a great accession of fame to the Bible Society. The University will not lend out my Ethiopic Gospel. You must send a person to transcribe it in the public library. If you should find any difficulty in the access, I will give you a note to the Vice-Chancellor."

The next subject to which the attention of Dr. Buchanan was directed was that to which he had devoted his memoir, and which he had ever considered as of primary and fundamental importance. This was the organization of a more extensive Ecclesiastical Establishment for British India. The time was now approaching for the renewal of the charter of the East India Company; and the friends of religion were anxious to improve this opportunity of pressing the consideration of the measure in question upon the attention of government and of the legislature. It was evident that no man was better qualified to suggest the best method of proceeding upon this occasion than Dr. Buchanan. Some distinguished persons, who took a lively interest in this weighty subject, accordingly applied to him to prepare a sketch of what he might deem advisable with respect to the proposed establishment, for the purpose of submitting it to the consideration of his majesty's ministers, and of others particularly concerned in the determination of this question.

It was with this important point that the correspondence of Dr. Buchanan was occupied during the spring and summer of this year. The following extracts from his letters to Mr. Macaulay will exhibit not only his zeal, but his piety and judgment respecting the accomplishment of the great measure which he had so long advocated:

"KIRBY HALL, March, 1812.

"India has scarcely crossed my mind since I wrote to you last; I mean in regard to legislative measures. I do not expect to be able to do any thing till the warm weather approach. Mr. Wilberforce writes to me that the Anglo-Indians question the fact of the burning of women stated in my memoir; and I read in the British Review that they doubt that of the self-devotement of a man at Ishera, stated in my researches under the article 'Juggernaut in Bengal.' I shall pen two sentences below on each of these subjects, which you may use as occasion may serve.

"Short as the above letter is, I have been nearly two days in writing it; and I do not now find myself able to finish my two sentences. I hope to recruit in a day or two, when I shall send them."

The two sentences thus meditated, branched out into two sheets; the substance of which afterwards appeared in the Christian Observer.*

Dr. Buchanan's next letter is as follows:

* For April 1812. In this paper it is stated that the calculation in question as to the number of women burned in the vicinity of Calcutta during a given period, was inserted in Dr. Buchánan's memoir on the authority of an official report to the College of Fort William, when the officers of that institution were collecting information to serve as an authentic record upon the subject of this female sacrifice. The truth of the fact respecting the self-devotement at Ishera was declared to rest upon the authority of the late Rev. D. Brown, whose country-house was near the spot referred to.

"Kirby Hall, 13th April, 1812.

"My dear Sir,—I send to you and Mr. Wilberforce by this day's mail a Prospectus of an Ecclesiastical Establishment for India. I will thank you to submit it to Mr. Grant and Lord Teignmouth; and I shall be obliged to them to make such alterations in it as they shall think proper. If they suggest any thing which you and Mr. W. approve, be pleased to incorporate it, and to revise the whole according to your judgment.

"I then wish you to send one copy to Mr. Perceval, and another to the Archbishop of Canterbury.

"When you are ready let me know, and I will send a note to accompany each copy. From Mr. Perceval I have lately received a very kind letter, in which he professes to have 'a respect for my character and exertions.'

"If, after you have sent in the copies, you should think that any part of the prospectus might be useful to Parliament, you may publish it in such form, and with such addition as you please, with my name or without it.

"I am much obliged to you for offering to do me service, if I can move southward; but now that you have the prospectus, you will not want me. I certainly should not have written it, if you had not pressed the subject. I can scarcely at present walk down stairs without help. As soon as the season opens a little, I propose to go to Scarborough for the benefit of the warm baths at that place. I am now seeking the comfort of the Holy Scriptures, and their promises; and love to contemplate Augustine and Luther. I look forward to nothing in this life but these two things, repentance, with bitter tears for past sins, and joy in the Holy Ghost. These two blessings I am encouraged to look for, for they are promised to sinners; they are 'the gifts to the rebellious.' In the meantime I pray to do the will of God, and to use my voice, my pen, or my feet, as he wishes me, while these members have any strength for his service.

"My dear sir, very sincerely yours, C. Buchanan."

"*Z. Macaulay, Esq.*"

The sketch of an Ecclesiastical Establishment, mentioned in the preceding letter, was not only transmitted to his majesty's ministers, and to other distinguished individuals, but communicated to the East India Mission Committee of the Society for Promoting Christian Knowledge, through Mr. Wilberfore, on the 1st of June. It was received by them with expressions of approbation, and of entire concurrence in the views of its author; and an abstract of it having been reported by that committee to a general meeting of the society, held on the 23d of that month, a series of important resolutions, in support of the measure thus proposed, as well as in favour of the general duty of promoting christianity amongst our Indian fellow subjects, European and native, were moved and adopted.

The following passage from a letter to a friend, who had suggested an alteration in a part of his "Sketch," will show, amongst other instances of a similar nature, how far Dr. Buchanan was from an unbending or disputatious temper:

"I am just favoured with your letter, and am greatly obliged to you for writing it. I consent to the section being omitted, and to the word 'colonization' not appearing in the whole book.

"I am only anxious that the cause of God should have due honour, and that 'exclusion of christian teachers in Asia' should be plainly represented as repugnant to God's will and revealed word. These are days of great measures. When we stand upon the *Rock*, we need not fear the conflicting currents of public opinion. But it is right to avoid obnoxious terms if we can; and if an object is likely to be attained without fighting for it, it is best."

Dr. Buchanan was, however, at this time by no means sanguine as to the success of the proposed establishment, though he rejoiced in the progress of christianity in other quarters. The following is from a letter to Colonel Sandys in April:

"I had very little pleasure in writing further on the subject; but, as I had given a beginning, I thought I would give the end. It is not probable that any thing of importance will be done. We ought to be satisfied with the great doings of the present day. Indeed the Bible Society's triumphs have been so great of late, that it is time (according to the usual dispensations in relation to the gospel) we should look for a *check*, to humble us a little, and keep us in our proper place.

"Since my return from Ireland, I have been much engaged with correspondence from that kingdom. There is a fine evangelical spirit, even amongst the nobility. I had urged Trinity College, Dublin, to organize a Bible Society. The students were for it; the elder members against it. Matters, at this moment, are very interesting. The Irish want the Bible almost as much as the Hindoos.

"My affectionate remembrance to Mrs. S. and Miss J., not forgetting Claudius, (look into Milner's History, for the life of Claudius, of Turin. I have just discovered in a volume of Archbishop Usher's, that there is a manuscript Commentary on St. Matthew in the library of Pembroke Hall, Cambridge, by this very Claudius: a fact which Mr. Milner does not seem to have known,) who, for the reason stated in the parenthesis, must go to Pembroke Hall, as a student of divinity. My namesakes must not go about with *flint and steel.* There is a higher warfare for them; in which I hope you are all fighting, and are more than conquerors through Him who hath loved us.

"I am, affectionately yours, C. BUCHANAN."

The beginning of the following month was marked by the appearance of some symptoms favourable to the intended measure respecting India, but clouded by the melancholy intelligence of the assassination of Mr. Perceval. Dr. Buchanan's observations on that lamentable event will be read with interest.

"KIRBY HALL, 15th May, 1812.

"I had a note from Lord Buckinghamshire thanking me for the Prospectus, and acknowledging its importance; concluding with—'You may be assured that it will receive from me all the attention to which it is entitled.' Another note from Mr. Perceval to the same effect. Happy Perceval! if he have died in the faith, as I have long believed he lived. In my last letter to him (about a month ago) there is the following sentence. 'One thing is certain,' (I had been alluding to his difficulties, and the state of public affairs,) 'and it must be a subject of permanent comfort to your own mind, that however the course of affairs may lead you in future life, good has already been done under your administration, which cannot be undone; and *even if life itself should not be long vouchsafed*, you would depart with the consciousness,' &c. &c.

"I have been trying to move the general assembly to notice the extension of religion in India. I have also urged Cambridge to petition Parliament on the subject. If an university, which has permitted its members to portray so often the blessing of giving christianity to India, should hesitate to recommend the measure, who can be expected to support it?

"I continue in an equable state of health. I can walk for about ten minutes at a time, but my weakness is very great, particularly in my limbs, which start and throb very much in bed, sometimes during the whole night. Last night an experiment was made of applying leeches to one foot. The consequence was, the throbbing ceased in that foot, and was more severe in the other.

"I am happy to hear that ——— is better, and with you.

He may probably be offered a command in Asia, in the course of a year or two. In the meanwhile, time flies, assassins fire shots, and we hear the voice, 'Be ye also ready.' I doubt not but the death of Mr. Perceval will give life to the religion of many a man in England. Some men will feel it as sensibly as if he had been a member of their own family."

In the month of June Dr. Buchanan proceeded to Scarborough, from whence he proposed a visit to the Bishop of Durham, and then to the Bishop of Llandaff, and the lakes of Westmoreland. This latter plan, however, he was compelled to relinquish, on finding that the exercise of a carriage was as yet too much for him. From Scarborough he wrote the following letter to his daughters; ending with a confirmation of his hopes respecting India.

"SCARBOROUGH, 18th July, 1812.

"I had the pleasure to receive your letter, Augusta, by Dr. B., and was much gratified by the perusal; and I have seen Charlotte's letter to her mamma, which is equally pleasing to me; for in both letters I think I perceive a love of piety, or at least a wish that you *could* love it. It is indeed so amiable a quality in young persons, that I cannot contemplate them with any pleasure, if they be destitute of it. For what are all other acquirements or possessions compared with this? Nothing. I wish you both to possess that which will give you hope, and me comfort, in the prospect of your dissolution. I wish to see you smile, and have inward peace, when you are shutting your eyes on the glories of life. But they are not glories. They are vanities. *I* cannot make you believe this. The grace of God alone can teach you this truth. And this grace is given oftentimes to children as young as you. When Christ said, 'Suffer little children to come unto me,' and when he quoted the Psalms to the Jews, where it is said, 'Out of the mouths of babes and sucklings thou hast perfected praise,' he meant to intimate that the grace of God is communicated to young children as well as to old persons; and that children may adorn the gospel by the beauty and piety of their conduct as well as the aged christian. But how is this grace to be attained? It will not be given to you unless you intreat God to bestow it. That is an ordinance or rule of God. And it will not do to ask in words only, in a formal way; but you must 'lift up your voice' in your closet, and expect it earnestly, as if you expected 'a treasure.'

"Be so good as to tell ——— and ——— that I have received a letter from Colonel Macaulay this morning, informing me that a deputation of Messrs. Wilberforce, Grant, Babington, &c., had waited on Lord Liverpool on the subject of evangelizing India, and that his lordship surprised them by offering almost more than they wished. He intimated his intention to carry the three following important measures; 1st. To establish a seminary at each presidency in India for instructing natives for the ministry. 2d. To grant licences for missionaries, not from the Court of Directors, but from the Board of Control. 3d. To consecrate bishops for India.

"Your mamma joins me in love to you both; and I remain, my dear girls,

"Your affectionate father, C. Buchanan."

The following extracts from letters to several of his friends, will show the general state of Dr. Buchanan's health, feelings, and employments, during the remainder of this eventful year.

"Kirby Hall, 17th August.

"I am just returned from Scarborough, where I have been for the last six weeks trying the efficacy of the warm baths at that place. I have been strengthened a little, but am still very weak.

"I have hardly any news but what I find in the Bible; and that book is always new. I keep far aloof from the world; at least I wish to do so; and my present indisposition favours my wishes. But even in this evil world every week produces joyful events. The city of London has formed itself into a Bible Society; and the Chancellor of the Exchequer has stood forth boldly as the advocate and supporter of the religion of Christ. But if I were to recount all the blessings of God to this unworthy land, I should need a quire of paper: a quire! If all the blessings to this unworthy land were written, 'the world itself' (to use the bold hyperbole of St. John) 'would not contain the books that should be written.'

"I rejoice to hear that you find yourself fully employed from day to day, feeling the weight of the labour, and yet obtaining strength for the day. For this, believe me, is the happiest state of your existence. The exertion of mind, under parochial, domestic, and scholastic cares, is like the budding and blossoming of trees which promise plenty of fruit. By and by it will be the autumn for you and Mrs. K.; labour and sin and sorrow will cease, and a glorious state of felicity will begin: of which I pray, that all your children and all your pupils may partake!"

"14th November.

"Thanks to you for your kind letter. I am in much the same state I have been, but I cannot write a page without difficulty. The paralytic affection remains without sensible abatement in my right hand, foot, and side. I can however walk and ride a little : and I have preached regularly this last month. There is no hope of my acquiring *strength* soon, for I do not take sufficient *food*. I am therefore content to do a little, not knowing whether I shall obtain strength to do more.

"I have just had a letter from Mr. Owen, (to whom I had occasion to send sixty pounds for the Bible Society, and ten pounds for Serampore to Mr. Macaulay, from the family here,) in which he manifests great alarm about Mr. Brown. Mr. Thomason's letter stated, that he was not expected to live a week. But my letter is the latest I presume. You would hear of the Serampore conflagration. The missionaries will soon recruit their money ; but the work will be somewhat retarded."

"Dec. 17.

"I thought I was going on very well, but I was suddenly threatened with a return of illness. It has hitherto been mercifully prevented; but I am obliged to desist entirely from my labour in the ministry; and am forbidden to engage in severe study.

"I rejoice to see you working with so much alacrity and content while strength is afforded you. 'Be thou faithful unto death, and I will give thee a crown of life.'

"What a terrible retribution is the modern Senacherib experiencing on the wolds of Russia! What an event for the use and edification of the christian! I fear both nations and individuals will suffer morally from their exultation. May you and I live to God, whether Bonaparte live or die!"

"Dec. 19.

"What a loss will Mr. Robinson be to the christian world! How many has he blessed in various ways, by preaching, writing, and family exhortation! What a shining example to all the midland ministers! I esteemed him the greatest preacher in England; as Mr. Scott is the greatest divine.

"I rejoice to see you continue in a spiritual frame. It is the balm of life. If Mr. —— has seen and tasted that 'Christ is precious,' he will 'set his face like a flint.' If his convictions have only been general, he will not be very useful in a higher sphere."

"Dec. 29.

"I received your welcome note, and desire the best blessings may be your portion in return. I suffer at present from the effects of a blister on the neck, which has taken a strong hold of my constitution, and can only write a few lines. If I could write, I have only to say, that I join with you in your hallelujah to Him who came at this season to redeem lost man, and to make us kings and priests unto God. May our song which begins now, last for ever!

"I had not heard that H. Martyn was about to return. God, who ordereth all things well, will show us perhaps that all these events are conducive to his glory."

At the close of this year, and the commencement of the following, Dr. Buchanan was occupied, at the suggestion of some of his friends, in preparing a new work, in the prospect of the approaching parliamentary discussions on the renewal of the charter of the East India Company, with reference to some more direct and effectual provision for the promotion of christianity in our Asiatic empire. Before we proceed, however, with this important subject, we must advert to some events which deeply affected the domestic happiness of Dr. Buchanan during the first three months of the year 1813. These will be best related in his own words. In a note to Mr. and Mrs. Thompson on the 27th of February, he wrote thus:

"I dare say your hearts will be filled with joy on the event of dear Mary having been so safely delivered. As for the little one, who would only stay half an hour in this evil world, there is no reason that we should grieve for him. I am happy to say, that his dear mother is perfectly composed and resigned to the dispensation.

"May the God of this family, even the God of Abraham, Isaac, and of Jacob, who surroundeth us with his comforts, administer to you also the consolation and support you respectively stand in need of, and shine on your path till you become partakers of his glory!"

On the same day, Dr. Buchanan communicated this event to one of his friends, and accompanied it with the following notice of the afflicting intelligence which had been lately received from India, and of the dubious state of his own health.

"I presume you have heard of the death of the Rev. Mr. Brown, of Calcutta, and of Mr. Martyn. And so these good men have ascended up on high in the vigour of age and life. Let us aspire to follow them, and join the assembly of the first born!

"I have no news for you, being, like yourself, much retired

from the world. I continue in my former state, as to health; that is, I can make little progress in acquiring strength, while the danger of a third attack of paralysis (which is imminent) obliges me to take little nourishment, and yet to lose much blood."

On the 13th of March, Dr. Buchanan, in writing to another of his friends, added:

"Mrs. B. recovers well, and has been applying to herself St. Paul's reasoning on the advantages of being without the cares of a family. I tell her St. Paul's is a wonderful book—it suits *every state.*"

This favourable appearance, however, of recovery was but of short duration. The following brief narrative, drawn up by Dr. Buchanan for the consolation of Mr. and Mrs. Thompson, describes in simple but affecting language the sudden extinction of his hopes, and the repetition of the blow which had once before laid low his expectations of earthly happiness.

"Long before her last illness, my dear Mary had frequently contemplated the probability of her dying in early life. Her delight was to talk of things heavenly and spiritual, and her studies were almost entirely religious. Her spirits seemed to have been much chastened by personal and by domestic suffering; and her affections were gradually losing their hold of this world. After her last confinement, her heart appeared to be devoted to God in a particular manner. On the third day she wrote the following note to her dear mother:

"'You will rejoice to hear I am as well as can be expected, and that I feel a wonderful *serenity of mind.* I feel a want for my poor little babe. Yet I do not repine, for I have great need of all the Lord's chastisements; and if I gain one step towards heaven, I am abundantly repaid, and would joyfully go through all over again to-morrow to gain one step more. I have great need of correction; but why my dear husband should be a sufferer in these losses I cannot conceive, who is so much farther advanced in his heavenly course and experience in every way. Pray for me, that I may so run as to obtain the heavenly prize.

"'My kind love to my poor little girls. Tell them I hope, in the course of a day or two, to be able to see them. I have great cause for thankfulness in every way. Adieu, adieu.'

"Notwithstanding her continued indisposition, accompanied by a high fever, she greatly enjoyed my prayers and religious converse. Having lost her child, she frequently alluded to the pleasure she anticipated in forming the minds of Charlotte and Augusta, and preparing them for the heavenly state. We mutually expressed the hope of devoting ourselves to the service of God for the time to come, more affectionately and actively than we had done in time past. She looked forward, certainly, to the comfort of enjoying more the life of a saint on earth; but I do not think she expected so early to be a saint in heaven. The expectations and assurances of all her medical attendants were very flattering in regard to her recovery. A rapid recovery was prognosticated; but she more than once intimated that they did not understand her case.

"On the night previous to her death, while she sat on the couch in my study, she begged I would give her the Bible, and a little table, and a candle. She read one of the psalms very attentively, the 46th I believe, beginning with these words, 'God is our refuge and strength, a very present help in trouble.' And when I took the Bible out of her hands, finding it open at that psalm, I read it to her as a portion of our evening religious exercise.

"On the morning of the day on which she died, after I had kneeled by her bedside, as usual, and prayed with her, and had left her, she desired her maid to read a hymn to her. She began one, but immediately said it was a funeral hymn; to which she replied, 'a funeral hymn will suit me very well.'

"About an hour afterwards she was brought into my study, and took her seat in the arm-chair. About one o'clock her dear father and mother came to visit her. After her father had stayed sometime, he and I went out in the carriage for an hour, while her mother remained with her. On our return, her mother took her leave, and I accompanied her down stairs to the carriage. On my coming up, my dear Mary had just got up from her chair, and walked over to the couch with a quick step, assisted by her nurse, from an apprehension that she was about to faint. I immediately supported her in my arms. Slight faintings succeeded, but they were momentary. She complained of a pain near her heart. On my saying, I hoped it would soon be over, she replied, 'O no, it is not over yet; what is this that is come upon me?—send for mamma.' After a few minutes' struggle, she sat up in the couch with much strength; and looking towards the window, she uttered a loud cry, that might have been heard at a considerable distance. She then drank a little water; and immediately after drinking, without a groan or sigh, her head fell upon my breast. I thought she had only fainted; but her spirit at that moment had taken its flight. It was just three o'clock in the day.

"Thus died my beloved wife. She was ready for the summons. She had long lived as one who waited for the coming of her Lord. Her loins were girded, her lamp was burning, and the staff was in her hand. She had nothing to do but to depart.

"'Blessed are those servants whem the Lord when he cometh shall find watching; and if he shall come in the second watch, or come in the third watch, and find them so, blessed are those servants.' Luke xii. 37.*

"MOAT HALL, 13th April, 1813."

A few days after this afflicting event, Dr. Buchanan expressed his personal feelings more fully, and detailed, in his "Private Thoughts," with genuine christian humility, those "peaceable fruits of righteousness," which he was chiefly anxious to derive from his loss. The notice of some of them will, doubtless, interest many readers.

"My first emotions of thankfulness (when I could seek subjects of thankfulness) were, 'that her last trial was so short.' It was given me to witness for my soul's health, I trust; and it was awful indeed, but it was short."

"Monday evening, 29th March.

"I have passed this week in a mourning and disconsolate state. I have lost appetite for food, and dwell almost constantly on the circumstances of my loss.

"I suffer chiefly from the reflection, that I did not commune with her more frequently and directly on the state of her soul. * * * God ordained her personal and domestic sufferings to mature her for her approaching change. * * * * Mature in my heart, blessed Saviour, this affliction, and enable me to obey the new commandment, 'that ye love one another.'

"This love exercised towards a wife or children acquires a double force; natural affection co-operating with spiritual love.

"Teach me, O Lord, to love my children as I ought to do, both in a natural and spiritual sense."

"April 2d, 1813.

"My grief has been growing more and more faint and languid; but, blessed be the God and Father of our Lord Jesus Christ, my sense of things heavenly and my penitence for past sins, have rather increased. I am enabled to pray three times a day, and am not as usual driven hastily from my knees. O

* The inscription on Mrs. Buchanan's tomb, written by her affectionate husband, will be found at the end of the volume.

that this may continue! I have long prayed for a spirit of grace and supplication, and now the Lord hath been pleased to give it by means that I did not expect. However it comes, it is a long-lost blessing.

"The chief petitions in my prayers have been these:

"1. That God would strike the rock of my affections with his rod, and cause the waters to flow; that I might become tender hearted, truly humble and solicitous about the spiritual state of men.

"2. That I might open my mouth in the cause of God. Hitherto my lips have been locked in a torpid silence. There is, indeed, much that is constitutional in this taciturnity; and my late nervous indisposition has greatly increased it. Like Hooker, I can scarcely look my children or servants in the face.

"I have prayed that this unaccountable weakness may be removed; that I may become vocal for God at all times and in all places; that I may look earnestly into the eyes and countenances of men, and seek anxiously their salvation; that I may never forget the agonizing looks and powerful voice of my dear wife in the struggle of death; and that I may call forth some animation of soul in *my looks* and *words* during my *life*.

"3. That I may learn to seek the glory of God as the first object in my conversation in the world, and to pray earnestly for the conversion of all men.

"4. Let me look on every person whom my eyes survey with benevolence, loving my neighbour as myself, and utter a mental prayer for that person, 'May this be a vessel of mercy prepared unto glory!'

"5. That the spirit of grace and supplication may never depart from me; and that God may hear my morning, noon-tide, and evening supplication during every day of my pilgrimage.

"6. That * * * I may fix my love, hopes, and affections on God; and obtain that fellowship which I learn from scripture is attainable by man in his present state. Amen."

Dr. Buchanan's communications to his friends upon this melancholy occasion breathe the same spirit as his more private meditations, and will still, it is presumed, be thought interesting and instructive. The following are extracts from some of them.

"Kirby Hall, 2d April, 1813.

After replying to one or two points respecting public events, he adds:

"But I do not know what is passing in these days. The

death of Mrs. Buchanan has removed to a vast distance from my mind subjects which were familiar to it. . . . I could not have believed that I should have been so much moved by the event as I am, or that my affections would have been so powerfully awakened. May the spiritual impression I have received never be obliterated from my soul!

"Offer my christian love to your wife who is yet alive. And may you and she enjoy much spiritual communion with each other, before the hour of separation arrives!"

"4th April.

"My dear Sister,—Charlotte has shown me your kind letter. I thank you most sincerely for your tender sympathy on my late loss. The summons came suddenly for Mrs. Buchanan, but she was evidently matured for her new state of existence; and I believe she in some degree anticipated it. Her death has, I trust, been blessed to myself, and, I would hope, to my children.

"While your dear husband is spared to you, and you are spared to him, enjoy as much spiritual converse together as is possible. For when the separation comes, you will reproach yourselves bitterly, if you have not been tenderly communicative on this subject.

"I remain, my dear sister, very affectionately yours,

C. BUCHANAN."

"*To Colonel Sandys.*

"15th April.

"Accept my sincere thanks for your kind letter of condolence. Your topics of consolation are all excellent; and you point to the right source, the heavenly Paraclete.

"I shall not be able to make a journey into Cornwall. I return you thanks for your most obliging offer, which is a true mark of your personal friendship, and of christian regard. My infirm state forbids my moving from home for sometime, except in a case of urgent necessity.

"I can write but little. My pen refuses to say much since Mrs. Buchanan's death. But I hope I have been affected by it chiefly in a spiritual manner."

"*To Colonel Macaulay.*

"April 16.

"I thank you most sincerely for your kind letter. The mournful event has, I trust, been sanctified to me. Some such affliction appears to have been necessary to soften a hard and proud heart. I pray that the salutary effects may never pass away.

"I am happy to hear you speak so favourably of the disposition of government in regard to the extension of christianity in the East. Mr. Wilberforce has urged me to go up and give evidence at the bar of the House of Lords. I told him I am willing to appear; the only question is, whether it be physically practicable. The physicians oppose my going. I do not know what will be the event."

The latter sentence in the preceding extract leads back our attention to the great subject which occupied the minds of religious men during the former part of this year, and with reference to which, it has been already seen, that Dr. Buchanan was employed, when his thoughts were for a time diverted from it by the late afflicting event in his family. To this important subject, therefore, we will now return.

CHAPTER IV.

The light which had been thrown a few years since, chiefly by means of Dr. Buchanan's writings, on the state of religion in India, and the interest which had been in consequence excited upon that subject throughout the nation, produced a very general impression as to the duty of urging upon the attention of parliament the necessity of making some more effectual provision for the religious instruction of British India, and of increasing the facilities of imparting the blessings of christian knowledge to the unenlightened millions of our native subjects. To promote these most important objects, several valuable tracts were published by the friends of religion; amongst which may be particularly mentioned an admirable "Letter to a Friend on the duty of Great Britain to disseminate christianity in India, occasioned by the proposed renewal of the charter of the East India Company;"* and a masterly "Address to the Public," on the same momentous topic, by the Rev. Robert Hall.

The subject was also briefly but powerfully touched by an able and eloquent defender† of the general system of our East

* See the Christian Observer, vol. xi. p. 261.

† Robert Grant, Esq.

Indian administration; who, in combatting an insinuation of a valuable writer on the south of India, thus expresses his own views upon the subject of promoting christianity in the East.

"'The question respecting the introduction of christianity into Hindostan does not, it must be owned, fall precisely within the subject of the present work; but its high importance will justify a few words upon it, even at the expense of what may seem a digression.

"'The idea of *coercive* proselytism, however mild the compulsory means employed, merits all the epithets which the language of reprobation can attach to it; and even that of proselytism, by the simple exertion of state influence, seems, in Hindostan, to say the best of it, highly objectionable. But surely the idea of proselytism by the bare effect of conviction,—by the effect of an unforced, unbribed, and unbiassed acquiescence in truth and reason,—however visionary it may appear to some persons, can only by a very singular rule of arrangement be classed with unmanly, ungenerous, and unchristian deception. To such a pitch of refinement would this valuable author have us carry our reverence for the superstitions of Hindooism! Their sanctity seems to be like what is said of the priestly character, indelible. Their sovereignty is so essential and inherent, that they not only cannot be deposed, but cannot even voluntarily abdicate.

"'A few years ago this subject was debated with great heat; but at present will surely receive a calm attention. The accomplished Sir William Jones, who was equally distinguished for his acuteness, his philanthropy, and his candour, has given his sanction to attempts, cautiously and fairly conducted, for the introduction of the christian religion among the natives of Hindostan. If, indeed, as Colonel Wilks justly affirms, 'it never can be a question, whether the English or the Hindoo code of religion be entitled to the preference,' the wish must naturally suggest itself to every humane and unprejudiced mind, that the better system should have every chance of the wider diffusion. Only the distinction is ever to be carefully observed between making it a matter of *option* and a matter of *authority*; a distinction which, even as applied to this particular case, the experience of many years has now shown that the natives are perfectly able to comprehend. The uncompelled and tranquil circulation of the christian scriptures (the method peculiarly recommended by Sir William Jones) appears so free from all possibility of exception, that it ought to receive the fullest and most willing toleration from the Indo-British Presidencies. Otherwise they would indeed 'forcibly stand between' the

Hindoo population and the highest and deepest hopes that can be infused into the human heart. And surely no government calling itself christian can, without incurring a fearful responsibility, refuse to a christian missionary, so long as he shall demean himself with strict loyalty, steady discretion, and unimpeachable virtue, the opportunity of exerting his unbought and honourable labour among the natives of Hindostan."

It was natural, however, to look to him who had first awakened the public mind to the imperious duty of regarding the religious concerns of our oriental empire, to lead the way in an appeal to the legislature upon this subject. Accordingly, amidst the pressure of domestic sorrow and of personal debility, Dr. Buchanan composed and published, early in the spring, a work entitled, "Colonial Ecclesiastical Establishment: being a brief view of the state of the Colonies of Great Britain, and of her Asiatic Empire, in respect to religious instruction: prefaced by some considerations on the national duty of affording it."

Though the state of the question relative to the promotion of christianity in India was very materially and happily changed since the year 1807, when it was so fully discussed, and thoughtful and religious men were in general persuaded of the necessity and importance of that measure, Dr. Buchanan still deemed it expedient to commence his work by briefly but pointedly urging this duty upon a christian nation, and by arguing, from various considerations, that the voice of Providence was evidently calling upon Great Britain to undertake it. He next entered upon an examination of the means of thus diffusing christianity; and under the head of one of them, "the extension of the National Church," gave a sketch of a general colonial establishment, and of the state of religion in the West Indies. Dr. Buchanan then argued the question as to the policy of promoting christianity in India.

On the subject, however, of parliamentary interference, he stated, that it was not his intention to urge the legislature to adopt any direct means in the way of expensive establishments for proselyting the natives. All, he said, that was expected at present in regard to them was, that the governing power would not show itself hostile to the measure of instructing them. Great Britain, he alleged, owed her primary obligations to her own children. The work, therefore, is closed by a powerful appeal to parliament as to its duty and responsibility upon the approaching decision of this momentous question, and with the sketch of an Ecclesiastical Establishment for British India, which has been already mentioned.*

---

* See page 357.

Such is a brief outline of the contents of this volume, which was very extensively circulated, particularly amongst the members of both houses of Parliament, and made a strong and general impression throughout the country.

It was not merely, however, by the press that the friends of religion endeavoured to instruct and awaken the public upon this critical and momentous occasion. They resorted to the legitimate and constitutional measure of petitioning Parliament upon the subject, and nine hundred addresses from the cities, towns, and even villages of the united kingdom, crowded the tables of both houses, imploring the interference of the legislature in behalf of the moral and religious interests of India. The contest was long and arduous; but the voice of christian duty and of sound policy, which must ever be inseparable, at length prevailed. A resolution to the following effect was introduced by his majesty's ministers into both houses; and, after very full and lengthened discussions, in which Mr. Wilberforce, Mr. W. Smith, and Mr. Stephen, particularly distinguished themselves by their able and eloquent efforts in its support, it was, in the House of Commons, carried by a great majority, and, in the House of Lords, without debate and without a division.

"That it is the duty of this country to promote the interest and happiness of the native inhabitants of the British dominions in India; and that such measures ought to be adopted as may tend to the introduction among them of useful knowledge and of religious and moral improvement. That, in the furtherance of the above objects, sufficient facilities shall be afforded by law to persons desirous of going to and remaining in India for the purpose of accomplishing these benevolent designs."

A previous resolution had already passed, by which a bishop and three archdeacons were to be appointed to superintend the clergy of the established church in India; thus accomplishing, though not to the extent which he deemed necessary, the two great objects which Dr. Buchanan had so ably and so perseveringly pursued.*

It is to these important and interesting transactions that the following extracts principally refer. With the exception of the first, the letters from which they are taken were address-

* The establishment of the See of Calcutta has been attended with all the benefits which Dr. Buchanan anticipated, and has already added not a little to the lustre of the English Episcopacy from the character of the distinguished and pious bishops whose services it has, for a brief period, enjoyed. The fol-

ed to a friend, to whose judicious and zealous exertions much of the success which ultimately attended the cause must be ascribed.

"KIRBY HALL, Feb. 4, 1813.

—— "You go up, you say, to witness the battle between the government and the India Company. It rages very furiously at present. It is a fine trial of the honesty of religious men. It is true, indeed, good men often live and die the slaves of particular prejudices; but, generally speaking, conscience will take the alarm if we are not honest in our vote in a cause between *God and man.*

———— "God will direct the event according to his counsel. There may be no remarkable triumph at this time: but other parts of the great catastrophe (the revelation of Christ's kingdom) are approximating, and you may live to see its advance. The expiration of twenty years more is likely to be a grander period in the church than the present.

"I have just submitted to the insertion of a large seton in the integuments of my neck. So you see the constitutional propensity to paralysis continues. But this is the best state for me. I could not have *chosen* a better; and it does me a great deal of good. I need slow fires to purge away my dross. But the Refiner is merciful, and gives me strength to bear the heat of the furnace."

"KIRBY HALL, April, 1813.

"The circumstances of my health render it impracticable for me, at present, to move to London. But I shall probably afford you any information as satisfactorily by correspondence as if I were on the spot.

---

lowing are the dates of their respective consecrations, and of the deaths of the first four of the number:

Right Rev. THOMAS FANSHAW MIDDLETON, consecrated 1814, died 1822.
" REGINALD HEBER, consecrated 1st June, 1823, died April 2, 1826.
" J. T. JAMES, consecrated 3d June, 1827, died 22d August, 1828.
" J. M. TURNER, consecrated 1829, died July 7, 1831.
" DANIEL WILSON, consecrated 1832.

Serus in cœlum redeat, diuque læto intersit populo.

Since the appointment of Bishop Wilson the English government has yielded to the manifest necessity of increasing the number of bishops in India. The Right Rev. DANIEL CORRIE, whose life has been devoted to missionary labours in India, and who is well known as the friend and associate of Henry Martyn, was consecrated Bishop of BOMBAY on the 14th of June, 1835. The succeeding year was marked by the consecration of the Right Rev. THOMAS CAN as Bishop of BOMBAY.—AM. ED.

"Your accomplishing the object of a numerous meeting at the London Tavern was a grand measure, and the whole christian world is indebted to you for it. The resistance to your purposes will be most resolute. The public voice alone promises something. If every city and town in England and Scotland were to petition, (which is practicable,) the business would acquire a new complexion before the end of May.

"The duty, however, of a christian is to be obedient to the powers that be. To claim as matter of *right* the permission of preaching christianity to the Hindoos, is highly absurd; and the assertion of the *right* ought to meet with a rebuke.

"Mr. Wilberforce's speech in the committee on Catholic claims will produce some sensation among religious men in England. I am of opinion that he has judged rightly. Liberal concession to the Catholics and dissenters will be good medicine to some; and will favour measures for enlarging the spiritual church of Christ. We may be sure that the country will make no concession to the Catholics which will *materially* injure her. If she does, she can retrace her steps, as she has done before."

"May 15.

"Many thanks to you for 'Christianity in India.' It is drawn up in the manner I entirely approve, which I could not say of the former summaries. It comes in well after the petitions; and its perspicuity and brevity will fix and fascinate the careless eye. I begin almost to *sympathise* with your Indian opponents, the battering of religious Britain has been so tremendous.

Like you, I am not anxious as to the terms of concession in regard to the question. The deed is done. Britain has lifted her voice in her christian character, and the effect will be permanent and blessed. By this concussion religion rises at least two degrees in a scale of twenty, both in its character and interests. The Bible Society, too, shares in the triumph.

"Mr. Dealtry's sermon* was well timed; and would be, I doubt not, a *coup de grace* to the dying prejudices of some.

"I have just read Dr. Milner's Strictures; and have praised God who hath given such understanding to men. He is a host in himself; and the church will begin henceforth to view him in a new light. They will dread his principles less, and reverence his abilities more. I trust it will please God to spare his life for some years.

* Before the Church Missionary Society.

"The publication of the Society's India Reports is just what we want. It identifies them with us, and confirms the truth of facts.

"Spare your health, and take repose; for you know not but you may have as much to do next year."

"KIRBY HALL, June 2d.

———— "I congratulate you on your great triumph. Such a resolution proposed under such circumstances! The moment it actually passes the petitioners ought to unite in one national hallelujah.

. . . . "What does . . . think of *civilization* now? Lord Castlereagh has put the question to rest. He says the fear of it is a chimera."

"11th June.

"I am charmed with Whitbread, when he sounds the right note.

"I continue stationary at present. I have had blood abstracted twice by cupping within the last month."

"5th July.

"And so Mr. Venn is dead! What a varied scene has he passed through in the evening of life, permitted, no doubt, for his soul's health and eternal good. The church may mourn indeed for Venn and Robinson. Let us be followers of them, who through faith and patience have inherited the promises!"

"July 7th.

"I enclose an additional paragraph for the Remarks. Mr. Lushington having declared so gravely that I had recommended the Hindoos to be converted *by force*, perhaps it would be right to advert to a matter, which I had never thought it worth my while to notice before.

"I hope now to give you no further trouble. It must be a great relief to you when Parliament and their India questions break up for good; and I should be glad to hear that you had gone for a while to the Isle of Wight; whence, as from a safe haven, you might look back on the tumultuous sea you have navigated."

"July 24.

"I congratulate you sincerely on the issue of your campaign, far more interesting to thousands than that of Lord Wellington.

"And now we are likely to be all disgraced. Parliament

has opened the door, and who is there to go in? From the church not one man! Lord C. anticipated this *dénoument* in a very pleasant vein. We may hope that the Church Missionary Society will excite a new spirit in various places. And we must believe that the late great national movement, in behalf of Christ and his kingdom, will have a reward in the fruits of righteousness within the year."

The labours, however, of Dr. Buchanan in this great cause were not yet completed. In the course of the debates in the House of Commons, upon the question allowing efforts to be made by pious and benevolent persons to promote christianity in India, his name and his writing were introduced by several of the Anglo-Indian* opposers of that measure, in terms which can scarcely be excused even on the ground of their own sincere, though mistaken, apprehensions of the subject. He was represented by these gentlemen as the calumniator of the Hindoos, and as having given to the world a false, or at least an exaggerated, statement of their cruel and immoral superstitions. They, on the contrary, wished the house and the public to believe, upon the authority of their alleged local knowledge, that the Hindoos, though idolators, and enslaved by a blind and corrupt superstition, were still a very harmless and moral race of people, and, in support of the excellence of the Brahminical system, quoted a variety of passages from the Heetopades, and other Hindoo books, to prove what pure and exalted sentiments they entertained of the Supreme Being, and of the great duties of morality. Witnesses, however, without end, possessing more than all the boasted local information of these gentlemen, from Mr. Holwell to Sir William Jones, Lord Teignmouth, and Sir James Mackintosh, had already convinced every calm and unprejudiced inquirer, that, whatever may be the speculative merit of their sacred books, or the social virtues of individuals, both the religious system and the moral practice of the Hindoos in general were—what we might be certain from abstract principles as well as universal experience, the heathen ever must be—"corrupt, abominable, and unto every" really "good work reprobate." And it would, in fact, be quite as practicable and as just to charge the sacred writers themselves in their descriptions of the idolators of Greece and Rome, however distinguished for their advancement in learning and the arts, with exaggeration and uncharitableness, as the representations of Dr. Buchanan, on a similar painful and deplorable subject.

* Particularly by Sir Henry Montgomery and Mr Lushington; the latter of whom did not, however, vote against the resolution.

It happened, in the course of the examination of evidence upon the India question before the House of Commons, that Dr. Buchanan's Memorial to Lord Minto in the year 1807, together with the reply of the Bengal government to that paper, and the observations of the Court of Directors on both, were exhibited, and afterwards printed by order of the house. The account given by Dr. Buchanan of the atrocities of the idol-worship at Juggernaut was also opposed and attempted to be invalidated by Mr. C. Buller, M. P. for West Looe, in a way which will shortly be stated.

The unfounded allegations of the gentlemen first named were generously repelled by Mr. Wilberforce, in one of his admirable speeches in the house, in the following terms:

"It is unwillingly that I bring in the name of one other person; I mean Dr. Buchanan: but I should be extremely wanting in the office and feelings of friendship, did I not take this opportunity of vindicating the character of that excellent man. The other night, the house will remember that it was stated by a friend near me that I had not mentioned a single fact or proposition on the authority of Dr. Buchanan. This, however, was not because Dr. Buchanan was no authority with me; but because I knew there was a great, but most unjust outcry raised against him: as, indeed, it was natural to expect there would be against any man who had endeavoured, with his zeal, to draw the public attention to this great cause. Thinking, therefore, that my facts would be more readily admitted, if I supported them by other less obnoxious names, I did not mention the name of Dr. Buchanan, although his testimony would have corroborated all I said. But I should not do justice to my sentiments, if I did not say that I feel Dr. Buchanan to be a man who deserves to be spoken of in a very different way from that in which some gentlemen have chosen to mention his name. Lord Wellesley selected Dr. Buchanan to be Vice-Provost of the college of Calcutta; and he says of him—'I have formed the highest expectations from his abilities, learning, temper, and morals;' if, therefore, I think most highly of Dr. Buchanan, as I certainly do, I am not alone in thinking well of him. And let me here remind the honourable member that Dr. Buchanan did not, at least, act like a man who wished to deceive the public, and to obtain their assent to a false proposition; for Dr. Buchanan published that very work, which states most fully and particularly all the great circumstances of Hindoo enormity, while he yet resided in Bengal, and the book was in circulation there a year or two before he quitted that country. He himself presented to the supreme government of

India a copy of this work; I mean his Memoir in favour of an Ecclesiastical Establishment for India; by which he drew as much attention to the subject as he could, and, at least, manifested his desire that the real truth should be ascertained. And, in justice to Dr. Buchanan, I must observe that, notwithstanding the unjust and illiberal aspersions which have been thrown out in a general way against him, I have never yet heard him distinctly charged with any specific misstatement of any fact which he has brought forward."

To Mr. Lushington and Sir Henry Montgomery Dr. Buchanan wrote privately in vindication of his sentiments respecting the Hindoos. A copy of his letter to the former gentleman is here introduced, not merely for the purpose of defence and explanation, for this is by no means necessary, but to show his exemplary mildness and forbearance under violent and undeserved reproach.

"KIRBY HALL, BOROBRIDGE, 29th June, 1813.

"Sir,—I do myself the honour to address you for a moment, in consequence of my having been informed that, on a late occasion in the House of Commons, you censured my statements concerning India as being unchristian and unjust; or in terms to that effect. Had such a stricture been made by a person who was hostile to the introduction of christianity into India, I should have paid no attention to it; but coming from respectable authority, and from one who is friendly to that measure, I think it due to him and to myself to offer some explanation.

"As you are an advocate for instructing the natives of India, I must think that you approve in general of my endeavour to give some account of the state of the people, and of the nature of their superstition; for, without some account of this kind, how should our nation ever be excited to interest itself humanely in their behalf? I must believe, then, that you do not object to the giving such an account, but only that you disapprove of the *manner* in which it is done. I am not conscious that there is any thing intemperate in my manner of writing. Had I been intemperate, the nation would not have listened to me. It remains, then, for me to believe that you advert to insulated facts stated by me, which you consider untrue. If you will have the goodness to refer me to any book, or other respectable authority, which plainly invalidates any particular fact, I shall be happy to publish the authority in the next edition of my work, and to confess my mistake. I assure you it will cost me no more to retract an error publicly than to write this letter. My only object is to promote the cause of truth in the world, by legitimate means. My own fame (since all men possess not the same information and principles and cannot be equally pleased) ought to be of little moment, and is, I hope, a secondary consideration. But I beg you will do me the justice to remember that on these subjects there is a great diversity of opinion, even among those who are adverse to my general views. Scarcely two persons from two different parts of India will be found who will give the same account of what they have seen and heard. Nor is agreement to be expected in describing the various nations extending over three thousand miles of territory. But as to those passages in my own work which you characterize as unchristian or unjust, I am at as great a loss to know which they are, as if you had charged them with high treason.

"I understood some time ago that the statement in my publication which chiefly provoked animadversion, was that which referred to the burning of women. But you are aware on what authority I published that account; and I presume you are informed that subsequent indubitable statements very far exceed it, and set this question entirely at rest.

"Probably you may not have heard that a work has been recently published in Bengal, in four volumes quarto, entitled a History of the Religion, Manners, and Literature of the Hindoos, which has been bought up with avidity in India, has already passed through two editions in that country, and is now publishing at home. It was printed under the immediate eye of the Bengal government, (as you know it necessarily must be,) and possesses an unquestionable authenticity on the various subjects concerning which it treats. It takes the high ground of literal translations from the Hindoo books, recent facts, and living witnesses. Now this work not only confirms my statements in almost every case which was controverted, but goes far beyond them. In describing the atrocities connected with the burning of women, self-devotement, and the impurity of the Hindoo worship, I find I have scarcely entered the vestibule. Will those, then, who pause at my statements, be able to assail this authority?

"There is another consideration, to which I would request you would advert. Speculative strictures on the character of the Hindoos constitute a very inconsiderable portion of my writings. In three publications concerning India, I do not think that criminatory reflections on the Hindoo character in the abstract would occupy three pages. I treat, in general, of entirely different subjects. It was not till the other day that I was induced to give an exposition of a radical principle of an impure character in the Hindoo worship; and that exposition would certainly never have been given, but for the statement of Mr. Buller. From his representation the nation would have been left to conclude, that the indecent emblems on the temples of the Hindoos have no evil effect on the morals of the people. Now if I was entirely convinced that the contrary was the truth, would it have been right in me to aid, by my silence, the promulgation of such an error?

"I would flatter myself that, when you have read this letter, you will be disposed to consider the object of my writings more favourably. There is a particular reason why I wish to obtain from you an expression of approbation."

Here Dr. Buchanan introduced a reference to the charge which he had received from the late Sir Stephen Lushington, on his going out to India, which has been already mentioned in these memoirs. He then continues as follows:

"If you will do me the honour at your leisure to look through my writings, I think you will approve the motives and general design; and I hope you will pardon particular aberrations. If you do not, I shall regret it; but I bear no resentments; and shall trust that time, which produces great revolutions in sentiment, will abate, and not increase, your unfavourable opinion.

"I have the honour to be, sir, your most obedient and humble servant, C. BUCHANAN."

"*To S. R. Lushington, Esq. M. P.*"

Such was Dr. Buchanan's temperate and satisfactory address to Mr. Lushington. To Mr. Buller's allegations, he thought it necessary to reply more publicly.

This gentleman perceiving, in the course of the examinations which took place in the House of Commons, that the enormities practised at Juggernaut had made a deep impression on the minds of many members, deemed it his duty, from his personal and intimate knowledge of the subject, with a view of effacing that impression, to address a letter to the Court of Directors of the East India Company, intending that it should be laid on the table of the house; where it accordingly soon afterwards made its appearance. Mr. Buller's letter contained a plausible defence of the tax on pilgrims resorting to the temple of the idol in question, and an attempt to palliate the atrocities alleged by Dr. Buchanan to be customarily committed during the celebration of the Rutt Jattra. Of the indecencies said to be exhibited there, he professed his total ignorance.* This vindication of Juggernaut was probably intended, together with the defence of the Indian government, to discredit the testimony of Dr. Buchanan in this particular point, and thus to produce a general distrust of his statements. The failure of this scheme shall be given in the words of a writer in a valuable periodical publication before alluded to; which nobly redeemed its pledge, given some years since, never to abandon the sacred cause of promoting Christianity in India and throughout the world; and to whose pages in the year 1813 the author gladly refers for a complete and masterly view of this whole subject.

"Had it pleased Providence," said the Christian Observer,† "that the severe illness with which Dr .Buchanan has recently been visited had either deprived the church of his valuable life, or reduced him to an incapacity of employing his pen in her service, it would obviously have been difficult, if not impossible, to have effectually defended him from this assault. But while the pressure of disease confined him to his couch, and almost denied his tongue its office, the use of a hand was spared to him, and his mind retained its more than youthful vigour. In a few days his reply to Mr. Buller was in the hands of every member of the House of Commons; and it may be considered as no unfair presumption that the reply was complete and satisfactory, that in the parliamentary discussions which afterwards took place, not the most distant allusion was made to the letter of Mr. Buller, by any of his friends, although it cannot be doubted that, when first produced, it was intended to serve important purposes in debate. We do not deny that we may be fairly suspected of feelings of partiality towards Dr. Buchanan. Our cordial respect for his character, and our gratitude for the important services he has rendered to the christian cause, may very possibly give a bias to our sentiments in his favour. We think, however, that had we been mistaken in attributing to his reply correctness of statement and solidity of reasoning, we should ere this have heard that, either in Parliament or out of it, some one of those Anglo-Indians, who have been accustomed never to pronounce his name without some expression of vituperation, would have accepted the challenge of his

---

* If Dr. Buchanan's representations of this point needed any support, we might resort to the coincident and unconscious testimony of the Danish missionaries, particularly that of Mr. Hutteman, which is contained in the Report of the Society for Promoting Christian Knowledge for the year 1762.

†Review of Buchanan's Apology for Christianity in India, vol. xii. p. 648.

friends, and have descended from the convenient but impotent generality of hard names, to the specification of some particular misstatements of fact."

As soon as Dr. Buchanan's reply to Mr. Buller's letter had thus produced its intended effect in the House of Commons, he prepared to publish it, together with some other documents, to the world. It accordingly appeared in the course of the summer under the following title: "An Apology for Promoting Christianity in India: containing two Letters, addressed to the Honourable East India Company, concerning the Idol Juggernaut; and a Memorial presented to the Bengal Government in 1807, in defence of the Christian Missions in India. Printed by order of the Honourable the House of Commons. To which are now added, Remarks on the Letter addressed by the Bengal government to the Court of Directors in reply to the Memorial. With an Appendix, containing various official papers, chiefly extracted from the Parliamentary Records relating to the Promulgation of Christianity in India."

This valuable and interesting volume is so well known, and is still so accessible, that it would be unnecessary to do more in this place than refer those who may be desirous of investigating the important subjects of which it treats, to the perusal of its various contents. Two passages, however, deserve to be extracted. One is from the close of the first letter to the Court of Directors; and is worthy, as it has been justly observed, of so distinguished a combatant in this field of sacred warfare.

The annual waste of human life, from the causes that have been mentioned, in the territories under the dominion of the Honourable the East India Company, is a subject of appalling contemplation. Every friend of humanity must be often putting the question, Is this scene to continue for ever? Can there be no amelioration of human existence in India? Are there no means of mitigating the anguish of reflection in England, when we consider that the desolations of Juggernaut exist under our government? Yes, we answer, there are means. We have seen with what avidity the Holy Scriptures are received by the pilgrims. These pilgrims come from every part of India; some from Cabul, a distance of sixteen hundred miles, and some from Samarchand. They are the representatives of a population amounting, as we have seen, to 'two hundred millions.' They are of every caste, and many of them of no caste at all. The Bible is by the inscrutable providence of God at hand: it has been translated into the languages of India. Would it not then be worthy of the East India Company to order ten thousand copies to be distributed annually at Juggernaut, in any manner that prudence would justify and experience direct, as a sacred return for the revenue we derive from it, if it should be thought right that that revenue should still be continued? The Scriptures would thus be carried to the extremities of India and the East. Is it possible that the shadow of an objection should arise against such a measure, innoxious, as it is humane and heavenly, in its tendency? Are we afraid that 'the wretches who come to lay their bones within the precincts of Juggernaut' would mutiny and take away our dominion? Would not the consequence be, rather, that 'the blessing of Him that was ready to perish' would rest upon you?"

The other passage which it may be right to quote from the volume in question, is the following general defence by Dr. Buchanan of his Memorial to Lord Minto, with which the Bengal government was so much offended, and which did not escape the more gentle reprehension of the Court of Directors.

"Of the accuracy of the facts stated in the memorial, I think there can be little doubt. I challenged inquiry before I left Calcutta; but the government did not think it necessary to investigate them. They wrote their letter to the Court of Directors while I was yet on the spot without communicating their sentiments to me in any manner, although I was on terms of personal civility with every member of the administration; and they sent the letter home without my knowledge by the same fleet which conveyed myself. Nor did I ever see it, until it was recently printed by order of the Honourable the House of Commons.

"The second remark I would make refers to the charge of 'disrespect' which is preferred against me, in the letter alluded to, for addressing government at all on the subject; and to which they frequently revert with lively sensibility. I am not at all anxious about self-justification in this matter, except as the honour of religion may be concerned; and I hope little personal feeling will be visible in these remarks. But in regard to the charge in question I only request that the Bengal government will look back to the transaction, and survey the *nature* of the subject and the circumstances in which I stood. Let them say whether I had any personal interest in the cause at issue. Did I address government for my own advantage? Was it to recommend myself to the favour of the Court of Directors when I returned home? No. It was not my own cause, but that of revealed religion, which I maintained. Christianity had been dishonoured. Its teachers were oppressed and silenced; and there was nobody to appear for the truth. I stood for a moment the representative of 'Him who is higher than the highest.' And is this to be denominated disrespect; especially when the words of my address are perfectly respectful? I think that, in the judgment of candour and of enlightened minds, it will be thought that I barely did my duty. The public voice in the settlement of Calcutta was certainly in my favour; for the proceedings against the missionaries were very generally condemned."

It will now be necessary to return to the more private history of Dr. Buhanan, and for this purpose to recur to his letters to various friends. The following extracts are partly of a general nature, and partly refer to the subjects which have been lately discussed.

"*To Colonel Sandys.*

"KIRBY HALL, July 29, 1813.

"Many thanks to you for your letter. The last eleven years have indeed been eventful to you and me; and it is possible that the next eleven (whether in heaven or earth) will be equally marvellous. My health, concerning which you inquire, continues, we hope, to amend; but it will be long before I obtain much strength, even if there should be no relapse of paralysis, which can only be known to Him who said to the sick of the palsy, 'Thy sins be forgiven thee.' If I am able, I must go up to town about the end of autumn or the year, to superintend the publication of some Syriac works which I have commenced, viz. New Testament, Grammar, and Lexicon.

"Since Mrs. Buchanan's death I have enjoyed more distinct views of the heavenly state than I had before; and have attained to more emphasis in prayer. So far, that event has been blessed to me. May the fruits of righteousness grow and increase to the end, even as they do with you and the faithful children of God in every place.

"I rejoice to hear that you and your family are well. As for the spiritual state of those you love, that must be for the trial of your faith and hope, even unto the end. 'Remember David and all his trouble.' Children seldom show signs of grace until they grow up. David had one hopeful son, Solomon; and he became an idolater. What may have been his end is not well known. But I think the Preacher became a monument of grace.

"I am not surprised that Lord ——— was *sick* when you addressed a letter to him on Christian subjects. He is as remote from the right way as poor ——— and ———. And yet even these may be converted by Him who made the world, before they die."

"*To Z. Macaulay, Esq.*

"KIRBY HALL, August.

"I thank you for your letter of the 2d inst., and was much pleased with your favourable account of Mr. G.'s exertions in the christian cause. He gave me the persual of his admirable book a few days before I went to India; and I know not whether it did not lay some foundation in my mind for future investigations.

"I approve most highly of your patronizing Dr. John's plans of native schools. They are properly Mr. Swartz's plans. See the defence of them in the last Church Missionary Register. I visited some of the schools, patronized by government, and witnessed their operation. They may be justly termed 'Mediate Schools' for christianizing the Hindoos, though their effects be not immediate. I had the same plan in view in proposing the numerous schools attached to the Ecclesiastical Establishment in my last work."

"KIRBY HALL, August 20.

"I only received copies of the 'Apology' yesterday. The editorial part reflects great credit on your attention; and the various improvements which I mark in many places demonstrate your kindness to me, and affection for the cause in which I have been engaged.

"The battle is now, I hope, over; and I would gladly forget all that is past, and turn my face Zionward for the rest of my pilgrimage.

"Neither Sir Henry Montgomery nor Mr. L. has condescended (as the Scotch say) on a single instance of mistatement in my volumes. As to what Mr. L. has alleged which Mr. Smith should consider not *defensible*, I have not the smallest idea; unless it be, as Horne Tooke says, 'eating little children alive without being roasted.'"

"KIRBY HALL, 8th September.

"The strange circumstance of *your* being at a watering-place, doing nothing but bathing, mounting hills, and looking down on the tumult below, induces me to write you a few lines in the style of Pope, that is about nothing. What labours of mind that man Pope achieved in doing nothing! And yet he thought he did something. But Horace did as much as he. Johnson flattered himself he did a little more for virtue and the chief good than the other two. But, alas! he, like they, 'knew not the way to the city; and in vain attempted to show it to others. But I am likely to fail in writing a letter in the style of Pope, and shall therefore approximate a little to business.

"I had a letter from ——— lately, accompanying a present of his book on India. He had been reading my Apology, and says he thinks my two letters to the Court of Directors, particularly the second, and my remarks on the letter of the Governor General in Council, 'are the best of my controversial pieces.' He adds, 'I am the more glad of this, because it is an evidence that your long course of illness has not affected your mental powers, whilst it may have invigorated qualities of a still more important kind.' It is certain, however, that I have suffered from my illness. *Non sum qualis eram.* Would that this were true in the other sense to which he alludes! He further says, 'Something seems yet wanting to expose to the public the irreligious spirit which has animated the Anglo-Indians in the whole of this question of introducing christianity into the East.'

"I have answered, that I would not be an assailant any more. I seek peace and an oblivion of past scenes; and have suggested that he himself might probably have leisure now to send forth a few pages on that subject.

"——— mentions that one of the Directors, 'who is now removed to another world,' was a violent enemy of mine. I do not know what is his name; and so little have I been in the habit of inquiring what is passing abroad, that I did not know I had such a thing as a personal enemy in the world."

The two next letters were addressed to Colonel Macaulay; and while they manifest the lively interest which the writer continued to feel in the great work of diffusing Christian knowledge, it will be a subject of regret that the voyage in question was not accomplished either by himself or his friend.

"Kirby Hall, 24th August, 1813.

"My dear Sir—"I was not a little pleased to hear of your proposed voyage to the Mediterranean, both on account of your own health, and of the advantage which I doubt not will accrue to the christian public. You will have opportunities of learning how far, and to what extent, the distribution of the Bible may be practicable, and what other steps we may take in regard to the translation of the scriptures and of tracts, and to the disposition of missionaries in those regions. It is wonderful that the places consecrated by the travels and labours of the Apostle Paul, should be yet left in darkness, unexplored. If your health improve under that genial climate, I do not wish to see you home again.

"My own health continues to amend. It is now seven weeks since I lost blood, the longest interval since my first illness.

"Lord and Lady L——— and family are now with me. They are the zealous promoters of religious institutions in Ireland, and are returning provided with new books, tracts, and arguments. They consider five at least of their bishops as being enrolled in the cause. I have petitioned for two of them to countenance the Homily Society.

"If I should have no return of illness, I have thoughts of going up to town about the end of autumn, and propose in that case to call at Mr. Babington's and Mr. Kempthorne's in my way. But by that time I presume you will be upon the foamy deep. Wherever you are, I pray that a blessing may be upon you till the end of your pilgrimage; and remain,

"My dear sir, very sincerely yours, C. BUCHANAN."

"KIRBY HALL, 2d September, 1813.

"My dear Sir.—I have been favoured with your letter, informing me that your voyage to the Mediterranean is just at hand. There are several important objects of research, which the course of your route will enable you probably to attend to; a few of which I shall mention, according to your desire.

"1. We hardly know any thing of the state of Christianity on the African coast, where it flourished in purity in the third and fourth centuries. Hippo, of which Augustine was bishop, was the fountain-head. It is close to Carthage, (where the Christian Council was held,) and Utica, and Tunis; all which places are not much more than one hundred miles from the Sardinian and Sicilian coast. Your message to the Christians will be, that they may have copies of the Scriptures from Malta or England, if they chose to apply for them.

"2. The Jews inhabit almost every town on the African shore. The Hebrew Testament will be soon ready for them.

"3. The island of Cyprus is a grand field for Christian investigation at this era. 'The greater part of the inhabitants are Greek christians. Besides a multitude of Armenians, there are here a great many *Maronites*,' or Syrian christians. This is the account of the Abbe Mariti. He adds, 'The Latins are far from being so numerous, and consist only of Europeans, and the brotherhood of St. Francis, known throughout the Levant under the name of the Fathers of the Holy Land.' There are very few English here; and it is doubtless for this reason that they have neither a church or chapel, nor a minister of their religion. Should they happen to multiply, they will probably endeavour to procure *all these things*. * This is from an Italian priest! I trust you will be able to show us how we may 'procure all these things.'

"You may tell the Greek christians that the Greek Testament is ready for them; and the Syrian christians, that the Syriac Testament will be soon ready for *them*. I go up to London, God willing, to superintend the printing of it, and of a Syriac grammar and lexicon at the same time.

"4. It is said that *two-thirds* of the inhabitants of European Turkey are of the Greek, Syriac, Armenian, and Latin Church. A continual subject of inquiry will therefore be, how many of these denominations respectively live in any particular place, and how many copies of the Greek, Syriac, Armenian, (the Bible Society* has not thought of the Armenian yet,) and Latin copies of the scriptures, including the French and Italian, may be required as a primary supply? Parcels may be sent at a venture.

"5. An accurate enumeration of the *churches* (buildings) is important, throughout every mile of your route, beginning with Lisbon, Cadiz, and Gibraltar. A church is an object of correspondence, if we know only how to address the priest in the language of his place.

"I consider you to be the fittest man in Great Britain to go upon a voyage of christian discovery.

"I hope to avail myself of Mr. and Mrs. Babington's kind invitation, and to stay with them two days in my journey up to London. I cannot say how soon I shall be able to set out. Again I follow you with my best wishes; and remain,

"My dear sir, sincerely yours, C. BUCHANAN."

Dr. Buchanan appears to have left Kirby Hall towards the end of October. One of his first visits was to his friend and relative the Rev. J. Kempthorne, at Claybrook, in Leicestershire; the following account, of which by that gentleman cannot but be interesting to the reader.

"The last time," says Mr. Kempthorne, "that he visited,

* Mariti. vol. i. p. 8.

* Armenian Bibles and Testaments have since been printed by the Theodosian Branch of the Russian Bible Society.

us, which was in his way to Cambridge, I thought him eminently dead to the world, and, as it were, absorbed in heavenly things. His deep domestic afflictions seemed to have been greatly sanctified to him. He appeared to watch for every opportunity of seasoning our ordinary discourse with the salt of religion. When we were speaking of Carey's Atlas, he took occasion to refer, in a solemn and affecting manner, to the map of the heavenly city which St. John has given us in the Revelation. When I spoke of Bonaparte's late astonishing overthrow, he heard it with comparative indifference, and soon adverted to the importance of the conversion of the soul to God, as involving consequences of greater moment than the fall of emperors and the revolution of the greatest states.

"After our family prayer, he with much kindness and wisdom made some observations on my manner of expounding the scripture; and after he left me, he called on a common friend, and faithfully expressed his fears respecting the safety of his spiritual state.

"Yet I have heard a piously disposed person, who saw more of his domestic habits, regret that his conversation, which was highly edifying when he was called forth by pious visitors, was not more frequently and decidedly spiritual in his own family circle.

"With what exquisite sensibility of conscience does he himself lament this in his private reflections after his second wife's most distressing removal from him."

On the 3d of November, Dr. Buchanan wrote to one of his friends from Cambridge as follows: The remark in this letter respecting a motto which he had assumed, shows his readiness to receive any suggestion respecting his conduct, even on slight and unimportant matters.

"I have been favoured with your kind letter. I had heard of the ninth babe at Rothley. May the dew of God's blessing descend on your increasing family, and make you all heirs of glory!

"As soon as I had read your observations on the motto I sent for a carriage-painter, and erased it. We have had it nearly four years, and I never heard a word concerning its peculiarity.

"I have experienced very general and more than ordinary civilities from the members of the University, particularly from the Bishop of Bristol. His lordship introduced me to his family, as the man from whose books he and they had derived much instruction. He and Lord Hardwicke were sitting together at Trinity Lodge when I called, reading my letter to the

Court of Directors respecting Mr. Buller, not knowing that the Apology had been published since. It seems the book has been so little advertised that Dr. Jowett had not heard of it till the review in the last Christian Observer appeared. There is not a single copy of it, or of the Colonial Establishment, at a bookseller's in Cambridge. The bishop and his friends partake of the spirit which animates you concerning Juggernaut.

"I expect to be in London soon, when I hope to have the pleasure of seeing you. Your last letter proves that you are as desirous I should be without spot as yourself."

Dr. Buchanan appears to have stayed about ten days at Cambridge, and then to have proceeded to London, where he was chiefly occupied in his preparations for the Syriac New Testament. During his stay in town, he wrote the following letter to his daughters:

"22d Nov., 1813.

"My dear Charlotte and Augusta,—I return you many thanks for your letter. I am happy to hear thet you are both in good health; and I doubt not you are both making a due proficiency in your studies.

"I am very much pleased, Charlotte, with your proposal to give five shillings to the West Indian Mission, which I shall do when I find the treasurer of the society.

"I sympathize with you, Augusta, on the death of the pretty bird, Cherry. But our grief is in vain. Its spirit will never return. But when Augusta's spirit takes the wing, it will live for ever; and those who loved her on earth will once more love her in heaven, if she and they prove worthy of eternal life. Cherry, its seems, was singing a few minutes before its death. So, oftentimes, does the christian sing and exult in spirit at the thought of putting off the veil of flesh, and entering on the confines of immortality. May you and Charlotte, after you have accomplished God's will on earth, be enabled to sing your dying hymns!

"I may probably send your work-boxes, together with your Virgils, by the coach to Borobridge, before I return myself.

"Remember me kindly to Augusta; and believe me to be, my dear Charlotte, your affectionate father,

"C. Buchanan."

In December Dr. Buchanan returned to Cambridge, where he was diligently employed, not only in the learned work which he had undertaken, but in preparing an address, the occasion of which will be shortly stated. Of this, and, as it proved, his last visit to the University, his friend Colonel Sandys, who came from Cornwall to meet him, gives the following brief but edifying account:

——— "I found my friend the most interesting christian, while residing in the tower of Erasmus, at Queen's College, the winter before last; where I passed my evenings with him while busily employed on the Syric version.

"Here the learned divine was, as it were, absorbed in the humble follower of the Lord Jesus Christ; and here he disclosed to me those views of his faith which I found beneficial to my own soul. His whole dependence was upon Christ, for wisdom, righteousness, sanctification and redemption!"

The Dean of Carlisle, speaking of the same period, thus observes:

"I saw a good deal of him during the last months of his residence at Queen's College; at which time his constitution appeared to have suffered exceedingly, yet not so much as to induce one to predict a speedy dissolution.

"He was to the very last most indefatigable in his inquiries after eastern knowledge.

"You know how very entertaining and instructive he has made the printed reports of his travels and interviews with extraordinary persons: I had the good fortune to hear many of the same things from his own mouth."

From Cambridge Dr. Buchanan wrote to his eldest daughter as follows:

"Queen's College, 31st Dec., 1813.

"My dear Charlotte,—I am extremely concerned to hear of this accident to Mrs. Thompson, and accompanied with pain too. Tell her I truly sympathize with her. But, when we consider it in another point of view, we must not call it an *accident*, which you know means literally that which falls out by chance, for nothing comes from God by chance. We must view it as an evil permitted for some great good. I am pleased to see your assiduity during her confinement. I am also pleased, my dear Charlotte, that you have presented yourself at the table of the Lord. Your emotion on that occasion was very natural. I trust you will henceforward reap the spiritual fruits, and proceed in the way of the Lord rejoicing.

"I beg you will present to your grand-papa and grand-mamma, Augusta, and all the family, my affectionate congratulations on the new year.

"I pray that it may be a year of temporal and spiritual blessing to you all.

"I do not go forth to visit yet, as the charge I am composing is not finished. I must send it to London on Tuesday next.

"I fully enter into your feelings on your first alarm lest Mrs. T. should have been taken from you. But you see she is yet spared to you; for although you are not her natural daughter, I hope you maintain and pray for a higher relation. There is noting durable and eternal but that union which is from Christ. Friendship, or relationship by blood, except growing on this foundation, will soon die.

"I remain, my dear Charlotte, your affectionate father,

"C. BUCHANAN."

The employment which divided the time and attention of Dr. Buchanan with Syriac, during his residence at Cambridge, was the composition of a charge to be delivered, at the request of the Church Mission Society, to the Rev. Messrs. Greenwood and Norton, clergymen of the Established Church, proceeding as missionaries to the island of Ceylon; and to the Rev. Messrs. Schnarré and Rhenius, ministers of the German Lutheran Church, proceeding in the same sacred character to the coast of Coromandel.

The readiness with which the Court of Directors of the East India Company granted the requisite license to these pious men to proceed to the objects of their destination, was a proof of the benefits resulting from the late solemn legislative recognition of the duty of Great Britain with respect to the diffusion of christianity in its eastern empire; and the selection of Dr. Buchanan to address these oriental missionaries was equally judicious and appropriate.

The rapidity with which this admirable charge to them was composed, and the various information and important advice which it contained, proved the vigour of its author's understanding and judgment; while the pure and fervent piety which breathes in every page, manifests the maturity of the advanced christian.

The charge itself comprises an exposition of that with which our Lord sent forth his apostles to preach the gospel. It forms, in fact, a manual of sound wisdom and instruction; and deserves to be frequently perused and thoroughly digested by every one who aspires to the character and office of a missionary. Like the former productions of Dr. Buchanan, this address contains much important and interesting information; and, though primarily intended for the missionary, may be read with much advantage by every minister of the gospel, and by every private christian. The following extracts will afford a brief specimen of the spirit and tendency of the whole.

Speaking of the periodical accounts which the missionaries would be expected to give of their labours, Dr. Buchanan introduced the following important caution:

"Let every page which you write be consecrated by sacred truth. Beware of that powerful self-deception whose operation is sometimes commensurate with a man's zeal for his object, which leads him to deceive for God's sake, and to do partial evil, under the hope and plea that great good may come. If you would keep at a remote distance from such a temptation, avoid amplification and embellishment in what makes for the credit and honour of your personal labours, or of those of your fellow missionaries. Like great generals, who recount their victories in few words, let a modesty of description characterize your spiritual trophies."

After pointing out, in a faithful and striking manner, the various ways in which a minister, whether at home or abroad, may deny Christ, Dr. Buchanan thus continued:

"My brethren, you may preach to the Hindoos, and say, 'Repent, and be converted;' while, at the same time, indolence, or avarice, or sensual passion, seizes your own souls, and you are quite indifferent about their repentance or conversion, except as it adds to your own interest, or the fame of your mission.

"Some who have preceded you, and have been solemnly designated to the sacred work, have fallen away. They declined from sound doctrine, or they were seduced from pureness of living; and, instead of doing the work of an evangelist, they have lived an useless burthen on the society which supported them.

"I mention these things to warn you. But I have more pleasure in directing your view to other servants of Christ, whose bright example has illumined the East; who have been patterns of faith, diligence, prudence, and fortitude. From the ministers of the two churches to which you respectively belong, I shall select two illustrious characters, who have left a great example for them that follow. I mean the venerable Swartz, of the Lutheran Church, and the late Rev. David Brown, of the Church of England. These men did not deny Christ. They did not love father or mother more than Christ. They took up their cross and followed Christ. If you knew, as well as I do, the conflicts which they were called upon to sustain in the East, you would see how fitly the words of our Lord might be applied to them, 'Behold, I send you forth as lambs among wolves. But beware of men.' If you knew, again, the conjoined wisdom and innocence which they manifested in these conflicts, you would acknowledge that they studied to obey our Lord's admonition, 'Be ye wise as serpents, and harmless as doves.' The character of both was marked by an extraordinary liberality of sentiment in regard to the differences in religious profession; a liberality which others, in a confined sphere, could not well understand. In a word, they endured unto the end; and both of them were enabled to glorify God in their deaths, by the manifestation of a joyful hope in the view of their dissolution.

"I have thought that this short record of these good men would find find a proper place in an address to young ministers who are in your circumstances. 'Be ye also followers of them, who, through faith and patience, have inherited the promises!'"

The appendix to this excellent charge contains some notices of the last hours of his late valued friend and colleague, Mr. Brown, which serve to illustrate the heavenly and devoted mind of that excellent man.

The health of Dr. Buchanan rendering it impracticable for him to deliver his charge to the missionaries personally, that office was assigned to an eloquent friend, who did ample justice to the composition. On the 7th of January it was accordingly addressed to them before a general meeting of the Church Mission Society, and was heard with a degree of attention and interest which appeared to promise the happiest effects from its author's exertions.

It is to the circumstances which have been just related, that some parts of the following extracts to Colonel and Mr. Macaulay refer:

"Queen's College, 3d Jan., 1814.

"I have sent by to-night's mail, to Mr. Pratt, thirty-three pages of a charge to be delivered to the missionaries on Friday next. As I am quite unfit to go up myself, I have requested Mr. Dealtry to read the paper for me. He may select such parts as he thinks best for the occasion.

"Dr. Milner approves of the passage upon 'denying Christ;' but I do not know what others may think of it."

"Queen's College, 7th January.

"The Bishop of Chester has expressed his wish that I would retain the curacy of Great Ouseburn, which I was about to resign, under the impression that I could not conscientiously accept a license (under the new act) as a resident curate, when it was notorious that I am not resident. But the bishop is persuaded that the duties of the parish will be performed to his entire satisfaction by myself or by my direction. His diocese extends to our parish.

"I inhabit Erasmus' rooms. They are chiefly remarkable for an immense *corkscrew*, about a third of a yard long, which tradition assigns to that eminent scholar."

"QUEEN'S COLLEGE, 13th January.

"My dear Sir,—Many thanks for your letter. It is most satisfactory. I have constructed the note as you desired, without names or places. It is now round and smooth, like a perfect chrysolite, and will excite many a smile and many a frown.

"I was smiling to think what a fine long letter I drew from you. I see you can work, if we will only tell you what to do.

"I entirely approve of your flitting to southern regions this severe weather. I cannot look out at the window on the dreary waste of snow, but I think I see Bonaparte and his squadrons, half covered, retreating towards Gogmagog hills. The thermometer is at 12.

"Wishing you good fires, and every blessing, I remain, my dear sir, very sincerely yours, C. BUCHANAN."

"QUEEN'S COLLEGE, 13th January.

"It was indeed somewhat new to hear strains of commendation from the lips of Mr. T. in public. The whole assembly seem to have been in good humour. The view of the four missionaries, perhaps, melted their hearts; and the news of the allies crossing the Rhine had just arrived. Mr. Farnish says he enjoyed the occasion exceedingly.

"I consulted the college to day concerning the proposed admission of Mr. Lee, the Shrewsbury linguist. It was agreed to admit him at Queen's."

"QUEEN'S COLLEGE, 7th February.

"I see in the last Christian Observer that Schaaf's Lexicon is mentioned as preparing for the press by subscription. Will you be so good as to inform me who is publishing it? for I was about commencing the work at my own expense, and the printer had just sent me an estimate. But I shall be most happy if the work has been undertaken by another. Mr. Kelly, of Dublin, wrote to me last week to say that he was projecting something in the way of a Syriac lexicon; but he wished me not to delay my work on account of his, as he knew not when it would be finished.

"I propose to leave Cambridge for Kirby Hall on the 17th instant."

Dr. Duchanan returned into Yorkshire about the time just mentioned, and continued there till the month of July following. While there, he wrote thus to a friend: "I am stronger than I was; but my defect in utterance and breath remains, and also my want of memory; which shows that my illness affected the mind a good deal."

The committee of the British and Foreign Bible Society had now determined to print the edition of the Syriac New Testament, which Dr. Buchanan had been so anxiously endeavouring to obtain for the use of the Syrian christians on the coast of Malabar. With his usual zeal and liberality, he engaged to prepare the text, and superintend the execution of the work, at his own expense. For this purpose he again left Yorkshire, and took up his residence, first at Cheshunt, and afterwards at Wormley, and Broxbourne, in Hertfordshire, at which latter place the printer lived who had undertaken the work. Soon after his arrival, he wrote to Mrs. Thompson as follows:

"TURNFORD HALL, CHESHUNT, HERTS,
23d July, 1814.

"My dear Mrs. T.—I arrived here last Saturday, on which day I wrote you a few lines. Since that time I have been daily employed in superintending the press, and corresponding with the Bible Society, with the syndics of the University Press, Cambridge, and with friends respecting tutors for the two noble families which I lately visited.

"I live with a widow lady and her daughters. They never had boarders before; but, hearing that I wanted accommodation of this kind in the village, they received me. We have morning and evening prayers just as at Skelton Lodge. I have my meals by myself, being willing to husband my voice, in the hope that it will acquire some strength. I walk in the meadows by the side of the river Lee, and endeavour to meditate on things spiritual and eternal. There are few days in which I do not think of Mary, now among the blessed. I envy her happy lot, but yet I have just strength to pray that I may be enabled to serve God in my generation.

"Mr. Yeates is come from London to co-operate with me. It is not decided yet whether one half of my work is to go on at Cambridge or not. They, however, expect me at Queen's

College, and I think it probable I shall go there in about a month, if, indeed, I do not go nearer to London; for Mr. Watts, my printer, has just informed me that he is about to remove his printing establishment to the metropolis.

"I hope to hear that your foot is almost well. Jacob, you know, 'halted' to the day of his death; but then every false step would remind him of his victory with God. And yet this 'prince with God,' would not be comforted when he thought Joseph was dead! How encompassed with infirmity is man, even regenerated man; man, partaker of the divine nature!

"I hope that Charlotte and Augusta are happy and well. Jacob prayed, saying, 'God, which fed me all my life long unto this day, the Angel which redeemed me from evil, bless the lads.' That is a prayer which I would offer up for Charlotte and Augusta. *I* also have been 'redeemed from much evil' during an eventful life; and so have they, hitherto. A boy about Augusta's age is dying near us here. He broke his leg by some imprudent exertion, and the fever induced is likely to prove fatal. His mother sits by him and cannot eat. He belonged to a Sunday school, and desires those hymns to be read to him which speak of Christ's atoning for wicked children. My love to you all. Adieu. C. B."

The pensive tenor of a part of the preceding letter will appear peculiarly interesting, when it is considered that Dr. Buchanan was now fast approaching the confines of that world whither so many of those who were dear to him had gone before. Amongst others, the son of his friend, Colonel Sandys, for whose welfare he had been affectionately concerned, was about this time departing in the faith and hope of the gospel. He thus replied to the intelligence which had announced to him the delightful change in his views and feelings since the time when he had visited him in Yorkshire:

"What wonderful news you relate! Your dear son William speaks of 'the unsearchable riches of Christ,' and magnifies his Saviour in the eyes of men! This is certainly a great triumph of divine grace. However, I anticipated it, as you know; for I was persuaded he would be given to your persevering prayers.

"Be pleased to give him my most affectionate remembrance; and tell him he is about to be ushered into a glory which good men upon earth have been contemplating for many years, but have not yet enjoyed. He has obtained the victory without the battle; for the Captain of his salvation has fought for him.

May his faith be firm and ardent to the last, that he may persevere in and complete his glorious testimony!"

"WORMLEY, HERTS, 5th August, 1814.

"My dear Sir,—I rejoice that you have taken up the Prophecies for the Hindoos. Follow your own judgment and ruminate on your sofa, and you will possibly devise something new. The Hindoos want a short, clear account, a striking picture, solemn assertion, and dogmatic theology.

"'The holy prophet Isaiah, who wrote in poetic strains, lived in such an era. Though ignorant and unlearned persons of India know it not, yet the learned of Europe, who are acquainted with the histories of the world, are as well assured that Isaiah wrote his Prophecy in the times of King Ahaz, &c., as that such a man lived in the time of Gengis Khan, Tamerlane, or Akbar the Great.

'"So of Matthew and his host of witnesses.'

"Short sentences, and no involved construction, will do best for oriental translation and capacity. Let your picture suit a Thames street carman, and it will do for a Hindoo. A tract of ten octavo pages is a good size. But as you cannot easily confine within such small bounds all the fine things that may occur to you on the subject, proceed *ad libitum* to a pamphlet or book, which may be translated for the Brahmins and more learned. But the short tract is the book for use to the multitude. This you may express from the larger work when it is finished, as genuine spirit is drawn from the vat.

"* * * That the evidence of prophecy will convince the human mind is true: but that 'the leaves of the prophet quietly dispersed,' without concomitant illustration of historic argument and fact by preachers or writing, is not true.

"I hope you will not be in a hurry to deliver any thing to the society. Short tracts on other parts of the Old and New Testaments are wanted, so as to embrace the whole code in different striking and simple forms. Nobody has told the Hindoos yet what our Shaster is. They have not got the *whole* book to read. If they had, epitomes are yet necessary for infant and ignorant minds, epitomes of one page, two, three, four, ten, twenty, and fifty pages. The whole Bible will occupy 1400 pages of their ordinary character of writing. It is but charity then to tell them what is in it, and invite their study.

"I am, dear sir, very sincerely yours,

C. BUCHANAN."

"WORMLEY, CHESHUNT, Aug. 17, 1814.

"My dear Sir,—I have come to this place for a while, to superintend the printing of the Syriac works now in the press. I want the following books, which I cannot find in the public library at Cambridge; viz.

"1. Reusch's Syrus Interpres cum fonte N. T. Græci collatus. 1742.

"2. Michaelis's Curæ in Actus Apostolorum Syriacos.

"3. Storrius, on the Syriac Language and Versions.

"4. Michaelis (the father) De Var. Lect. Nov. Test. cautè colligendis.

"5. Gloster Ridley's Dissertatio de Syriacis Versionibus.

"6. Amira's Syriac Grammar; and

"7. Professor Bode's Pseudocritica Millio-Bengeliana. 1767.

"Now if your own library, or if the Oxford Libraries through your means, could supply me with these or some of them, you will confer on me a particular obligation. I have perused some of them at the British Museum, but I cannot have them here.

"I rejoice to hear from time to time of your labours, and of the triumphs of the gospel at the church of St. John's. It is a theatre of grander events than the General Congress.

"My own health is slowly improving, but I am yet wholly incapable of vocal exertion.

"I remain, my dear sir, very sincerely yours,

C. BUCHANAN."

The succeeding extracts from letters to different friends describe the general state of Dr. Buchanan's health, feelings, and employment during the remainder of this year:

"*To Mrs. Thompson.*

"WORMLEY, HERTS, Aug. 2, 1814.

"I have been twice bled, I think, since I wrote, and must, I fear, suffer further depletion. With returning strength my constitution brought with it, what was to be apprehended, a tendency to fulness. And possibly I must soon revert to abstemiousness and the painful seton. But the Lord's disposal is the best for this world and for the next. I seek to do his will.

"*To his Daughters.*

"August 22.

"I am not very sure that I shall be able to execute what I have undertaken by the time proposed. There are three printing presses at work, and I am obliged to read and correct every word in Syriac, Latin, and English."

"*To Colonel Macaulay.*

"WORMLEY, 8th September.

"Two Cochin Jews, who recollect you very well, are in distress for a passage back to India. I would try to aid them if I knew to whom to apply. But I fear the company are not in the habit of giving a passage to persons of their description. You will know better than I what to recommend them to do.

"Since the peace you have been passing through many countries, and doing good. I, on the other hand, have been stationary, travelling slowly through the regions of the New Testament, I congratulate you on your equable health. My own was well confirmed for a while; but it is again in a critical state."

"*To Mrs. Thompson.*

'WORMLEY, September 14.

"I know not God's will. I think less of seeing another autumn than at any former time. If, however, I live, I shall most probably go to Ireland, or to the continent; I mean Paris and Rome. I wish I could have visited both these latter places before I had commenced my present work."

"*To Miss Buchanan.*

"BROXBOURNE, 7th December.

"My dear Charlotte,—Many thanks to you for your letter. I am glad that Augusta's queries have afforded Mr. Graham so fair an opportunity of displaying his classical powers. But the true Virgilian model requires the first words to be *Sic vos non vobis.* Would that poor Virgil could have understood the distich which Mr. G. has written. But, alas! that *divine* poet, as he has been called, never heard of an atonement for the sins of men. He had, however, some confused idea of the coming of a Messiah, or Prince from heaven, who should regenerate an evil world. This you will see in his Polilo, one of the Bucolics; which I will thank you to read as soon as you have finished the sixth book of the Æneid.

"I am happy to hear that you read a little of the sacred language on Sunday. As there is no Italian teacher at present in York, you must postpone your acquaintance with the 'modern Roman' till an opportunity offers.

"I hope you will not leave thorough bass till you understand it *thoroughly*.

"You ask me for Mr. Slater's drawing. I sat to him two mornings, but contrived to have a sheet of Syriac placed in the direction I was to look. He complained that I was thoughtful. I told him of the talent of Sir Joshua Reynolds; who by his fascinating discourse contrived to keep his *patients* (a proper term *I* think for persons subjected to this operation) in a state of high good humour, particularly with *themselves*, which showed itself in their beaming and expanded looks. When Mr. Slater had done, I looked in vain for the beaming and expanded look. Mr. S. accused the Syriac. I told him, I thought the picture was that of an ill-looking man. He said he thought it was *a good likeness*. I only saw it for two minutes, after sitting to it two days. I told him he might send it down to Mrs. Thompson, and he should be at liberty to engrave it, if it obtained *her* approbation. I desired him to send with it, as a present to you and Augusta, a print of Mrs. Hannah More: that you may have before your eyes a lady who made so good an use of her opportunities for study between the fourteenth and seventeenth years of her age, that the world has been benefitted by it ever since.

"Yesterday Mr. B. and Mr. S. spent the whole day with me. Their object was to procure my name as secretary of the Jewish Society. But I had radical objections to the constitution of that society in its present form, and suggested renovation and improvement.

"I should like to be present at the famous duet for *three voices*. I hope I shall be with you shortly after Christmas. I must superintend the printers till the day they break up for their own holidays, which I suppose will be on Christmas day. Besides, I wish to see the four Gospels finished if possible before my long journey.

"I have not seen the Velvet Cushion. The ladies tell me it is a very amusing and instructive work.

"My love to Mrs. T. and Augusta; and I remain, my dear Charlotte, your affectionate father, C. BUCHANAN."

"BROXBOURNE, HERTS, Dec. 17, 1814.

"My dear Sandys,—I thank you for your letter of the 12th, which informs me that you and seven children are well. There are a great many blessings comprehended in that expression.

"I am glad that you have been enabled to write a narrative of the rise and progress of religion in the soul of William.

Under whatever form it eventually appear, I doubt not but it will do good. Particularly among his young relatives in Cornwall, such a record must appear as a solemn witness.

"My health continues much the same. I take a little exercise on horseback, live low, go to bed early, and rise generally to read by candle-light. By such means, under the blessing of God, I am enabled to carry on my present undertaking. But a slight return of indisposition would suspend the whole. I therefore would live a pensioner on God's mercy for the hour.

"A letter from Mr. Udny informs me that Miss. F. died lately, and had peace in death, 'her heart having been long previously weaned from the world.' He speaks with satisfaction of the effect of a work I published two years ago, entitled 'Colonial Ecclesiastical Establishment.'

"I beg to be affectionately remembered to Mrs. S. and to Allan. The purpose of the latter to cultivate his mind by classical knowledge is very gratifying to me.

"I am very affectionately yours, C. BUCHANAN."

"*To Mrs Thompson.*

"BROXBOURNE, Dec. 24.

"My dear Mrs. T.—I write to say that I hope to be with you in the course of the first week of the new year. It is, however, doubtful whether I shall not be detained till the 9th or 10th of January. I shall at all events write before I set off.

"What detains me is the wish to complete the four Gospels before I leave this place, lest I should never return. 'For what is our life?' saith St. James, 'It is even a vapour, that appeareth for a little time, and then vanishes away.'

"I have had another visit from Mr. S. and Mr. L. W. on the subject of the Jewish Society. I proposed that the institution, in whatsoever degree supported by church members, should be exclusively a Church of England Society. I declined, however, pledging myself for its support, further than by offering my best advice. I desired them to communicate their plans and wishes to all good and eminent ministers in the kingdom, to request useful hints and affectionate support, and to do nothing of themselves:—not to call their society, 'for conversion of the Jews:' but a society for the education of Jewish children; for diffusing the New Testament among the Jews; for corresponding with them concerning the Messiah in all lands; and for the diffusion of Jewish literature. Lastly, to connect the institution with the Church Missionary Society, the end being the same.

"I have just received letters from India. Sabat, who had left his christian society, and it was feared would never return, has returned to Calcutta, and is again translating the scriptures. He confessed to Mr. Thomason that he could find no rest for the soles of his feet.

"Mr. T. sends me the third annual Report of the Calcutta Auxiliary Bible Society, which I shall take down with me, if I remember it. My love to all till I see you.

"Your very affectionate son, C. BUCHANAN."

Dr. Buchanan's visit to the north was but of short duration. On the 19th of January, 1815, he returned to Broxbourne; from whence he wrote to Mrs. Thompson as follows:

"My dear Mrs. T.—I could have reached this place yesterday, but I reserved seventeen miles for this morning. I slept on Monday night at Carleton Hall. I travelled about a hundred miles next day in post chaises; and, though it snowed, I was warm and comfortable all the way. My only mishap was losing my diamond pin somewhere, which I have had for ten years. I now use one of those Augusta gave me. Thus we cease to sparkle.

"I found all at home well. One of the letters on my table was from Mr. John Thornton, nephew to Mr. Henry Thornton, informing me of the illness of his uncle, and requesting letters of introduction to his brother going to India.

"Another letter was from Mr. Macaulay, mentioning the increasing illness of Mr. Thornton, and comparing him, after twenty-two years' acquaintance, rather to the character of the saints in the next life, than in this; 'the just man made perfect.'

"I request you will alter any thing in my written or oral instructions to Charlotte and Augusta, according to your discretion. If the verse in the morning appear to be an unfruitful task, it may be discontinued by both.

"My love to them; and believe me to be, my dear Mrs. T., your affectionate son, C. BUCHANAN."

"Thus I have been enabled to accomplish a journey of four hundred miles with health and strength. Bless the Lord, O my soul, for all his goodness. May I only live to his glory!"

A letter to Mr. Macaulay, on the same day on which the preceding was dated, briefly but emphatically notices the fatal termination of Mr. Henry Thornton's illness, and the anxiety of Dr. Buchanan to pay the only tribute of respect which remained to his memory.

"BROXBOURNE, Thursday, 19th Jan.

"My dear Friend,—On my return from Yorkshire this morning, where I have been for a fortnight on a visit to my family, I found your letter of the 11th inst. lying on my table.

"The first intimation I had of Mr. Thornton's illness was on Monday last at Carleton Hall, Workshop. On my arrival here, I found your letter, and one from Mr. John Thornton confirming the painful intelligence. I was just going to sit down to request that he would communicate to his uncle my feelings on the occasion, and my request to go to town to visit him if he had strength to see me, when, casually looking into the paper, I found that he had died on the Tuesday. All I can now do is to attend the funeral of this good man, my earliest and most particular friend and benefactor. I have requested Mr. John Thornton to let me know on what day the funeral takes place. In case of mistake, will you have the goodness to mention to me the time and place, and I shall go out early in the morning, and return in the evening, as my present work will not permit me conveniently to be absent a night

"I desire to thank you most unfeignedly for your kindness to the two Cochin Jews.

"With kindest regards to Mrs. M., I am very affectionately yours, C. BUCHANAN."

On the 22d Dr. Buchanan wrote to Mr. Macaulay as follows:

"My dear Friend,—I have just received your note, and I propose to go on Tuesday morning, so as to be at your house by twelve o'clock, if I should not have joined the procession before that time. I shall be happy to dine with you, and to take a bed at your house, and return next morning after breakfast.

"Yours, ever affectionately, C. BUCHANAN."

It was upon the solemn and affecting occasion thus referred to, that the author of these memoirs met Dr. Buchanan for the last time. A crowd of other friends, distinguished by their talents, rank, and piety, united in lamenting the loss of the eminent person around whose tomb they were assembled. Amidst that mourning throng, it will readily be believed by those who recollect his obligations to Mr. Thornton, as well as his just appreciation of the various excellencies of his revered friend, that no one shed more sincere tears over his grave than

Dr. Buchanan. Doubtless he then felt, as he seemed to feel, in common with a multitude of other persons, that another of those ties by which he had been linked to this world was destroyed. The writer of these pages remembers, with sensations of melancholy yet pleasing regret, the peculiarly holy and heavenly strain of conversation with which Dr. Buchanan cheered and edified his friends on the evening of that mournful day, and on the morning of his return into Hertfordshire; little thinking that it would be the last opportunity of their enjoying that privilege.

Of this short and affecting visit to Clapham, the following interesting anecdote has been communicated by a friend at whose house Dr. Buchanan took up his abode:

"He was relating to me," observes this gentleman, "as we walked together from the church-yard where we had deposited the mortal remains of Henry Thornton, the course he was pursuing with respect to the printing of the Syriac Testament. He stated that his solicitude to render it correct had led him to adopt a plan of revision which required him to read each sheet five times over before it went finally to the printer. The particulars of the plan I do not very distinctly remember. It was, however, something of this kind: He first prepared the sheets for the press. When the proof was sent, he read it over attentively, instituting a comparison with the original, and looking into the various readings, &c. A revise was sent him, which he carefully examined, making corrections. This was submitted to Mr. Yeates. When it came from him he read it again, adopting such of his suggestions as he thought right. When the printer had made the requisite correction he sent a fresh revise, after being read, to Mr. Lee, and reperused it when it came from him. A third revise was then procured, which he again examined before it was finally committed to the press. I do not know that I am precisely accurate in this statement, but it was something of the above description.

"While giving me this detail he stopped suddenly, and burst in tears. I was somewhat alarmed. When he had recovered himself he said, 'Do not be alarmed. I am not ill; but I was completely overcome with the recollection of the delight which I had enjoyed in this exercise. At first I was disposed to shrink from the task as irksome, and apprehended that I should find even the scriptures pall by the frequency of this critical examination. But so far from it, every fresh perusal seemed to throw fresh light on the word of God, and to convey additional joy and consolation to my mind.'"

How delightful is the contemplation of a servant of Christ

thus devoutly engaged in his heavenly Master's work, almost to the very moment of his transition to the divine source of light and truth itself!

The pious and elevated frame of Dr. Buchanan's mind is evident from another incident which occurred at this time.

In passing through London on his return to Broxbourne, he spent a few hours with a friend whom he had met upon the solemn occasion of the preceding day. In the course of their conversation, his friend observed, how affecting was the consideration of the removal of so many great and good men, whom they had lately had occasion to lament, in the prime of life and in the midst of their usefulness. To this observation Dr. Buchanan replied, "So long as they were still on earth, and the divine will was not known, it was our duty fervently to pray for their recovery and lengthened life; but, when once that will has been discovered by the event, we should rejoice and praise God that he has received them to himself, and hasten to follow them to his heavenly kingdom." It was not long before he himself afforded another illustration of this remark; which, though not unfrequently made, was peculiarly characteristic of that spirit of calm and habitual submission to the will of God, and of lively faith in the realities of an eternal world, by which he was distinguished.

The extreme severity of the weather had excited some apprehensions in the minds of many as to the probable effect of Dr. Buchanan's exposure to it during some hours of the preceding day. He did not, however, appear at the time to have suffered by it, and reached Broxbourne on the 25th of January in safety.

On the first of February he wrote to Mrs. Thompson, informing her of the solemn scene at which he had lately been present, describing the numerous and respectful attendance at the funeral of Mr. Thornton, and expressing his earnest desire to follow him to the same blessed inheritance.

This was the last communication of Dr. Buchanan to his distant friends. The time of his departure was now fast approaching. He continued, however, his christian undertaking to the last. On his return from Yorkshire, he had proceeded with the preparation of the Syriac version of the Acts of the Apostles, and had advanced, on the day preceding his death, to the twentieth chapter; in which the zealous and affectionate apostle, in his address to the elders of Ephesus, expresses his conviction of his final separation from his friends in these remarkable words: "And now, behold, I know that ye all, among whom I have gone preaching the kingdom of God, shall see my face no more." The chapter which thus closed the labours of Dr. Buchanan, and in which he seemed to bid farewell to every earthly association, was but too prophetic of the event which was about so shortly to take place. Of his few remaining days, and of his sudden removal to that higher world, for which he had long been ripening, the following letter to the Rev. Mr. Kempthorne, from his confidential servant, who was his only attendant in Hertfordshire, though unavoidably inadequate to the anxious wishes of his friends, affords a minute and faithful account.

"Broxbourne, 12th Feb. 1815.

"Rev. Sir,—In case of your not having been made acquainted, through the public papers, of the decease of my dear master, Dr. Buchanan, I feel it my duty to write to you on the subject.

"The doctor's state of health, as you may have understood, had improved during his residence here, up to the time of his late visit to Yorkshire; but the fatigue of that journey, probably added to an attendance, in a week after his return, in bad weather, at the funeral of Mr. Henry Thornton, brought on an apparently slight indisposition, which the doctor himself, I believe, considered merely a cold. On Thursday last, however, while making a morning's call on some of the neighbours, he was taken with something of a fainting fit, which passed off without his considering it of consequence enough to require medical assistance. As the sickness came on again towards evening, I took the liberty to disobey my master's orders, and to send for the medical gentleman whose skill had so much appeared in the improvement of the doctor's health in the preceding months. This gentleman was with him about nine o'clock in the evening, and did not express any apprehension of danger. Dr. Buchanan retired a little past ten, saying he was better; and, as he expected to get a little sleep, wished me not to disturb him to take the second medicine till he rung the bell. About half-past eleven, sitting on the watch for the summons, I fancied I heard something of an hiccough; which induced me, contrary to orders, to enter the chamber, and to inquire if he was worse. He signified he *was* worse. On which I instantly alarmed the family, and sent for assistance; and then returned to the bedside, where my master appeared labouring under a spasm in the breast. He intimated a wish for me to hold his head; and in this posture, without struggle or convulsion, his breath appeared to leave him; so that before twelve, by which time Mr. Watts, the printer, Mr. Yeates, and a few other neighbours, were with me, we were obliged to conclude that our excellent friend's spirit had joined the glorified saints above. I should have mentioned that, on returning home in the morning after the fit, Dr. Buchanan seemed lame on the left side; but, as it went off, he did not think it of any consequence. I have reason to think it might be a third attack of paralysis. The medical man, on his coming after my master's dissolution, said it did not surprise him. A letter was immediately forwarded, by express, to communicate the melancholy intelligence to my master's family in Yorkshire; from whence some one is hourly expected. Mr. Macaulay was also written to; and Mr. Simeon at Cambridge. On Saturday Mr. Babington, the member for Leicester, came down, and approved of the precaution and arrangements taken immediately after the departure of my master; both as to putting seals on the drawers, study, &c. &c.

"With the greatest respect, I beg to subscribe myself, Rev. Sir, your most obedient faithful servant, T. VAUX."

Such was the sudden summons by which, on the 9th of February, 1815, in the 49th year of his age, this eminent servant of God was called to his heavenly rest. To himself it could scarcely be said to have been unexpected. The debilitated constitution which he brought with him from India, and the repeated shocks it had subsequently sustained, led him habitually to regard his continuance in life as extremely uncertain and precarious; while his various afflictions, personal and domestic, had tended to withdraw his thoughts and affections from the world, and to fix them on spiritual and eternal objects. We have seen that in fulfilling the important engagement which terminated his earthly course, he evidently appeared to be working while it was called "to-day," and to be constantly anticipating the near approach of "the night," in which he could no longer work. Of his habitual preparation for the hour of his departure, no one can entertain a doubt, who has marked the scriptural foundation of his faith, and the unquestionable evidences of its sincerity, in the long and uniform tenor of his truly christian career. It might, perhaps, have been desirable, both for himself and for others, that some interval, however short, had been vouchsafed; in which this "good and faithful servant" of his Lord might have had an opportunity of renewing his repentance, of testifying his faith, of perfecting his patience, of purifying and exalting his charity, of bidding a more solemn and express farewell to "things seen and temporal," of preparing more deliberately and devoutly for an immediate entrance upon "things unseen and eternal."* Such an interval, however, so precious to the generality of mankind, and usually so important, the divine wisdom did not see fit to grant to the subject of these memoirs. Neither, indeed, can it be said to have been necessary. The readers of the preceding narrative have already observed Dr. Buchanan in India, upon what he strongly, though erroneously, believed would prove his death-bed; and they have witnessed the deeply penitent, yet resigned and peaceful frame of mind which he then exhibited. Such, as we are evidently authorized to conclude, only of a mature and heavenly nature, would have been his testimony and his feelings, had he been allowed again to express them. In the absence, however, of any such opportunity, we must be contented to recur to that scene; and, together with the recollection of his subsequent "work of faith, and labour of love, and patience of hope," endeavour to enter into the full meaning of the following brief sentence, which occurs amidst a few other "private thoughts," and in which its author appears plainly to have anticipated the probability of some final stroke, which should impede the exercise of his faculties, and prove the prelude to his departure. "If," said he, "my mind and memory should be affected by illness of body, I shall look to my head, Christ. I am but a member." From any painful infliction of this kind Dr. Buchanan was mercifully spared, and, after having paid the last sad tribute of affection to the friend and benefactor of his early years, was removed almost contemporaneously and reunited to him, and to other kindred spirits of the "just made perfect," in regions where sickness and sorrow, change and separation, are for ever unknown.

In consequence of a wish he had expressed to Mrs. Thompson, not long before his death, the remains of Dr. Buchanan were removed from Broxbourne to Little Ouseburn, in Yorkshire, and deposited near those of his second lamented wife. A monumental inscription, written by the Rev. W. Richardson, of York, records in plain but expressive language the leading particulars of his life and character.†

It may, perhaps, be expected that a more definite and comprehensive review should be given of both at the close of these memoirs. The length, however, to which they have been already extended, and the distinctness with which the events of Dr.

* See the exquisite defence, by the pious and learned Hooker, of the petition in the Litany against "sudden death." Ecclesiastical Polity, vol. ii. p. 175.

† See the end of the volume.

Buchanan's life and the features of his character have been marked, will only require such a general recapitulation as may assist the reader in forming a correct judgment of the whole.

In reviewing the history of Dr. Buchanan, our attention must be first directed to his religious character. It was this which originally introduced him to our notice, and by this he was principally distinguished throughout his benevolent and useful career. The deep and solemn impression of religion, which, through the grace of God, was made upon his mind in his twenty-fourth year, formed the commencement of a life devoted to the service of Christ. We have traced the effects of this great spiritual change in the course of his studies at the University of Cambridge, during his various labours in India, and his continued exertions after his return to this country. Amidst these diversified scenes and engagements, an energetic conviction of the infinite importance and value of the gospel, and a lively sense of his own obligations to that grace which had made him effectually acquainted with its blessings, were the commanding principles which actuated his conduct.

Those who know little of real christianity may, perhaps, attribute his earnestness and activity in religion, as they would that of the great apostle himself, to enthusiasm, zeal for proselytism, or the love of fame. But the whole tenor of this narrative sufficiently proves that no corrupt, weak, or worldly motives swayed his mind. The great object to which he devoted his life, engaged him in an unceasing contest with the principles and the prejudices of those whom a regard to his worldly interest would have led him carefully to conciliate; and, though his benevolent exertions undoubtedly procured him many valuable friends, few men of such sober and practical views, and of such genuine philanthropy, have gone through a greater variety of "evil" as well as of "good report." With still less justice can the activity of Dr. Buchanan in the great labour of his life be ascribed to a controversial or innovating spirit. He was, on the contrary, disposed, both by constitution and principle, to avoid rather than court opposition; while, during several years the languor of declining health was continually urging him to self-indulgence and repose.

Amidst such powerful inducements to a very different line of conduct, it is scarcely possible not to percieve that Dr. Buchanan could only have been actuated by pure and disinterested motives. The love of Christ and of the souls of men, and a fervent desire to be the instrument of imparting to others that unspeakable blessing which he had himself received, were in reality the springs both of his public and private exertions.

These were the principles by which he was animated, and which supported him with equanimity and patience amidst labour and reproach, infirmity and sorrow, and even rendered him joyful in tribulation.

Combined with these motives, Dr. Buchanan possessed a spirit of lively and vigorous faith, which substantiated "things not seen," and led him to think and act under a strong impression of their truth and reality. He was therefore eminently a practical man. Though inclined by natural taste, and the habits of a learned and scientific education, to indulge in speculative pursuits and pleasures, the strength of his faith, and the ardour of his love towards objects of spiritual and eternal concern, rescued him from their fascination, and taught him to account all knowledge, and all occupation, vain and unimportant, compared with that which tended to render himself and others "wise unto salvation." Hence, from the period at which the religious necessities of his own countrymen in India, and the moral state of its benighted native inhabitants, first impressed his mind, the life of Dr. Buchanan exhibits a continued series of strenuous, self-denying, and disinterested efforts to supply the deficiencies, and to ameliorate the condition, which he lamented.

For the accomplishment of this great purpose, he was admirably qualified both by natural and acquired advantages. Sagacious and observant, calm and persevering, resolute, yet mild and courteous, he took a penetrating and extensive survey of the various objects around him; and, omitting points of inferior consideration and importance, fixed his attention on the grand and prominent features by which they were distinguished. The temper also and habits of Dr. Buchanan were peculiarly calculated to soften the asperities, and to remove the prejudices, of opponents, to treat with men of every rank upon their own grounds, and to engage them in promoting the great objects which he himself had in view; while the comprehensiveness of his mind, and the munificence of his disposition, enabled him both to conceive and execute designs of no ordinary difficulty and magnitude.

We have accordingly seen in the course of these memoirs that, by the publication of authentic documents and convincing statements, by the proposal of magnificent prices, by the active excercise of his influence with those who respected and esteemed him, and by personal exertions, which included a journey of more than five thousand miles, amidst many difficulties and dangers, he endeavoured to extend and perpetuate among the European population of India the national faith and worship; and, unmoved by the obloquy of opponents, and by the want of cordial assistance on the part of some who might have been expected to support and cheer him, laboured unceasingly to diffuse among millions, immersed in the thickest darkness, "the light that leads to heaven."

Nor did he labour in vain. Whoever has attended to the state of public opinion, and to the course of public events, in this country and in India during the last twenty years, must perceive the revolution of sentiment and feeling, which has taken place in that period upon these important questions. The general acknowledgment, and the recognition in Parliament, of the solemn duty of attending to the religious interests of British India; the establishment of our Episcopal Church, and the facilities afforded to the efforts of Christian piety and zeal to promote the knowledge of the gospel in that extensive empire; and the progress which has been actually made in this great work, demonstrate the truth of this assertion. It is equally certain that to the able and persevering exertions of Dr. Buchanan must this happy change of opinion and these salutary measures be principally attributed. Of his claim to the merit of having successfully pleaded the cause of an Ecclesiastical Establishment for British India, and thus of having prepared the way for the most effectual civilization and moral improvement of the natives, there can be no doubt; and of his zealous participation in the great plan of oriental translation, his original proposal of the Malayalim version, and of a new edition of the Syriac Testament, and his generous and self-denying exertions to promote both those important works, are proofs which neither can nor will be forgotten. Millions yet unborn will, doubtless, on account of these and many other great and truly christian services of this eminent man, have reason to rejoice, and will hereafter "rise up and call him blessed."

The qualifications of Dr. Buchanan as a writer were peculiarly suited to the task which he had undertaken. Bold, perspicuous, and decisive, he is distinguished in all his works by the accumulation and display of new and striking facts, connected, for the most part, by brief, pointed, and sententious observations. Even in his writings, which are more strictly theological, he adopted a similar plan; seldom pursuing a long train of reasoning, but laying down certain undoubted facts, truths, or principles, and arguing from them directly and practically to the conclusions which he had in view. The style, however, of Dr. Buchanan, though in general simple and unambitious, was, as we have more than once had occasion to notice, frequently dignified and eloquent. But upon this point we may refer with advantage to two most competent and respectable authorities. The first is that of Dean Milner; who, in speaking of Dr. Buchanan, observes as follows:

"I perfectly well remember that the circumstance which very soon marked his character, even in the early part of his residence, as an undergraduate, was plain, sober, good sense, with a perspicuity and brevity of expression in all his English compositions on religious and moral subjects. He had no pretensions to elegance; but he was altogether free from that vicious, flowery style into which young students are apt to fall. Buchanan had always too much matter to allow him to be very wordy."

The other testimony to which a reference has been made is from the review of one of his works in the Christian Observer.*

"Dr. Buchanan is characterized, as a writer, by ease, and by a colouring of the picturesque, with which he contrives to invest his subject. Some great writers have laboured to clothe fiction in the garb of truth: Dr. Buchanan's peculiarity is, that he gives to truth many of the charms and ornaments usually appropriatad to fiction. In consequence of this, he has, we think, eminently the power of touching some of the best feelings of the mind, and of winning over those whom dry reasoning might not convince."

The subjects to which Dr. Buchanan devoted his attention did not require or even admit the display of learning, strictly so called. It has, however, sufficiently appeared that, without affecting the character of a consummate scholar, from which he was precluded by the duties of an active and laborious profession, his attainments in European literature and science were of no ordinary nature, and such as qualified him to sustain with credit the important offices to which he was appointed in India. His acquaintance with oriental learning, if not critical or profound, was extensive and considerable. After making some progress in the Persian language, he relinquished it, from a conviction of its comparative inutility to himself, soon after his arrival in India; but with the Hindostanee he was familiar; and of the Hebrew, Syriac, and Arabic, he possessed a very competent knowledge. His grand object, however, being popular and practical, his chief excellence consisted in the collection and exibition of important and various information, and in bringing it, by convincing and luminous deductions, to bear upon some weighty and interesting question. In this talent

* Vol. xii. p. 242.

he stands nearly unrivalled; and to this must be in a great measure ascribed the success of his appeals to the understanding and the heart upon the great subjects discussed in his writings.

The sentiments of Dr. Buchanan as a divine have been for the most part fully developed in these memoirs. They have appeared to be truly scriptural, and in perfect unison with the doctrines of the Church of England. With respect to one point, which, for the very reason that it is now for the first time noticed, evidently formed no prominent part of his creed, he was what, for the sake of distinction, may be called moderately Calvinistic. The avowal of his belief in the doctrine of personal election does not occur in any of his publications, and was in very few instances introduced into his discourses from the pulpit. It appears, however, somewhat remarkably in the preamble to his last will; which is expressed in the following words:

"I, Claudius Buchanan, of Little Ouseburn, make this my last will and testament. I commit my soul and body to Jesus Christ, the Saviour of lost sinners, of which sinners I am one, the chief of sinners: but I trust I have obtained mercy; and I look for eternal salvation through the obedience of Christ unto death, even the death of the cross. I account the origin of my salvation to be the love of God the Father, who loved my soul in Christ its head before the foundation of the world. I renounce all works as a claim of merit. All my works have been mixed and sullied with sin and imperfection. Whatever has been acceptable to God is his own, even the work of his Holy Spirit; it is not mine. Glory be to God the Father, Son, and Holy Ghost, for ever and ever. Amen."

Such is the emphatic declaration of his faith, with which the eminently pious subject of these memoirs bade adieu to every earthly concern, and anticipated an eternal world. While the grand truths of which it consists accord with the sentiments and feelings of every real Christian, it undoubtedly recognizes a position with which many will not agree. Though Dr. Buchanan was thus reserved upon this mysterous subject, it was, however, one on which he had thought and read much. He left behind him an unfinished work, in which it was fully but cautiously discussed.

It is easy to dispose of this great controverted question in a summary way, and to deny that there is any scriptural foundation for what is termed the Calvinistic view of it: but those who are aware of the difficulties in which the whole subject is involved, whatever may be their own sentiments respecting it, will be neither surprised nor offended at those of Dr. Buchanan. That he was far from being the retailer of other men's opinions, or from blindly and indiscriminately adhering to the tenets of an earthly "master," is evident, not only from the general tenor of his character, but from his express declaration in a note to one of his published sermons;* in which, referring to the general propensity to render the religion of Christ a human system, and to enlist under the banner of some celebrated leader, he observes that the enlightened Christian acknowledges no name but that of Christ; and exclaims with indignant surprise, "Calvin and Arminius! Is it not an insult to men of intelligence and learning, humbly receiving the revelation of God, to suppose that, instead of drawing pure water from the fountain-head, they should drink from such shallow and turbid streams!"

Of human guides to the knowledge of divine truth, Dr. Buchanan was undoubtedly disposed to follow the decisions of the church of which he was a member; and upon no other point more readily than upon the doctrine of the divine predestination, as contained in the seventeenth article. He considered that admirable composition as expressing nearly in the language of scripture the mysterious truth of which it has been seen that he declared his own solemn belief; and as doing this in so guarded a manner, as to preclude all objection and abuse, except such as is corrupt and wilful. Whether right or wrong in this interpretation of scripture and of our church, may be a matter of discussion; but if he erred in his view of the doctrine in question, let it not be forgotten that he erred with many of the greatest divines and brightest ornaments of the church; with Whitgift and Hooker, with Davenant and Hall, with Usher and Leighton. And where, it may be safely added so far as mere human authority is concerned, are more illustrious names to be found? Or who will venture to throw contempt upon opinions thus accredited and adorned?

Dr. Buchanan's view of this profound subject, like every other sentiment which he entertained, was far from being merely speculative. Whenever he thought it right to inculcate it, which, as it has been observed, was but seldom, it was not crudely or exclusively; but with reference to certain specific marks of the christian character, in connexion with other scriptural truths, and especially such as declare the obligations and responsibility of man, as an intelligent and accountable being, and in harmony with the general promises of the gospel.

* The Healing Waters of Bethesda.

The observations which have been already made, as well as the specimens which have been given of his discourses, render more than a single remark upon Dr. Buchanan as a preacher unnecessary. His delivery was slow, but impressive, and though far from being studied, was yet pleasing and persuasive. His sermons were often doctrinal, but more frequently practical and experimental; and generally interesting, either from the historical or parabolical form, or from the simple yet energetic and affecting style in which they were composed. So far as mere popularity of manner is concerned, he may not be considered as entitled to much distinction. But if success be admitted as any test of merit, he must be allowed to rank high as a preacher. Both in India and this country he was honored as the instrument of converting many from "the error of their way," and of instructing and edifying others in the faith of the gospel.

Preaching was not, however, that by which Dr. Buchanan was chiefly distinguished. His peculiar excellencies as a public character were of another kind, and are to be discerned in his enlarged and truly christian philanthropy, in the extent and acknowledged importance, utility, and disinterestedness of his plans, and in the boldness, generosity, and ability, with which he laboured to accomplish them.

Of his fidelity, diligence, and activity, in the fulfilment of his official duties, the conduct of Dr. Buchanan, as Vice Provost of the college of Fort William, is a striking and satisfactory instance; and it is no slight proof of the value of his services, that the year in which they were superseded by the abolition of this office is distinctly marked, by a very competent witness, as the period of the declining usefulness of that important institution.* During his residence in India, independently of his acknowledged value as a public servant, he was, according to the memorialist of his excellent colleague, "beloved and admired by many of every rank for his fine abilities, and for the estimable qualities of his heart;" and, after his return to this country, his uninterrupted labours in the cause of christianity, amidst accumulated infirmities and sorrows, equally secured him the respect and esteem of all who are capable of appreciating pure and exalted virtue.

Dr. Buchanan, however, sought not "honour from men." His faith enabled him to "overcome the world," and rendered

---

* See Mr. Fraser Tytler's "Considerations on the State of India."

him comparatively indifferent to its applauses and its frowns. He lived

"As ever in his great Task-master's eye;"

and appeared on all occasions supremely anxious to fulfil his appointed duties, and to hasten towards the heavenly prize. "He carried about with him," observed one of his intimate friends, "a deep sense of the reality of religion, as a principle of action; and, from various conversations which I recollect with him, I could strongly infer how much he laboured to attain purity of heart." His last commonplace book contains various proofs of his simple, devoted, and progressive piety. Observations occur, chiefly founded upon passages of scripture, on the great doctrines of the gospel, particularly on faith in the atonement, on divine grace, on holiness, on the love of God and of our neighbour, on humility, on communion with God, and on the world of spirits.

One brief extract, entitled "A general Topic of Prayer," may serve to show the practical piety, and the humble and subdued disposition of its author.

"Let us," says this excellent man, "endeavour to seek happiness and contentment in our own place and condition, not looking abroad for it. Let us seek and expect it in existing circumstances; contented with little domains, little possessions, a little dwelling; that we may prepare for a less house, a smaller tenement under ground."

If we descend to the more private features of his character, the reader of his memoirs must be struck by his patience under protracted weakness and suffering, and his submission to the will of God under frequent and severe privations of domestic and personal happiness, and by his extraordinary liberality and diffusive charity. Of the more remarkable instances of these virtues, sufficient notice has been already taken; but Dr. Buchanan was cordially and habitually generous; and, independently of those munificent acts which were unavoidably public, the writer of this narrative has met with many other instances, scarcely less noble, of which the world never heard; while, in addition to his liberal support of various christian institutions which adorn our country, there were, no doubt, numerous exertions of private benevolence, which were utterly unknown.

It may seem scarcely necessary to add that Dr. Buchanan, from deliberate conviction and choice, was warmly and steadily attached to the established constitution of his country, both in church and state. Of his exertions to extend the one throughout the British empire, the reader needs not to be reminded; while his loyal and zealous support of the other is abundantly testified by his Jubilee Sermons, and by various excellent discourses both in India and in England.

His social virtues require only to be mentioned. His invariable kindness and candour, his forbearance and readiness to forgive, together with all the charities of domestic life, are excellencies which, though happily too common to be much dwelt upon, will long live in the recollection and regret of his family and friends. To him, indeed, in these, and in some other points which have been noticed, may not improperly be applied the tribute of a Roman historian to a man of eminent merit in degenerate times, "Civis, maritus, gener, amicus, cunctis vitæ officiis æquabilis, opum contemptor, recti pervicax, constans adversus metus."*

An enemy, however, for such it seems he had, or even a less partial friend, might here be disposed to say, with a celebrated French annalist,† when describing a man of extraordinary qualities, "Tournez la médaille." To such a proposal there can in this case be no objection. It is by no means necessary to the just appreciation of Dr. Buchanan, to represent him as a faultless character; and if it were possible for him to interfere with so unwise and unchristian an attempt on the part of any of his friends, he would be the first to deprecate and to resist it. His defects were such as are incident to the talents and dispositions by which he was distinguished. Naturally bold and ardent in his conceptions, feelings, and expectations, he unavoidably communicated his own impressions in his delineations of human good and evil. Hence he has been accused of sweeping and undistinguishing severity in his strictures on the ecclesiastical negligences and deficiencies of our eastern administration, of a dictatorial tone in his suggestions, and of exaggeration in his representations of the religious state of India, and of the probable results of the measures which he recommended.

"Il y a dans cela," to adopt an expression of a celebrated personage, "un fond de vérité." Let us, however, define the nature and extent of the admission. If it be meant by such animadversions to insinuate that Dr. Buchanan either intentionally, grossly, or even materially misrepresented or over-stated any facts or incidents which he has undertaken to relate, his friends would have no hesitation in denying the charge, until some specific proof of such allegations be adduced; and, in the meantime, they would express their calm and un-

* Tac. Hist. lib. iv. c. 7.

† The Duc de Sully.

doubting acquiescence in the result of a full and impartial examination. It may be added that a man of so much integrity and ingenuousness as Dr. Buchanan, when, at the close of his life, he was urging upon the attention of the missionary* the importance of a strict and cautious adherence to simplicity and truth in his periodical reports, could scarcely be conscious of any personal failure in the performance of a similar duty.

If the objections in question refer merely to the warmth of colouring which pervades his descriptions, the reply has been anticipated in the sanguine nature, complexion, and character of his mind; which would as necessarily produce such a style, as the opposite temperament of another writer would naturally lead to colder and less vivid representations. If this consideration should be deemed unsatisfactory, it can only be lamented that what in writers, who have but little else to recommend them, is freely forgiven, and even admired, is severely visited upon one whose claims to general credibility and regard are of no ordinary magnitude. But it is remarkable that, while the world will readily approve the coldest and most inadequate statements upon religious subjects, the man who treats them with any degree of fervour proportioned to their importance, will be discredited and condemned. That Dr. Buchanan should have been resisted and misrepresented by those who consider his zeal for the conversion and salvation of men excessive and enthusiastic, and his plans and expectations visionary and extravagant, not to say rash and dangerous, ought not to excite our surprise. Time, however, and that which it will doubtless bring with it, additional information and experience, will, it is confidently presumed, gradually dissipate these illusions, and prove to the satisfaction of all, who are not under the influence of inveterate prejudice, the substantial correctness as well as importance of his statements; though, as it will ever be more easy to cavil than to disprove, to criticise the productions of others than to add to the general stock of knowledge and happiness, it is vain to expect that minute and pertinacious objectors will either be satisfied or silenced.

"I ever considered," observes a friend,† whose testimony is peculiarly valuable, (in speaking of the efforts which have been made to depreciate the authority of Dr. Buchanan,) "such attempts as the effect of dislike to the plans in which he was engaged. I apprehend no one will ever be able to invalidate any of the facts recorded by Dr. Buchanan, though some, who possess not his spirit, will not view the circumstances as he

* See page 394.

† The Rev. D. Corrie.

viewed them, and, therefore, will not speak of them as he did." This latter remark forms, in fact, the key to the greater part of the injurious charges and insinuations which have been circulated respecting the subject of these memoirs, and at the same time furnishes an antidote to their poison. Let but the spirit of faith in the gospel, and of love to the souls of men, animate those who are now inclined to treat with negligence or contempt the statements and reasonings of Dr. Buchanan; and it may be asserted, without incurring the charge of uncharitableness, that they will not be long in acknowledging the truth and correctness of the one, and the force and value of the other. Let men, in short, only be convinced that ignorance of the true God is the grand cause of all the moral evil in the world; that to "know Him, and Jesus Christ whom he hath sent, is *life eternal*;" and that multitudes are everywhere "perishing for lack of" that "knowledge;" and they will at once be disposed to admit that there can scarcely be any exaggeration in describing the wretchedness of those who are destitute of it, or any excess in their zeal who labour to make known to every creature under heaven that gospel which has the "promise of the life that now is, and of that which is to come."

If the imperfections of Dr. Buchanan, as a private christian, have not been studiously exhibited, it is because, from his remarkable simplicity, and, if the expression may be allowed, his careless confidence of integrity, the defects as well as the excellencies of his character can scarcely fail of being sufficiently noticed by an attentive reader of these memoirs. The assistance also of a biographer is seldom required to point out the errors of men who have acted a prominent part in the world; while the benefit of such representations, in works not sanctioned by infallible authority, is very doubtful; mankind in general standing much more in need of being animated by the exhibition of eminent merit, than consoled or gratified by the disclosure and delineation of defects inseparable from the condition even of the most advanced christian. Of those which were incident to his own character, no one could be more humbly sensible than Dr. Buchanan, more watchful for the discovery of unknown faults, more anxious for their correction, or more diligent in endeavouring, under the influence of divine grace, "to perfect holiness in the fear of God."

After all the deductions, therefore, which may be due to the paramount claims of truth, or urged by the severer demands of a less friendly scrutiny, there remains to the subject of these memoirs a residue of solid, and undoubted, and indefeasible excellence, of which the conviction and estimate will, it is firmly believed, be gradually and certainly augmenting. He may be slighted by some, and misrepresented or misunderstood by others; but among those who can justly appreciate distinguished worth, genuine piety, and enlarged and active philanthropy, there can surely be but one opinion—that Dr. Buchanan was "a burning and a shining light," and a signal blessing to the nations of the East. We may, indeed, safely leave his eulogy to be pronounced by future generations in Great Britain and Hindostan, who will probably vie with each other in doing honour to his memory, and unite in venerating him as one of the best benefactors of mankind; as having laboured to impart to those who, in a spiritual sense, are "poor indeed," a treasure

——— "Transcending in its worth
The gems of India."———

But if it were possible that men should forget or be insensible to their obligations to this excellent person, he is now far removed from human censure and applause; his judgment and his work are with God; his record is on high, and his witness in heaven. He has "entered into peace," and will doubtless stand in no unenvied lot "at the end of the days;" when "they that are wise shall shine as the brightness of the firmament, and they that turn many to righteousness as the stars for ever and ever."